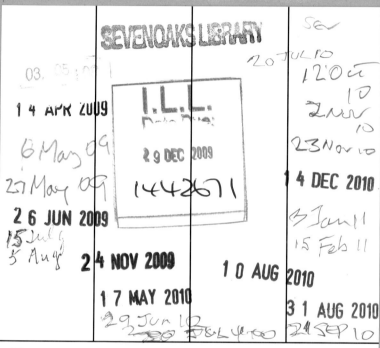
Please return on or before the latest date above.
You can renew online at *www.kent.gov.uk/libs*
or by telephone 08458 247 200

_____

_____

CUSTOMER SERVICE EXCELLENCE

Libraries & Archives

Kent
County
Council

00884\DTP\RN\07.07   LIB 7

Settling Scores

German Music,

Denazification, &

the Americans,

1945–1953

DAVID MONOD

The University of North Carolina Press

Chapel Hill and London

Settling Scores

© 2005

The University of North Carolina Press

All rights reserved

This book was published with the assistance of
the William R. Kenan Jr. Fund of the University of
North Carolina Press.

Designed by Richard Hendel

Set in Galliard by Keystone Typesetting, Inc.

Manufactured in the United States of America

The paper in this book meets the guidelines for
permanence and durability of the Committee on
Production Guidelines for Book Longevity of the
Council on Library Resources.

Library of Congress Cataloging-in-Publication Data

Monod, David, 1960–

Settling scores : German music, denazification, and
the Americans, 1945–1953 / by David Monod.

   p. cm.

Includes bibliographical references (p.) and index.

ISBN 0-8078-2944-7 (cloth : alk. paper)

1. Music — Germany — 20th century — American
influences. 2. Germany — History — 1945–1955.
3. Denazification — Germany. I. Title.

ML275.5.M66   2005

780'.943'09044 — dc22   2004029685

09 08 07 06 05 5 4 3 2 1

FOR MICHAEL KATER

CONTENTS

ILLUSTRATIONS

ACKNOWLEDGMENTS

Two very different military occupations imprinted themselves on these pages. The first, which occurred a half-century ago, raised perplexing questions about the American authority's confusion over goals, rapidly changing priorities, diminishing commitments, difficulties with establishing legitimacy, and ambivalent successes. The second occupation, which occurred as this book was being written, helped me recognize some of the answers to those questions. Music is not one of the concerns of the American administration in Iraq, but it was an issue for the occupiers in postwar Germany. The peculiarity of that concern is what first drew me to the subject; my fascination with issues such as the moral responsibility of the artist and the value of music as a communicator of ideas sustained me during my ten years of research; and the frustration I felt watching America's current engagement with occupation government stimulated and shadowed my writing.

The present has also impinged on this study in other, and more pleasant, ways. I was tremendously fortunate to have been able to interview a number of the men and women who had been involved in the administration of music in postwar Germany. Talking to the subject of one's research inevitably changes one's perception of the archival material, and I am glad that my own thinking was challenged, grounded, and, I believe, humanized by the interviews. I admit to having been captivated by the generosity, intelligence, and spirit of the individuals I interviewed and, most important, having come to appreciate their deep musicality. Music, I quickly realized, was not simply the subject of their endeavors in Europe: the men and women I spoke to could not have been administering mining or health care. Music was something tangible for them, a social force with its own power and culture and moral attributes. Though not uncritical of their fetishization of music, I understand and respect it and even see it as strangely ennobling. My great regret is that many of the individuals I spoke with have not lived to see the publication of this book. My profound gratitude to Carlos Moseley, Mateo Lettunich, Virginia Pleasants,

John Bitter, Edward Kilenyi, and Newell Jenkins for what they taught me about Military Government, music, and themselves and to John Boxer, Henry Pleasants, Suzanne Arco Heidsieck, Sir Georg Solti, and Isaac Stern for their memories and reflections on music, their colleagues, and Germany.

I was also extremely fortunate in that all of the archives I approached, with the exception of the Orff-Zentrum in Munich, did their utmost to facilitate my research. I am especially grateful to Becky Colyer and Amy Schmidt at the National Archives in Washington for their assistance over many years. I am also grateful to archivists at the Hoover Institution on War, Revolution and Peace; the Harry Ransom Center; Yale University Archives; the Library of Congress Performing Arts Division; the Dwight David Eisenhower Library; the Harry S. Truman Library; the Oskar Diethelm Library of Cornell University; the Jerome Lawrence and Robert E. Lee Theatre Research Institute at Ohio State University; the Washington State University Archive; the Stadtarchiv Stuttgart; the Stadtarchiv München; the Staatsarchiv Ludwigsburg; the former Stadtarchiv Berlin; the Landesarchiv Berlin; the Institut für Zeitgeschichte; the Hauptstaatsarchiv Stuttgart; the Hessisches Hauptstaatsarchiv; the Bayerisches Hauptstaatsarchiv; and the Akademie der Künste for making material available and for ensuring that my visits would be memorable. Although the archivists I dealt with in all of these places were unfailingly helpful, I must single out Volker Viergutz and Klaus-Dieter Pett at the former west Berlin Stadtarchiv who, recognizing the high cost of international travel, allowed me to keep researching even on days when the archive was officially closed.

My research was supported by a major grant from the Social Science and Humanities Research Council of Canada and by a number of smaller awards from my home university, Wilfrid Laurier. I am also grateful to the Deutscher Akademischer Austausch Dienst for a German Study Grant and to the German Historical Institute, Washington, for inviting me to spend a memorable summer at the German-American Center for Visiting Scholars. Wilfrid Laurier University also awarded me a Book Publishing Grant, which assisted in the final preparations of the manuscript.

While I was researching this book a number of people — some of whom I still hope to meet in person — took the time and trouble to send me information and documentation. Much of this material had taken them years to accumulate, and without their generosity it would have remained well beyond my reach. The Knappertsbusch biographer, Kazuhide Okunami, provided me with valuable documents regarding the conductor's denazification; Claudia Maurer Zenck supplied me with an amazing collection of her notes on new music performances in Berlin; W. Howard Cotton Jr. sent me a package dealing with the first music chief in Bavaria, Harry Bogner; Jean Massud dispatched a stack of War Department photocopies pertaining to the New York Field Office; David Farneth gave me a bundle of material from the Weill-Lenya Research Center on Otto Pasetti; and Reuben Silver shared his memories of his former colleague, Benno Frank. I was also privileged to have enjoyed the hospitality of Jeremiah Evarts and his family, who allowed me to live in their home while I studied the remarkable and moving diary and memorabilia of John Evarts. I am grateful to Carlos Moseley for sending me copies of the letters he wrote home in the late 1940s; to John Bitter for allowing me access to his scrapbooks; and to Mateo Lettunich, Carlos Moseley, Virginia Pleasants, John Bitter, Newell Jenkins, and Jeremiah Evarts for allowing me to reproduce their personal photographs.

Because I was sure I had used up my share of good fortune during the researching and writing of this book, I did not expect a smooth passage through the publication process. I am so pleased to have been proved wrong. The staff at the University of North Carolina Press is a terrific bunch: courteous, intelligent, and professional. The manuscript went through its various appraisal and editorial stages with startling efficiency. One could not want a more supportive or knowledgeable editor than Chuck Grench or a more warmly enthusiastic person fielding one's questions than assistant editor Amanda McMillan. With green pen and sharp pencil, Brian MacDonald did a superb job of copyediting the manuscript, and Ron Maner, UNC's managing editor, guided the book and me through the stages of publication with little fuss and a great deal of positive encouragement.

A large number of friends and colleagues also shared their expertise and advice and read portions large and small of the manuscript. The book would have been infinitely poorer without the time and knowledge they brought to that task. I am grateful to Joan Evans, Celia Applegate, Toby Thacker, Elizabeth Koch Janik, Jeffry Diefendorf, Thomas A. Schwartz, Michael Kater, Boris von Haken, Carol Gruber, Michael H. Gray, George Urbaniak, Paul Monod, Michael Sibalis, and Guido Heldt for their comment, criticism, and cheer. To Toby, a special thank-you for sorting out so many of the research questions I could not solve; our email correspondence is now something of a military government archive in itself. Michaela, Adam, and Emma endured months of my absences on research trips and tolerated, without too much complaining, my monopolization of the computer. Michaela also put up with endless questions regarding German grammar and endured (still endures) a burgeoning list of undone household jobs. I am so grateful to you for your laughter and conversation and hugs and for the privilege of having such a close and loving family.

Finally, this book is dedicated to Michael Kater, whose support was crucial to its completion. Michael's willingness to sponsor a newcomer in his field placed me in vital and early contact with an exceptional community of scholars and invaluable sources of funding; his archival knowledge (and private archive) filled in the blanks in my research, and his scholarship served as a model for my work. Michael's sense of history is personal, immediate, and alive; he hauls it up from the archives and engages his audience with it provocatively and vigorously. What a pleasure it has been to experience his enthusiasm and to take directions from his intellectual compass. This book is a partial thank-you.

ABBREVIATIONS

ABSIE	American Broadcasting Station in Europe
ACC	Allied Control Council
ASCAP	American Society of Composers, Authors and Publishers
BPO	Berlin Philharmonic Orchestra
CDU	Christlich-Demokratische Union (Christian Democratic Party)
CIC	Counter Intelligence Corps
CSU	Christlich-Soziale Union (Christian Socialist Party)
GDB	Genossenschaft Deutscher Bühnenangehöriger (theater workers union)
GEMA	Gesellschaft für musikalische Aufführungs (copyright society after 1949)
HICOG	Office of the High Commissioner for Germany
ICD	Information Control Division
IIA	International Information Administration
ILL	International Lending Libraries
ISB	Information Services Branch
JCS	Joint Chiefs of Staff
KPD	Kommunistische Partei Deutschlands (Communist Party of Germany)
MG	Military Government
NSDAP	Nationalsozialistische Deutsche Arbeiterpartei (Nazi Party)
OMGB	Office of the Military Government Bavaria
OMGUS	Office of the Military Government United States
OSS	Office of Strategic Services
OWI	Office of War Information
PAD	Public Affairs Division
PWD	Psychological Warfare Division
PWE	Psychological Warfare Executive
RIAS	Radio in the American Sector
RKK	Reichskulturkammer (Chamber of Culture in the Third Reich)

SA   Sturmabteilungen ("Storm Sections" of the Nazi Party)
SED   Sozialistische Einheitspartei Deutschlands
            (Socialist Unity Party of Germany)
SHAEF   Supreme Headquarters Allied Expeditionary Force
SMAD   Sowjetische Militäradministration Deutschland
            (Soviet Military Government in Germany)
SPD   Sozialdemokratische Partei Deutschlands (Socialist Party)
SS   Schutzstaffel ("Defense Squad" of the Nazi Party)
STAGMA   Staatlich genehmigte Gesellschaft zur Verwertung
            musikalischer Urheberrechte
            (copyright board prior to 1949)
SWNCC   State-War-Navy Coordinating Committee
ToK   Tarifordnung für die Kulturorchester
            (orchestral pay scale regulation)
USFA   U.S. Forces Austria
USFET   U.S. Forces European Theater
USIS   U.S. Information Service

Settling Scores

Introduction

As president of the American Society of Composers, Authors and Publishers (ASCAP), which licensed works and collected royalties on behalf of composers and music publishers in the United States, Deems Taylor felt he had to respond. The implication, after all, was that his organization was helping the enemy. And so he chose to address the biggest audience he could: listeners to his regular intermission commentary for the Sunday radio broadcast of the New York Philharmonic. What he couldn't understand, he told listeners on 22 February 1942, was how Erika Mann, daughter of the novelist Thomas Mann, "whose father's books are being burned in Germany," could advocate censorship over here. If people didn't want to listen to German performers, Taylor argued, that was fine; but they mustn't smash their records: "[I]t's a Nazi technique. . . . Don't imitate those barbarians." He then focused on Richard Strauss, the best known of Germany's living classical composers, whom Mann had recently declared was "putting his genius at the disposal of the enemy" by "conducting for storm troopers," while Americans "sheepishly" listened to his music and ASCAP collected the U.S. royalties that it would hand over to him at the cessation of hostilities. Art, Mann insisted, should not take precedence over politics: after all, if Hitler's pictures were really good, would that justify exhibiting them during the war in American art galleries? Taylor's defense was to try to separate the composer from his work and to insist that, while Strauss might be a bad man, his work was still worth hearing. Why ban Strauss's music? "[W]e're not fighting music, we're fighting Germany, Italy and Japan." If the democracies were to prevail, he continued, they had to practice the kind of civilization they were defending and that meant *renouncing* the tactics of the enemy. He quoted with approval the conductor Bruno Walter's recent comments on Strauss: "I detest him as a person, and I abhor everything for which he stands," but he "is a genius, and some of his works are masterpieces. I cannot in all honesty boycott masterpieces because I detest their composer."[1]

The problem Taylor, Mann, and Walter were addressing is still relevant to our appreciation not just of midcentury German music but of the cultural expressions of all those whose values we find repugnant. During the early years of the Cold War, many people in the West felt they should not listen to the works of Dimitri Shostakovich because he was thought to be a model Soviet composer; some today cannot bear the hallucinogenic novels of Céline, a French fascist, while others remain disturbed by D. W. Griffith's films because the director was a white supremacist. Today, it has to be admitted, assertions such as Walter's that the composer and his work must be kept separate seem somewhat trite, for ours is a time when the politicization of the arts and the identification of producer and product are increasingly taken for granted. Contemporary Western culture, which genders the gaze and deconstructs the racial and social foundations of the artistic canon, which sees a Coke can and a Chagall as equally significant message carriers, and which has to debate whether a crucifix floating in urine is art or obscenity, has become less hospitable to people like Taylor and Walter and their idealistic assumptions concerning the value of art in itself and for its own sake.

But if time has been on Erika Mann's side, Taylor's view still serves to check the prejudices that so easily accompany her perspective. Art may no longer rise pristinely above the context of its production (or its reception), but whether out of nostalgia or for the sake of openness many still cherish the hope that it might do so. Moreover, as historians, we need to recognize not just the importance of Taylor's view but also its audacity. Amid wartime hardship's terrible vindictiveness (for while the Americans in February 1942 had yet to engage the Germans, their forces were being overwhelmed in the Pacific), Taylor spoke in favor of tolerance and liberality. He did not approve of musicians who chose to perform in Nazi Germany—and he followed Mann in singling out the pianist Walter Gieseking—but he continued to feel that their art could give pleasure and enlightenment to Americans. Although Taylor can be criticized for pretending music was nonpolitical and for accepting the artistic genius of an enemy people, his defense of free speech at a moment of xenophobia, war, and fear remains commendable.

What Taylor lacked, however, was an actual plan for how to be liberal and tolerant. Mann's position had clear political ramifications: ban the cultural products of the Third Reich and seize the assets of its citizens. Taylor's had only negative ones: do nothing and let the public decide. He did not condemn those people who stopped listening to German music because they were uncomfortable doing so, but that was as far as he would go; even ASCAP, he insisted, could not appropriate the royalties of enemy composers, although he did advocate first using them to compensate American artists who were not receiving payment for works of theirs that might have been performed in occupied Europe. But decency of Deems Taylor's kind has always been more of an attitude than a plan for action.

Fortunately for both Taylor and Mann, they did not have to make policy or implement regulations; they were able to debate the issues without really sorting out how to put their views into practice. The same was not true, however, for the officers who had to assume control over the arts in Germany once Hitler's Reich was defeated. Suddenly, American bureaucrats were confronted with the very real problem of what to do with an arts sector that had made peace with the most repulsive regime imaginable. They had to judge who was guilty and of what and to what extent, and they had to decide if the Germans should be given the chance to listen to the same music that had entertained them through fascist tyranny and war. They had to remove Nazi controls from cultural life and to chart a new relationship between the artist and society. Moreover, once they determined what constituted artistic freedom, they had to design laws and appoint people capable of maintaining it. At the most basic level, they had to take a stand in the debate between Taylor and Mann and to put their beliefs into action.

This study deals with the results of their endeavors in the American occupation zone in western Germany. It documents the complex, confused, and often contradictory efforts of the American authorities to punish musicians for the things they had done in the Third Reich while establishing the foundations of a democratic cultural life. The conflict between the American occupiers' two goals — punishment and freedom or, put another way, control and democracy — is the central theme of this work. What this study shows is how difficult it was to establish freedom within the context of military rule, to democratize the arts while controlling them, and to find a usable middle ground between Deems Taylor and Erika Mann.

The culpability of the artist working under tyranny was unquestionably the most complicated and contentious of all the problems those supervising Germany's cultural sector addressed. Even at the time it was a question that provoked fierce debate. Most of the prominent musicians who remained in the Third Reich had made deplorable choices, even if one can today understand the expectations, fears, and weaknesses that made them do so. Those Americans who pushed for a complete denazification of German artistic life — through the removal from public performance of all those artists who had compromised with Hitler — had sound reasons for desiring a cultural revolution. But it was naive of the occupation authorities to feel that culture should or could be completely "purified," and the radical denazifiers' drive to ostracize all those tainted by fascism was simplistic and bound to fail. In fact, their heavy-handed efforts at revolutionizing German music had the unfortunate effect of encouraging artists to obliterate their own past by lying about what they had done. While this enabled German music to recover rapidly from the shock therapy of denazification, it also perpetuated myths concerning music's unpolitical nature, the innocence of the artist, and, worse, the fundamental incompatibility of Nazism and *Kultur*. Only now, with the death of almost everyone who enjoyed a notable career in the Third Reich, are the myths being punctured. And this reversal, in so many ways, comes too late.

This book is not devoted to naming names or exposing lies; other scholars have undertaken that important task.[2] Rather, my interests lie in exploring the debate over what should have been done with Germany's tainted generation of musicians and its debased culture. As a work of history, it confronts the moral questions not in their abstract, as Mann and Taylor debated them, but as they were dealt with at the time by American officers working in Germany with restricted resources, competing objectives, and imperfect knowledge. Without denying that the decisions the occupiers made were often poor ones, as a historian, I am interested in what led people to make them and in the consequences of their actions. The book asks readers to confront the question of the culpability of the artist, but it wants them to do so in the context of a time and a place and to understand what was possible, what was known, and what was thought then to be right.

This study of music politics under American occupation, however, does not deal with the type of twentieth-century music that the United States has dominated. For a variety of reasons, wartime planners decided to leave popular music alone and to make classical music the focus of postwar controls. The ramifications of that decision were far-reaching. Instead of being instruments of Americanization—pressing swing and boogie-woogie on the Germans and manipulating mass tastes—Military Government (MG) personnel were agents of reeducation. The American music officers in Germany were not there to sell their own popular culture but to reform German *Kultur*: the high culture of the educated classes. The Americans, who came from a society in some respects even more segregated—in a cultural sense—than Germany's, took for granted the distinction between high and low culture even if they realized the terms had a particular resonance in Europe. For Germans, *Kultur* was part of the national identification. Where Americans often looked to business, scientific, or political leaders, such as Lincoln or Ford or Edison, when thinking about who they were, the Germans tended to refer to artists and philosophers: to Beethoven and Bach and Goethe.[3] Because American policy makers understood this, they made classical music one of the targets of their reeducation efforts.

Understandably, for all its intrinsic interest and cultural significance, music control remained one of the least important elements in military government. For postwar planners in London and Washington, music paled in significance next to such administrative nightmares as feeding the German population, collecting reparations, demobilizing the army, rebuilding the education system, and reforming the economy. And yet, while considered unimportant within the broader context of occupation policy, music control dealt with moral issues of equal complexity to those confronting decartelizers and educators. As a result, its career mirrored that of most of the U.S. administration's larger sections. All of the units involved in reorientation, whether they dealt with journalism, theater, book publishing, education, or film making, experienced a similar trajectory. All began by wiping clean the slate: closing schools, shutting down theaters and movie houses, and stopping presses. Operations were then resumed under new German management, using personnel whom the Americans had screened to ensure their political cleanliness. At the same time, in the late summer of 1945, the Americans launched a major purge of cultural personnel and imposed blacklists of Nazis, militarists, and nationalists. During the winter of 1945–46, after the first wave of the purge was completed, American supervisors put specially chosen artists, educators, and journalists to work creating a democratic culture; domestic film producers were the last to be rehired, in early 1946. Then, in the spring, things began to come unstuck. In March 1946, by order of the military governor, denazification was returned to German control, and many of those whom the Americans had blacklisted were cleared by the *Spruchkammern*, or local denazification courts. The newly elected *Land* and municipal governments then moved to reappoint these recently cleared people to their former jobs and to shunt aside those whom the Americans had installed. Briefly, in the fall of 1946, some of the cultural divisions fought back and a second purge followed, but it was short-lived. By early 1947, military government had ordered a winding down of controls, and American influence was being sharply curtailed. In fact, the year saw a transition in policy from rule to role modeling as MG dictated that its remaining personnel should influence Germans by example and advise rather than control. The accelerating conflict with the Soviets over the latter half of 1947 only added a further dimension to the new task: that of convincing the Germans that the Americans and not the Russians were their friends. The transition was gradual and uneven, but by 1948–49 all of the cultural divisions had been themselves reoriented to the task of winning German loyalty and support. Denazification, which had been a diminishing concern of Military Government for two years, was quietly put to rest.[4]

The brevity of America's controlling season and the suddenness with which it was transformed into something altogether different and more familiar (the containment of communism) make understanding its impact especially challenging. For historians, the occupation period rests indecisively in twentieth-century west German history between the compelling blackness of the Nazi Reich and the chromium brightness of the economic miracle. It has been generally seen as a transitional time when, depending on how critically one approaches the subject, Germany's past was either mastered or suppressed. Because the Americans put a quick end to denazification — and there is an unfortunate tendency in the literature to see the foreigners who handed responsibility over to the locals as somehow more culpable than the German *Spruchkammern* that actually did the deed — some historians accuse them of allowing the crimes of the Third Reich to be whitewashed. Time here is often foreshortened, and MG's interest in closing its own book on Nazism is attributed to its desire to get on with the job of Americanizing German business or fighting communism. Historians who feel a new Germany did emerge after 1945 also see the occupation period as an in-between time: it either laid the groundwork for what was to follow or temporarily obstructed its development. Military Government is particularly significant to these scholars because it helped embed capitalist and consumerist values, though some find this a happier development than others.[5]

The indefinite status that has been accorded the occupation period can be justified, in part, by the confusion it encompassed. The decision makers appeared to have no long-range plans and goals or to have issued insufficiently detailed short-term guidelines. Multiple huge American bureaucracies — the War Department, the State Department, the Treasury — had fingers in the German pie, and the Office of the Military Government (OMGUS) itself generated a vast quantity of poorly organized paper but little in the way of consistent policy. Critics of Military Government generally point to the contradictory lines of authority and the confusion over directives to explain why the whole thing was such a mess. In fact, some have suggested that the best one could say for OMGUS was that it phased itself out reasonably quickly. Others use an even sharper point and suggest that Germany became a democracy partly because the locals had to exercise their political rights in order to battle the oppressive and incompetent Americans.[6] So dominant has this negative assessment become that it has forced those wanting to defend the idea of a positive American influence on Germany to look below the policy level and study local interactions and attitudes. Today we are left with the muddied image of overall policy failure combined with the success of a grass-roots, unplanned Americanization and democratization.[7]

Underlying these various interpretations regarding the importance and impact of the U.S. occupation is the debate over continuity and change in German history. Those who deplore the survival of traditional German values in the 1950s, the authoritarianism of the country's political culture and the continuing power of its prewar elites, tend to criticize the Americans for not having done more to revolutionize the country. Others, who see a new society under construction in the postwar period, point to the subversive influence of American GIs, American movies, and American values. Conservative Germans, they point out, may have regained control and resisted these trends for a time — condemning the relations between American soldiers and German girls, lamenting the popularity of rock 'n' roll, and regulating against changing gender relations—but eventually even they were forced to assimilate a postwar world of American design. Germany did change, according to this interpretation, but its transformation was gradual and not fully achieved until the 1960s.[8]

In recent years, some scholars have argued against the dichotomization of continuity and change in postwar German history. They have suggested that the conservative restoration and the new "Americanized" values were connected (not opposed) and that real societal change could only have been achieved without America. They point to a brief moment in 1945–47 when the elements of a truly new and homegrown democratic Germany began to assemble themselves. These "golden hunger years" were marked by the appearance of authentically democratic and antifascist political movements, an artistic awakening, and a spiritual rebirth. One writer has likened this *Stunde Null* to the rousing of a long-slumbering princess, while another has written of a rising "historical movement that had at last brought enlightenment, emancipation and a radically questioning discourse to this belated nation." But to these historians, the moment soon passed, a victim of the Cold War's quickening. MG authorities were unwilling to accommodate true democracy, the conflict with the Soviets allowed the old elites to rise like scum to the surface, and American popular culture swept in, obliterating the fragile cultural renaissance and turning Germany into a caricature of the United States.[9]

This book is designed to build upon, modify, and add to the substantial edifice that now constitutes occupation studies. It too has at its heart the question of continuity and change after 1945 and addresses such issues as the long-term contribution of Military Government, the efficiency of the American administration, and the centrality of the policy shift from denazification to anticommunism. The following chapters argue that, in the cultural field, MG did have a lasting impact on Germany, though they also suggest that the Americans' most positive contribution was in promoting structural changes in arts administration and in subtly affecting certain values. I do not find any significant shift in musical tastes, despite MG's efforts to promote a new repertoire, nor do I find that denazification was handled effectively or OMGUS run efficiently. Further, while this study shows that a modest cultural regeneration was observable in the classical music sector in 1945–47, unlike most historians, who depict it as occurring despite the boorish occupiers, I argue that it was in large measure due to the policies and actions of the American officers and the people they appointed to guide the country's regeneration. Moreover, and more contentiously, this book suggests that the postwar cultural reawakening was largely possible because of the truly revolutionary and transforming impact of denazification. In fact, it was the decision to end American control over denazification that allowed more traditional musicians to regain their positions within cultural life and first turned art back on a more conservative axis. One year after the end of radical denazification, the crippling effect of currency reform completed the reactionary drift, destroying whatever elements of experimentation remained in the mainstream by emptying the concert halls and opera houses. In the music field, concertgoers no longer wanted to pay to hear pieces they did not recognize or to see unknown performers. So far as classical music's repertoire and artistic personnel were concerned, currency reform and the *Spruchkammern* together propelled a conservative restoration.

This study offers a more positive assessment of the American occupation than is common in the scholarly literature. MG did make an important contribution to the musical arts in Germany, even if its most obvious successes were short-lived. Much more could have been achieved. Denazification, as it was initially conceived, would have transformed German music life over time, but it was curtailed too soon and so badly that its ultimate impact was overwhelmingly negative. Moreover, the program was implemented so crudely that, even if it would have worked over time, it would have been at the expense of other important undertakings and policies and at great cost to many innocent people. In the cultural field, OMGUS's failure to find a middle ground between the hard-peace and soft-peace advocates meant that neither side was able to achieve as much as it might. The confusion within MG, a result of the conflicting lines of authority, poor organization, and rapidly changing policies, was a major factor in weakening the effectiveness of the occupation. In other words, it was not anticommunism that derailed the effort to transform Germany but the failure of Military Government itself to decide on goals and methods. In view of this, the Americans' modest achievements in the musical field were somewhat remarkable.

I tell the story of classical music's reconstitution in postwar Germany in six chapters organized thematically and (to a lesser extent) chronologically, the main body of which can be grouped into three substantive sections. The first chapter introduces some of the problems the Americans faced in Germany in 1945 and shows why the occupiers' directed their efforts at "serious" (as opposed to "commercial") music. The next two chapters deal with the high tide of American influence in 1945–46. The first looks at the activities of those who adopted the Erika Mann approach — radical and punitive denazification — while the next focuses on those Americans who resisted censorship and pushed for modest reform rather than revolution. The second substantive section, also composed of two chapters, traces the gradual easing of MG control and the return of German authority over the arts in 1946–50. Chapter 4 concentrates on the ending of the denazification program, and chapter 5 deals with the way the retreat from revolution together with the currency revaluation constrained efforts at reform. The third substantive section (chapter 6) deals with the period after 1947 when American attention shifted from transforming a culture that had produced Nazism to encouraging German resistance to communism. In the music field, Cold War tensions manifested themselves primarily in the effort to convince the Germans that the Americans, exemplified by touring U.S. artists, were "just like them." The book closes with a brief discussion of the impact of the occupation on German music life through a critical evaluation of the new Bayreuth Festival of the 1950s, an institution that symbolized both German music's corruption and its regeneration.

In sum, although the American cultural officers were deeply divided and lacked clear policy guidance, they did push through important structural reforms and encouraged new thinking about the freedom of the arts and how to ensure them. Their failure to reach consensus in the debate between Deems Taylor and Erika Mann hurt their efforts, but it did not prevent them from doing valuable work. Many of the reforms they implemented took root and provided the structural foundations for a more democratic and liberal administration of cultural life. Less successful were their attempts to broaden hidebound tastes by importing American compositions and touring American performers. Most Germans continued to regard America as suffering from severe *Kultur*-deprivation, and few went out to hear the artists who visited. Still, even here, a few seeds of change were planted, and not only in new music centers like Darmstadt. Further, although the Americans' steel-plated denazification program survived just a few months, it did have a powerful effect on Germany's artists. Most of those who had enjoyed prominent careers in the Third Reich felt threatened enough to want to black out all memory of their Nazi-era selves. In multiple ways this development was unhealthy, but it helped create the image, fiction though it was, that the postwar arts were clearly and cleanly separate from the prewar — an illusion that, for all its subsequent costs, helped the Federal Republic move ahead and allowed marvelous music to sound again.

1 Preparing for Music Control

For John Bitter it began in silence. A former intelligence officer attached to the 4th Armored Division, Bitter had come to Berlin three months after Germany's surrender as a new addition to America's Military Government. Disgorged from a C-37 at Tempelhoff airport with a jeep and three other soldiers, Bitter headed north, eager for a look at the remains of Hitler's Berlin. Unable to proceed around military roadblocks or along rubble-congested streets, the GIs circled west of the administrative center and north of the Tiergarten park. Although it was growing dark, Bitter hoped to get a view of the city and climbed onto what was left of a wall. "I'll never forget this," he recalled, "because this was in Moabit, an old industrial part of Berlin. There was not a sound. I'll tell you, for a musician to hear absolute silence is very odd. There is always some tone. You will hear the fan or the air conditioner or the wind or something and airplanes pass by. But here, not a sound. No lights. And it was like a moonscape."[1]

A few days before, instead of going back to his job as conductor of the Miami Symphony Orchestra, Major Bitter had volunteered to join the American Military Government and remain in Germany. Telford Taylor, a friend of his from college days at Yale who was heading the team assembling material for the Nuremberg trials, had recommended him to one of his colleagues, General Robert McClure, the commander of the Psychological Warfare Division (PWD). On the lookout for men with fluency in German and expertise in specialized cultural fields, McClure approved his appointment.[2] And so the kind, doughy-faced American arrived in Berlin as a member of one of the more peculiar elements in Germany's postwar military administration: the music control branch of the Psychological Warfare Division.

Part of an omnibus field unit that included Theater and Film, the branch John Bitter joined was charged with the duty of coordinating the denazification of German musical life and reorienting it according to democratic principles. His job was to serve as a kind of sentinel watching over the birth of artistic freedom. As a music officer, Bitter was to ensure that no works endorsing fascist or militarist ideals were performed, that compositions suppressed in the Third Reich (such as Mendelssohn's) were restored to the concert hall, that artists celebrated by the Nazis were blocked from further performances, that the influence of the state in the cultural sector was minimized, and that German audiences were taught that the music of other nations and cultures was as valid and worthy as their own. Music control aimed at creating a rupture in German cultural history by shattering the public's sense of superiority in Germany's musical achievements and by promoting performers and works that had been neglected or banned under Nazi rule.

In undertaking all of these tasks, music officers in the American occupation zone were participating in a massive undertaking whose goal was to obliterate the culture of Nazism and reorient German thinking. This was considered necessary because PWD planners believed they had to eliminate the forces that made Germany such a warlike and expansionist power. They considered the notion, popular at the time in Germany, that the Third Reich's atrocities and the war were caused by a small group of Nazis much the same as the country's effort in 1919 to deny its war guilt. "A repudiation of Nazism," a SHAEF Joint Intelligence Report concluded in July 1945, "is one of the ways in which the average German can avoid [an] unpleasant feeling and the only fault they acknowledge is that they once trusted Hitler and add that they can hardly be blamed for failing to see how things would turn out."[3] Forcing the Germans to accept their collective responsibility for the crimes of Nazism was considered essential for the country to achieve a more peaceful future. "Our goal," President Truman's secretary informed the theologian Reinhold Niebuhr, is to "teach the Germans a lasting lesson by treating them as a defeated nation and pariah." This, however, depended on the occupation forces' ability to compel the defeated to accept that Nazism was simply the latest manifestation of their own innate aggression and chauvinism and that peace would only come to Europe once the Germans reformed their character.[4] In order to achieve this, wartime planners prepared for the control of all aspects of German cultural expression: film, theater, museums, literature, radio, and newspapers. The idea was that if the Allies could supervise the news and entertainment media for long enough, prevent expressions of German patriotism and intolerance, and bombard the population with democratic and guilt-inducing messages, in time the country would be reformed.

WHY CLASSICAL MUSIC?

For most of the war, it had been the job of the U.S. Office of War Information (OWI), rather than the U.S. Army, to engage the enemy in cultural warfare, which it did by broadcasting messages from its London studios into the occupied countries. Here the idea of using the media to change German attitudes was first explored. As Virginia Pleasants, who worked for OWI's American Broadcasting Station in Europe (ABSIE), remembered, "we scoured London for people with languages, because all kinds of expatriates [had] fled to England, and for GIs who spoke a foreign language. They would come and make short talks: morale building or information, something like that. . . . It was really propaganda, you know, because the announcer would say: 'Here is somebody who speaks a dialect,' but in reality he was a GI."[5]

As part of its radio campaign, OWI sent music banned or disfavored by the Nazis and performances by American ensembles, both classical and popular, over the airwaves. Popular music — "the best of boogie-woogie and the baritone of Bing Crosby" — dominated OWI's trans-missions, composing almost 50 percent of its broadcast time, but clas-sical music was also prominently featured. In fact, ABSIE had initiated its overseas transmission with a Stephen Foster tune played on the banjo followed by a Toscanini recording of Beethoven's Seventh Sym-phony. These two dimensions — the popular and the serious — were each considered important to the war effort. In addition to attracting audiences with varied musical tastes and boosting morale among Eu-rope's subject people, they were intended to show the Germans that the United States was a vital and enviable musical superpower. The American composer Roy Harris, who headed OWI's music program, emphasized that the agency had a two-pronged mission in Europe: first, "to show the interest, appreciation, understanding and activity in the performance of the music of the European nations as it is practised in this country. The second part concerns the development of a native music."[6] In effect, those in occupied Europe would gain hope and the Germans despair on learning that U.S. bands could not only play Brahms and Beethoven but also really jump and stomp.

OWI's offices were once described as a "palace of culture, wisdom and swing," and it seems fitting that the three categories were itemized separately. Although Harris was sympathetic to popular idioms, and the head of ABSIE's music division, Marc Blitzstein, was a composer who explored the middle ground between popular and classical forms, the agency kept its musical offerings carefully segregated: *culture* and *swing* were presented as separate sound worlds, at different times of day, and in dissimilar formats. And while it was popular music that filled up the day and later evening, the prime-time broadcast hours were largely devoted to "the Music of the Great Masters." The implicit rank ordering of OWI's musical propaganda was echoed in the press, and it was always the popular idiom that the critics who doubted the value of OWI's broadcasting ridiculed. "Occupied Europe dances while the American taxpayer pays the bills," snarled one hostile press report in early 1945, while another mocked, "[A] German who can't be cured by hot jazz or Harlem rhythm will bear watching. . . . It is the world's tragic misfortune that the OWI music division didn't start operating on Hitler and Himmler several years ago." Interestingly enough, there was little or no press criticism of the broadcasting of classical music, a reflection of both the reluctance of the American intelligentsia to recognize the artistic value of the popular idiom and the inadequacies Americans still felt in presenting their homegrown culture to Europeans. Most Europeans, they felt, looked down on Americans as uncultured, a view substantiated by the country's popular music. Many in the American establishment were vaguely embarrassed by OWI's support for a music they found primitive. Even Roy Harris occasionally betrayed doubts, as when he told the press that he thought the most enthusiastic foreign audience for jazz broadcasts might be found among "many of the tribes of the Pacific."[7]

Despite the symbols of equality Americans cherished, their music culture was deeply stratified. Classical music recordings and broadcasts had a sizable audience, which included large numbers of working-class immigrants, and conductors like Toscanini and Stokowski and soloists like Heifetz and Rubinstein were real celebrities. Indeed, as the popular columnist George Marek remembered, the audience for serious music in the United States had been growing in the interwar years: "[A]s more homes were equipped with radios, more people listened to symphonic broadcasts. As more people listened, more orchestras took to the air. Attendance at concerts leaped to a new spectacular high." But while classical music did have a widening public, the fine arts establishment in the country remained centered in the East Coast and was presided over by such influential arbiters of taste as the newspaper critics Virgil Thomson and Olin Downes. In the late nineteenth century, concertgoing had become, for the affluent, an emblem of their status and a mark of cultivation. Their financial support maintained the country's musical institutions. Well-to-do Americans often measured their sophistication in terms of their suffusion in European culture, and they believed (as did elite Germans) that classical music had an enlightening effect. Listening to serious music, it was suggested, made one a better, more cultured and more spiritually alive person.[8] Views such as these had, by the mid-twentieth century, become part of classical music's image, despite the efforts of many contemporary composers and musicians to challenge their rather hidebound associations. Consequently, although many people enjoyed classical music, it had a reputation for being high-brow, educational, and somewhat stuffy.

Prevailing attitudes to the classical repertoire helped shape responses to and the image of popular music in early twentieth-century America. Even though many well-to-do people enjoyed commercial music and jazz had a sizable audience among the young white-tie crowd, its associations were hardly refined. American race prejudices were central to popular music's construction and the black origins of jazz made it and its offshoots seem unclean and base. If classical music was considered uplifting, popular music was connected in its public imagery with drink, drugs, sex, and miscegenation. Its defenders argued that it was all good fun and pure entertainment, but this too, with the commercialism it implied, tended to debase its coinage. In the 1930s, Tin Pan Alley had been legitimized somewhat by the crooners — such as the pipe-smoking, golf-playing Bing Crosby and the debonair Fred Astaire — and jazz had achieved a measure of respectability thanks to the efforts of Paul Whiteman, who led his orchestra (not band) with a baton, but popular music continued to suffer comparison with the status-enhancing classical sound. If the boundaries segmenting American culture were starting to become more fluid, and if a new midbrow terrain was emerging on the turf occupied by the popular classics, Broadway musicals and swing, traditional associations continued to dominate tastes. As a result, OWI had a much harder time convincing American critics that its boogie-woogie broadcasts were as important as its classical programming.

If owi had difficulty establishing the propagandistic importance of popular music, it had even greater problems convincing the army that it should play any role at all in the upcoming campaign for Europe. owi's great limitation, as U.S. ground forces began engaging the enemy, was that as a civilian agency it had no connection to Eisenhower's headquarters (shaef) and no mandate to operate in combat areas. owi, together with the American secret service agency, oss, had initially demanded and financed, in September 1942, a liaison unit, the Information and Censorship Section, that was attached to shaef. The new section's job was to keep the two civilian administrations aware of the army's needs and to help direct their propaganda efforts, press releases, scores of war correspondents, and secret service operations to military purposes. As the new unit would be coordinating both British and American propaganda efforts, the promotion of Robert McClure, former military attaché at the embassy in London, to the section's command made a good deal of sense. As McClure explained, the job of the various leaflet writers, radio and press correspondents, and censors under his command was to disseminate propaganda "designed to undermine the enemy's will to resist, demoralize his forces, and sustain the morale of our supporters." McClure's untidy unit was first employed in a combat situation in Morocco, but it was in Sicily where, he believed, it really proved its value by helping to break the morale of the Italian troops.[9]

In early 1944, with the prospect of an invasion of France nearing, Eisenhower approved the creation of a new division, with greater autonomy from the civilian agencies and with more military associations. The new Psychological Warfare Division was to assume responsibility for "all psychological warfare activities against the enemy and all consolidated propaganda activities in liberated countries." Although the division, under McClure's command, continued through the first half of 1945 to operate largely through civilian-controlled channels, distributing owi pamphlets, transmitting over the American Broadcasting Station, and employing former owi officials in its senior positions, it was slowly militarizing its ranks by recruiting soldiers with language and technical specializations. These activities geared up in the winter of 1944–45 when the decision was reached to make pwd, rather than owi or another civilian agency, responsible for media control and censorship during the military occupation phase in Germany. As a result, by April 1945, the psychological warfare functions of OWI were gradually "dropped in the ashcan," although its influence continued to be felt for some time to come.[10]

Headquartered in Paris, PWD began in February 1945 to train personnel to run Germany's information and entertainment sectors. Initially, the new division would control the press, radio, and entertainment industries, but the full range of its responsibilities still had to be specified. In January, SHAEF drew up Military Government Law 191 which prohibited all film, theatrical, and musical entertainment in Germany that was not authorized by the military administration through the issuance of a license. Two months later, PWD composed its own plans for a three-phase psychological warfare offensive in Germany. According to initial planning, the army was going to occupy Germany for only a short time and had to be prepared to "pack up on 24 hours notice." PWD therefore recognized the need to establish rapid controls over German media services to be followed by a lower-level surveillance phase that could be continued under State Department authority over the long haul. In phase one of the occupation, PWD would issue propaganda to demoralize enemy combat units and broadcast orders to civilians in occupied areas. It was also charged with assembling information regarding potential insurrections, encouraging anti-Nazi sentiment, and easing German fears regarding the occupation. In phase two, PWD was to get the production of newspapers under way, initiate radio transmission, and lay the groundwork for a licensing system. In phase three, Germans whom the division had vetted regarding their political allegiances would be allowed to assume responsibility for the various information services under PWD's supervision.[11] The entertainment industry was to receive precisely the same treatment as the radio and print media, although at this point no one had yet defined what "entertainment" was supposed to mean.

Several factors, however, were combining to narrow the scope of PWD's understanding of entertainment. In the first place, PWD began seconding personnel with experience in arts administration from OWI, the most important of whom were drawn from America's East Coast establishment. The first chief of the Radio Section was Davidson Taylor, the former head of classical-music broadcasting at CBS, and his deputy was Sam Rosenbaum, a wealthy Philadelphia lawyer and vice-president of the Philadelphia Symphony Orchestra. The first chief of the Entertainment Section was the eminent stage and film producer

John Krimsky, another OWI official who before the war had produced, among other classic films, *Three Faces of Eve* and *Emperor Jones*, as well as the New York premier of the *Three Penny Opera*. The division's London-based cultural expert, who participated in the discussions with the British over what aspects of German culture to control, was Warren Munsell, who prior to enlistment had been the producer for the New York Theater Guild and who, among his many credits, had managed the Boston and New York premiers of *Porgy and Bess*.

These men appear to have shared the general American belief in the difference between "legitimate" and "popular" entertainments. Munsell's Theater Guild, for example, was a self-conscious promoter of art theater. Born as an experimental playhouse in Greenwich Village, the guild moved uptown shortly after World War I and developed a subscription-based program dominated by such European authors as Shaw, Ibsen, and Strindberg. American dramatists, like Rice and O'Neill, did find a place in the guild's repertoire, but Europeans were always its centerpiece. By the end of the 1930s, the guild had established itself as the premier art theater in New York and as the fashionable alternative to Broadway's commercial entertainments. Munsell and his colleagues promoted the idea that drama and show biz were antithetical forces, and they underlined their contempt for the Great White Way by describing themselves as members of the "legitimate theater." Not surprisingly, then, when Munsell was asked to participate in allied planning discussions regarding German theater and music, he accepted the distinction made by his British colleagues between classical music and "pure entertainment." Military Government, the planners concluded, needed to concentrate its attentions on propagandizing allied achievements in the European repertoire as the Germans would get "their fill of light music and jazz" from the British and American troops. As another cultural affairs official announced, PWD could best attack Nazi sentiments in the music sector by showing the Germans that Americans could sing Wagner better than they. There was no need to promote U.S. achievements in the more commercial media, for "popular music manages to find its own way. Nobody thought that America didn't have popular music. . . . But serious music was another matter."[12]

Developments in America's international cultural mission served to reinforce these views. In early 1945 the Roosevelt administration decided to wind up OWI's operations and transfer its overseas branch to the Department of State. The plan was to merge OWI's European operations with the State Department's cultural affairs branch, the International Information Agency (IIA), and create a new organization to be known as the U.S. Information Service. USIS would take over the propaganda effort in liberated countries and, it was assumed, replace PWD when the army relinquished control over Germany to the Department of State. If PWD would oversee the initial phase of rebuilding the defeated's cultural life and purging it of Nazi influences, USIS's job would be long-term reeducation through a promotion of the cultural achievements of the democracies. This was a continuation of State Department programs that had hitherto aimed at creating international capital for the United States by advertising its cultural achievements through visiting lecturers, touring exhibitions, and the establishment of lending libraries. Under its music program in Latin America, the IIA operated twenty libraries holding classical music scores and books, and it sent one or two consultants a year on tour to lecture on American music. Although the agency began, in the mid-1940s, to distribute recordings of American folk music, it had no popular music program. Because PWD planned to surrender its cultural operations to USIS, it was closely tied to the civilian agency. In fact, until July 1946 the division continued to receive policy instructions and supplies from the Department of State rather than the army. This was why PWD had, from the outset, adopted OWI / IIA's goal of working to "destroy long-standing and unfortunate impressions held by Europeans that American cultural achievements are well behind the nation's industrial development." The Nazis, explained Edward Barrett, OWI's overseas director, "have been telling Europeans that America is backward, barbaric, decadent, and is not to be included among the progressive, civilized nations of the world." To fight this, "the United States must busy itself convincing Europe that America has a culture."[13]

Clearly, culture was becoming a more important concept in postwar planning than entertainment. The conviction within the various policy-making circles was that it was the serious cultural media, the legitimate theater and the classical music sectors, that needed attention, rather than the commercial arts. Popular music, like Broadway theater and comic books, was not considered a "cultural" achievement so much as a business success. Its influence would flow through commercial activities and not at the cost of taxpayers.

From the perspective of long-term reorientation, it was in many ways unfortunate that the Allies adopted this position. Fighting the battle to reorient German culture on a terrain which that country had long dominated disadvantaged the occupiers from the beginning. By 1945 the Americans were already leaders in the popular cultural field, and PWD disregarded that advantage. But given the cultural divide in America itself and the views and backgrounds of the people involved, the decisions they made were unavoidable ones. After all, the psychological warriors argued, those Germans who listened to popular music had already demonstrated their willingness to break with their country's traditional chauvinism and accommodate North America. It was the committed cultural elitist, the believer in the preeminence of German *Kultur*, whose intolerance PWD really had to combat. And so culture became the primary operating concept, even if music had yet to be singled out as a particular target of PWD control.

Music first attracted the attention of PWD in October 1944, when American forces liberated Luxembourg and the division came into possession of one of Europe's most important and centrally located transmitters, a 150,000-album record collection, and intact recording and broadcast studios. The radio station, while serving listeners in liberated areas, also had the capacity to broadcast into much of western Germany, making it a powerful propaganda weapon. The Luxembourg government hoped the station would one day be returned to its control and was particularly concerned with saving its celebrated radio orchestra. Through OWI Lend Lease funds were secured to keep the musicians working, but PWD determined what they would play. Davidson Taylor, whose primary concern was with breaking German morale, directed the station to broadcast recorded music by the finest allied orchestras, to have the Radio Luxembourg orchestra perform with American and British conductors and soloists, and to spotlight the works of non-German composers. In order to assist in this mission, Rosenbaum, who was placed in charge of the station, recommended the transfer to PWD of an intelligence officer he knew in the 101st Airborne, a fellow Philadelphian, Edward Kilenyi.

A pupil of Ernö Dohnányi, Kilenyi was an exceptionally gifted pianist who had enjoyed an impressive concert career prior to his induction in 1942. An elegant, nonobtrusive, gently sarcastic young man, Kilenyi was conservative in both his attitudes and his musical preferences. Although his father (an eminent music teacher) had for a time taught George Gershwin, Kilenyi had no taste for jazz or popular music. The presence of Rosenbaum and Kilenyi, both of whom were classical in their musical tastes, helped shape Radio Luxembourg's broadcast policy and influenced PWD's thinking about music control. In particular, the people Rosenbaum assembled at Radio Luxembourg became lobbyists within PWD, pressing the importance of music in German entertainment and urging policy guidance on its postwar control. Their efforts were aided by the fact that on Davidson Taylor's insistence and with OWI's support, PWD was assembling a library of scores and recordings that was overwhelmingly classical in content. By June 1945 the division had collected enough classical recordings by allied artists to fill 160 broadcast hours but only 60 hours of popular music.[14]

Although PWD's involvement in Radio Luxembourg meant that its classical music stock was steadily rising, as late as mid-February 1945 the Entertainment Section still claimed not to know the extent of its job in Germany. Finally, in early March 1945 McClure responded to the combined voices from Paris and Luxembourg and asked for input into whether the division should undertake the specific control of music. By the end of the month, the Psychological Warfare Executive, a British committee that was developing plans for the occupation, had heard a report on Nazi influences in German classical music life. Warren Munsell, attending the PWE meeting as an American liaison, relayed the report to PWD. On the basis of his London notes, Rosenbaum compiled a "Draft Guidance on [the] Control of Music," which was submitted to McClure in April 1945. By May the necessary changes had been implemented, and the former Entertainment Section had been reconstituted as a Film, Theater, and Music unit with three separate branches under a single chief. McClure's headquarter staff then amended, to include music, the standard control instructions prohibiting the dissemination of information and art "associated with Fascism, the NSDAP, Pan-Germanism or any of the German Armed Forces," forbidding the employment of people who have been "notorious or active Nazi[s] or ardent Nazi sympathizers," and outlining conditions for the licensing of artists. In May, Davidson Taylor was appointed first chief of the new section.[15]

Between October 1944 and April 1945, the momentum of events and the prejudices of people had worked a trick on entertainment and transformed it into classical music, film, and the legitimate theater.

Although music officers would spend some of their time supervising the cabaret and circus, their primary concern was with opera and "serious" orchestral music. Dance bands and musicians performing in clubs that served food or drink were specifically exempted from their administration. *Show business* was allowed to follow its own course, whereas *culture* came in for regulation and control. This approach was in harmony with the one being developed by the public affairs officers in the Department of State and owi, and it reflected the preferences of the arts patrons and performers who now wore the uniforms of pwd officers. But the choice was in many ways a strange twist in strategy, because the psychological warriors were neglecting the great number of Germans who preferred jazz bands to chamber ensembles and crooners to symphonies. Some, such as the usfet liaison officer in Vienna, found the approach adopted a mistake. As he later remarked, "most American officials didn't have a feel for what younger Europeans wanted. . . . they were interested in us as Americans, but we were interested only in showing them that we were good Europeans."[16] As a result, American confidence (which among pwd's planners was mingled with contempt) in the power of free enterprise and the influence of the GIs won out. Germany's high-brow culture would be reconstructed by design; its popular music would be reoriented by the sheer force of America's swinging sound.

MUSIC AND NAZISM

By the time the decision was made to include classical music in the reorientation program, American soldiers had already fought their way into Germany. Despite this, pwd's main planning documents — MG Law 191 and the Information Manual — provided only the most general information concerning the cultural profile of Nazi Germany. pwd officers knew that Nazism had contaminated cultural life and, as soldiers, they anticipated the damage of war and the hostility of the locals. But no instruction or preconception prepared them for the multiple and daunting tasks they now faced.

What the Americans found was that most of the larger centers in their zone, the south German *Länder* of Bavaria, Hesse, Württemberg and part of Baden, had been destroyed by bombing and ground fighting. Municipal services did not function, streets were impassible, bodies decayed among the ruins, and there was no food or water or fuel. Remarkable pockets of life — buildings that had miraculously avoided the bombs and fires — speckled the wreckage and most of the houses in the leafy neighborhoods beyond the centers remained untouched. But the destruction was nonetheless staggering and would take many years to clean up. When he first toured Munich in April 1945, Edward Kilenyi asked his German driver to show him Richard Wagner's former house; he was taken past a pile of rubble. Three years later, one of Kilenyi's successors made the same request and was shown a big hole in the ground.[17]

Because concert halls and theaters were mostly located downtown, the American music officers found almost all the larger ones bomb-damaged, with Wiesbaden possessing the only fully functioning house in the American zone. Everywhere, costumes and opera sets had been destroyed or scattered, musical instruments lost or crushed in rubble, scores burned, and companies and orchestras devastated by deaths and dispersals. Most concerts in Germany ceased following Goebbels's 20 August 1944 announcement of total war, and many of the major opera companies and orchestras had not worked full-time for the last eight months. Some organizations, such as the Berlin Philharmonic Orchestra, continued to perform at special concerts designed to boost morale, but they did not run regular seasons. Several groups shut down completely. Ordinary musicians with less celebrated ensembles found themselves drafted into the army or serving in civilian defense units; many were dispersed or wounded or killed. The disruption that resulted was devastating and it was difficult after the war to find the musicians to staff most of the larger ensembles. Not that there were many places for them to play, even if they could be rounded up. Any hall that survived with a roof over it was being used by the army as shelter: in Munich, the seats on the balconies of the minimally damaged Prinzregenten Theater had been ripped out to make room for GIs to sleep; in Bayreuth, the Festival House was serving as a billet for soldiers of the 11th Tank Division.[18]

Nowhere was the destruction greater than in the Berlin John Bitter toured in late July 1945. Ravaged by years of Allied bombing and devastated by ten days of bitter street fighting at the end of the war, the city had just endured two months of savage Soviet occupation. The Red Army, which pummeled its way through Berlin in the last days of April, only withdrew from the city's western half on 11 July to make way for the British, American, and, eventually, French troops. When the Americans arrived, thousands of bodies still lay unburied and rot-

The foyer of the Munich Staatsoper, 1945
(Photo courtesy of Jeremiah Evarts)

ting, clogging cracked sewers and subway tunnels and feeding the proliferating swarms of rats and flies; the water was foul and contaminated, the streets narrowed by debris, the population starving. For weeks, Soviet soldiers had ransacked the city, removing everything of value and raping the terrified women they found hiding within the ruins. It was, according to Lucius Clay, commander of the American military government, a city of the dead. As one of his officers remarked, "there remains nothing human about it. The water is polluted, it smells of corpses, you see the most extraordinary shapes of ruins and more ruins and still more ruins . . . people in civilian clothes among these mountains of ruins appears merely to deepen the nightmare." As late as 1949, an American visitor to Berlin observed, if "one were let loose to walk on the surface of the moon, to trudge through a lunar landscape of craters and jagged peaks, up-heaved against the black of empty outer-space, perhaps one might begin to sense the comfortless, forsaken quality of these pulverised sections of the city. All life had crept out of those areas which take in the biggest part of the city. No trees in the Tiergarten. The Siegesallee a cemetery of unburied marble mutilations, only the Siegesäule bolt upright carrying its gilt angel with uninterrupted audacity. The Reichstag, the Kroll Oper, tangles of twisted girders, resembling empty bird cages. Beyond the Brandenburg Tor, the blocks seem to be made of brown sugar that has gone hard in lumps and streaks." To this observer, it felt like a city "buried above ground." Blasted into a living death, it was a metropolis "hushed to a whisper."[19] No wonder John Bitter remembered his major challenge as one of raising music out of the silence.

Reassembling the pieces of a disrupted art was the first job undertaken by the music officers. They had to secure halls for performances, vet artists, and determine the terms on which music would be organized. Costumes and scores had to be gathered and a mechanism for circulating them established. But the Americans also had to figure out who was to take responsibility for hiring musicians, paying them, and rebuilding the damaged theaters. Although the *Länder* and municipalities continued to exist as organizational entities, they functioned with local administrations appointed by the Americans and without intrinsic political authority. Because full German self-governance had been terminated, the Americans had to determine the role that governments would assume in cultural life. Unlike in the United States, where theaters were mostly privately organized and financed, in Germany they were traditionally supported by public subsidies and their senior personnel were government appointees. As occupied Germany no longer had wealthy patrons who could underwrite the costs of private organizations, some form of government subsidy was accepted as necessary. But an overweening state was perceived by the Americans in 1945 as

one of their former enemy's hereditary ailments. The Germans' pre-
disposition to subordinate themselves to the will of the state, they
believed, largely explained their willingness to elect Nazis and accept
their tyranny. Allowing a government to reassert its financial and administrative authority over the entertainment sector was therefore a
dangerous proposition. For German cultural life to be reconstructed
according to democratic principles, the power of the state in the arts
would have to be held in check by the rights of the public and the
freedom of the artists. Somehow, then, governments had to be brought
to accept the necessity of paying the piper without calling the tune.

In seeking to limit government authority over the arts, the occupiers confronted what they believed to be innate German predispositions. But they felt they had to persevere because they saw in the
Third Reich not primarily a "racial state" (whose first principle was
racial purification) but a bureaucratic behemoth. The Nazis had established layer upon layer of bureaucracy within the arts, each held together by the desire to realize party purposes and every one of them
peppered with party loyalists. Musicians were strongly encouraged to
join Nazi cultural associations, and all were required to have membership in the regime's professional union for musicians, the Reichsmusikkammer, or one of its associated chambers. Everything from the
artists' pension fund to the copyright association was coordinated by
the Propaganda Ministry to serve political goals. The Nazi state was
never all that rationally organized and its administrative structure was
byzantine, but the ideal that each part worked toward the center (the
Führerprinzip) was essential to its functioning. For the Americans,
then, eliminating party influence meant more than simply outlawing
Nazism; it entailed fostering a connection between the state and the
arts that rested on principles of decentralized authority and democratic
checks and balances. Only in this way, they believed, could the public
sector manage and fund music life without manipulating it for political
purposes.

Even as they grappled with the problem of democratizing the arts
bureaucracy, the music officers had to ensure that specifically Nazi
influences were removed from the opera house and concert hall and
that party supporters and profiteers were punished. This was not easily
done because, as the Americans discovered, Nazi influence within music life was pervasive. In the 1930s, the Nazis purged the entertainment
sector of Jews, utterly skewing its character. Jewish artists were segre-

gated, ostracized, and driven out, and the works of Jewish composers, even those central to the repertoire, were banned. Because the regime suffered severe international criticism for its actions, the maintenance of artistic quality in a Jew-free arts sector became a focus of national pride. Consequently, all those musicians who continued to perform in Germany after the Jews were barred from appearing with or before Gentiles were, in fact, accomplices in the crime of "Aryanization." By continuing to excel musically, they were legitimizing the Nazi claim that "true" German art did not need the Jews.

Musicians could not but have known what the regime was up to in this: they knew that Jews were being isolated and abused and murdered, that anti-Nazis were disappearing, and that the Gestapo was an instrument of torture and death. One could not really claim not to have understood what the Nazis were about, even if awareness of the ultimate extent of their genocidal depredations was limited. Certainly Goebbels used the German musical canon as an advertisement for the regime, and artists often heard their own talents used as an explanation for the war. As Goebbels declared in an April 1944 radio address, "our natural superiority makes us hated and disliked . . . [but the] hymns of hate against the Reich . . . are only the stammerings of their [the Allies'] inferiority complexes." This was a view that the psychological warriors found many Germans had assimilated: "[T]hey are fond of finding comfort in times of misfortune in the thought that their misfortunes are undeserved," one report noted. "They are fond of asking why it is that other nations so dislike them and giving the satisfying answer that it is the tribute of envy to their universally recognized excellence."[20]

The difficulty the music officers now faced was one of deciding for themselves the degree of guilt involved in the artists' complicity in the crimes of National Socialism. Should they hold to any extent responsible the violinist who occupied a position in an orchestra once held by a Jew? Had that violinist not profited from the racial purge and contributed to the normalization of life in this racially perverted state? Even more critically, what should the Americans do with the conductor who led the ensemble, who performed before Nazis and accommodated himself to the racial remodeling of his orchestra? Was the fact that many of the more prominent musicians helped ease the Jews out, by writing letters of recommendation, or giving them money to leave the country, to their credit or discredit?

The distressing truth was that the great majority of Germany's lead-ing non-Jewish musicians remained in the Third Reich and contin-ued to enjoy enormous public acclaim. All of them continued work-ing only because the government—in most cases, Joseph Goebbels's Propaganda Ministry—approved them for the posts they occupied. Those musicians who enjoyed a rising salary, awards and prizes, and the right to perform at special concerts before and for party officials did so because the regime recognized the value of their contribution to the patterning of life under dictatorship. When these people traveled abroad, whether to occupied countries or to Germany's wartime allies, they were touring with the permission of the Foreign Ministry and as ambassadors of the regime. The repertoire they performed generally conformed to Nazi ideological preferences: they did not play works by Jews or by those modern composers whom party officials deemed "degenerate," nor did they include compositions by nationals of coun-tries Germany was battling. Because little evidence exists of groups actually having their programs censored, and some artists did quietly continue to play proscribed works, the overall restrictions on the re-pertoire seem to have flowed largely from the artists' own fears that they not overstep what they perceived to be official limits.[21] Conse-quently, opera and orchestra directors, chamber musicians, and solo-ists accepted the racial reconstruction of both performance life and their repertoire even when not explicitly told to do so. As most of the prominent soloists, directors, and conductors could have found work outside the Reich—and here their options were greater than those of ordinary choristers or orchestra members—their decision to remain under the terms set for them by the Nazis suggests they should be held more culpable. This, however, implied that people should be punished simply for not giving up their jobs and emigrating for political or moral or artistic reasons.

Collaboration was never an absolute. Some artists clearly accepted the Nazis' demands more fully and compliantly than others. The diffi-culty for the occupation forces lay in tracing and measuring their be-havior. When the war ended, the documentary evidence was scattered and American officials knew it would take months, if not years, to recover and read. Much of the crucial evidence had also been de-stroyed. People, of course, remained and they were remarkably willing to talk, but could one rely on such oral evidence when judging collab-oration without appearing to be engaged in a gestapo-like witch-hunt?

One option would have been to close down all entertainment facilities for as many years as it took to sort things out, but this was never seriously considered. The army was the first to realize that a people deprived of entertainment outlets and opportunities for cultural expression would be very hard to manage. And once again, would the Americans not seem to be as exterminatory in their approach to German culture as the Nazis had been in the territories they sought to annex and repopulate? Germany would have to be purged in some way but ideally without making the victors appear as brutal and insensitive as the defeated had been.

Because theaters and concert halls had to be kept operating, another solution was to bar from performance life only those people who had chosen to actually join the party. Very few of Germany's most celebrated artists had done this, but some were *Parteigenossen*. Unfortunately, while the cases of these party members might appear less ambiguous, few of them really were. What the Americans discovered, to their distress, was that most Nazi artists claimed they had had no choice but to join, that they had been told they could not work or succeed unless they joined. Most insisted that they never believed in Nazi ideology, that they never did anything for the party, and that they continued to work just as before. A majority of them professed to have defied the regime all the time in little ways and to have done everything they could safely do to help Jews and others demonized by the Nazis. And many of those musicians who did join the party were young and insisted they could not get ahead without a membership card. Should the occupiers regard their actions sympathetically, or should their opportunistic bid for career enhancement be more harshly condemned? Further, even the military governors knew that many artists who rose to favor under the Nazis and made public statements supportive of the regime never joined the party. Was it fair to punish the "nominal," "opportunistic," or "*muß*" (those who felt they had no choice but to join) Nazis and leave such strong supporters or profiteers unpunished?

In addition to the myriad problems regarding individuals, the music officers had to deal with the critical issue of disengaging music culture itself from Nazi ideology. This was not just a matter of restoring a censored repertoire. Members in some groups, such as the Berlin Philharmonic or the Munich Staatsoper Orchestra received higher pay than other musicians because of their importance to Nazi officials. The status of these groups, and of certain favored soloists, had been enhanced in Germany, but what should be done with this legacy of Nazism? Should the rank ordering of organizations and people be consciously reversed as a way of undoing Nazi influences? Should pay scales be adjusted and an effort made to limit the careers of those most revered in the Reich? And what should be done about a culture that accepted the prominent place of the state and its apparatuses in artistic life?

Disentangling Nazism also meant confronting the fact that music had served propagandistic functions. It had been used to legitimate Nazism by demonstrating the Third Reich's continuity with Germany's past: the prominence of German performers and composers in Western culture was promoted as evidence of Aryan superiority, and Nazi veneration of a canon of eminent musicians was used as proof of fascism's connection with the nation's glories. If the occupation powers wanted Germany to make a fresh start, somehow postwar German music had to be disengaged from its prevailing ideological construction. Beethoven, for example, had been venerated in the Third Reich as an Aryan titan, a visionary outsider, and a symbol of virility, of revolutionary intensity, and of mastery through suffering.[22] If this reading of what Beethoven's music represented had embedded itself in the popular imagination, how could one continue performing his works without affirming values the Allies now hoped to excise? Music, it seemed, would have to be released from the images and ideas that encrusted it if it were to be reformed.

And then there was the problem of what to do with living composers whose works had been popular in the Third Reich. If the Allies allowed the compositions of such people as Werner Egk or Carl Orff to be performed, were they not symbolically accepting the legitimacy of the successes these artists had enjoyed in the Third Reich? Would they be able to set contemporary German music on a new course without relegating its current champions, who were perfumed with evil, to history's dustbin? The trouble was that if the music officers banned works by selected composers, they would be accused of doing what the Nazis had done. This meant they had to find a way of forcing German audiences to listen to music because it had been banned and not listening to works the Nazis praised without appearing to be tyrants themselves. Which raised a related issue: should they even identify a work as having a Jewish or non-German composer? Wasn't that just legitimizing the racial myth they otherwise denounced?

The endless questions reveal how terribly complex the issues facing the occupation authorities really were. The Americans had to find some method of controlling a foreign country in an evenhanded way; they had to remove wrongdoers and set a new course without tarnishing their own reputation as democrats; they had to resolve for themselves the difficult problem of whether an individual can contribute to the public life of a totalitarian state without bearing a measure of responsibility for the existence of that state; and, unlike most of us, they had to find their answers under difficult and pressing circumstances. Not surprisingly, they reached no consensus on how to proceed. Many American officers had been hardened by the war and were convinced that the social and cultural forces that inclined the Germans to support fascism had to be eliminated. Democracy, they believed, could never take hold so long as the roots of the Nazi cancer survived. Others believed that it would be impossible to persuade the Germans to accept democracy if the Americans behaved like dictators. While they accepted that Germany's cultural life had to be trimmed of its Nazi branches, they did not believe it was rotten to the core. Still others took an even more moderate line, doubting that culture had much to do with Nazism at all and suggesting that artists were too unimportant for the occupation to bother with. In short, there was little agreement on how to proceed with the result that each officer had to find his own way through the country's tangled moral ruins.

A QUESTION OF GUILT

Because PWD was the vanguard of American reeducation efforts, and because it was civilian rather than military in origin, it was a division with some unusual features. Unlike other MG personnel and soldiers, PWD officers were not bound by SHAEF regulations prohibiting fraternization with Germans. As a result they were able, from the outset, to develop close working relations with locals and to socialize with them as well. Unlike other Americans, PWD officers were not prohibited from going to shows attended by German civilians. Adding to these singular privileges, and to PWD's image as the division that went native, was the fact that its officers were by and large German speaking and were authorized to wear civilian clothes in public rather than uniforms. Finally, although its officers were paid out of MG's budget, its supplies were obtained through a civilian agency, the Department of State, and its operations were largely financed from revenues derived from the sale of books and newspapers, from movie tickets, and from radio subsidies contributed by the *Länder*. In the first eight months of 1945 alone, the division raised over $2.5 million from its retail operations — as much as it received from Congress — and this encouraged its singular sense of autonomy within the Military Government administration.[23] That autonomy continued even after August 1945, when PWD was dissolved and its operations assumed by a new unit, still under McClure's command, the Information Control Division (ICD).

ICD remained, like PWD before it, a loosely managed organization with McClure a distant commander who, though of firm convictions, never tried to regiment those working under him. Even after it was decided that the army would retain control over Germany for some time, and planning for a transfer to the State Department halted, McClure remained relatively aloof. He never attempted to resolve differences within his peculiar command, possibly because he recognized the difficulty of harmonizing the views of the various artists, newspapermen, professional soldiers, and corporate executives with whom he worked. As he told his former deputy chief, C. D. Jackson, who had returned to his job as vice-president of Time-Life, he was supervising, by mid-1946, the biggest media enterprise in the world with authority over 37 newspapers, 6 radio stations, 314 theaters and 642 cinemas, and 237 book publishers: it was an odd job for a professional soldier![24] But McClure's remove from the field units meant that important policy questions within the division were never settled, which continually disrupted its work. In particular, and despite his own feelings on the matter, McClure never managed to prevent advocates of a soft peace from influencing ICD policies.

For an officer charged with assuring German reorientation, it is remarkable how little confidence McClure expressed in the population. In his view, they had "ceased to be a civilized people," and he doubted whether there were very many "good Germans . . . waiting for a chance to prove their democratic attitude." As he really did not believe that the licensing system would work, to the extent that the Americans would not find the anti-Nazis needed to run the country's arts and information sectors, he adopted the pragmatic line that his division should maintain tight controls for the foreseeable future. In direct contrast to his superior, Military Governor Lucius Clay, who believed in turning over administrative responsibilities to the locals as swiftly as possible, McClure thought that the Germans "do not have to form their own opinion — the Germans have to be told."[25]

The general's tough stance on Germany was echoed by his Intelligence Section chief, Alfred Toombs, who was in charge of the denazification program. Intelligence, unlike the other units in PWD/ICD, was more closely connected to OSS and army Intelligence, and it saw its role as one of exterminating Nazism rather than promoting democracy. Under Toombs's vigorous leadership (and his attitudes may have been influenced by the fact that 12th Army Group intelligence officers under his command were the first Americans into the Buchenwald concentration camp), ICD became the most ardent force of denazification in the American zone, and it purged German culture and the media of all those it thought had joined, believed in, sympathized with, or profited from the Nazi Party. McClure's and Toombs's approach was to use ICD as a revolutionary instrument: they sought to eliminate Germany's cultural elite and educate a new generation in democratic values. According to their thinking, ICD control should be remorseless, comprehensive, and long-term.

Behind ICD headquarters policies was the conviction that Germans had waged war and committed heinous atrocities because they were culturally predisposed to aggression and a hatred of others. McClure argued that ICD's ultimate mission was "to cause the individual German to renounce the doctrines of Nazism and militarism by making him aware of the moral issues involved in German aggression and of his personal share in the collective German responsibility for the acts of the Nazis and militarists." It had to be made clear to the population that "we have waged war against Germany and not only against the Nazis" and that "we condemn them on account of their aggressions and war crimes." Punishment — which involved identifying all those who had associated themselves with the goals of the regime or held chauvinistic, militaristic, or antidemocratic views and compelling them to work as manual laborers cleaning the rubble and burying the dead — was simply a symbolic way of stripping away "German misconceptions about Germany and its relationship to the world." America's wrath would fall on the most prominent, not because they were necessarily the worst, but because their punishment would serve as a lesson to all. Reeducation, McClure maintained, could only begin once ICD had "aroused in the Germans a sense of collective responsibility for Germany's crimes." Indeed, "the Germans can look forward to a decent, civilized future only if they learn from the lessons of the past. By accepting Germany's guilt as a nation as his personal guilt, the individual begins the task of personal reconstruction." Only at this point would the defeated be able to appreciate "the reasonableness and justice of American views and the decency and attractiveness of American institutions."[26]

McClure was not alone in condemning the Germans as collectively guilty for World War II and the Nazi's crimes against humanity. It had been a long and cruel war, and few who fought the Germans, at least until the final weeks, doubted their absolute commitment to the struggle. As the battle-hardened cartoonist, Bill Mauldin, observed, "our army has seen few actual Nazis, except when they threw in special ss divisions. [But] we have seen the Germans — the youth and the men and the husbands and the fathers of Germany — and we know them for a ruthless, cold, cruel, and powerful enemy." Even so sympathetic an individual as Hans Speier, a German-born sociologist who emigrated to the United States in the 1930s and returned to Germany in 1945 as an ICD intelligence officer, insisted that his former countrymen accept their collective guilt for Nazi aggression and genocide. Speier was deeply disturbed when he spoke with his old philosophy professor at the University of Heidelberg, Karl Jaspers. The eminent existential philosopher was at the time writing a treatise on the question of German guilt and had managed to distinguish, in his own mind, between *collective liability* and *guilt*. "He did not speak about what the Germans — as distinguished from the Nazis — had done," Speier reported sadly, "that is to say, he did not dwell on what they had done or left undone to make it possible for criminals to prosper and command respect . . . nor did he talk of the millions of Germans who shared in the looting of Europe." Why, he asked himself, was Jaspers himself not "worn down by doubts on this issue, if not silenced by grief and horror." Why did the old philosopher not ask himself: "When did I make an unnecessary compromise? When did I look away?" Why, Speier wanted to know "did [he] not leave Germany in 1933? Any university in any country . . . would have extended a welcome." Jaspers, he sighed, was probably "among the best Germans we left behind us in 1933," but even he was unready for democracy, for even he appeared "not to have realized what the Germans [as opposed to the Nazis] did to Europe."[27]

Not everyone in PWD/ICD was as convinced as McClure or Toombs or Speier of collective German guilt or of the need for absolute American control. Unlike Intelligence, which was established to judge people and punish them, the division's functional units — Radio, Film, Theater, Publications, and Music — were expected to find trustworthy Germans and work with them. Explicitly charged with rapidly reactivating cultural life "in order to prevent possibilities of social tension," they were also under orders to entrust "suitable Germans" who combined "expert knowledge [and a] willingness to accept our ideas" with licenses to perform and publish.[28] In other words, ICD's field units were supposed to initiate reeducation through German intermediaries even though their commander believed hardly any reliable locals could be found.

The fundamental disagreement over the method of information control was present from the beginning. The Music Branch's original planning document, the "Draft Guidance on Control of Music," which Sam Rosenbaum had prepared on the basis of the PWE document in March 1945, had explicitly set the unit on a course contrary to that favored by McClure. Adopting the approach advanced by OWI and IIA, Rosenbaum directed that the branch "should not give the impression of trying to regiment culture in the Nazi manner . . . we should not try to compile a complete index of political music," or indeed blacklist composers, conductors, or artists, with the exception of "those who have proved themselves to be ardent Nazis." Instead of regimenting musical life and excluding artists who remained active in the Third Reich (even those who "occupied prominent positions giv[ing] implicit support to the regime"), PWD/ICD must influence German culture "by positive means, i.e., by encouraging what we think beneficial and crowding out what we think dangerous." Crowding out would not be achieved by dictate, however, but by "introduc[ing] and reintroduc[ing] the German public to the large musical world from which they have been cut off for so long. . . . [In this way] performances of [undesirable] music should . . . be crowded out with more desirable music." In addition to rejecting censorship, the branch refused to specifically press the works of Jewish composers, insisting that attention should not be drawn to them for fear of creating the impression that they were in some way distinct. Instead, "they should take their place in a balanced program. We suggest that it be part of our practice to encourage the restoration to the repertoire of works which were banned under the Nazis, whether Jewish, Russian, British, American, or what-not." Consequently, even though ICD officers found that "the Germans are so anxious to please they would play Mendelssohn, Offenbach and Goldmark all the time if we didn't halt them," the Music Branch feared the results of this and "tactfully suggests more diversity in the programs." This applied to artists as well, and branch chief Davidson Taylor instructed that even "Jewish musicians should be employed on the basis of ability" and not to right wrongs or teach the Germans a lesson.[29]

What the Music Branch's internal guidance recommended was that German reorientation be allowed to occur through a normalization of performance life. The works of composers from outside Germany, of banned artists, and of Americans were to be promoted by discrete methods while those of artists who had been especially popular in the Reich could not be "built up by special concerts." Similarly, performers whose careers had suffered under Hitler would be offered opportunities, should their talents warrant them, while those who had profited from Nazi rule would be prevented from holding licenses or running organizations, although they could still pursue their art. As one field officer in Wiesbaden explained, "we destroy only Nazi culture, not German culture." According to branch officers, the goal of music control was not to punish a defeated people, it was to "restore the exchange of ideas between Germany and the world outside it" and encourage German reeducation through democratic means. "We must be informative without boasting and self-assured without smugness . . . we must try to [reeducate] . . . without preaching and without facile righteousness," OWI advised PWD units in Germany. By "projecting the strength and virtues of democracy," rather than by control and recrimination, the cultural officers hoped they could "induce the Germans to reconsider their basic political beliefs and prejudices."[30]

If the approach to German reorientation adopted by the Music Branch in early 1945 originated with OWI and IIA, it was supported by the soldiers PWD/ICD recruited to staff its field units. Most of them were young artists and arts administrators who shared a certain idealism about music and its place in society. Edward Kilenyi, who served as Music Branch chief in Bavaria from June 1945 to April 1946, was thirty-five years old when he assumed his post. He had studied piano in

Philadelphia and at the Liszt Academy in Budapest, having his concert debut in Amsterdam in 1939 and his American debut in Philadelphia, one year later. By the time he was drafted in 1942, he had already performed with many notable European and German orchestras and his recording of Liszt's *Totentanz* had won him a Grand Prix du Disque. The son of an eminent Austrian-born sculptor, John Bitter, who ran the Berlin branch from August 1945 to September 1948, was thirty-six at the end of the war. He had studied at the Curtis Institute in Philadelphia and had been an assistant to Leopold Stokowski. In 1934, at the age of twenty-five, he took over the Jacksonville Symphony Orchestra and six years later he moved over to the Miami Symphony. Bitter joined the army as a tank driver in June 1942 and by 1945, because of his fluency in German and French, was made a G-2 (intelligence) officer attached to the 9th Army. The branch chief in Württemberg-Baden from January 1946 through August 1947 was the conductor Newell Jenkins. A pacifist, he had enlisted in the Field Ambulance Service in 1942 and served in the North African and Italian campaigns. Born in Connecticut in 1915, Jenkins had received his musical education in Nazi Germany: in Dresden (1932–34) and under Wilibald Gurlitt at the University of Freiburg (1934–37) and Carl Orff in Munich (1938). Returning to the United States as war approached, he studied with Paul Hindemith at Yale and, for a year prior to enlistment, conducted and worked in arts administration in New York.

John Evarts, who succeeded Kilenyi as branch chief in Munich and went on to lead the Theater and Music Section from 1948 to 1951, was the grandson of a celebrated New York senator and secretary of state in the Hayes administration. Born in 1908, he graduated from Yale in 1930 and went to Germany for language and music studies. In 1934, he secured a job as professor of music at an experimental college being set up at Black Mountain in North Carolina. There Evarts worked alongside such eminent émigré German artists and educators as Josef Albers and Erwin Straus. Although a charming man and inspired teacher, Evarts was ostracized at Black Mountain once his homosexuality became public knowledge, and to escape he joined the army in 1942. Because of his language skills, Evarts served in radio intelligence in the signals corps. Other branch officers had similar peacetime backgrounds: Jerome Pastene, at the Heidelberg post, was a conductor and music critic; William Dubensky, in Wiesbaden, was a young violinist whose future career had been cut short in 1944 by a bullet through the hand; William Hinrischen, who was chief of the Music Branch in the American zone in 1946–47, was the former owner of the Peters music publishing house in Leipzig. A Jew, Hinrischen had been forced to flee Nazi Germany and surrender his business a decade before. Eric Clarke, Evarts's predecessor as commander of the combined Theater and Music Section, had been the administrative secretary of the Metropolitan Opera in New York City.

It was a distinguished and knowledgeable team of college-educated, German-speaking, music professionals that ICD assembled. But the very similarity in their backgrounds meant that they shared a culture that predominated in artistic circles and included, among other things, a belief in music's healing value. As John Evarts wrote, music might not be able to tame savage beasts or prevent the destruction and horror of war, "but if ever the beasts of war are tamed, it will be music which will grant us the strength of heart and soul to do it." The social value of music, Evarts believed, lay in its ability to arouse sympathy and to bind people together in the mutual experience of their humanity. It could be abused—manipulated in such a way as to make groups identify with their nation or region and feel superiority over others—but, in itself and if left alone, music was an "international language" that would inspire empathy and fraternity among peoples. Listening to the music of Shostakovich, John Bitter explained, made one feel kinship, not just with the Russian peoples, but with all mankind. Consequently, although it might be used for propagandistic purposes, music was inspirational, not political. This was why it was ridiculous to think of prohibiting works like Strauss's *Ein Heldenleben* or the funeral march from *Götterdämmerung* because of their Nazi associations. If these pieces were thought to be sullied by Nazism, Sam Rosenbaum declared, then so too were such popular works as the second movements of Beethoven's Third and Seventh symphonies.[31] Because of convictions like these, the branch officers repudiated censorship, arguing that a rapid reactivation of concert life was the first step in German rehabilitation.

But if music was not itself political and generally served positive emotional and spiritual ends, the same could not be said about musicians. The American cultural officers accepted that even great and inspiring artists might be unpleasant people or have done bad things. Kilenyi, for example, sized up many of the more prominent musicians he met in an article published shortly after his return to the United

States. For composer Richard Strauss, he suggested, "all questions of politics and humanity boiled down to whether Axis or Allied royalties showed more promise"; for Hans Pfitzner, whom, he said, "had violent altercation[s]" with the Nazis, the only point of conflict was the regime's "insufficient appreciation of Pfitzner's works." Artists, Kilenyi admitted, "from [the] world-famous . . . to peasant band accordionists . . . represented fantastic varieties of convictions. There were Nazi thugs, mystics, careerists, people compelled to join [the party] to safeguard self or relatives and others who just managed to walk the tightrope without compromising their integrity." But if one thing characterized most of the artists he met, it was their political naiveté. Even Elly Ney, an ardently Nazi concert pianist, Kilenyi rated a political unsophisticate. Henry Alter, PWD's first cultural officer in Berlin, agreed: "European artists have always been flattered by the existing government without giving them any true allegiance and without, in fact, ever acquiring a political conscience. . . . that they continued to work is partly due to the professional vanity without which they would not be artists, partly to the lack of political conscience, and finally to the varying degrees of pressure exerted by the government."[32]

The convictions of the professional musicians and arts administrators staffing ICD's Music Branch were therefore completely in harmony with the orders they received from OWI and the Department of State. This is why they saw their work, from the beginning, in a positive light: their mission was to sift the rubble for the least tainted Germans, rebuild the concert halls, and place the public administration of the arts on a democratic basis. The cultural officers did not feel they had to control German music but to reform it by example and by promoting what the Nazis had suppressed. If McClure and Toombs hoped to resolve the complex questions involved in reorienting Nazi Germany through rigid controls and a sweeping purge of the cultural leadership, the branch officers sought to nudge the occupied into democracy without humiliating them. Unfortunately, because headquarters never imposed one approach to the problem at the heart of reorientation, the Music Branch continued to act as it preferred; but because more powerful units in the division maintained a contradictory position, it was also continually being overruled. This result was distressing for local artists and administrators and revealed to them MG's confusion over goals and methods.[33]

The issues involved in Nazi Germany's cultural transformation were profoundly complicated, and they inevitably provoked dramatic and oversimplified solutions. It is to the credit of the music officers that they were committed to finding a middle ground between the extremes: they decried censorship, endorsed a case-by-case approach to blacklisting, and promoted the notion that the good could be encouraged without prohibiting the bad. Convinced that they might only advance democracy by acting like democrats, they suggested leaving the ruins of Nazism where they were and encouraging without compelling positive artistic sentiments. They pushed these ideas as quintessentially American: tolerant, positive, and responsible. The structural reforms they suggested had at their core such similarly American notions as the need to maintain checks and balances and the responsibility of government to the taxpayers. But at the center of the music officers' beliefs was the idea that the Germans had to be participants (though never determinants) in their own reeducation: "Military Government has not come to graft on to the German nation the 'American democracy,' but to help the German people see to it that despotic forces do not again crush the democratic aspirations which have their roots within Germany itself."[34] This was, needless to say, an idealistic vision. Branch officers adopted a definition of collaboration sufficiently weak as to allow them to find good Germans even among Hitler's supporters. They insisted they were encouraging the Germans' own love of freedom, but the model of democracy they used was thoroughly American. And while they asserted that they had to act like democrats to teach democracy, they neglected to mention that the locals only complied with their wishes because they had bayonets against their backs.

Four months after John Bitter and his team absorbed the terrible silence of Berlin, Edward Kilenyi was sent to appraise conditions in Bayreuth. Unable to contain his curiosity, the music officer took time out from his evaluation of the damage to theater facilities to visit the battered estate of the Wagner family, Wahnfried. There, in the garden behind the house, he expressed, in a tiny act not taken, his own disgust for Nazi Germany and his undimmed idealism about music. "It's funny the way things develop, you see," he later recalled, "I was in the backyard . . . and there was a bunch of rubble and a bathtub in the backyard too, oddly enough. And there was a small book, *Der Fall Wagner*, by Nietzsche. It was quite a souvenir. But somehow, the idea of taking that souvenir repelled me — it seemed unclean — so I just left it there."[35] It was an absurd moment: standing outside a bomb-blasted monument of German music history, with its open-air bathtub, quiet gardens, and the grave of one of the world's most celebrated composers. But Kilenyi, who appreciated the comedy, could still not bring himself to defile this shrine of music through theft. Something unpleasant, he remembered, lingered about the book, a filth that had sullied Germany's artists and that he was determined would not compromise him. Perhaps the issues engaged in the tract — its critique of Richard Wagner's anti-Semitism — were simply too painful to this Hungarian American Jew; perhaps it was just that this book had once belonged to a family he knew had been fouled by Nazism. Whatever it was, he would not trophy-hunt nor would he stoop to book burning by throwing the thing away. In keeping with the directions he had received from OWI, Kilenyi wanted to reform Germany without compulsion, by the sheer moral force of his democratic beliefs and moral rectitude. And so, in the end, he left the book where it was. In so doing, perhaps, he made a small contribution to the undermining of the revolution that his commanding officer insisted Germany so badly needed, but his inaction was the honorable thing to do.

Silent wastes, shattered cultural icons, and destroyed traditions. This is how the music officers remembered the Germany they found in 1945. The task of rebuilding was to them a task of revitalization. They would fill a silence with new sounds, populate a music library with unknown works, create a democratic foundation for the arts. They had a naive confidence in the reforming power of music and in the intrinsic goodness of the democratic way of life. They somehow believed that ordinary Germans would embrace new sounds and accept as equal an American culture that they had hitherto viewed with disdain. They apparently thought that prominent artists of the Nazi period would acknowledge that their day had passed and would step aside gracefully. They felt they could inspire government officials to act democratically by treating them with courtesy and respect. These were overly optimistic beliefs, reached by men more comfortable as artists than as uniformed administrators. Although the field officers' efforts to chart a middle course were commendable, they were no less idealistic in their endeavors than the extremists with whom they argued. In the end, what can perhaps be said for them is that, within the limits of their own understanding of the term, they tried to behave decently. Simple though it may seem, in the aftermath of so terrible a war and in the face of so many extreme approaches to its ending, it was something of an achievement.

Otto Pasetti felt the old man was suicidal. Over eighty and in uncertain health, Germany's most famous living composer, Richard Strauss, had recently been placed on Information Control's blacklist. Though his compositions could still be performed, he could receive no personal honors or recognition and he could not conduct or appear before the public. While on the blacklist, he was also prohibited from collecting royalties on performances of his works. For a man who had spent much of his life fighting for authorial property rights, these penalties were hard to bear. It grieved him that the world considered him a Nazi, and he was desperately fearful for the future. Within a month of the issuance of the blacklist, in November 1945, Strauss fled the American zone and sought refuge in Switzerland. But he could not so easily cast off his tribulations, and the Swiss newspapers continued to bait him, calling for his deportation and charging him with Nazi sympathies. Early in December, shortly before Pasetti's visit, the Basel *Nationalzeitung* published a brief poem the composer had written in adulation of Hans Frank, the murderous Nazi governor of Poland. The poem had been composed as a thank-you to Frank after he had intervened to prevent the Strauss estate from being used to house displaced persons (DPs), but its Swiss publication was almost too much for Strauss to bear.[1]

Pasetti, the American music officer in Salzburg, left the composer feeling that he had been harshly treated. Strauss appeared old and weak and, as Pasetti realized, he had never held Nazi sympathies. True, he had eagerly served the regime—composing a hymn for the 1936 Olympics and festival music to honor Germany's ally, Japan; agreeing to conduct on short notice when others withdrew or were dismissed for political or racial reasons; traveling abroad as a self-acknowledged advertisement for the regime; and energetically serving as first president of the Reichsmusikkammer, the Third Reich's musicians' organization. But he had also defied the government in his collaboration with Stefan Zweig, the Jewish librettist of *Die schweigsame Frau*, and, in so doing, had fallen into disgrace. Moreover, many in his Jewish daughter-in-law's family had been interned and in one instance the composer had traveled to Theresienstadt in a futile effort to secure the release of her grandmother. Strauss made friends with several prominent Nazi officials, but he used those contacts to protect his "racially mixed" children and grandchildren. He ingratiated himself with the regime to secure his income, to guard his family, and to advance his relatively narrow vision of German culture. He tried to do so without compromising his beliefs or his art and, while he failed in that ambition, by the early 1940s he was too tainted by his Jewish connections and too set in his ways to remain a Nazi favorite. Performances of some of his works were prohibited, his family was harassed, and his appeals for protection were treated off-handedly.[2]

Strauss served a regime that didn't much like him effectively and well, even if he suffered terrible anxiety and fear for himself and for those he loved. But the information control officers who compiled the blacklist were unmoved by the ambiguities in his case. Their mandate was to revolutionize German society, not to right individual wrongs or rehabilitate particular people. Convinced that the job of distinguishing the finer shades of guilt was impossible in the confused early months of the occupation, ICD's denazifiers applied simple standards. Those who had been prominent under the Nazis, who appeared to have profited professionally, and whom the public would have recognized as major cultural figures in the Reich were blacklisted. Only in this way, the Americans believed, could the Germans be shown that the new day had dawned with its new culture born. This hard, punitive approach grew out of the conviction that most Germans held a fundamentally baleful world view. Strauss was therefore on the mandatory removal list because the denazification officers believed he symbolized a malign culture.

But not everyone agreed. In fact, many in the American forces treated Strauss with deference and sympathy. His estate in Garmisch was not requisitioned and, as he happily noted shortly after the appearance of U.S. troops in May 1945, "the Americans are extremely kind and friendly, and I can hardly avoid the autograph-hunters—I have often had to write down the waltz from *Rosenkavalier*, and, on one occasion, the Don Juan motif." Among those who visited the composer in Garmisch was Harry Bogner, the first chief of the Music Branch in Bavaria, who came down to see what he could do to make the old fellow comfortable and to collect his autograph. Even after Strauss was blacklisted, in October 1945, his property was not seized, and, quite amazingly, he was issued a travel permit for Switzerland. Travel visas were almost impossible to obtain in 1945 and required multiple levels of approval; for someone on the mandatory removal list to have been provided one was extraordinary and revealed the discomfort many Americans felt with the composer's blacklisting. Quite possibly, senior officials feared for the celebrated composer's health and did not want him to die on their watch. But the kindness shown Strauss by those who met him was honest enough. Certainly, Otto Pasetti felt nothing but sympathy.[3]

Strauss's works were beloved in the United States, particularly his "waltz opera," *Rosenkavalier*, but that was not the only reason the composer encountered Americans both compassionate and hard-boiled. In fact, presenting just such a Janus face to the Germans was a common practice for the occupiers, especially in the Information Control Division, whose operations depended on its competing personalities. As Robert McClure described it, ICD had both "positive and negative functions," which he believed would dominate different stages of the occupation. During the initial "control" phase, cultural and information sectors would be shut down and purged of their Nazi elements, an exercise referred to in the Potsdam declaration as "the negative process of extirpating Nazism and militarism." Once cleansed, the arts and news media would be revived and "encouraged" along democratic lines as part of the "positive" stage of German reconstruction.[4]

Remaking Germany's culture therefore involved both denazification, intended to cut the umbilical cord connecting the postwar zone to its depraved past, and a promotion of new attitudes and visions. Denazification was the most purely "negative" face of reconstruction, as Richard Strauss discovered, combining "the mandatory removal of symbols and leaders" and a program to "arouse" in the population "a sense of collective responsibility for Germany's crimes." The positive side, reeducation, required teaching the Germans "to understand to evaluate the products of Kant, Goethe, Bach, Beethoven, Heine, Schubert" as models of "liberal ways of thinking" and also involved exposing the defeated to "the best" in foreign music and literature in order to break down any notion of German national superiority. Admittedly, this two-stage model was never as clean in fact as in theory, and for most of the occupation both positive and negative elements operated coterminously. It was less chronology that distinguished Information Control's two functions than structures. Whereas the Music Branch officers busied themselves with promoting international music and encouraging liberal thinking about Bach, Beethoven, and Schubert, the Intelligence Section took on the job of purging Germany of its Nazi artists.

INTELLIGENCE

During the war, the Intelligence Section of PWD interrogated captured soldiers and civilians and monitored German radio in order to measure enemy morale. It also assembled a partial list of individuals in the media who were considered active Nazis for eventual dismissal under the occupation. Once across the Rhine, Intelligence continued these functions and added the job of compiling the necessary background information on surviving media facilities and personnel. In August 1945, when PWD was dissolved and ICD created, the Intelligence Section began sifting the cultural field, investigating applicants for employment and expanding its earlier white, gray, and black lists. The lists were used to determine employability: persons on the "black" and "grey unacceptable" lists were to be denied any work above manual labor (these were the "mandatory removals"); those on the "grey acceptable" list were to be allowed to work at their profession but not to hold "policy-making or executive positions"; and those on the "white" list were to be free to take any job that was offered. The first lists were published on 10 October 1945, and a supplement appeared in December. By the summer of 1946, Intelligence had compiled files on 10,000 individuals in the media and arts sectors.[5]

Initial plans for the occupation had stipulated the need to eliminate Nazism through the removal of National Socialists from all public and private positions. Identifying a Nazi proved more difficult than had originally been imagined, however, and as a preliminary guide, in April 1945, PWD provided a list of organizations whose leading members could be treated as Nazis. Among these organizations was the Reichsmusikkammer in which most musicians had been required to hold membership. This simple approach was complicated somewhat by the Potsdam Agreement of July 1945, which, without revoking the previous instructions, added the stipulation that "all public and semi-public office[s] and . . . positions of responsibility in important private undertakings" should be purged of anyone who had been "more than nominal participants" in the political life of the Third Reich. This created the problem of determining whether one was nominal or active in the party or one of its affiliates. In the interests of resolving this difficulty, the Joint Chiefs of Staff (JCS) in September 1945 circulated JCS 1067/6 which included the following clarification and guidance: "Persons are to be treated as more than nominal participants in party activities and as active supporters of Nazism and militarism when they have . . . voluntarily given substantial moral or material support or political assistance of any kind to the Nazi party or Nazi officials and leaders." The directive of the Joint Chiefs was implemented in Germany as MG Law #8 (in late September 1945), which codified the new definition of guilt and established investigation and appeal procedures.[6]

For the remainder of 1945, the Potsdam Agreement, as defined by JCS 1067/6 and as implemented under MG Law #8, provided official guidance to the Intelligence Section in its purge of the informational and cultural sectors. Clearly, neither policy statement was a calibrated instrument for measuring Nazi sympathy, as words like "voluntarily," "substantial," and "moral" were open to wide interpretation. Richard Strauss, for example, was a past president of a prohibited organization and had provided moral support to the regime through his conducting, policy direction, and travels. The major question revolved around whether he had done so "voluntarily," given his family situation, but the Americans felt that he had already demonstrated his willingness to serve the Reich prior to his family coming under threat and that the latter had not motivated the former. Judgments like this one struck many in Information Control as harsh, but Intelligence prided itself on its ability to root out Nazis whom no one else could see. Significantly, many of those working in the Denazification Branch of ICD Intelligence had themselves been victims of totalitarianism. In Bavaria and Hesse the top intelligence officers in charge of interviewing musicians were Czech, Polish, and Hungarian refugees. In Stuttgart, Intelligence was in the hands of an Austrian Jew and a German émigré. In Berlin, where eavesdropping on the Soviets was considered as important as understanding the Germans, both senior officers were refugees from Bolshevism, one being an Estonian Jew and the other a Russian aristocrat. Most of these officers knew Germany before the war and all, inspired perhaps by their rigorous section chief, Al Toombs, favored an inclusive definition of Nazism. Real opponents of the regime would have emigrated, the intelligence staff thought, and anyone weak enough to have served the Nazis was inappropriate material for the job of reconstructing Germany. As the section noted of itself, "high standards of personal selection were maintained by ICD despite differences of opinion, some within ICD itself. . . . [S]eldom . . . did [the] Intelligence Section temper its judgment with expediency, and as a result of this strong policy, information services were sometimes criticized for not using the ablest German available."[7]

ICD Intelligence imagined itself fighting in the vanguard of a revolution. The war had not ended for these officials in May 1945; in fact, Intelligence liked to refer to a "combat phase of the War with Germany" and a "Military Government phase." As one directive noted, "just as Psychological Warfare made use of the information media to drive home each fact which would help to break down the enemy's will to resist, Information Control should reinforce every educational program in an effort to reach all sectors of the German population with material designed to eliminate Nazism and militarism and make possible the growth of peace and democracy." Destroying Germany's armament industry or limiting its industrial power "will not alone abolish aggressive tendencies on the part of the German people. It is not the machine itself that makes war, but the mind behind the machine."[8]

For ICD's revolutionaries, the occupation's ultimate purpose was "the eliminat[ion of] the fundamental conditions in German life which have made her a recurring menace to the peace of the world." To achieve this, "not only must the basic social attitudes of the German people be changed but also political and economic power must be shifted from the ruling groups in German society during the Nazi regime to other groups in whom we may justifiably have greater confidence." Cultural change was seen as crucial to this revolution because the Nazis justified waging war on their neighbors with the assertion that they were superior to everyone else and were doing the world a service by pushing less enlightened peoples aside. The dominance of German thinkers and composers and the supposed preeminence of Germany's performers were used by nationalists as evidence of the country's superiority. Why should a people capable of producing Beethoven accept second-class status in Europe? And why would any of Germany's neighbors feel aggrieved at being conquered by so evidently superior and enlightened a people? The sublimity of German music, which was seen by many as the preeminent manifestation of the "national soul," was used during the war to disprove charges that the Nazis were cruel and oppressive. Music pointed Germans toward their true selves: profound yet organized, spiritual yet disciplined.

ICD was charged with the control of the arts and media to eliminate attitudes such as these. In time, it was believed—and the division initially thought in terms of a twenty-five-year American presence—the redirection of the cultural and news channels would effect a transformation in German thinking. As its goal was the elimination of a culture conducive to war making, it is not surprising that Intelligence broadly interpreted the orders mandating its activities. ICD's "long term task . . . the destruction of all that remains of the Nazi and militarist influences" could only be achieved through the forceful removal of anyone who gave "substantial moral support" to or "benefitted to any serious extent" from National Socialism or who "before 1933 actively supported any party advocating German nationalism."[9] In other words, any musician who continued to conduct or compose or perform as a soloist or orchestra member could be judged severely because his art made an evil regime seem normal. Denazification, which is generally considered to imply a kind of individual purge, like going through a detoxification treatment, was actually alien to the ICD approach in 1945. Artists and journalists were not denazified by the Americans; they passed through screening and were either cleared to work or barred from meaningful employment. Intelligence was not interested in rehabilitating people. Quite the contrary, it screened the population in order to identify and ostracize the Nazis. ICD had bigger goals than cleansing individuals; its officers were charged with denazifying a society and its culture.

The process followed in denazifying the arts was straightforward enough. In the first two months of the occupation, prior to ICD's creation, a fairly ad hoc approach prevailed, with temporary political clearance coming to all those who convinced the Americans of their anti-Nazi convictions. Music officers generally asked CIC units to investigate job incumbents or candidates and determine whether individuals had been members of prohibited organizations. Talking to artists and a simple security check were the primary, if unreliable, weapons in this phase of the war against Nazism. Because the reach of PWD offices during this period rarely extended beyond Wiesbaden,

Munich, and Stuttgart, in most cities local liaison or special services officers simply took charge of the situation. Only infrequently did these soldiers bother with even a basic intelligence screening.

When, in June 1945, Edward Kilenyi and Arthur Vogel of Munich's Music Branch finally made it to Nuremberg, they found the opera in full swing, offering two performances a week to an average of 500 servicemen a night. According to one report, the 610th Tank Destroyer Battalion, which occupied the city center, "now employed the local opera company, which included many Nazis, to give variety shows for military personnel." Kilenyi, who attended one performance, was shocked by the show and noted with disgust that "all exhibitions of Teutonic femininity were greeted [by the GIs] with howls and whistles of approval." Even more disturbing was the fact that the city had withdrawn its financial subsidy for the opera and that it was surviving, still under the management of its Nazi-appointed *Intendant*, Willi Hanke, and under the baton of its previous conductor, SA *Sturmführer* Alfons Dressel, entirely through American largesse. On Kilenyi's order, the house was closed, a new conductor and *Intendant* were appointed, and negotiations for a revival of the opera company under municipal sponsorship were initiated. But after a week, the cultural officers were gone, and the situation remained in shambles; the opera limped along for more than a year as a private enterprise with inadequate municipal support.[10]

This kind of disorder prevailed in the American zone until August 1945. Only with the establishment of ICD and the full staffing of its Intelligence Section were the necessary procedures instituted to standardize denazification. Now anyone who wanted to work in any capacity in the performance arts needed to visit an office of the Film, Theater and Music Section and fill out a series of forms including four *Fragebögen*, or personal information questionnaires, four business or career questionnaires, three MG questionnaires, and four application to work forms. An ICD intelligence officer would then attempt a detailed verification of the information supplied and, if the artist was a potential agent, employer, or director, would interview the applicant. Copies of the forms were sent to the Counter Intelligence Corps and the Public Safety Special Branch for checking against captured Nazi Party records. Only after this screening, which took anywhere from three weeks to six months, was an individual cleared for work. Those currently performing were generally authorized to continue until ICD had processed their applications for clearance. It proved a time-consuming process and one in which the intelligence officers had great discretionary power. Even if musicians' *Fragebögen* appeared clean, they might be blacklisted if in their interview they did not convince the American interlocutor of their anti-Nazi sympathies.

The first and most important people to be vetted were those seeking licenses to direct or administer others: conductors, artistic agents, cultural administrators, and the like. Next on the list were prominent soloists and, after them, ordinary technicians and orchestral musicians. Few in this last group were actually interviewed by intelligence officers; most of them were cleared or dismissed after checking their *Fragebögen* with CIC and Special Branch. Even so, the task of denazifying the arts proved immense and even Intelligence was eventually forced to rely on those it had already vetted to cleanse the organizations they managed. After the passage of MG Law #8 in September 1945, ICD demanded that already cleared conductors, directors, agents, and administrators ensure that none of their employees were former party members. License holders were required to register the names of all their employees, and if any of them were subsequently discovered to have been *Parteigenossen*, their license to perform could be revoked.[11]

As a result of all these changes, by the fall of 1945, officers in the Music Branch played no significant role in denazification decisions, though they continued to do much of the preparatory work. Music officers helped artists fill in their *Fragebögen*, conducted preliminary interviews with suspect musicians, and issued and administered licenses. Under MG Law #8, they also established and supervised the German advisory committees that steered artists through the tangle of forms and relayed appeals to the Intelligence Section. In general, music officers provided central coordination for the denazification process but they made none of the decisions themselves. An unfortunate consequence of this was that the music officers began to sense their own second-rate status. They were in the frustrating administrative bind of having to assemble applications for clearance, represent ICD to German officials, and deal with musicians, but without holding any actual decision-making authority. Intelligence officers, in the meantime, often developed an aloofness and arrogance befitting their highly judgmental and secretive detective work. They made decisions in isolation and had minimal contact with artists after interviewing them. Of all the branches of ICD, theirs most retained the features of wartime espionage; not surprisingly, some intelligence officers later became important operatives for the CIA.

To German artists, denazification proved an almost unbearable trial. They understood how much hinged on their successful negotiation of the process, but they also realized that ICD left few passages clear. It was not enough for musicians to claim that they were innocent of wrongdoing; they had to actually prove that they had not supported the Nazis morally or politically and had to demonstrate that they had not profited from their rule. As proving this meant showing that their careers had suffered during the Third Reich, something almost impossible for Germany's leading musicians, they relied on a series of subterfuges to demonstrate that they had suffered without showing it. The Intelligence Section's definition of collaboration was so broad and its moral outrage so deep that it all but forced artists to dissemble. Applicants for denazification were compelled to appear to accept collective guilt without acknowledging their own.

Whenever they could, German artists corroborated common assumptions about their political naiveté and concern for little beyond their work. Wilhelm Furtwängler, the country's most famous conductor, maintained that it was "my conviction that art has nothing to do with politics, with political power, with the hatred of others or with that which arises from a hatred of others." He decided not to leave Germany, he said, because the Nazis bowed to his insistence that he remain "a non-political artist." The theater and opera director Herbert Maisch protested that "politics lies outside the cultural field, to which he devotes himself," and he used this to explain his passive acceptance of the Third Reich. And Heinz Drewes, who joined the party in 1934 and served until 1937 as the president of the Reichsmusikkammer and head of the Music Section in the Propaganda Ministry, insisted that he, like all other musicians, was "non-politically minded." Even Elly Ney, a pianist, who gave preconcert speeches in praise of Hitler, was said "to be like all great artists, naturally unpolitical. Her friendliness towards the regime was only in the interest of music."[12]

Political naiveté was, however, only one of the excuses musicians offered in defense of their actions. In order to prove their opposition to fascism, a few even claimed participation in the resistance, though the smart ones, like Heinz Tietjen, the once powerful *Intendant* of Berlin's Preussische Staatsoper, corroborated their stories with lots of notes and remembered conversations with people who were already dead. The composer Carl Orff chose a different gambit. He was clever enough to avoid telling anyone in an official interview that he had been in the resistance, but informally he did convince Newell Jenkins, his former student and chief of the Theater and Music Branch in Stuttgart, that as a friend and associate of Kurt Huber (who had been executed for subversion in 1943), he was a resistance fighter. Although Jenkins was theoretically powerless to influence Orff's denazification, he was so impressed by his former teacher's claim that he managed to get him admission to a special vetting center that had been established to screen MG employees. In this way, Orff actually avoided a hearing with ICD Intelligence.[13]

Orff and Tietjen were unusual in claiming adherence to the organized resistance, but it was common for artists to insist on their opposition to Nazism. Most tried to prove this by demonstrating that the fascists did not really like them. Anticipating the perspective that any disagreement with a totalitarian regime implied opposition or nonconformity, musicians made the most of their international reputations, their disagreements with Nazi arts administrators, and their relationships with individual Jews. In fact, they made hay out of every conflict or bad press notice they ever had. Even those who were celebrated by the Nazis tried to emphasize that they had really been opponents. The conductor Wilhelm Furtwängler, who was exalted in the Third Reich and could not distort that fact, nonetheless argued that his performances had to be understood as gestures of defiance that the Nazis could not comprehend. He portrayed himself as a resister because he conducted Beethoven in a singular way. Similarly, Karl-Maria Zwissler, a conductor in Mainz, attempted to prove his resistance to the regime by referring to his performances of the works of Stravinsky, who had been included in the "Degenerate Music" exhibition of 1938. Zwissler, however, did acknowledge that he had applied to join the party in 1937 and received his membership card in 1942. Like Zwissler, the onetime conductor in Aachen, Herbert von Karajan, who joined the party in 1933, tried to demonstrate his spiritual opposition to the Nazis with reference to his performances of Bach's music, which, he asserted, the city's *Gauleiter* had forbidden him to conduct.[14]

Musicians suggested their independence from the Nazis in other ways. Winifred Wagner, guardian of the composer's shrine in Bayreuth, who joined the Nazi Party in 1926 and enjoyed a close personal relationship with Hitler, spoke to the Americans of her attempt to prevent war with Britain, her efforts to help Jews flee persecution, and her misgivings about both the Führer's politics and Nazi ideology. She managed to get both of her boys out of the Hitler Youth and considered her insistence that her oldest son, Wieland, not serve in the army partial proof of her opposition to the war. In his interview with an intelligence officer in Munich, the baritone Gerhard Hüsch advanced a threefold defense of his actions: he omitted to mention his connections with the Nazi Party, emphasized his disagreement with racial politics, and stressed the international nature of his career. The Augsburg conductor Max Hahn, who joined the party in 1938, emphasized his Catholicism (he "kept playing in Catholic masses"), his tolerance (he "never believed in Nordic superiority and loved Spanish architecture [and] Slavic music"), and his passivity ("I am not a fighter") as proof of his discomfort with Nazism. For all of these people, independence from the regime could be demonstrated by their skepticism about its cultural policies or military ambitions, and they offered their artistic reservations (bad reviews in the press, conflicts over programming, and the like) as further evidence of their opposition to Hitler. It was crucial to maintain, as one of soprano Elisabeth Schwarzkopf's friends insisted, that one could be "Pg [*Parteigenosse*] but not Nazi."[15]

Young and less prominent artists who joined the party often defended their actions by insisting that they had no choice but to become Nazis. As one PWD interrogator discovered, "the current line is that one *had to be* a Nazi." Indeed, "those who stated that they had been Party members invariably qualified this admission by the remark that, after all, one pretty well had to be a member to live." The problem with this line was that PWD considered "this self-exculpation largely responsible for the total absence of a genuine sense of defeat, and its implications, among Germans. . . . This tendency to make the Party a scapegoat for all evil, is a purely theoretical scrap of meat thrown at the occupying lion. For a *Muß*-Nazi, who was forced to join the Party against his will, feels that he surely cannot be held responsible for crimes ordered by the high Party leadership." The fashionable expression was *belogen und betrogen* (deceived and betrayed) when explaining the support one had previously given the party.[16]

For German artists, however, establishing a record of friendly and professional contacts with Jews was believed to be the litmus test of independence from Nazism. Because those seeking clearance were almost all soloists, conductors, or arts managers who had important careers prior to the Nazi seizure of power, it was apparently not hard for most applicants to solicit testimonials from former Jewish colleagues. The vast majority of those testimonials came from musicians whom the artists had helped to escape Nazi Germany or from people who wrote as character witnesses asserting that they never heard the individual in question make racist remarks. Even the conductor Karl Böhm, who often expressed pro-Nazi sentiments, presented at his denazification hearing "a very large number of testimonials in his favor" and stressed the difficulties he had faced because of his connection with Jewish conductor Bruno Walter. Similarly, after reviewing the case of the Austrian maestro Clemens Krauss, the Americans conceded that the conductor had established that, while he enjoyed "the most powerful position in the musical life of the Third Reich . . . [t]here is evidence that he helped some Jews." In fact, Krauss did nothing to stop rumors that one of his parents was Jewish, and Richard Strauss testified that the conductor "was the only one who could keep his . . . Jewish daughter-in-law free from persecution." As the opera director and longtime party member Rudolf Hartmann explained, Krauss "was never a nazi-ideologist. He helped Jews." Similarly, the singer Maria Cebotari, whose husband was a party member and who closely connected herself to the prominent Nazi official Hans Hinkel, brought up her part-Jewish cousin whom she claimed to have used her influence to protect. This commodification of Jewish contacts was a way of demonstrating an artist's lack of sympathy for Nazism. What the musicians were trying to prove was that no matter what bounties they might have enjoyed in the Third Reich, they remained, in their hearts, uncorrupted.[17]

For German artist, the extent of one's adherence to ideology was the indicator of guilt. Only the true believers — the xenophobic anti-Semites — should really be considered culpable as Nazis. In other words, where McClure and ICD's Intelligence Section proposed treating musicians en masse and judging them against fixed standards, the artists themselves insisted that their cases had to be individually considered. They wanted to be assessed not for who they were but for what they believed and how they behaved toward others. As one PWD officer remarked, "they rely upon every possible argument — their Roman Catholicism, their [regional] loyalties, their participation at one time or another in opposition parties — anything to convince the interlocutor that they are nothing more than innocent by-standers at the scene."[18] And so, unlike Toombs and McClure, who believed few Germans had resisted Hitler, Germany's musicians presented the distance between the collaborator and the outright opponent as very slight indeed. But, in a way, Intelligence had left them no choice.

THE IMPACT OF REVOLUTIONARY DENAZIFICATION: BAVARIA

While the denazifiers busied themselves removing the rot from artistic life, the Music Branch set about restarting concert activity. Unfortunately, it authorized performances under the ad hoc system of denazification that prevailed before the first blacklist was issued and many of its decisions would subsequently be reversed. The problem was that the two missions of reactivating music life and purging it were fundamentally incompatible: while one group of Americans authorized musicians to work, another ordered them fired. Neither seemed to know what the other was doing. The resulting chaos proved disastrous to MG's reputation and confirmed the beliefs of German arts patrons and officials that the Americans were tyrannical, disorganized, and lacking in cultural refinement. ICD never recovered.

Prohibiting all music activity until the regulations governing political clearance had been finalized in October 1945 would have made more sense, but that option was never considered. In the first place, PWD's music officers felt they had no time to waste in beginning their work because concertizing was already under way in most places under the authorization of Special Services. This section of the U.S. Army was responsible for troop entertainment, and as soon as U.S. forces entered an area, Special Services swept in, requisitioned facilities, and engaged local performers like the pianist Walter Gieseking and the conductor Hans Knappertsbusch. In Austria, when Special Services needed money to pay for the local artists it employed for troop entertainment, it actually began to open its shows to ticket-buying locals, something that not only placed it in competition with the indigenous theaters but also contravened military regulations concerning fraternization.[19] Often Special Services ordered concert halls converted into movie houses for soldiers, leaving companies — including big ones like the Berlin Philharmonic Orchestra — without a home. In some cases, such as in the Stuttgart Staatstheater, it would take the cultural officers years to get the army's entertainment branch out of the building. In a sense, PWD/ICD saw itself engaged in a race against time to salvage what was left of Germany's cultural life before Special Services completely absorbed it.

But the thirst for GI entertainment was not alone in propelling PWD to speedily restart musical activity. The division also moved swiftly because, as one officer announced, rumors were circulating that "the Americans will not allow any entertainment in retaliation for atrocities [and] that there will be no Festivals or Philharmonics because the Americans are cultural barbarians."[20] This perception was taken seriously because the division's commanders believed it would be difficult to convince the Germans of the need to change their culture if they thought the Americans had none of their own. Reeducation, after all, could not be achieved by force; it had to result from the kind of subtle persuasions and encouragements more familiar to Madison Avenue advertising executives than to soldiers. But a good sales pitch, as even the crudest persuader knows, is impossible if the recipient feels more knowledgeable than the salesman.

Speed in reversing America's image in Germany was also believed essential, according to McClure, because the other occupation governments had quickly reintroduced public entertainment. The Russian policy, in particular, "has at its basis an almost fanatical reverence for art and artists coupled with a belief that artistic creation is almost intrinsically good, and an urgent need of human beings in times of uncertainty and suffering." Soviet and French moves to activate musical life only highlighted PWD's relative reluctance and rubbed raw American feelings of cultural inadequacy. Paradoxically, the conquerors were still intimidated by the cultural authority of the defeated, even though they insisted that Germany's artistic life was misshapen. According to one senior American official, he was often "embarrassed and chagrined" in his efforts to reeducate the Germans and suggested one of the things that would "strengthen us immeasurably" would be for "each of our State legislatures or Congress" to do what the Europeans did "and allocate funds for municipal and state symphonic orchestras and operas." Complex feelings such as these were not often openly expressed by the music officers; mostly they simply justified their efforts in strictly military terms. Security concerns would be eased, they maintained, if German morale were higher and the locals' "hunger for music and theater and movies" satisfied. Art was a balm to a crushed and starving population, or as one PWD officer quipped: the maintenance of social order requires bread and circuses and the Germans were already being limited in their bread.[21]

McClure hoped that the major musical organizations would be vetted and concerts reintroduced by 1 July 1945. PWD's first Music Branch, its Munich detachment, pressed to meet this deadline, announcing that it would "begin activities anew, no matter how modestly or on how small a scale." Early in July 1945 the branch authorized the municipal orchestra, the Munich Philharmonic, to begin offering weekly concerts in the bomb-damaged Prinzregenten Theater. Although the branch was acting, in this regard, in accordance with official PWD policy, there can be no doubt that it moved too soon.[22]

The first challenge lay in finding a conductor for the orchestra. Austrian-born Oswald Kabasta, who had led the philharmonic since 1938, was ruled out for the simple reason that the division would not allow a leading artist to occupy "the same position under American control which he held under the Nazis" — at least not until "extensive investigation" had cleared him. Hoping that this would soon happen, the city continued to pay Kabasta's salary and to negotiate with the Americans for his reinstatement. But this became a virtual impossibility when Kabasta admitted to having applied to join the Nazi Party as a precondition for getting his job, even though he added that he had never been issued a membership number and had always been "inwardly" anti-Nazi (the conductor neglected to tell the Americans that six years before he had also applied for membership in the Austrian Nazi Party). And so, despite his appeals, in October 1945 the conductor's name appeared on the Intelligence Section's blacklist, and Kilenyi ordered the city to discontinue his pay. An impulsive musician with a bad heart and an unsteady temperament, Kabasta was devastated by his dismissal. From his hospital room he issued mournful appeals to the Americans and the city for rehabilitation; but ICD remained firm. Four months after his blacklisting, the conductor killed himself.[23]

Even before this tragedy unfolded, ICD had to deal with the problem of whom to employ if not Kabasta. The city, which funded the Philharmonic, had placed the orchestra in the temporary care of Adolf Männerlich, Kabasta's assistant conductor and himself a former party member. Munich's mayor had stalled taking further action, arguing that because Kabasta's contract was still in force, he could not be replaced. Bavaria's music chief, Harry Bogner, agreed not to interfere and told city officials that the Americans had no desire to "meddle in theater and music life, but merely to exercise supervision over the organizational and political side . . . and to ban overtly Nazi works and reinstate previously prohibited pieces." Unfortunately, Bogner's colleagues in Theater and Music did not support his passive approach to denazification and control. His fellow officers regarded him as "grossly incompetent" and lacking in the necessary missionary zeal; further, they were angered by his deference to the city government. In a shocking exercise of an authority he did not possess, the chief of the Theater Branch decided that because Bogner was unwilling to "launch [the Music Branch] into battle," he would. Without consulting his colleagues in the office next door, the officer ordered Männerlich's dismissal and appointed the orchestra leader Robert Edenhofer to replace him. Five days later, the section chief placed the philharmonic under temporary Military Government control, relieving the city of management responsibility. Bogner promptly returned to the United States and, while his subordinates, Arthur Vogel and Edward Kilenyi, were relieved to be rid of him, relations between the music and theater personnel had soured.[24]

The difficulty was that, although Edenhofer was a "likeable young man" and a satisfactory rehearsal leader, Kilenyi rated the job of music director "beyond his present capability." Moreover, the Music Branch had already determined that Edenhofer had himself been in the SS, even though he claimed to have "quit . . . in disgust." Embarrassed and at something of a loss, the branch cast around for alternatives. Its first choice was Eugen Jochum, an "energetic, successful man of 42 with a sympathetic personality." Although *Generalmusikdirektor* of the Hamburg Philharmonic, Jochum had returned to his family's Munich home in the last days of the war. Unfortunately, the conductor insisted that he had to return to Hamburg and only agreed to serve as the philharmonic's principal guest conductor. And so, Edenhofer temporarily continued as *Kapellmeister*. The arrangement was not entirely satisfactory, and Jochum did little to keep the Americans in his corner. Kilenyi, who replaced Bogner as branch chief, reported that the conductor was "happy about never having been a party member, explaining that he is an artist and that he is glad to perform wherever he is wanted, as he had [during the war] in Holland and France, and [that he] is ready and pleased to do the same 'for the enemy.'" His wife gently corrected this little faux pas. He talked freely of how he had artists and associates exempted from military and labor service by using his influence with Goebbels, and having friends freed from prison in Holland through Seyss-Inquart."[25]

But even the unsatisfactory arrangement with the indiscreet Jochum soon came unstuck. In the second week of July, as the CIC finally got around to cross-checking the *Fragebögen* of Munich's orchestra personnel, it discovered twenty party members, including Edenhofer. All would now have to be dismissed, and Jochum, fearful for his own position, promptly returned to Hamburg and the lenience of British zonal administration. Performances of the philharmonic were canceled and, in a temporary move, Hans Knappertsbusch, whom the branch had already appointed to lead the Staatsoper, was given control over the philharmonic as well. Knappertsbusch was the Music Branch's trump card: a conductor beloved in Munich whose career had apparently suffered at Nazi hands.[26] Anxious about making another mistake, the music officers carefully screened the roughhewn musician, the local Intelligence Section interviewed him, and Special Branch cross-checked his record and cleared him for employment.

Knappertsbusch told the Americans he had been dismissed as *Generalmusikdirektor* of the Staatsoper by the *Gauleiter* of Bavaria in 1934 because of his closeness to the *Intendant*, von Franckenstein, whom he insisted the fascists disliked, and because of several anti-Nazi statements he had made while on tour in Holland. Only in 1936 did the Reich again endorse him, after the Foreign Ministry requested that he be allowed to accept an offer to perform in Barcelona. Knappertsbusch was not, however, awarded another conducting post in Nazi Germany and, after his return from Spain, he moved to Vienna. To the Americans, the towering, hard-edged Knappertsbusch appeared a "strong, energetic person which [*sic*] is very much impressed with itself . . . he considers himself a martyr and expects to be treated as such." They welcomed his hostility to the Nazi Party and were delighted by the malicious gossip he spread about such rivals as Clemens Krauss (who had replaced him, on Hitler's personal instruction, as conductor of the Munich Staatsoper) and Wilhelm Furtwängler, but they were appalled by the fact that he seemed not to "understand the collapse of Germany and that things have changed . . . [he] behaves as if he was far above the present plight of his country." For the cultural officers, Knappertsbusch was a valuable artistic asset, though "an impossible person."[27]

To an extent, Knappertsbusch deceived the Americans. While it was true that he had been driven from Munich by the Nazis, the move had done more injury to his pride than to his career. Until 1943 Knappertsbusch remained a dominant force at the Vienna Staatsoper, and after the Anschluss he had successfully rehabilitated himself in Nazi eyes. In fact, it was common for the Propaganda Ministry to "break in" musicians by demoting or retiring them for a time and then restoring them to favor. But for the fact that Knappertsbusch had been kept away from the opera house in Munich, his rehabilitation had been total. He was often invited to conduct in Berlin and was awarded the prestigious Martial Order of Merit. He conducted in occupied countries, including Holland and France, and at party functions and in honor of Hitler's birthday. On such occasions as the Vienna Mozart Festival in 1941, he led his orchestra in concerts following speeches by Goebbels and other Nazi officials. There is strong evidence to suggest that Knappertsbusch was anti-Semitic and that he played a role in the campaign to drive Jewish conductor, Bruno Walter, out of Munich. The Music Branch knew little of this, but it did realize that he had done better in the later years of the Reich than he claimed and noted that by touring and accepting honors he had "contributed much to the Nazi boast that they were a *Kulturvolk.*" On the other hand, because Munich audiences were aware that he had been dismissed from his position in their city, they regarded him as "a symbol of anti-Nazism" and Knappertsbusch shared that perception. The Americans sensed the hollowness of this claim, but as the intelligence officer who interviewed the arrogant Maestro sighed, "his record is still better than that of most of the other top artists which [*sic*] remained in Germany."[28]

The "idol of Bavaria" was, however, unable to manage both a Staatsoper, reeling from the mandatory dismissal of 40 percent of its personnel, and a depleted and demoralized philharmonic. In any case, he was never a good administrator, being too headstrong and impulsive and domineering to bother with budget constrictions or with the feelings of those who worked with him. It was on Knappertsbusch's recommendation that the Munich office approached Hans Rosbaud, then living in Stuttgart, and offered him the directorship of the philharmonic. Rosbaud was a lucky find: he was neither famous (like Furtwängler, Krauss, or Knappertsbusch) nor a party member. Even more happily, he was known to be a friend of such modernists (and American residents) as Stravinsky, Schoenberg, and Hindemith, and an ardent promoter of new music. As one cultural officer recalled, "Rosbaud . . . was a really great musician and tremendously interested

Hans Rosbaud and the Munich Philharmonic
(Photo courtesy of Carlos Moseley)

in contemporary music . . . I mean Rosbaud was right and with it." At the time the Munich detachment found him, the conductor was under consideration for a position in Stuttgart, and he had already composed an ambitious proposal for the overhaul of the city's musical life. The Music Branch in Württemberg-Baden found those ideas intriguing and they urged the government to offer him a contract, but the ministry hesitated, so the Munich office scooped him up.[29]

With Rosbaud's acquisition, the Music Branch finally felt that it had everything in order. But its officers could not have been more wrong. On 10 October 1945 the unthinkable happened, and the branch found itself rear-ended by its own Intelligence Section. When an American-controlled radio station in Bern broadcast ICD's first blacklist, the Munich detachment discovered that Hans Knappertsbusch had been included "on the wrong list." In a staggering display of administrative incompetence, no one had thought to warn the music officers of the impending catastrophe. Indeed, only three months before, the chief of the Theater and Music Branch had met with his counterpart in the Intelligence Section in Bad Homburg and reached "complete agreement" on vetting procedures. Kilenyi was understandably furious: "[W]e hold no brief for Mr. Knappertsbusch . . . [but] it is going to be hard to explain locally how a man can be thrown out first by the Nazis and then by the Americans. The fact that we were the last . . . to know of the Blacklist leaves us looking very stupid." Did ICD's command really believe, he snarled, that "as we are strictly operational, German speaking and anonymous little moles we should be kept in the dark[?]"[30]

Knappertsbusch's mandatory removal, together with the gutting of Munich's orchestras, had a "paralyzing effect . . . on musical life" in the city. Kilenyi considered the situation "acutely embarrassing for this organization. After having encouraged them with their first concerts, we are now forced to castrate and behead the body." The Knappertsbusch case, in particular, was a community-relations catastrophe, for not only had he been hired to run the Staatsoper and, for a time, the philharmonic, but he had also performed in special concerts with and for American military personnel. Knappertsbusch's blacklisting served particularly to "undermine [the German public's] confidence in the validity of our licenses and appointments." Indeed, in the wake of the announcement, Kilenyi found that local "ambition to rebuild their musical life seems to have gone."[31] The branch's anger was justified on administrative grounds, but the denazifiers had sound reasons for blacklisting the conductor. Well aware of both his performances in occupied countries and of his conducting at Nazi-sponsored functions, the Intelligence Section determined that the big man had provided "moral support" to the regime by representing it internationally and at home.

Because headquarters decisions could not be appealed, only revoked, the Music Branch had no alternative but to cast around for Knappertsbusch's replacement. In the meantime, protecting Hans Rosbaud, the newly appointed leader of the philharmonic, became an even-more pressing task. As Arthur Vogel remarked, "with the blacklisting of practically every prominent German musician," Rosbaud had become "the one good conductor . . . available in the U.S. zone and hence a musical plum." Rosbaud was not particularly well known in 1945, and his name had not appeared on the October blacklist, but there was no reason to expect that Intelligence would ignore him for long. Rosbaud had, after all, been the leading opera director in wartime Alsace, a French province that the Nazis had annexed to the Reich and made the target of a Germanization campaign. Like Knappertsbusch, he had suffered in the early years of Hitler's rule: as the orchestra director at Frankfurt Radio he had been vigorously attacked by Nazi polemicists for his patronage of music and musicians considered degenerate. He tried to emigrate to the United States but failed to secure a position and so remained in Germany, quietly doing what was necessary to get ahead. And Rosbaud succeeded: in 1937 he accepted a position in Münster that was less prestigious but better paid than his job in Frankfurt and, having endured this "demotion," three years later the Propaganda Ministry rewarded him by approving him for the job of *Generalmusikdirektor* of the theater orchestra in Strasbourg. Although Rosbaud's decency impressed his new orchestra—he spoke French to them, protected musicians who feared dismissal, and saved some from military service—the conductor also imposed a heavily Germanic repertoire and performed works by Nazi composers. Like Knappertsbusch, he conducted concerts in occupied France and Belgium, at Nazi-sponsored festivals, and following party speeches.[32]

Rosbaud abhorred Nazism (and here he differed from Knappertsbusch, who simply found the Nazis inferior and stupid for their failure to appreciate him), and he appears to have known that his brother, a physicist, was passing information to the Allies. Still, there can be no doubt that because of his position as a German conductor in an occupied territory and because of the promotions he had enjoyed, he would be blacklisted. Dodging that fate now became a major concern not only for the conductor but also for his patrons in music control.

Newell Jenkins, who had just taken over as chief in Stuttgart, unexpectedly offered his colleagues in Bavaria a way out. At the moment the Munich Branch was pushing for Rosbaud's denazification, Jenkins was trying to secure the *Intendant*'s job in Stuttgart for his mentor, Carl Orff. Because Jenkins needed a fast decision on Orff if the composer were to get the job, and because screening by Intelligence could take months, Jenkins hit on the idea of sending his friend to the Screening Center ICD had recently established for its licensees at Bad Orb. The center, also known as the ICD School, was one of the Intelligence Section's more peculiar experiments: a psychiatric clinic devoted to uncovering Nazi personalities. The center actually traced its origins back to the 1930s and to the belief among some psychologists that fascism was the social excrescence of "authoritarian personalities." If Nazism was an expression of psychological deviance, the psychiatrists argued, then it was obvious that by careful testing one could detect and enumerate the personality traits that characterized the Nazi. David Levy, the doctor who managed the center, was influential in wartime intelligence circles, having previously screened OSS agents for overseas assignments, and he had also, in his New York practice, been enumerating fascistic personality traits since 1942. Unlike most intelligence officers who attributed Nazism to cultural and social forces, the psychiatrists tended to see it arising among children with stern, often physically abusive fathers and distant, frightened, and unaffectionate mothers. "The German alternatively commands and scrapes," the doctors declared, "this is obvious in the family, where the father, dominating his wife and children, no sooner leaves the house than he bows to his superiors." Nazis were particular products of this environment; they felt "not a rebellion against the powerful, but an envy, and an aspiration. Also [because of their own repressed backgrounds] they feel identification with the socially deprived" of their own kind and "hostility displaced from the father" toward social outsiders and rivals.[33]

Opened in October 1945, the center was designed to vet applicants for press licenses and for staff jobs in ICD offices. Those attending the center were subjected to up to five days of psychological screening ranging from Rorschach tests to composing autobiographical essays to interviews and monitored group discussions. Bad Orb attendants were not just licensees; "school graduates," as they were sometimes called, were to constitute the cadre of German intellectuals on whom MG would rely. Great discretion was used in selecting those to be screened at the center with "only the most valuable candidates [being] sent." Decisions of the center were "to be binding on all agencies, military and civilian, Allied and German" and could not be overruled by other sections in ICD.[34] Still, because Bad Orb shifted the ground from who one was to what one had done and what one believed, it allowed individuals to exculpate their actions. Only for the handful who passed through Bad Orb was denazification a personally meaningful phrase; only here could the Germans explain their actions and inactions and receive psychological absolution.

Like most of those who underwent screening in Bad Orb, Rosbaud kept a great deal to himself, lied when necessary, and justified his collaborations as best he could. As with most of those interviewed, he underestimated both the amount of information that had been collected on him and the intelligence of the psychiatrists interviewing him. Rosbaud claimed that he had been offered the Strasbourg position through his agent and that it was a private deal struck "against the will and without the consent" of the Propaganda Ministry. This the Americans knew to be false and they also understood that, as a German in Strasbourg, Rosbaud "was playing a propaganda role." The conductor further asserted that he had not toured internationally under government auspices, but the Americans knew that all Germans performing in occupied countries required the permission and support of the Foreign Ministry. The psychiatrists also recognized that Rosbaud's salary increased steadily in the Third Reich and that he had "satisf[ied] his personal ambitions" by accepting the jobs he was offered. More troubling, the psychiatrists detected in Rosbaud elements of an authoritarian personality. He was "self-controlled to the point of masochism . . . cold and independent . . . in attaining his ambition, he has been absorbed in his work and has let nothing stand in his way." On the other hand, the conductor was rated as philosophically anti-Nazi and a critical thinker, and his application for clearance was endorsed by several prominent "anti-German" artists.[35]

The psychiatrists rated Rosbaud as "Grey-Acceptable," by which classification he could work as a conductor but would not be allowed any executive responsibilities. Technically speaking, the Music Branch could therefore allow him to continue as *Generalmusikdirektor* of the philharmonic but not as its license holder. To have an exception made, the branch lobbied hard to have him continue as chief administrator and conductor, and Intelligence ultimately agreed to allow Rosbaud a probationary license. For three months he was not allowed to hire or fire personnel without the approval of the municipal *Kultusreferent* and the Music Branch. John Evarts (who had just succeeded Kilenyi as branch chief) found this decision "vindictive . . . and mightily childish," but he was relieved the application had at least been approved.[36] That Rosbaud emerged reasonably clean from ICD denazification was somewhat miraculous, and it had only happened because of his end run around the blacklist. Very few were as lucky. Most of the more prominent musicians had been barred by the Intelligence Section's first list, and only a handful ever made it through Bad Orb. In fact, the psychologists closed the door to musicians soon after Rosbaud's denazification, arguing that they were not sufficiently vital to the occupation to warrant the special education the school provided.

Although the philharmonic was finally in competent hands, the Staatsoper remained without a music director. Stuttgart was also now in chaos, because the psychiatrists pegged Carl Orff "Grey-

Acceptable," by which standard he could not hold a license as *Inten-dant*. Unlike Rosbaud, who was already running the orchestra and got through "on probation," Orff would be a new appointee to a higher-profile position and neither the ministry nor the Music Branch thought Intelligence would accept him. Denazification was proving a blunt and brutal instrument. Not only did it alienate local administrators and Music Branch officers, but it left in shambles the work that had already been done toward revivifying German performance life. Orff might have made a superb *Intendant*, but three days at the ICD school were enough to make irrelevant the months of debate within the Kultmi-nisterium. Similarly, Knappertsbusch was an inspiring opera conduc-tor and Jochum a popular orchestra leader; Richard Strauss would certainly not have caused trouble if left alone in his house in Garmisch. But the intelligence officers understood that revolutions are not easily achieved, and they were determined to put an end to the Germans' aggressive proclivities. They believed that it was "impossible to sustain in Germany any effective alternative to an authoritarian and externally aggressive nationalistic government" and took seriously the job of purging a culture in order to allow its democratic potential to develop. They were convinced that while "a real revolution might help," a "fake" one "which left the junkers, militarists and monopolists hidden but potent, might do more harm than good."[37] How could German music be set on the right course if the old guard were left in charge? The people ICD silenced may have been great artists, but others, the Intel-ligence Section asserted, would emerge. As revolutionaries, the intel-ligence officers thought big thoughts and had little sympathy for sal-vage operators like the apostates in the Music Branch. Consequently, their methods and their attitudes provoked defiance not just among German artists but also among those in the operational sections with whom they had to work.

DENAZIFICATION AND ALLIED RIVALRY

The rough way in which denazification was introduced and its damaging impact on work already completed caused abiding resent-ments and served to undermine the long-term effectiveness of ICD's reeducation policy. It exposed the Germans to the peculiarity of some Americans trying to enforce rules while others worked to get around them. In the eyes of Newell Jenkins, this only served to "befuddle" most artists.[38] German musicians were especially confused by the fact that the Americans' zeal did not seem to be shared by their allies. Eugen Jochum, as musicians and informed concertgoers knew, may have been a mandatory removal in the American zone, but he was still concertizing as *Generalmusikdirektor* in Hamburg; the pianist Walter Gieseking was performing and teaching in the French zone, even while under blacklist in the American; and the conductor Joseph Keilberth, who was blacklisted for his party membership and for leading the German Orchestra in occupied Prague, was nonetheless employed by the Russians as chief conductor in Dresden; in Berlin, Robert Heger, who was on ICD's list as a *Parteigenosse*, conducted a few blocks north of the American sector at the British-controlled Städtische Oper. Didn't these facts make the actions of the Americans seem all the more wrongheaded, arbitrary, and cruel?

In truth, the Americans were deeply perturbed that their allies did not share their zeal for cultural denazification. This was especially true in Berlin, a city divided into four sectors, where the incongruities in policy were readily apparent to the locals. As late as January 1946, half the members of the Städtische Oper were party members, including its two principal conductors, while in the Soviet sector, prominent opera singers known to have been Nazis continued to perform at the Staatsoper. The Americans urged the dismissal of *Parteigenosse* musicians, but the British officers argued it would be impossible to function without them, while the Russians maintained theirs had already been denazified. No one else, it seemed, was particularly interested in going after artists. British Information Services did periodically circulate mimeographed blacklists, but they were much more modest than the American, "the British explanation being that their denazification laws are not as strict as ours." The French were never much of a concern for ICD, because in Berlin their sector contained no significant theater or performing arts organization, while outside the city, in the French zone proper, they tended, at least until the fall of 1946, to officially accept the American blacklist, even if they rarely enforced it. Between the Soviet and American intelligence officers there was little communication and virtually no agreement. Russian policy confounded the Americans because Soviet officials were at once uninterested in removing most former Nazi artists and then went far beyond any of the other Allies in punishing others. But if one rule seemed to shape the Soviets' handling of denazification, it was their ambition to present German audiences with the artists they preferred to see. According to Michael

Josselson, one of the intelligence officers responsible for denazifying Berlin's arts and media, the "Russians are trying to beat the Western Allies . . . [by demonstrating] their own efficiency and good will towards the German people."[39]

The Soviets appear to have understood how far they had to travel to rebuild respect for their forces. They were the soldiers the Germans most despised, they were the ones most responsible for Nazism's defeat, and they were the ones who captured Berlin. The depredations of the Red Army—the lootings and murders and hundreds of thousands of rapes—as well as the cuts and stabs involved in the Stalinization of the territory under their occupation, made it difficult to argue for the singular bestiality of the fascists. The Soviets appear to have agreed with the Americans that the occupation was going to be a long one, but they also realized, as the Americans initially did not, that successful indoctrination depends on both force and understanding. In the rebuilding of the Soviet occupation zones, the adherence of the most malleable intellectuals and elites to the new administration was regarded as crucial. Music was viewed as one of reeducation's "soft" dimensions: it could be used to build a sense of "fraternity" between Russian and German peoples and to blur some of the crueler elements of political indoctrination and military occupation. "Overtly, towards the Germans, they began from the very outset to play the role of patrons of German arts, German music and German culture," the intelligence officer Nicolas Nabokov observed, and "as a corollary to this propagandistic *Kulturträgertum* [carrying the banner of culture] they began secretly to castigate the Americans and British as suppressors of German culture." The historian Elizabeth Koch Janik agrees: "The Soviets successfully cast themselves as supporters and promoters of German cultural tradition to a degree that the Americans initially had difficulty challenging."[40]

In Berlin, a city divided into four occupation sectors, the Americans had to deal most openly with the Soviets. In fact, the arts establishment they found in the city had really already been largely reconstructed by the Russians prior to their arrival in July 1945. Berlin's premier opera company, the Staatsoper, had been performing for six weeks; the Staatskapelle Orchestra had given its first radio performance a few days after the capitulation; the Städtische Oper had mounted a ballet on 15 June; and, about the same time, the Berlin Philharmonic began concertizing under a new, Soviet-appointed *Ge-*

neralmusikdirektor. The Russians made hay out of all this, emphasizing through the Soviet-controlled press and radio that they were trying to restore normal life in Berlin as quickly as possible. For the first Soviet *Kommandatur*, under General Bersarin, the revival of performance activity appears to have been a priority, and days after the city's capture, on 14 May, he held a reception to introduce his administration to 200 artists of stage, film, and concert hall. Even the Americans recognized that the reopening of the theaters just two weeks after the German surrender "represents quite an achievement" and that the Soviets had done it "as a task of prime importance, not only because they needed the soothing effect on the population, but also because they are genuinely convinced of the necessity of such activities to humanity." McClure was patently concerned by all this, and he warned his British associates that he remained "convinced that we must be firm in our approach to the Germans and by no means allow Russian propaganda to push us too far into reversing policies which have been carefully thought out."[41]

Two things struck ICD's officers as they first explored Berlin's cultural terrain. First was the realization that because of Soviet actions, Berlin had become "one of the most prominent window displays in the field of theater and music," a place where the Allies would have to compete, like Renaissance princes, in their patronage of the arts. Second, and following from this, the Americans recognized that in Berlin zonal regulations could not be fully applied because of the need "to adjust U.S. viewpoints and experiences to the requirements and interests of the other three Allies." And the most notable viewpoint they learned that needed adjusting was ICD's prejudice against allowing the Germans to denazify themselves.[42]

By the time information control officers arrived, the denazification of artists in Berlin was already under way, and the Americans found it being run "almost exclusively by Germans."[43] The Soviets had appointed as director of the municipal Amt für Volksbildung, with jurisdiction over education, theater, and music, Otto Winzer, a Berlin communist who had returned with the Red Army after twelve years in Moscow. His assistant, Erich Otto, was a syndicalist and president of the Genossenschaft Deutscher Bühnenangehöriger (GDB), the organization that represented stage artists. The *Kulturreferent* for music was Kurt Bork, another communist. As had the Americans, the Soviets' initially denazified in fits and starts. By military order, many suspected Nazis were simply dismissed, and some were rounded up and jailed; but there was little apparent logic to the process and where one was arrested another was allowed to perform. Although interventions of this type did not stop, the Soviet Military Government's (SMAD's) position appears to have been that denazification was to be made a German responsibility as swiftly as possible and that it should be undertaken by reliable opponents of the Reich. Because most of the anti-Nazis considered trustworthy were communists, many of whom had spent the Hitler years in Russia, the approach served broader Soviet purposes. Still, the Soviets had found an imaginative method for reviving communist influence after twelve years of suppression, while at the same time distancing the Soviet Military Government from a potentially unpopular process and convincing the Germans that SMAD intended to treat them like adults.

The rebirth of Berlin's cultural life was vested by the Soviets in the Kammer der Kunstschaffenden, an organization of artists, stage and screen performers, cultural administrators, and technicians founded on 30 May 1945. The Kammer's functions were broad and ill defined; according to Paul Wegener, its president, the organization "serves art, and therefore serves an idea. The Chamber demands a spiritual outlook, which in a higher sense, will serve in the education of the whole German population." Wegener was seventy years old and a highly respected actor who had kept a fairly low profile in the Third Reich. His view on art was "uncompromising," and he was committed to the idea that theater and music were the media "by which Germany can, must and will be reeducated and by which she will earn a new place in the family of nations." Assisting the president in this task was his deputy, Wolfgang Harich, a member of Berlin's communist underground (antifas or antifascists), who was appointed as Wegener's "political mentor," and a five-person managing council that included Winzer, Erich Otto, and Fritz Erpenbeck, Winzer's cultural adviser and another refugee back from Moscow. Founded as "a ready instrument for the speedy revival of the arts in Berlin," the Kammer was given control over the process of renewing the city's culture. Anyone seeking to work in film, theater, or music needed a permit from the Kammer. Applicants were required to complete a questionnaire and, if necessary, to submit to screening by a denazification committee. On this committee, Harich, an "uncompromising political foe of the Nazis," even in the eyes of the Americans, served as attorney for defense, and Wolfgang Schmidt, another member of the Berlin underground (but a Social Democrat), and an equally fanatical antifascist, was the prosecutor.[44]

The Kammer was, however, more than simply a licensing committee: it was far bigger than that. The organization believed its mandate extended to the coordination of all of Berlin's cultural life: it vetted applicants for such jobs as theater director and ordered individual appointments, it oversaw and approved theater repertoire, and it adjudicated disputes between management and labor. Most important for artists, it also assigned ration cards and determined the amount of food one was entitled to receive.[45] In short, the Kammer assumed many of the same duties as the Reichskulturkammer and it shared with it its functional divisions—music, theater, film—its powerful secretariat and figurehead president, and the vesting of its administration in the hands of the dominant political party. These points of similarity were only strengthened by the fact that the Kammer occupied the RKK's old offices on Schlüterstrasse and maintained, for denazification purposes, its predecessor's files. But the Kammer, although run by communists, was part of a Soviet effort to create a more broadly based and popular anti-Nazi front. On its various subcommittees were many respected artists holding a wide spectrum of political views.

In a very short time, the exceptional range of the Kammer's power proved too much for city officials. The organization played a valued role in the chaotic days following the capture of Berlin, but as the Amt für Volksbildung established itself, Winzer came to see it as a rival. So much responsibility had been handed over to the Kammer that the city had little left to do except pay for its operations. Soon the *Magistrat* was signaling that the Kammer was "too large and too ineffective to justify its existence" and, with Russian agreement, the groundwork was laid for its elimination. On 26 June 1945, another organization, the Kulturbund zur Demokratischen Erneurung Deutschlands, was founded by another group of repatriated communists led by the writer, Johannes R. Becher. The more important of the Kammer's directors were included, but the organization was clearly dominated by refugees returned from Moscow. Unlike the Kammer, the Kulturbund assumed for itself a merely advisory role and defined its mission in chiefly ideological terms: to achieve "on the basis of culture and humanism an indestructible union of intellectuals" that might pry Germany free from "the reactionary filth of its history." In essence, the

Kulturbund was to serve as an old-style popular-front organization that would bind intellectuals together and manipulate them in support of communist causes. In contrast to the Kammer, however, it recognized that the Amt für Volksbildung had to be responsible for actual cultural administration and, while mobilizing artists, it shied away from such official duties as denazifying artists, licensing them, or issuing their ration cards.[46]

Significantly, the leadership of the Kulturbund tended to exclude the very people who dominated the Kammer: the former members of the Berlin resistance. For Winzer and his colleagues in the city bureaucracy, the local communists were too powerful and independent and difficult to control; for the Soviet military authority they were something of an annoyance. Ardent and stern in their anti-Nazism, the antifas were unwilling simply to toe the line for either the Communist Party (KPD) or its Soviets rulers. To people like Harich and Schmidt, the continued employment of former Nazis and prominent collaborators was unthinkable: in their minds a reborn Germany had to gain strength from the sacrifice of its elites. As one member of the Kammer announced, "the public does not want to see the 'favorites' of the past twelve years and should get used to entirely new faces and ideas." This was a view ICD Intelligence would have found congenial, but the same could not be said of the Soviets, who bridled at charges that they were not taking seriously the job of denazifying the arts. Harich, a committed Stalinist and equally intense antifa, appeared especially confused by SMAD's reluctance to punish talented artists who had compromised with Hitler. On the one hand, he told the Americans, if anyone "should be lead [sic] by artistic considerations to tolerance towards nazi [sic] artists it was his, Harich's, job to stop him." But at the same time, he had to acknowledge that "politically grey people" and "even some black ones" were being allowed to work, and even to assume leadership positions. As PWD's first deputy chief in Berlin observed, where the Kammer's denazification committee "is strongly anti-Nazi and is determined to clean up the profession," the Russians' "foremost interest at the moment seems to be 'activity at all costs.'"[47]

There was considerable truth in this charge. In the initial days of the occupation, the Soviet *Kommandatur* had actually extended rather than curtailed the authority of cultural administrators who had been prominent in the Reich in order to achieve a preliminary centralization of information. Heinz Tietjen, for example, who had run the Staatsoper for Goering, found an equally genial boss in Nikolai Bersarin, who charged him with reactivating the city's entire classical music life.

Unfortunately, Tietjen ran afoul of Leo Borchard, whom Bersarin had appointed music director of the combined forces of the Berlin Philharmonic and the Staatsoper orchestra, the core of which concertized as the Staatskapelle. An antifa who was also a leading figure in the Kammer der Kunstschaffenden, Borchard was a dangerous man to alienate, and he promptly unleashed on the *Intendant* what Tietjen called "an avalanche of slander and lies." Borchard feared Tietjen's efforts to entice more famous and Jewish rivals back to Berlin and opposed his proposal to amalgamate the Staatskapelle and the philharmonic. He also knew that Tietjen was interested in getting rid of him because the *Intendant* never liked employing someone closer to the regime (Borchard spoke fluent Russian) than he was. Borchard therefore revealed to SMAD information concerning the *Intendant*'s collaborations with the Nazis and engineered his dismissal just three weeks into his office. The conductor may not have wanted Tietjen to destroy his chance-of-a-lifetime leadership of Berlin's two major orchestras, but to the man who took over as *Intendant* of the Städtische Oper, Michael Bohnen, another leftist and Kammer member who had remained in the Third Reich, there was a different explanation as to why his predecessor had to go: "[H]is continuing was not an option if we were to rebuild German opera on a new and democratic foundation."[48]

Although the Soviets had quickly corrected their error, they did so only under pressure from the antifas and the "Tietjen case" left a lasting impression. Harich rationalized it as a purely tactical maneuver: "[T]hese people," he explained, and "he gave the example of Tietjen," can be "used to get together the members of a certain theater or branch of the film industry, and . . . as soon as the initial job is performed, these people will be . . . purged." But Harich was wrong. One year into the occupation, a full half of the Staatskapelle were still former party members, and none had been dismissed; while at the Staatsoper, twenty-seven former Nazi choir members and such prominent fascists as Tiana Lemnitz, Josef Greindl, and Willi Domgraf-Fassbaender continued to sing. The Russians left Hans von Benda, notorious (according to ICD) for his pro-Nazi sympathies, in charge of his Berlin chamber orchestra, and although it appointed Borchard to the philharmonic, they retained his old friend, the former Nazi, Robert Heger, as principal guest conductor. Ironically, complaints about Soviet resistance to revolutionizing theater and orchestral life clearly bothered the KPD's cultural spokespersons. When the Americans were introduced to Winzer in early July 1945, one of the first things he said to them was that because "theatrical and musical life . . . had to be revived immediately and urgently in order to get the population of Berlin out of its complete apathy and induce them to work . . . a certain amount of leniency had to be applied in the beginning." However, he assured the newly arrived Americans, more hopefully than truthfully (and in contrast to Harich who felt that while the problem was real, a purge was imminent), a "gradual weeding out process is in progress . . . and at present there exists only a limited number of borderline cases."[49]

The Kammer's needling only added to the resentment generated by the organization's apparently unlimited administrative power and guaranteed its demise. With the Kulturbund in place, the *Magistrat* moved swiftly to close down the Schlüterstrasse organization, cutting off its financial support in early October 1945 and then demanding the dismissal of administrative officers and the surrender of its powers. At the same time, the Amt für Volksbildung established its own cultural affairs bureau, headed by a *Kulturreferent*, together with a denazification committee to take over its rival's functions. The Kammer was then dissolved by direct order of the Kommandatura, on the advice of Winzer, because it had failed to "cooperate properly" with his cultural affairs committee. Adding insult to this injury, Winzer accused the Kammer of being too much like the former Reichskulturkammer and an intrinsically fascistic organization.[50]

Unfortunately, the Americans, who appeared in Berlin in the midst of these battles, were slow finding their feet. Only too late did they realize that control over denazification was about to pass to the city and the fount of cultural inspiration to the Kulturbund. Only too late did it dawn on the zealots in ICD Intelligence that their true soulmates were the antifas on the Kammer's denazification committee. A week after the Kammer's dissolution, the Intelligence Branch in Berlin tried to cripple the increasingly powerful Amt für Volksbildung by ordering Winzer removed after his department published a magazine that had not received Kommandatura authorization, but the Soviets blocked the attack. ICD did, however, prevent four-power recognition of the Amt für Volksbildung's authority over denazification, which meant that the defunct Schlüterstrasse committee remained the only group as yet recognized by all the Allies. This gave ICD something to reorganize and recoup after the fact of the Kammer's demise. Because the old Kammer's offices in Schlüterstrasse were in the British sector, the RKK's files remained there, and Schmidt and a few others were retained by ICD's British analogue, ISB, to administer them. Then, in February 1946, the Americans agreed with the British that they would reactivate the Kammer as a consultative body on denazification, and John Bitter, the music officer, convinced Wegener to resume his duties as president. The U.S. retreat had now begun to firm up: "Our opposition to the closing of the *Kammer* is frankly this: that [because] both trade unions and the department of cultural affairs in the *Magistrat* are under the complete direction of . . . Moscow trained German communists . . . it would be unwise on our part to permit these people to take complete control over the situation." The British and Americans also hit on the good idea of boosting the new Kulturkammer's profile by opening a restaurant in the building where licensed performers could buy dinner for cash without using up their ration coupons.[51]

The trouble was that the Berlin officers could empower the Kammer no further, because by the time they grasped their missed opportunity, McClure's revolution was under way. With the issuance of the blacklist in October 1945, denazification became the exclusive jurisdiction of the Intelligence Section and its counterparts in Special Branch and the CIC. In Berlin the procedural reform caused particular problems because the city government, backed by SMAD, claimed responsibility for vetting its own people. A compromise of sorts had to be reached, and in late October the Allies agreed to the creation of a cultural committee attached to the Kommandatura with veto authority over municipal denazification rulings. The trouble was that each power had its own rules in this matter and each refused to sacrifice them for the sake of the others. Consequently, while the Americans blacklisted everyone in sight, the other Allies continued much as before. Nor did the agreement settle the issue of the Kammer, which, for political reasons, the Americans needed to keep alive. The Berlin office seemed determined to continue giving it some function and proceeded, in late 1946, to use the Kammer as an appeals tribunal as defined by MG Law #8, but for months ICD in the zone refused to recognize its authority. And so, yet another element of madness was introduced into the process of denazification, as artists blacklisted by

ICD who were cleared in Berlin were allowed to perform in the American sector of the city but prevented from doing so elsewhere in the U.S. zone.

Denazification, in the eyes of Intelligence Section officers, had to be comprehensive and unequivocal. Exceptions to rules were intrinsically unfair, and no artist should be allowed to escape responsibility simply because he or she was talented or popular. Because of their dogmatism, ICD officers were often considered simpleminded and incapable of understanding the complexities of European art and society. But while it is true that in removing the Nazi cancer the Intelligence Section employed a chain saw instead of a scalpel, it had sound reasons for adopting that approach. It was time-consuming to find and process the documentary information available in 1945–46, individuals were lying to protect themselves, and knowing who and what to trust was difficult. Moreover, denazification's grim exponents were so tough not because they were ignorant, but because they appreciated the horror of Nazism and sought to crush it completely and irrevocably. They had no interest in making excuses for the war or the Holocaust; they considered all Germans who had not repudiated the chauvinistic and nationalistic culture that produced Nazism as sharing in its crimes. To appreciate revolutionary denazification one must understand the cultural assumption (that Nazism was the logical and terrible extension of popularly held attitudes and beliefs) that underpinned it.

Alternative approaches were, however, available. The Music Branch officers and most Germans, for example, believed that culpability should be determined on a case-by-case basis. Although they did not agree on the measure of a Nazi, they both felt that individuals, not society, needed denazification. Wherever they could, the music officers used loopholes in ICD's regulations — such as those offered by the Screening Center in Bad Orb — to get individuals they believed "clean" denazified. The Soviets in Berlin also presented ICD with an alternate approach to denazification. Their method was more arbitrary, insofar as the Russians tended to clear the people they considered most important, but equally ideologically driven. In consequence, in Berlin, where ICD Intelligence struggled to impose its approach on a system not of its making, the results were friction among the Allies and a grid-locking of denazification's administration.

It is by no means clear, however, that a more case-sensitive American program would have produced a fairer or less controversial result. True, ICD's revolution was costly to art and damaging to many musicians (Kabasta's suicide being the saddest example). Moreover, through its extremism—its failure to distinguish between levels of collaboration—it all but forced artists to lie. This only made it harder to separate the big lies from the smaller. But would a more individualized approach on the part of the occupation authorities have produced a more just result? Were the music officers right? Would individual rather than cultural denazification have lessened the conflict with the Soviets? Fortunately, we can go some way toward answering these questions because the Americans did employ an alternate approach in Austria, the only other European nation that fell under quadripartite military rule. And this makes the contrasts between the two countries illuminating.

DENAZIFICATION IN ¾ TIME: AUSTRIA

In Austria a very different set of cultural assumptions produced a much-subtler concept of denazification than in Germany. Instead of overturning a society, the Americans there satisfied themselves with cleaning up a few bad neighborhoods. As the Austrian case shows, America's denazifiers were not, as has often been charged, incapable of distinguishing guilt from innocence or recognizing musical greatness. In Germany they had revolutionary goals; where they did not work to achieve social or cultural change, they were subtle and compassionate in their approach. Intriguingly, however, the more surgical approach to denazification pursued in Austria did not prevent injustices or lessen the conflict with the Soviets. Unlike the Americans, who treated Austria and Germany differently, Soviet cultural administrators in both countries implemented much the same program, and their methods were equally antithetical to the Americans'.

Austria, the *Military Government Handbook* asserted, was a "treasure house of culture," a splendid remnant of European art still largely unaffected by fascism and war (this was written before the Americans actually saw Vienna). Although the cultural life of Austria "badly needed a coat of fresh paint after the discoloration of the Nazi regime," inwardly it was considered "sound and rested on its ancient foundations." In Austria, unlike Germany, the Nazi tumor was thought benign and easily extracted. In music, for example, the American cultural officers maintained that "the traditional classical program itself was impregnable against Nazi ideology and with the restoration of

*The Vienna Staatsoper, Auditorium and Proscenium, 1946
(Photo courtesy of Virginia Pleasants)*

Mendelssohn, Mahler and Offenbach to the repertoire, the structure [will be] as good as new." Where the Germans were believed to be brutal and calculating, the Austrians were seen as lighthearted and peaceable. Although they had gone along with the Nazis, American officials told themselves, it was only because they were too good-natured to object. In contrast to their counterparts in Germany, Military Government personnel in Austria were advised to be patient and understanding with their charges. In fact, MG officers were instructed that unlike the Germans, "Austrians hate regimentation and discipline, that they appreciate good manners and a cheerful air and have a highly developed sense of the ridiculous." Moreover, and this must have been hard for military men to swallow, "they are deficient in the sense of responsibility, [and] they attach little importance to efficiency," though one did have to admit that "there is a streak of cruelty that underlies their otherwise very genuine culture and civilization."[52]

Austria was in a peculiar position after the war. In Moscow, in October 1943, the Allied foreign ministers publicly committed their governments to the restoration of the country's independence. In so doing, they agreed to rank Austria's 1938 annexation by Germany over its wartime collaboration with the Nazis. Yet the one never fully obliterated the memory of the other. True, Austria was a conquered country, but it had also fielded thirty-five Wehrmacht divisions, supplied a number of generals, and spawned the Führer himself. In part because the right had scattered the socialists and communists even before the Anschluss, the country also failed to produce the kind of resistance movement that would at least serve as evidence of its subjugation. The Allies' decision to treat Austria as a country to be "liberated" was therefore an act of wishful remembrance, and the Soviets were not alone in doubting it was justified, despite their acquiescence to the Moscow Declaration. Indeed, the very fact that Austria was at once liberated and divided, like Germany, into four military government occupation zones, was peculiar testimony to its indeterminate status. As the American's *Military Government Handbook for Austria* explained, U.S. forces had a mandate both subtle and complex: to reestablish the country's democratic government and to "remind" the population that it had a "responsibility . . . for participation in the war at the side of Hitlerite Germany." The Soviets had a more concrete understanding of this duality than the Americans, for no sooner had the Red Army entered Austrian territory than it started liberating the country of its economic infrastructure.[53] Ultimately, however, the two occupiers were agreed that Austria was only partially culpable for the actions of the Axis powers.

The Red Army was the first to enter the Austrian capital, and, as in Berlin, it proved reluctant to allow the Western Allies admission. It was a full four months before the Americans were to establish themselves in Vienna, by which time the Soviets had already set up an interim government under Karl Renner. Their decision to declare that government a national one, even though Russian troops occupied only a small portion of the country, and to announce that free elections were to be held in November 1945, had far-reaching consequences.[54] Although they clearly hoped that the interim government would mobilize support for the left and that a snap election would result in a victory for the Austrian Communist Party, in deciding that the country would have one rather than four or more zonal administrations, the Soviets were gambling. Should the Austrians elect a leadership antagonistic toward their interests, a potent political entity with support in the West and authority over all four zones would be created. Unlike Germany, it would then be difficult to simply do what one wanted within one's own zone of occupation.

Of course, the Soviets were not thinking that far ahead. As with the other Allies, they anticipated an early settlement of the state treaty negotiations that would end the war and reestablish the independent Austrian nation. Doubtless, they moved quickly to strip their zone of its resources because they didn't know how long they would control it. If their gamble yielded pay dirt, then they could withdraw their forces, leaving a pro-Soviet government in control. If the election produced a less favorable result, then the Russians would have to improvise some new strategy. American planners were thinking along much the same lines, although, because they came late to Vienna and had not organized the national government or precipitated the election, they were in an even less secure position. Still, like the Soviets, the Americans did not expect a prolonged occupation. This simple fact was crucial in determining American denazification policy.

In Austria, the equivalent of OMGUS Information Control Division was called the Information Services Branch and the name reveals a lot. ISB bore the mark of Austria's indefinite status as a belligerent victim of Nazi aggression. During the war, control over culture and the media in conquered areas was vested in the Psychological Warfare Division, but in liberated countries OWI initially ran America's propaganda effort. This separation could not really be sustained in Austria, which was at once conquered and liberated, and so the civilian agency and the military unit worked in tandem. ISB's chief, General A. J. McCrystal, had commanded PWD in Italy, but he worked with a liaison officer from OWI. Similarly, the first director of OWI operations in Austria was a PWD officer, and OWI personnel such as Margot

Pinter and Virginia Pleasants moved over to the Theater and Music Branch of Military Government. Because the Americans planned on a relatively rapid transition to civilian control, OWI maintained an Austrian branch and it was assumed that, with the imminent demise of Military Government, the civilian agency (reconfigured as a branch of the State Department) would take over its work. These plans changed in August 1945, when Congress voted to terminate OWI's operations without giving the State Department the means to absorb its overseas functions. State continued, as in Germany, to supply and guide ISB programs, but the division remained a branch of MG. And yet, because everyone was waiting for the withdrawal of all American forces—something that in the end took years—there was little impetus to reconstruct Austria's cultural life radically. Consequently, in the case of ISB's work, the "positive," or reeducational, aspect remained far more important than the "negative," and the branch's primary tasks were to reactivate musical life and give it a new look. This explains why the Americans pressed the Salzburg Festival back into operation so quickly after the end of the war and triumphantly broadcast the results.[55]

In Austria, then, it was the demand for normalization that put a strain on the process of denazification. This is not to imply that denazification was not taken seriously, only that its goal was limited. Here there was no talk of revolution; instead, the aim was to make the politically immature Austrians understand that they should not have collaborated with Hitler. Being a collaborator in Austria was not seen as evidence of irredeemable nastiness; even party members, rather than being judged summarily, were individually examined to determine whether they subscribed to Germanic values or had simply demonstrated the typical Austrian trait of tagging along. As one former ISB officer explained, in Germany everything seemed white and black, in Austria it was all tones of gray. The differences mystified, delighted, or appalled participants in ICD's revolution in Germany. Some, like Berlin's first theater and music officer, Henry Alter, put in for transfer to Vienna. Others, such as his successor as theater officer, Edward Hogan, were not quite sure what to make of it all. After one spring 1946 visit, Hogan noted that, while the quality of singing at the Staatsoper was higher than what one might hear in Berlin, it was largely because "no one gives a hoot about Nazis, who pursue an even course as though nothing had happened."[56] Still, Hogan found the climate congenial enough, and in 1948 he applied to take over Alter's job in Vienna.

By quadripartite agreement, denazification was to become an Austrian responsibility as soon as the national government passed the necessary laws. Although the Allies maintained veto authority over local decisions in their respective zones, it was the Austrians who put people on trial. The approach to denazification ultimately adopted by the conservative, pro-Western Figl government, which won the November election, was modeled, interestingly enough, on the one introduced by the Renner interregnum and therefore bore traces of its original Soviet design. The job of denazifying the cultural field was entrusted to committees of experts that, like the Kammer in Berlin, were appointed by the government. In December 1945 the Ministry of Education, which had authority for the arts, established committees in Linz, Salzburg, and Vienna to hear cases in the American zone. Unfortunately, because each military government had to approve Austrian decisions in its own zones, a similar situation to that in Germany arose, with one occupation authority banning an artist who had been cleared by another. And, because the Allies in Austria had no quadripartite committee until the spring of 1946, there was even less harmony here than there was up north. For example, when the director of the Salzburg Festival requested that Julius Patzak and Elizabeth Schwarzkopf be engaged to sing at the first festival, the Americans vetoed their clearance because both artists were former Nazis. But this did not prevent the two singers from performing at the Theater an der Wien, which, though in the "International Sector" of Vienna, was for the moment predominantly under Soviet care. To resolve this difficulty, and because the election had returned a government congenial to the West, the Americans pressed for a national denazification law "which will be valid in all cases." This approach, Henry Alter maintained, was necessary because "for the time being utter confusion reigns as to who is bound by our directives. . . . How can we effectively ban a person in the American zone if, for lack of proper coordination with the Austrians, all he has to do is to move to another theater and continue his activities."[57] It would, however, be a long time before such coordination was achieved because the Soviets refused to accept a law that would embarrass them in their own zone. In the meantime, the disputes among the Allies over the applicability of Austrian tribunal decisions made the fights in Germany look like teething trouble.

Conflicts among the occupation authorities were not the only things complicating the denazification of Austrian artists. Because the Austrians did most of the work, ISB was not fitted with an intelligence section and it was Military Government's Special Branch or the army's Military Intelligence Division (G-2) that ordered removals and issued requests for trials. ISB officers supplied the names of individuals to Special Branch and G-2 and compiled basic briefing information, but it could not itself issue the removal order. ISB therefore had no formal blacklist, even if it did compile a register of the most important people in the arts and documentation concerning their activities in the Third Reich. It also adopted ICD's list to the extent of agreeing that mandatory removals in Germany could not be cleared in Austria unless they were Austrian nationals. ICD, however, refused to allow Austrians it had blacklisted to perform in Germany no matter what ISB thought. Though limited in all these ways, ISB still had the power to approve or reject decisions of the Ministry of Education's denazification tribunals, at least in most cases.

As in Germany, the major difficulty was that most of the more popular musicians had either attained or sustained their profile under the Nazis by accommodating themselves to the regime. "European artists have always considered it their privilege to be honored and flattered by the existing government," Henry Alter noted, and they made no exception for the Nazis; as a result, Alter continued, "we are dealing with an artistic generation which is guilty in toto of having 'collaborated' with the nazis [*sic*]."[58] The Austrians were even less sympathetic to the removal of this generation than the Germans, in part because no one regarded the failure to give up one's career for political reasons as "grounds for prosecution" and in part because Austrian music had recovered its golden glow in the last years of the Reich. Clemens Krauss's departure from Vienna to Berlin in 1937 had been a double blow to the Staatsoper as he had taken away with him several of the city's best singers, and the philharmonic had languished somewhat under the Nazis. But when Baldur von Schirach became *Gauleiter* of Vienna in 1940, the city's musical fortunes began to reverse. Furtwängler's installation in that year as Vienna's musical plenipotentiary and permanent conductor of the Vienna Philharmonic Orchestra was a major coup, as was the Staatsoper's 1943 acquisition of Karl Böhm. Restoring the postwar music scene to its previous level of achievement became an issue of national pride. Indeed, because Austria controlled its own denazification process, the government attempted to fast-track the clearance of such blacklisted Germans as Furtwängler and Strauss in order to secure their presence in Vienna.

Austrian support for prominent artists of the Nazi period — Böhm, Furtwängler and Krauss, Patzak and Cebotari — revealed more than just a refusal to consider the politics of music important. The revival of musical life was as much about Austria's return to the community of nations as it was about music making. A Staatsoper led by Böhm or Krauss would serve as international acknowledgment that the Austrians had done nothing wrong and that the Allies accepted the innocence of their cultural leaders. To the Americans, the 1945 Salzburg Festival was meant to reveal the birth of a new Austria, but to local administrators, who proposed mounting much the same program with most of the same people that they had under the Nazis, it was a theater of exoneration.

The Soviets understood this urge and were willing to satisfy it. By the time the other Allies were allowed into Vienna, they already had a short list of musicians they wanted to see rehabilitated. At the top of that list was the revered conductor Wilhelm Furtwängler, who they really hoped would return to the Berlin Staatsoper, but whom they would happily see at the helm of the Vienna Philharmonic as well. For Vienna's Staatsoper, the Soviets backed its brilliant former *Generalmusikdirektor* and Hitler favorite, Clemens Krauss. The presence of these men at the top of the Soviet's list determined the names of those at the bottom: Krauss's arch-rival, Hans Knappertsbusch, and Furtwängler's nemesis, the man he perceived as his chief rival, the young star, Herbert von Karajan. These two men were deemed "unacceptably Nazi" by the Russians. Unfortunately for the Soviets, all of these people, the good and the bad, were for the moment out of their reach: Furtwängler was in Switzerland and Krauss, Karajan, and Knappertsbusch were in the American zone. And ISB's music officers were astute enough to recognize the leverage that accompanied possession, and they kept the musicians most interesting to the Soviets under wraps for as long as they could.

Of course, Soviet preferences put ISB in an impossible position. Because the artists most favored by their eastern ally were on ICD's German blacklist, Military Government could not easily allow their return. Moreover, those at the top of the Soviet list — Krauss and Furtwängler — were considered by the Americans to be among the most tainted collaborators of the concert hall. They had been *Reichskultursenatoren*, had been Hitler's two favorite conductors, and had occupied the top musical positions in Germany. In Krauss's case, there was past evidence of "violent anti-semitic" feelings. Krauss's wife, the singer Viorica Ursuleac, was also known to have been a close friend of Göring and Bormann, and the conductor had often bragged of his personal relationship with the Führer. He distributed personally dedicated copies of *Mein Kampf* to singers in Munich who had been awarded medals for long service.[59] As with the Soviets, the preferences of the Music Branch officers were determined by their reactions to these two men, so they promoted Knappertsbusch and Karajan, the one in Munich, the other in Vienna.

In Munich, ICD's officers sensed that the crude Bavarian maestro was less clean than he maintained, but they also accepted that he had suffered career setbacks during the 1930s and they realized that he was widely considered an anti-Nazi by the public. ISB in Vienna had fewer excuses when it came to Karajan, who won over the Americans by poise, lies, half-truths, and musical ability. Because ISB officers were willing to judge each case according to its merits, and because they were sensitive to Austrian wishes, they allowed themselves to be gulled by the young conductor. And Karajan's performance in the first year of the occupation was masterful. Unlike Böhm and Knappertsbusch, he never harangued the Americans for their stupidity in not recognizing his greatness. Instead, when they first refused to let him conduct, he congratulated them for taking their job as seriously as he took his and for sticking to their convictions. When he was blacklisted, he volunteered to work behind the scenes, helping out wherever he could, asking for no recognition, and making himself indispensable. When approached by Walter Legge, a British EMI record producer attached to its Swiss affiliate, with a contract to record, he "was in no hurry to sign, even though he had no money and no work — and no possibility of work"; such, Legge thought, was his "inner sense of repose." Certainly, he made a point of appearing calm; when his third appeal for rehabilitation was rejected, he announced he was going skiing in the mountains. As the conductor informed an awestruck Henry Alter, "my time is sure to come and I await it, calm and confident." For a time the music officers did not know how to handle the controlled and dapper young conductor. As one of them remembered, "he used to drop around to the office, perfectly dressed. Like a city gentleman. And Vienna was in rags. And here was Karajan with hat and umbrella and gloves. . . . I'll never forget him coming and paying his visits."[60] But Karajan was no dandy, and his style of dress was as carefully considered as the story he told the Americans.

From what Karajan said, and on the basis of the information they had available, his case was not beyond redemption. Although he admitted to having joined the Nazi Party in 1935, at the age of twenty-seven, he maintained that he had only done so in order to secure a major conducting job in Aachen. He said that he had been "pressured" to do so earlier, when he was working in Ulm (1928–34), but had only joined in order to secure the Aachen promotion. He maintained that the local *Gauleiter* had told him to join, and his secretary had applied for him as "he himself did not care about this matter." Later in life he would compare becoming a Nazi to enrolling in a ski club in order to work with a particular instructor. Claiming never to have been a good joiner, he informed the Americans that he refused to play works by Nazi composers when in Aachen, despite being urged to do so by the authorities. In 1938, he asserted, he lost his position because of opposition to him from within the party. Later, he would list the date of his dismissal from Aachen correctly, as 1941. Sometime between 1938 and 1941, Karajan said, his problems began with the powerful and the powerfully connected. Heinz Tietjen brought him to Berlin to conduct at the Staatsoper and promoted him as a rival to Furtwängler. This only served to incense Hitler and Goebbels, who regarded Furtwängler as the supreme exponent of German music culture. When the pressure on Tietjen increased, Karajan maintained, the wily *Intendant* dropped him to second billing. He then lost out on an opportunity to succeed Böhm in Dresden, and the number of concerts he was hired to conduct in Germany fell from sixty to six a year (at another point he declared the number had fallen by half). In these years, the conductor declared, he survived through guest concerts in Hungary and Italy. His marriage, in 1942, to a *Mischling 2. Grades*, a quarter-Jew under the Nuremberg Race Laws, provided the killing blow to his career. He claimed that he was brought before a Nazi tribunal, where, in an outrage, he quit the party. According to Pasetti, Karajan's hard luck proved that he had "made good his joining the party by his attitude later on."[61]

Karajan's petition for denazification was forwarded by ISB with a positive recommendation to the Ministry of Education's Salzburg Commission for the Political Investigation of Artists in early December 1945. The Music Branch—Henry Alter, Margot Pinter, and Otto Pasetti—were convinced that he had both a new enough face and an ambivalent enough record to become the musical personality Austria needed. Unlike Krauss or Furtwängler, a Karajan in charge at the Vienna Staatsoper or Philharmonic (the same orchestra was used in both houses) would signal the arrival of a new era. But not everyone in Military Government agreed, and Henry Pleasants, the USFA G-2 officer responsible for cultural affairs, filed his opposition to Karajan's denazification. Nonetheless, the Austrian commission thought well enough of the maestro and, in late December, recommended his clearance. With no higher MG office yet established that might oversee or coordinate denazification findings, ISB's Music Branch approved the Austrian tribunal's recommendations, and Karajan was scheduled to conduct four concerts in Vienna in January 1946. The Russians, however, realized they were being outmaneuvered by the Americans, and days after Karajan's clearance was announced, the Vienna Staatsoper Orchestra unanimously voted to approve the still blacklisted Clemens Krauss as its music director. This failed to move ISB and so, on the morning of Karajan's first concert, the Soviets refused him permission to perform. They claimed that the municipal *Kulturamt* had issued the request for the concert's cancellation. When Pinter and Pasetti appealed to them to let their man perform, the Russian music officer replied that they would not allow Karajan to be denazified before Krauss. Ultimately, a compromise was reached. Aware of the poor publicity they had generated among the musically starved Viennese by canceling the concert on short notice, the Soviets agreed to allow Karajan to conduct his next two concerts, but they refused to recognize his denazification.[62]

Still hoping for an early settlement to the case, Karajan was rebooked to conduct the philharmonic in early March 1946, but by then the jig was up. Two hours before his next Musikverein concert, the Soviets again ordered its cancellation. This time the gesture was purely a way of embarrassing ISB, because they had weeks previously found the chink in the Music Branch's armor and might have notified them sooner. In fact, the Ministry of Education had already considered the issue the Russians now identified and had ruled it nonapplicable. The problem, the Soviets announced, was that Karajan was technically an

Illegaler, a party member during a time when the NSDAP had been banned in Austria. Consequently, under Austrian law, he could not hold a "leadership position" without the approval of the *politische Kabinetsrat*. And so, as ISB and the maestro waited, his case was forwarded to the Austrian Interior Ministry for reconsideration; in the meantime, the newly organized Internal Affairs Committee of the Allied Kommandatura agreed to bar Karajan from all conducting pending referral of the ministry's verdict. Only the English delegate, possibly influenced by the fact that Walter Legge had just signed him to a recording contract, dissented and supported his clearance.[63]

ISB's Music Branch had by now been humiliated by the Soviets twice and had been abandoned by its own superiors. From the perspective of its officers, Karajan had been cleared by an Austrian denazification tribunal, and its decision had been approved in the usual way. The Soviet charge that Karajan was an *Illegaler* was discounted as the conductor had at the time been a member of the German party and not its banned Austrian equivalent. Unwilling to betray a man in whom it had invested so much, the Music Branch allowed him to be employed as musical director of the Salzburg Festival; however, it emphasized that while he might rehearse with the band and singers, he could not be permitted any public appearances or recognition for his efforts. Revealing typical poise, the conductor accepted these terms, but in the end he was unable to contain his urges once back on the podium. Karajan slipped now for the first time, and he began behaving as though he had "already been cleared for public appearance," opening his rehearsals to the public and "allowing" his name to be slated for twelve concerts during the 1946 festival. Karajan's activities attracted too much attention, and the Music Branch was compelled to order his name off the festival playbill. It told him to cease rehearsing with the orchestra and singers but allowed him to remain as an unnamed artistic consultant.[64]

By now the *politische Kabinetsrat* had agreed to recommend the conductor's clearance, but the Allies had had enough. The Kommandatura's Internal Affairs Committee, meeting in June 1946, refused to allow Karajan's denazification on the simple grounds that he had been a party member since 1935. Any further consideration of his case would have to await approval of the country's national denazification law. There was general agreement on this, with the French and Soviet delegates opposing Karajan's clearance most strenuously, and the British delegate being the most supportive. The Americans, who had not been united on his case from the beginning, seemed content to allow the others to make the decision.[65]

In the end, of course, ISB had completely misjudged the Karajan case. In their eagerness to have him cleared, they ignored his scheming and never really checked up on his story. Karajan did not join the party as a condition of employment in Aachen; he joined two years before, in Salzburg, and then he rejoined in Ulm when he moved to Germany. He was therefore twice over a Nazi prior to his appointment in Aachen. When he first joined, just three days after his twenty-fifth birthday, and a month after the election that gave Hitler power, the regime was too new for him to have figured that his membership would benefit him professionally. Consequently, he must have had political rather than career-related reasons for becoming a Nazi. His father, a prominent Salzburg physician, was also a party member. Nor is there any evidence to support his claim that he was "dismissed" from his job in Aachen or that he was grilled by a party committee after marrying a "non-Aryan," and his record of membership remained intact. In fact, contrary to his claims, his wife was not even a "non-Aryan" according to the 1935 Nuremberg Race Laws. By 1949 the Americans were learning other things about the conductor: that he "never wavered" in starting his concerts in occupied countries by conducting the *Horst Wessel Lied* and that he refused now to take American music seriously. The Americans even began to doubt the maestro's claim of indifference to politics; "he is a mature and highly intelligent man," the theater and music officer noted, and "it seems absurd to assume that so intelligent a man should have been completely unaware of the meaning and the consequences of becoming a party member."[66] By 1949, of course, American opinion no longer made any difference; Karajan had been finally and irrevocably denazified under Austria's new National Socialists Law one year before.

As Karajan's case demonstrates, the American music officers in Austria, like their counterparts in Germany, attempted to chart a delicate course between whitewashing and blacklisting, revival and renewal. Karajan was considered tainted but not black — at least not as black as his more prominent compatriots, Böhm and Krauss. But what really tipped the scales in his favor was that he was seen as new and therefore a potential symbol of cultural rebirth. He was discovered during the Third Reich, but his career success was restricted and that made him seem a victim. In this sense, ISB hoped to use Karajan as an instrument of both denazification and reeducation, even if the maestro was unsuited to both goals. Although the conductor was willing, in these early years, to play some unusual works by a few contemporary composers — von Einem and Walton being examples — he never contemplated moving his career down an unconventional path. Ambitious and arrogant enough to fancy himself the successor to Furtwängler, something elements in the Berlin press had already proclaimed, he knew he had to make his name in the traditional repertoire. His political record, moreover, was one of the worst among prominent conductors, and it would be a stretch to see his clearance as anything like "a purification through remorse."[67] To get through the process, Karajan lied about his party membership and continued to do so throughout his career. It is hard to consider his actions a sign that he was really prepared to master his own past and move forward. Nor is it clear from this case that a more sensitive approach to denazification necessarily yielded better results.

Although ICD in Germany forced a revolution and ISB in Austria pressed for renovation, in both countries the Americans and Soviets came into conflict. The Russian cultural administrators in Germany and Austria had very different ideas from their American counterparts about what they might achieve through music. In the short term, they were clearly the more interested in providing local populations with what they most wanted: performances of familiar music by celebrated artists. In the longer term, they hoped to infiltrate cultural organizations and align them with Communist Party priorities. But the two objectives were to a large extent separate and followed independent trajectories: the one was a matter of maintaining morale among subjugated populations; the other was an issue of building long-term support for Stalinism. Inevitably, however, both brought Soviets and Americans into conflict. In Germany, ICD resented SMAD's rejection of revolutionary denazification; in Austria, ISB was entangled in a struggle for popularity and influence and could not allow the Soviets to gain the advantage. In both countries, denazification provided music making with a Procrustean bed. In Austria, the goal of promoting the new led ISB to stretch the definition of political cleanliness beyond the breaking point. In Germany, the policy of denazifying artists by blacklisting them induced ICD's Intelligence to simply lop away music's overextended parts.

Denazification raises important questions about the complicity of citizens in the crimes of their government. Artists in Germany and Austria were state or municipal employees; they performed in concert halls beneath swastikas and were surrounded in their work by the emblems of the Reich. When they performed abroad, it was because the Nazis saw benefit in their doing so; when they obtained promotions or won honors, it was because Hitler's administration supported them. They were not unaware that the regime they worked for was pursuing an inhuman racial pogrom: all of them knew and worked with Jews who lost their jobs, who suffered public humiliation, and who died. All of them also would have known that the Nazis were being denounced around the world for their barbarism and that the regime was anxious to foster the arts as a way of glorifying German achievements. When they appeared before the public and performed well, they were sending out a message to audiences that the contributions of the Jews and other "undesirables" were not needed — that *pure German art* was perfect in itself. Although many of them helped Jews leave quietly, this was an easier course than objecting to their removal or leaving oneself. In all these matters, the musicians made choices; they were free not to participate in the cultural construction of the Third Reich, though that decision was harder for some to make than for others. Those who did look to escape, such as the conductor Hans Rosbaud, deserve a measure of respect, if only for trying.

But what was to be done with this tarnished generation? For the revolutionaries in ICD, the answer was simple: the old had to be discarded to make space for the new. ICD's denazifiers wanted and needed quick solutions to big problems and so they turned to psychology and sociology and simple inconsistency in blacklisting musicians. They were true zealots and did not worry if the Germans had to live without their eminent artists or if the country's musical tradition was shattered; in fact, that was the very point of their actions. It is easy to criticize their violent assault on high culture, but as the Karajan case reveals, individual considerations did not necessarily produce a more just result. Revolutionary denazification cut through German music in great swathes, and one might conclude that if the Americans had been more refined in their approach, they could have done a better job. This is, however, what ISB attempted in Austria, and what the psychiatrists strove to do in Bad Orb. The results of their efforts do not build confidence. It was just too hard to know whom to trust in 1945: detailed information was lacking or took too long to collate and process, and judgments were not being made in the cool light of reason. Germany and Austria were ruined nations, corpses were decaying beneath the rubble, and people were hungry and demoralized. American Military Government personnel harbored understandable resentments against Germany; they had trouble moving around the country, the phone lines didn't work, they were short-staffed, and many of them spoke the language inadequately. It would be naive to suggest that in this environment sensible and well-thought-through decisions would be made by reasonable and informed people. If revolutionary denazification obliterated distinctions between black and gray and the shades of each, can we be so certain that a more case-sensitive approach would have produced fewer injustices?

The Music Branch officers thought so, and they resisted ICD's revolution from the beginning. As the Austrian and Bavarian cases reveal, if the music officers had had their druthers, they would have taken a very different approach to the denazification of artists. To most of them, people and not their art had committed the crimes of Nazism. As musicians themselves, they found it impossible to conceive of censuring a music culture in which they had been nurtured. They accepted that there were chauvinistic elements in German (if not Austrian) attitudes to music, but they thought they could eliminate these through education and exposure to the art of other lands. Their thinking was close here to that of local administrators and musicians, most of whom saw nothing wrong with collaboration, except in the case of *ideologically* committed Nazis. Branch officers and locals alike rejected the notion that a culture had to be denazified by removing its symbols and called for "punishment only of those who are accused of specific crimes." As Pasetti explained it: one should not "ban every artist who was performing under the Nazi regime and especially the great artists, because each of them was once invited [out] by a Nazi official or shaked [sic] hands with him, [one must] check each case carefully and find out the artists [sic] mentality, especially if he did any denouncing or other harm to non-party members or opponents of the regime."[68] Punish the person, not the culture, for the crime.

For the time being, however, neither the branch officers nor the Germans exerted much influence over denazification, although individual artists did work to obstruct it by lying. In time, however, the locals would gain more influence over the process, and the resentments they harbored would boil over. Once they were back in charge, German artists and administrators would abandon cultural denazification and undo the revolution. In so doing, they would also reveal the distance they had traveled from ICD's moderates. Although they had not wanted to revolutionize music culture, the branch officers had believed that culpable artists should be punished. Unfortunately, what the Germans would undertake was a whitewashing of music life so indiscriminate that even the music officers would find it disgraceful.

3 Reforming Music Culture, 1945–1946

In their war on Nazism, ICD officers were guided, however vaguely, by a series of official directives. Although the 1945 *Military Government Handbook*, the Potsdam Declaration, and JCS 1067 (the occupation's basic guidance document) said little about the actual workings of ICD's denazification program, they at least defined its scope. That denazification was to purge German society of its Nazis and *Nutznießer* and remove them from powerful and public positions was implicit in the orders shaping Military Government activities. But the positive dimensions of the occupation were less clearly etched in 1945. Not until July 1947, when authority for ICD's cultural programs passed from the State to the War Department, would the Joint Chiefs issue a policy paper on reorientation, by which time the fundamental structures of postwar governance had already been established. Consequently, ICD field officers operated in the first year of the occupation with no firm idea as to how they might begin to promote structural reform in arts administration. OWI and the State Department's IIA had issued basic instructions on the purposes of cultural control, but no one told them how to reorganize the Third Reich's copyright system; no directive informed them as to what role the state should play in cultural life; no order instructed them on how they were to broaden the musical tastes of the German public or combat nationalist sentiments. Instead, past practice emphasized the importance of promoting American culture abroad, but this was difficult in Germany because the rules controlling fraternization also prevented American artists performing before locals. As a result, although its connection to the civilian agencies helped preserve the focus on reorientation among those field units (Film, Radio, Publishing, Theater, and Music) that had originated in OWI, it did little to actually guide ICD's officers in their work.

What the music officers had been issued was the ICD Manual,

which, while silent on the whole question of music organization, offered important insights regarding denazification and censorship and the nature of artistic life in the Third Reich. Unlike their counterparts in Intelligence, who considered themselves midwives of a transformed nation, Music Branch officers operated under the instruction that, although cultural life had been "perverted under Nazi control," there was a "*genuine* German cultural activit[y]" that might still be recovered. This was a significant observation, because implicit within it was a shift in emphasis from demolition and new construction to salvage and rehabilitation. And the field officers took it to heart. In their reflections on German history, branch officials maintained that the performing arts before the Nazis had achieved "unusually high artistic standards and great integrity" and that the theater had been, as Schiller observed, a "moral institution." Opera houses, concert halls, and theaters were, before the Third Reich, "inseparable part[s] of education and cultural life" — places where people could witness "the noble and the ignoble, the eminent and the base, the illustrious and the sordid counterpoised" and confront alternative solutions to existential problems. In light of this, they concluded, "Hitler's accomplishments in the theater were largely negative," making ICD's real job one of restoring Germany culture to its formerly elevated position.[1]

The music officers did, however, footnote this positive reflection with the observation that chauvinism and nationalism had tainted cultural life even before Hitler's seizure of power. They deplored the conservatism of public tastes: "[F]or the majority of them one has the impression that music written after 1905 ceases to be meaningful"; and they derided "the strong feeling of arrogance and superiority among Germans in regard to their own music and their own prowess."[2] What made the Germans' pride in their own musical accomplishments so pernicious was that it served both to fertilize Nazi aggression and legitimate the actions of Hitler's Reich.

It was a widely held belief among Americans that nationalism was the primary cause of the European wars that had twice compelled U.S. intervention. Containing nationalism was more than just a way of curing Germany of its aggression; it was the mechanism for ensuring European peace. Consequently, American policy makers were strong supporters of European integration and the blurring of cultural boundaries. In particular, they believed that Germany must be transformed into a crossroads for European cultural influences if war was to be permanently eradicated. The music officers shared this view and were committed to the quintessentially liberal idea that familiarity produced empathy. Thus, music, the ultimate international language, was a means of ensuring Europe's peaceful development. But ICD officers had other reasons for wanting to extinguish the defeated population's national pride. Since the late nineteenth century, the cultural officers argued, German music had been contaminated by chauvinism and xenophobia. Part of the Wagnerian inheritance, they opined, was the conviction that "holy German art" was superior to all others. "The German spirit has transformed itself into sheer bestiality," noted the musicologist, Alfred Enstein, "and Wagner's art, which deserved a better fate, has become the intoxicating drug of nationalism." Edward Kilenyi concurred; music, he wrote "furnished unlimited material for racist, mystic incantations" and "[i]t served as an emotional inspiration for the intense nationalism so typical of the German nation." Most artists and concertgoers, he added sadly, would still agree with Goebbels's dictum that "music must not be merely good, but German."[3]

Clearly, this situation was not beyond repair as there was a "genuine" and "humanist" tradition in Germany that might yet be recovered. Music itself was open to manipulation, but it did not predetermine the interpretations that were assigned to it; consequently, it might "be used by men of artful politics to foster rabid emotions or by magnanimous men of humanism to foster virtue and spiritual sublimity." The first problem was one of eliminating those proclivities among the Germans that would lead them to embrace racist and chauvinistic approaches to art. Foremost among these, according to ICD, was the Germans' reluctance to question those in authority or to challenge powerful leaders. "Even before the Nazi rise to power," the ICD Manual explained, "the Germans were a people who tended to exalt the state above the individual." It was "an immutable German habit," the division's historical officer agreed, "that the majority follows where the aggressive minority leads."[4] Creating a democratic culture was therefore largely a matter of encouraging people to think for themselves and critically evaluate the actions of their officials. At this moment in America's history, its soldiers were willing to teach that unquestioning patriotism and an absence of dissent were antithetical to democracy.

In their efforts to encourage critical thinking, religion was a particular fixation. A broadly religious people themselves, and one for whom freedom of belief was considered a bedrock of democracy, Americans were culturally predisposed to see religious sentiment and subservience to the state as antithetical. Even the denazifiers felt that one could not be a Christian and a Nazi, as conviction appellants as diverse as Hans Rosbaud, Eugen Jochum, and Herbert von Karajan recognized. Rosbaud said his transfer to Münster, "a Catholic city," provided him with "artistic freedom," and Jochum insisted that as a Catholic he could not have supported Hitler. Karajan used his programming of Bach's compositions as evidence of his refusal to cooperate with the Nazis. This struck a chord, because the American officers looked kindly on performers interested in Bach, whom they regarded as a great Protestant humanist.[5]

The other tradition they supported was represented most powerfully by Goethe, whom the Americans interpreted as a liberal, and by his musical counterpart, Beethoven. Where German nationalists had celebrated Beethoven as the Aryan titan, the Americans urged them to reconceive him as a democrat: an opponent of arbitrary state power and a champion of individual rights. Not surprisingly, *Fidelio* appeared on the first season playbills of most opera houses in the American zone. The Germanic countries had produced heirs to the tradition of Goethe and Beethoven, but the bulk of them—Thomas Mann, Artur Schnabel, and Bruno Walter were most often named as the prime examples—had sought refuge in the United States. It was, however, their influence, once thought to have been all but extinguished under the Nazis, that the Americans sought to recover.[6]

What linked this "positive" strand in ICD policies with the revolutionary denazifiers' "negative" approach was the emphasis on replacing bad people. While Music and Intelligence differed over standards, the basic policy of finding "clean" Germans was supported by all ICD officers. That some locals had to be trusted with the business of rebuilding the country's cultural life was self-evident. "The long-term education" of Germany, the ICD Manual declared, "can be accomplished only by the Germans themselves. And those few Germans willing and able to do it can be successful only if, under our supervision, media of information are opened to them and closed to those in whom the spirit of aggression survives." The success or failure of ICD's programs hinged on finding appropriate artists—people who believed in freedom of speech, who had "faith in the dignity of the individual against the preeminence of the State," and who were convinced that crimes against civilized standards of morality were intolerable — and placing them in charge.[7]

During the initial phase of the occupation, compliant Germans "with expert knowledge" were simply appointed to major artistic positions. In order to ensure a good fit, committees were established to advise the Americans on local issues and personalities.[8] The key artistic personnel were made responsible to and beholden to the occupation government, and it was expected that ICD would closely monitor their activities. Indeed, theater administrators were required to present their programs to the branch three days prior to each performance. Although there is no record of a music officer actually rejecting a program, "preperformance censorship" was considered an important symbol of Military Government authority. In time though, and it was unclear exactly when, planning documents instructed that once the right people were in place, preperformance would be supplanted by postperformance scrutiny, steering and consulting committees should be transferred out of American office spaces, and arts administration would be exercised under American supervision rather than control. ICD set for itself a target date of April 1946, at which point, it was hoped, democratic Germans would occupy all the major positions, and control would give way to supervision. In the end, ICD understood that "reeducation should be accomplished by Germans, but the Occupying Authority should make it possible for [them] to accomplish it."[9] The music officers' task in 1945–46 was therefore to appoint the people and establish the structures that would underpin the development of a democratic culture.

DECENTRALIZING AUTHORITY

In the early months of the occupation, licensing and registration were the prime instruments of Music Branch policy. So important were they to ICD thinking that some initially believed they could alone serve as the building blocks of democracy. By issuing registration cards only to those who could establish their democratic leanings, ICD anticipated eradicating nationalist and militarist tendencies in the theater. Artists who were blacklisted, for example, were to be denied a registration card and so barred from employment. At the same time, theater owners, directors, and leaders of musical ensembles were required to hold a license. Licensing essentially provided ICD with control over all important appointments in the arts. By only authorizing liberal-minded conductors, directors, and administrators who would, it was presumed, present works of an ennobling kind in an empathetic way, the division would indirectly inspire democratic and fraternal feelings among the public.

In the short-term, the major challenges ICD officers confronted were how to license and whom to license. The disagreement between the Music Branch and the Intelligence Section was only one aspect of the personnel question; even more decisive, in the long run, was the issue of deciding which job classifications needed licensing in the first place. Unlike in America, where opera companies and symphony orchestras were private organizations, in Germany most of them were public. Although a few cities and states had been running musical organizations for generations, the greater number had inherited them between the time when Germany was unified and the end of the First World War. State and municipal authorities took over court orchestras and opera houses that had been created in an age when German nobles were thick on the ground. Consequently, musical organizations were often in close proximity to each other and of such venerable lineage that they were hard to shut down. The Nazis had succeeded in reducing the number of Germany's theaters (in large measure by closing the more politically radical or artistically modernist or Jewish-owned), but the Americans in 1945 were still staggered to find major opera companies in cities as close together as Mainz, Wiesbaden, Darmstadt, Giessen, and Frankfurt.

Like their aristocratic forebears, municipal and state governments in the Weimar period maintained control over the theater through appointed administrators, or *Intendanten*. The *Intendant* was a government employee responsible to his employer for planning and budgeting the season's entertainments. In most *Länder*, the *Intendant* reported directly to the Ministry of Culture, which maintained a *Referent*, or cultural adviser for the arts, to oversee his actions. Cities also maintained an arts *Referent* who reported, in larger places, to a cultural department and in smaller, to the mayor or council. Although theoretically independent in artistic matters, *Intendanten* were regularly removed when they spent too much or presented too many unpopular works. They were also often replaced when one party followed another in office. In the Weimar Republic, the relationship between the *Intendanten* and their government employers was complex and politically charged, and it became even more so under the Nazis. Rather than abolishing the old structure, the Nazis added more layers to it: except in Prussia, a national bureaucracy, the Propaganda Ministry, had to approve all appointments, and various factions in the party joyfully entangled themselves in theater management. The result was that only the most cunning of *Intendanten*—one thinks of Heinz Tietjen in Berlin—were able to preserve a measure of independence, though even they had to do so by playing one level of governance off against another. The problem for the Americans in 1945 was what to do with the remains of this system, so unlike their own.

Given its background, it was inevitable that ICD should officially endorse the privatization of German theaters. In fact, its music officers were specifically charged with giving "all possible support . . . to the small number of independent theaters." About 400 privately owned theatrical organizations had existed in the Weimar Republic, including a few opera houses and a handful of independent orchestras. The Americans hoped to revive some of these and they made early contact with impresarios such as Hans Adler in Berlin and Erwin Russ in Stuttgart. But they were realistic enough to recognize that a private organization of any size would be difficult to sustain in war-ravaged Germany, if for no other reason than because war and denazification had so thinned the ranks that it was impossible to staff even the state-subsidized musical ensembles. Indeed, some of the private groups, such as Berlin's Tchaikovsky Orchestra, which flitted wraith-like from sector to sector, included a number of blacklisted performers. Although they could not be offered contract positions, it was difficult to police private organizations that hired artists without registration cards by the night. And so, although they provided encouragement to several chamber orchestras, such as Stuttgart's, when they did find, as in Nuremberg, a larger ensemble without public support, they tended to press the municipality to assume at least some of the financial responsibility. Where the traces of U.S. interest in the private theater could be found was in the Music Branch's insistence on free competition in the arts and in its efforts to ensure performance venues for private musical groups. It could also be found in frequent lectures to German audiences on the merits of free competition. As one typical lecture instructed, were free competition to exist, "the public would be empowered to make decisions about what they wanted to see and they would not be subject to the opinions of some failed schoolteacher (in other words, the *Kulturreferent*)."[10]

It is fair to say, however, that enthusiasm for privately owned musical organizations remained largely unsatisfied during the occupation. The refugees and European-trained artists who populated the Music Branch gave lip service to privatization but saw nothing wrong with the public theater. Senior officials like Benno Frank and Walter Hinrischen, who had lived in the United States for just a decade and who had experienced the crisis of America's theaters during the Depression, could hardly be expected to initiate a major change to the German system. Although they struggled to restrict government influence over arts management, they mostly recognized the immediate need for the security state ownership provided.

In fact, the ICD Manual and early MG directives endorsed their efforts to restore rather than revolutionize music life. The division's initial directives had stipulated that all producers of live entertainments "includ[ing] municipalities," required a license. Although the authors of the *Manual* did not anticipate the existence of *Land*-controlled theaters, they implicitly acknowledged that publicly funded theaters administered by state-appointed *Intendanten* were to be the norm. And yet, at the same time, ICD officers were instructed to "foster German information services on a decentralized basis free from control by German governmental bodies."[11] The initial policy guidance therefore provided justification for the continuation of almost every opera house, symphony, and philharmonic organization under their preceding form of ownership and control, while at the same time enjoining Military Government officials to curtail the state's direct influence.

For the first few months of the occupation, the implications of American policy were unclear because local German administrators appointed the *Intendanten* chosen for them by the Americans. Most of those selected had been *Intendanten* in the pre-Nazi Republic, but a few were simply theater people who struck ICD officers as efficient and compliant. In all cases they tended to see themselves as answerable to the Americans who issued their license, rather than to the German authorities who paid their salaries. In Stuttgart, the American's inherited the Staatsoper's *Intendant* from the French, whose preceded them in the city. But Albert Kehm, like his counterpart in Munich, Arthur Bauckner, had been a Weimar-period *Intendant* and so fit the predominant pattern. Wiesbaden's first American-appointed *Intendant* was Carl Hagemann, one of Germany's more prominent directors and, according to the Music Branch, "a well-known anti-Nazi since the inception of the Party."[12] But if the early going proved fairly easy, finding a balance between the government's right to appoint administrators and the Americans' duty to prevent a politicization of culture soon developed into a bigger problem.

The Americans knew that they would exercise absolute control for only a very short time and so they had to find mechanisms for ensuring the depoliticization of music administration once German responsibility for hiring was restored. In fact, by December 1945 McClure had already made clear to the branches that licensing authority would soon be placed under German administration, with ICD retaining supervisory and veto power. But if locals were to play a larger role in administering the arts, how were reorientation goals to be guaranteed? Would German authorities continue to appoint the "right people" once they were in control? Was veto power enough? William Dubensky, the music chief in Hesse, spoke for his colleagues when he complained that "the prospect of turning all but the final control of licensing over to the Germans" made it imperative that some institutional restraint on state power be found. This could only be done, he felt, if ICD's licensing power was vested in "some [nongovernmental] agency with the responsibility of assisting in the licensing of worthy candidates." Previously ICD had not been forced to consider this issue, so it was not until January 1946 that branch headquarters even began discussing the "change in policy . . . [that will] put more of the burden back into the hands of the German authorities."[13]

Benno Frank, Theater and Music's deputy chief, who had been active in the Berlin *Volksbühne* during the Weimar Republic, felt that "in spite of direct control of theater and music by city and land authorities, [the] free and democratic development [of the arts] could still be guaranteed" by the creation of local licensing committees, run by members of the performers' unions — the Deutscher Musiker Verband and the Genossenschaft Deutscher Bühnenangehörigen. If these committees were granted authority over the licensing of *Intendanten* and senior administrative personnel, Frank argued, they would be able to veto (by refusing to license) state appointments that struck them as inappropriate or politically motivated. Unfortunately, many of the music officers were not so sure. They were suspicious of unions and feared devolving too much power onto them. Some officers also worried that the communists and socialists were infiltrating the labor movement and were trying to turn it into a "political battlefield." Most significantly, Eric Clarke, the branch commander, disagreed with his deputy. As the former administrative secretary of the Metropolitan Opera he was, not surprisingly, interested in ensuring that the *Intendanten* remained responsible to the people paying their bills. At the Metropolitan, Clarke had "fostered the principle that the Met is a public institution not the prerogative of the Social Register." In a memorandum issued one week after his deputy chief's, he implicitly contradicted Frank by suggesting that authority over the *Intendant* should be fully in the hands of the politicians. Information Control, he advised, "must recognize the obligations of . . . licensees as public functionaries and their duty towards the taxpayers"; consequently, "the right to engage and supervise (as well as the right to discharge) *Intendanten* . . . [should] be vested in the *Ministerpräsidents* and any and all violations of Information Control regulations . . . [should be] referred to them for appropriate action."[14] Where Frank suggested institutionalizing a check on state authority, Clarke believed the democratic process would itself control government power.

Meeting in late January 1946, ICD's branch chiefs announced a compromise. The chiefs resolved that while "it would be wrong to transfer to the *Lander* [*sic*], or any of their subdivisions, sole responsibility" over appointing *Intendanten*, it would be equally wrong to vest too much authority in the performers' unions. Rather, the chiefs called for "independent" licensing commissions, "chosen by [each *Land's*] *Ministerpräsident*, with the advice and consent of Information Control from lists submitted by various German organizations." The minister or his *Kulturreferent* might be members of the committee, but they were to be "non-political in character" and self-perpetuating to the extent that they would elect their own replacement members. ICD would reserve a veto over licensing to itself and would thereby supervise the process. The committees were, however, intended to be powerful. In addition to licensing, they were expected to monitor ticket prices, taxes, building repairs, and the allocation of state funds.[15]

While headquarters debated policy, the first major test of ICD's ability to check state influence was already under way in Hesse. Wiesbaden was an important music center for the Americans in 1945 as it not only housed the headquarters of the Western District Information Control unit that administered Hesse and Württemberg-Baden, but also contained, in its Deutsche Operhaus, the only largely undamaged opera in the American zone. The acquisition of Carl Hagemann as

Intendant was icing for the ICD cake. Sadly, the Deutsche Oper's fortunes failed to rise. The opera house had been taken over by Special Services in June 1945, and it provided entertainment only for U.S. servicemen; locals wanting to hear concerts or attend operas had to go to the Catholic community hall. The Hessian government did not oversee the house at this point, and it survived on small state and municipal subsidies and through American support. The opera was therefore very much a plaything of the occupation forces, which made it only the more embarrassing when Hagemann, who was anxious to maintain the artistic quality of his company, proved reluctant to dismiss a number of formerly Nazi theater personnel. By early October 1945, following reports that Hagemann was "getting out of line," the Music Branch ordered his removal on the grounds that he was no longer "politically reliable." Finding a replacement was not easy, however, so the music officers selected as interim director Richard Payer, a Viennese *Heldentenor* who had been with the company since 1933 and who had impressed them with his artistic talents and popularity. What they did not know was that Payer had worked as an assistant to the opera's Nazi *Intendant*, Max Spilcker, the son-in-law of Robert Ley, head of the Nazi Labor Front. Payer's questionable past was revealed to the Music Branch within a few weeks of his appointment, but it made the practical decision to retain him while it searched for his replacement and conferred with Special Services to resolve the opera house question.[16]

William Dubensky, who had taken over as Hesse's music chief after the district was split into two units in January 1946 and the Württemberg-Baden detachment moved to Stuttgart, understood that Wiesbaden would never attract quality artists as long as its primary house remained in army hands. He urged the Hessian Ministry of Culture to assume control of the Deutsche Oper (which was soon renamed the Hessische Staatsoper), and endorsed its loosening ties with its other two operatic charges: the theaters in Kassel and Darmstadt. At the same time, Dubensky negotiated a gradual withdrawal of Special Services from the Wiesbaden house; by March 1946 it was finally opened to German concertgoers on selected days. With the Hessian state now involved in the question of appointing Payer's successor, Dubensky continued on a conciliatory course. He helped locate a suitable candidate in Friedrich Schramm, a former *Intendant* in Düsseldorf who was working at the time in Basel. Unfortunately, neither the ministry nor the opera's employees were taken with Schramm, even though their preferred candidate, an *Intendant* in Leipzig, had to be dropped because he failed to clear Intelligence. Working with Dubensky, Benno Frank then put the ministry in contact with a theater director in Wilmersdorf, Otto Henning, who proved popular and was soon secured.[17]

The Wiesbaden hiring was important as a test case for the Music Branch in the zone (Berlin was always exceptional). It involved the kind of hands-on supervision branch directives suggested, showed that different groups could be involved in the hiring process, and kept the state's power in check. This was how positive administration was supposed to work. It helped that Dubensky was well regarded in the Hessian capital and that he was able to assist the administration by easing the army's grip on the opera house. It also helped that the government still remained dependent on the occupiers for legitimacy, having not as yet mounted the hustings. But the goodwill shown by both the Americans and the Hessians proved that informal arrangements could work, even if they were never repeated. In the spring of 1946, ICD moved away from the Music Branch's ad hoc approach and implemented the more structural solution to the problem of containing state power that it had debated over the winter.

For Newell Jenkins, the creation of the first totally German licensing committee, in Stuttgart in March 1946, was the "most important development in the *Land* if not in the entire American zone of Germany." Now an arms-length agency existed that would at one and the same time relieve the Americans of the job of licensing and supervising government patronage in the music field. It was a promising development, but the Americans quickly discovered how hard it was to control the situation once they were no longer making all the decisions. This was especially true in Bavaria where ICD had had difficult relations with the Kultusministerium since the Knappertsbusch debacle. Just three months after licensing was turned over to the locals, branch officers discovered that the committees had become tools of the Kultusministerium, which had packed them with party loyalists. Unfortunately, ICD found that the committees were approving everyone nominated by the ministry and raising obstacles in the way of licenses for private theater directors and operators. Suddenly, the "state and city control [had emerged as] a menace to free enterprise and . . . unless very carefully watched in the future it will grow like a snake-weed and choke off any flowering of a democratic system in the Bavarian theater." Although ICD could still veto committee decisions, the problems the division suddenly faced getting the Germans to nominate the right people and their inability to prevent bureaucratic obfuscation brought home the point that they could not depend on licensing alone to limit the influence of the state and provide a counterweight to patronage.[18]

The Americans faced a further challenge because even as they struggled to find a way of controlling the Bavarians, the *Länder* made a bid to have *Intendanten* exempted from the need to secure a license at all. The *Länder*'s position was that *Intendanten*, as public-sector employees, managed theaters for the state; they did not own them and therefore refused to enshrine in law the licensing-committee structures that the Americans had imposed on them. Frank, who negotiated for ICD with the assembly of the states (the *Länderrat*), insisted that *Intendanten* did need to be licensed and pressed to have agencies even more fully independent of the government placed in control of licensing. His efforts, however, failed. Ultimately, Württemberg-Baden passed legislation that affirmed the authority of semi-independent licensing committees with union representation, but Bavaria did not. The Bavarians made clear that they would abolish all licensing committees as soon as they were no longer bound by MG directives. Both states also eliminated the licensing requirement for *Intendanten*. The Hessians, in the meantime, refused to pass any law regulating the process of appointments in the cultural field on the grounds that they did not yet need to, but promised they would legislate the American regulations when U.S. control ended. If nothing else, the frustrating experience of trying to turn licensing into the bedrock of artistic freedom taught the field officers that they needed to distance the theater even more fully from government power. As the Military Government's liaison officer told the *Länderrat*'s theater committee, it was now firmly of the opinion that "the less [state] control the better."[19]

The evident weakness of licensing as a bulwark for democracy encouraged ICD to experiment with other initiatives designed to ease the structural links between the various ministries of culture and their *Intendanten*. In places where individual incumbents were too easily controlled, ICD pushed for multiple and overlapping appointments. In Bavaria, for example, governmental authority over the entire state theater apparatus — theater, operetta, and opera — was invested in one man, who served as both state adviser and artistic director. Here, in the fall of 1946, Military Government forced a "minor revolution" when the Bavarian Kultusministerium agreed to detach the post of *Referent* from that of *Intendant*. Six months later, the *Land* agreed to abolish the post of *Generalintendant* and created three different administrators for the opera, operetta, and theater.[20] At the opera, the *Intendant*'s power was further hemmed in by the presence of two American-backed conductors, one who worked as principal conductor and the other as opera director.

Another solution was to force a decentralization of the actual hiring process for theater and music administrators. In this way, ICD would counter the state's influence over licensing by weakening its absolute control over hiring. In Württemberg-Baden and Hesse, for example, the various state-supported theaters and their *Intendanten* were each saddled with two committees, a *Betriebsrat* and a *Verwaltungsauschuss*, which oversaw appointments and all business decisions affecting their institutions. The *Intendant*, artistic directors and performers were represented on the committees as were the city and ministry and the theatergoing public. The two committees not only supervised the management of the theater but also were responsible for nominating candidates to senior positions and approving ministry appointments. Further limits on *Land* authority came through the independent press, through the business managers whom the Americans insisted each theater must appoint, and even through the courts.[21]

The aim of the administrative committee structure was to decentralize power, one of the goals specified in both the Potsdam Declaration and JCS 1067. As the Americans regarded the Germans as unhealthily deferential, committees were seen as a way of changing the national character. Committees, it was hoped, would become forums for the exchange of ideas and for free debate. By involving stakeholders such as the municipalities and unions in the decision-making process, they would provide working lessons in democracy. Because all municipalities subsidized their public theaters, even those run by the *Land*, the mayors demanded input into theater policies and hiring decisions. The committees provided them with official access to theater management, even though some of them preferred to work behind the scenes. Unionized employees might also make good use of the committee system to challenge an *Intendant*'s power. This occurred in Kassel where an *Intendant* who tried to streamline the theater ran so far afoul of his *Betriebsrat* that he lost his job.[22] In other places, theater directors used the committees to wage war on their boss.

In Stuttgart, for example, the Kultministerium, under Theodor Heuss, was anxious to define a new role for itself and the arts.[23] Unfortunately, the *Staatsintendant*, Albert Kehm, was unsure how to accommodate the new democratized structures. Artists felt under pressure to be new, to contribute to the emergence of another Germany, but Kehm appeared to them a fragment of the past, forever "hesitating, weighing, maneuvering and displaying the lack of commitment of an experienced cabinet politician." The orchestra, in particular, was pressing Kehm to secure a new *Kapellmeister* and director, but he stalled. Kehm's refusal to consider hiring the conductor Hans Rosbaud, whom he regarded as too ambitious and willful, also alienated a potential ally, Stuttgart's Mayor Klett. Strained relations between the directors and the *Intendant* exploded in late December 1945 when Kehm tried to fire one of them and replace him with someone less truculent. With two American Intelligence officers in attendance, the new management committee of the theater proposed a compromise, but at the next meeting, with no ICD officers present, the agreement collapsed. The Americans liked Kehm because he was an energetic denazifier, but the ministry, which had located what it hoped would be his replacement in Carl Orff, decided he must go. Heuss insisted that a new spirit had to be kindled in the theater and that Kehm, as one of his advisers observed, was not the man for the job: "[T]he past has shown that important moments in theater were not achieved by the weighty hesitations or crude diplomatic tactics of *Intendanten.*" But the *Intendant* held onto his post by protesting to ICD that the state was trying to obstruct him in his duties as an "American licensee in a free and democratic Germany." The branch agreed and refused to allow his removal. The crisis in the theater continued into the new year: Kehm faced a revolt of his own directors backed by the city, and the ministry declared its inability to resolve the crisis because the *Intendant* was a Military Government appointee. Because Kehm's contract would soon expire, the business of the theater ground to a halt: the *Land* refused either to replace him or to renew his contract; the artists who worked for him wanted him gone; and the Americans, who interpreted the whole thing as an effort to stymie an active denazifier, refused to allow his removal. It took the new branch chief, Newell Jenkins, to break the logjam. In February 1946, Jenkins, influenced by his relationship with Orff, reversed the branch's position and indicated that Kehm was expendable.[24] The

*Jerome Pastene, Newell Jenkins, and Carl Orff in Stuttgart, 1946
(Photo courtesy of Newell Jenkins)*

Intendant promptly left his position, but when Intelligence failed to clear his successor, the theater was plunged into crisis once again.

As the example shows, committees could have debilitating effects on arts management, but they did serve the purpose for which they were designed. The American goal was to establish a system of checks and balances and, in so doing, to decentralize authority and limit governmental control, and committees went some way toward achieving this. In Kehm's case, the committees worked as they were intended to do, but the results were mixed. Not only would the Stuttgart Staatsoper be for months without an *Intendant*, but it also lost its most active proponent of denazification. Decentralization was, like denazification, an American priority and the dilemma in Stuttgart was that the one policy invalidated the other.

Although the Music Branch placed heavy emphasis on developing institutional limits on state power, it also recognized that the best guarantee of artistic freedom was to place the right people in charge of the major cultural institutions. No matter how many checks and balances ICD imposed, it remained the people who mattered. This was why the Americans considered "a willingness to accept our ideas" as one of the essential qualifications for those seeking leading positions in music life. It was also why they used all the influence they had, so long as they retained it, to place people of real artistic merit in key positions. Good artists with democratic attitudes, they believed, would be harder for the state to remove and this would ensure a strong voice for artistic freedom. But finding good artists who cleared the intelligence hurdle, were willing to comply with Music Branch priorities, and were able to win the support of the German authorities was no easy task, and the Americans sometimes discovered the right man in unusual places.

One lucky find was made by John Bitter, the branch officer in Berlin. The BPO's conductor question had supposedly been resolved before U.S. troops arrived in the city, with the appointment of Leo Borchard. But on 23 August 1945, as Bitter escorted the conductor home from a party, their German driver failed to stop at an 82nd Airborne checkpoint and the sentry opened fire, drenching the American in Borchard's blood.[25] John Bitter was a good conductor and a fine teacher, and these qualities stood him in good stead now as he considered Borchard's replacement. In late July, Bitter had heard Sergiu Celibidache, a thirty-three-year-old Romanian, lead the Berlin Chamber Orchestra in a Tchaikovsky concert. Celibidache had spent the war years as a student in Berlin and had survived the last few months living in a cellar and working as a private music teacher. He was in poor health and, according to Bitter, "he was so thin and gaunt, and with his hair parted in the middle like those renaissance paintings, he looked like Jesus Christ." Bitter had been at the Curtis Institute with one of the cellists in the BPO and through this intermediary he urged the orchestra to try out the young conductor. Naturally, what the occupation authorities ordered, the philharmonic was in no position to refuse and, after working briefly with him at one rehearsal, it agreed to Celibidache's appointment. This might seem odd, but at this point the orchestra was performing one-half of all its concerts exclusively for allied servicemen and it had recently been relocated to an American-requisitioned movie house, the Titania Palast. As the conductor imposed by the Russians was dead and its interim conductor, Robert Heger, was a former party member, the orchestra was in no position to argue. Nor did the city, which had taken over the philharmonic from the Reich government when the war ended, do more than snarl over the contract it was instructed to offer Celibidache.[26] This implausible opportunity for someone at the start of his career also proved to be good fortune for the Americans. Celibidache turned out to be a musician of true concentration and fire, and under his direction an orchestra that had been devastated by wartime losses was transformed into an instrument of exceptional power and agility, even though it never warmed to the maestro's suspicious and hard-driving nature.

Equally fortuitous was ICD's eventual resolution of the crisis following Knappertsbusch's removal as music director of the Bavarian Staatsoper. A Christmas vacation in Switzerland led to a chance meeting between one of Bavaria's theater officers and a refugee Hungarian voice coach and pianist living in Zurich, Georg Solti. When Edward Kilenyi, who had known Solti as a student in Budapest, learned where he was, he invited the young musician to come to Munich. Bauckner, the opera's *Intendant*, agreed to give him a trial but would not accede to American pressure and offer the conductor more than a guest appearance in *Fidelio*, even though he was at the time without a *Generalmusikdirektor*. Years later, Solti recalled Kilenyi being "furious" at the interview and he remembered Bauckner's repeated insistence that "we don't need him." While waiting for his premier in Munich, Solti performed *Fidelio* in Stuttgart and made a tremendous impression on Jenkins, who immediately urged the ministry to appoint him principal conductor. But the Kultministerium was still hoping to save money by securing Carl Orff as *Intendant* and conductor, and it voiced concern over public reaction to Solti. As the American officer later remembered, the ministry's *Referent* protested: "But you know Solti is a Jew and a Hungarian" and Jenkins' retort — "What has that got to do with the price of beans? We just fought a war about that. It makes no sense, you can't get anyone better. Take him" — made no impact. In the end the ministry did offer Solti a limited contract, but it waited too long and (as with Rosbaud) the opportunity was lost.[27]

Solti's debut in Munich was as electrifying as his performance in Stuttgart. John Evarts observed that "the improvement in playing of the orchestra was little short of miraculous. Mr Solti himself said that with only two rehearsals it was practically improvised, implying he *could* have made a much better job of it." Even the cautious *Intendant* was momentarily exhilarated and enthused that, after searching so long for a music director, "this is our man." Possibly under pressure from the ministry, however, which still hoped to hire the blacklisted Bavarian Eugen Jochum, Bauckner reneged. In the end, Solti was offered a two-year contract as chief conductor. He would direct a limited number of performances over which he would have complete artistic control, but he would not run the orchestra. As that arrangement allowed the maestro to maintain a foothold in Switzerland, and as he was concerned about surviving as a Jew in Germany, he accepted the position. In many ways, Solti was a symbol for the new Germany ICD hoped to build: a young, untried outsider and an explosive talent. But he also had the disadvantage of inexperience, and while not unwilling to essay the occasional modern work, he was building his own repertoire in Munich and gravitated to the pre–World War I classics. Moreover, his constant commutes between Germany and Switzerland would prove trying on the Americans, as would his strong will and intractable character.[28]

The Americans achieved other notable successes in the appointment of the talented Hungarian conductor Ferenc Fricsay to the RIAS Symphony Orchestra in Berlin (which also performed in the Titania Palast), and in the eventual acquisition of Ferdinand Leitner as music director in Munich. All were young men at the start of important careers and ICD's officers revealed their skill by identifying their musicianship. But significantly, several of the most prominent conductors employed in the U.S. zone in 1946 were foreigners. So devastating had the impact of denazification been that it had, as had been intended, obliterated a generation of performers who had passed their galley years in the Third Reich. There were, however, several important advantages to be gained by choosing outsiders. In the first place, ICD took a major step toward achieving its goal of internationalizing German musical life. Although Solti would disappoint in his repertoire, Celibidache, Rosbaud, and Fricsay were fervent advocates of new and non-German music. Furthermore, both foreign conductors and locals were conscious of their dependence on the Americans for their jobs, which made them more willing to work with ICD in constructing a democratic and international music culture. Ultimately, the relationship between the Americans and their musical charges would become close and comfortable and mutually supportive. As one of Bavaria's music officers remembered: "Karl Amadeus Hartmann was their [Bavaria's] leading composer and we used to gather at his house at night and play games. . . . Rosbaud would play all kinds of obscure opera excerpts and other things on the piano and we — Solti would be amongst us — would be guessing what they were. We had a lot of fun . . . those were really good times."[29]

Taken together, the various American-inspired reforms achieved their objective by loosening the state's grip on the public theater. Although none of the policies was an unqualified success — licensing committees were never independent enough and the appointment and administrative committees sometimes undercut the *Intendant*'s authority and created a series of rival power blocks under his administration — they did serve, when taken together, to limit the government's influence over the arts. Moreover, by installing the right people in key artistic positions, the Americans laid the foundation for real cultural change. It all worked well enough as long as the various interests were in harmony or, at least, understood the extent of their relative power. Establishing licensing and theater committees, hiring business managers, and employing new, often foreign, musicians were, for their time, imaginative and innovative undertakings. What ICD failed to anticipate — and how could it — was the degree of German resistance to its efforts that would emerge when the *Länder*'s economic problems became critical and American power collapsed.

REEDUCATING THE PUBLIC

ICD's Music Branch did not limit its reformist efforts to containing the influence of the state but also sought to change attitudes among the public. "The basic objective of the occupation requires the democratization of the German government and people," declared one directive, an approach that involved "teaching democracy to the individual German." Where denazification would force each person to "renounce the doctrines of Nazism and militarism by making him aware of the moral issues involved in German aggression and of his personal share in the collective German responsibility for the acts of the Nazis and militarists," cultural products might be employed to "strip away German misconceptions about Germany and its relationship to the world." Initially, "music, opera and ballet will be given preference over other forms of entertainment" in this public reeducation program, as these forms provided few "opportunities for subversive propaganda" and might be "designed to restore the exchange of ideas between Germany and the world outside it."[30] Just as ICD directives suggested that there was a salvageable core to German music culture and that state-subsidized institutions could be democratized through reform rather than revolution, they also implied the existence of a receptive public that could be made to appreciate new and foreign music. Effort had to be made to humanize and demote the country's cultural titans and show the local population that central Europe was not the repository of all that was best in music history. In particular, concertgoers had to be taught that during the preceding twelve years far more interesting music was composed outside Germany's borders than within.

"Adolph Hitler," the branch declared, "[had] succeeded in transforming the lush field of musical creativity into a barren waste." During the Third Reich, the occupiers believed, most of Germany's best artists were abroad, the country was "completely isolated from international development," and its own composers were "produc[ing] nothing . . . [but works] psychologically effective to the Nazi cause." Under these circumstances, pressing a new and internationalized musical repertoire on German audiences was considered good therapy. "There is still a strong feeling of arrogance and superiority among Germans in regard to their own music," the Americans concluded, which a broader repertoire would help to destroy. Listening to the modern music of different countries "will introduce . . . breadth of outlook, international understanding and non-political attitudes." Music Branch officers were fairly broad-minded in the repertoire they suggested, as promoting the music of all of the Allied nations (and they included in this group the works of émigrés such as Toch and Martinů and Menotti and Bartók) was seen as important in "help[ing] to stress the significance of an unpolitical art in Germany."[31]

But before this could be done, a functioning agency for the collection of royalties had to be established. The American League of Composers and ASCAP, which policed copyrights in the United States, made very clear that they would not allow unauthorized or unrecompensed performances of works, no matter what their presumed educational value. The institution that handled copyright in Germany, STAGMA, had been a Nazi organization attached to the RKK and under the direct control of the Propaganda Ministry. The party paid a lump sum each year for rights to perform any music it wanted in propaganda films or at official functions, and STAGMA, in turn, was required to use the party's contribution to subsidize musicians and organizations specially selected for it by the Propaganda Ministry. Although a servant of Nazi racial policy, the agency was such a cash cow that when the war ended everyone from the city of Berlin to the GDB to the Kammer für Kunstschaffenden lobbied to take it over. While the Allies decided what to do, two senior executives of the Nazi period, Erich Schulze and Pierre Cretin, maintained STAGMA's operations, though they were generally unsuccessful in their effort to convince artists and theater directors to pay them for performed material. The actions of Schulze and Cretin did, however, help ensure that STAGMA rather than a new agency would continue to collect fees, and the Americans temporarily backed them as alternatives to state control. The whole process of negotiating a structure for the new agency lasted months, in large measure because the Soviets had little use for a private collection agency and were unsure whether to support it. So it was not until late summer 1946 that all four powers agreed to recognize the private organization's exclusive right to administer royalties. In the meantime, ICD needed another solution if it were to launch Germany's cultural reeducation. In December 1945, therefore, the division opted to act alone: it appointed a director of STAGMA for the American zone, established branch agencies in different cities, and ordered all performers and theaters to pay royalties only to that agency. By Christmas, ASCAP had negotiated terms of payment with the American zone STAGMA (renamed GEMA in 1949), clearing the way to performances of U.S.-copyrighted works. In addition to this function, the German agency was charged with collecting all royalties for the performances of works by blacklisted composers and holding them in a closed account until such time as the individuals were cleared.[32]

With copyright now protected, musical material began to flow into Germany in January 1946, but it came in strange packages. OWI's former overseas offices, now being liquidated or absorbed by the Department of State's IIA, contributed a large number of scores and recordings, but this arrangement changed when the army took control and ICD was placed under the operational control of the Civil Affairs Division. Unfortunately, CAD, which stood at the head of OMGUS's supply line, did not appoint a music administrator until March 1946, further delaying ICD's field operations. When the scores and parts did arrive, they came as microfilm, requiring enlargement and photoduplication at the headquarters of ICD's Film Branch in Munich. The process proved time-consuming and some of the material was unreadable, requiring new photographing. All of this served to slow the dissemination of American music in Germany, and by July 1946 ICD had only about 100 compositions, as compared with 600 made available by the Russians and 300 by the British. One important advance in facilitating the use of Military Government's supply of scores came with the creation of an Interallied Music Lending Library in Berlin in September 1946. Located in the state library in the Russian sector, it provided a central lending point for music supplied by the occupation powers.[33]

As most of the first generation of music officers had studied in Europe and lived in the northeastern United States, they included in Germany's cultural tonic works by Stravinsky and Milhaud, Shostakovich, Hindemith, and Bartók. This was the modern music the officers heard in Boston and Philadelphia and New York performed by such European conductors as Koussevitsky and Rodzinsky, Toscanini and Stokowski. A few, like John Evarts and John Bitter, were knowledgeable about American composers, but to others, like Newell Jenkins and Edward Kilenyi, it was unfamiliar terrain. Still, the music officers were all fairly catholic in their tastes and through their supplier in 11A, they secured scores by Prokofiev, Bartók, Honegger, and a host of others for their German licensees.

American music, in the eyes of senior planning officials was, however, always thought to have a special role to play in Germany. This was especially true for State Department authorities, who saw American culture as the vanguard of democratization. According to an influential report on reeducation activities: "Germans, weak in their political tradition, tend to judge American political democracy by the kind of cultural life they imagine it to produce, and as they are convinced that it produces nothing of value, their minds are for the most part closed to the suggestion that they adopt it for themselves. . . . If Germans are once convinced that America does have a culture of its own, and moreover one that has progressed beyond theirs in certain fields in which they have prided themselves, they will begin to listen with more interest to talk of political democracy."[34] Breaking down the Germans' sense of cultural superiority would therefore be more effectively achieved through American music than through the works of other nations.

The music officers agreed with this and promoted works by Piston and Copland and Harris and Schuman, without abandoning their more internationalist goals. But by the summer of 1946 their effort to supply modern music, as opposed to narrowly American works, had run into a major obstacle. When the War Department finally assumed full responsibility for ICD, it appointed Harrison Kerr as its music administrator in its New York field office and the job of supplying scores was transferred from IIA to the Civil Affairs Division. Kerr was a composer and former administrator of the American Music Library, and he had a far narrower concept of the Military Government's mission in Germany than the field officers or his predecessors in IIA. His job was to purchase the supplies needed for reeducation purposes and he, not the music officers, controlled the budget and exercised final decision-making authority. Kerr refused to authorize the dispatch of music by non-Americans or even of émigrés such as Hindemith, Martinů, and Křenek, even when asked to do so by the field officers. In Kerr's opinion works by these composers were not sufficiently representative of America and would have no reeducational value. The branch officers did not agree with Kerr, but they had no official alternative to the New York office. Whenever they could, they ordered scores from Switzerland and England, and one of them, who had previously been in charge of IIA's music program, continued to use the old channel and had material shipped through the Music Division of the Library of Congress. But the American officers had to pay for much of this material themselves or make use of friends and donors in the United States.[35]

ICD's officers worked hard to provide German performers with music from Europe and the United States, but they were not always so selfless in their actions. On a number of occasions, they took advantage of their positions to showcase their own work or ability. John Bitter led the Berlin Philharmonic three times and his third string quartet premiered in the city while he was still a music officer; Pastene conducted frequently in Heidelberg; and John Evarts started writing a chamber piece for a Munich ensemble until ordered to stop by Kilenyi, his fastidious superior. Harrison Kerr shipped a disproportionate number of his own works to Germany, including big ones like his forgettable First Symphony. William Castello, who worked with Jenkins in Stuttgart, was reportedly heavily involved in the black market. Activities like these do not reflect well on ICD's officers, though the urge of musicians to make music and of composers to promote their wares is not unusual. Still, like so many others, they were hoping to lay the

John Bitter conducting the Dresden Philharmonic Orchestra, 1947
(Photo courtesy of John Bitter)

foundations of their post-MG careers by enhancing their resumes with some European credits. A great number of Americans did exactly the same thing, including army officers who used their authority to conduct leading orchestras; amateurs who ordered Europe's top musicians to give them lessons; musicians with stalled or stillborn careers who moved to Switzerland in the hopes of descending on Germany or Austria the moment travel restrictions were lifted. Not all of these were artistically unworthy; Erich Leinsdorf, for example, a gifted if hard-driving opera conductor, whose career in America had been derailed by military service, slipped into Vienna in the hopes of landing a top job. On the scale of things, the abuse of power shown by those ICD officers who conducted or pushed their compositions was relatively inconsequential, if nonetheless inexcusable.[36]

Directing an orchestra oneself did have the advantage of allowing a music officer to choose his repertoire, and it is noteworthy that Pastene, for one, performed American pieces whenever conducting in Heidelberg. The first American works performed in Germany were played before Allied service personnel: in early September 1945 the black activist, composer, and clarinetist Rudolph Dunbar led the Berlin Philharmonic on invitation of Leo Borchard, and conducted Still's

Afro-American Symphony in an Armed Forces concert. In a subsequent concert, early in December, John Bitter and the same orchestra performed Barber's *Adagio*. But convincing German licensees to try out an American composition was never easy, even when the musician was as cooperative a person as Rosbaud or Celibidache. American music was, at the time, virtually unknown in Germany, and most artists shared the national bias that it could not be very good. Even friendly musicians complained that the style of American music was too unfamiliar or that they could not induce their orchestras to give it a try. Consequently, it was not until spring 1947 that Solti performed his first American works, Barber's *Essays for Orchestra*, and Rosbaud only directed his first (Copland's *An Outdoor Overture*) in September 1946, five months after Celibidache conducted Barber's *Adagio* in Berlin. The less prominent orchestras proved more forthcoming: what appears to have been the first orchestral work presented to a German audience was Piston's *Incredible Flutist Suite*, offered in Heidelberg on 8 March 1946; a few days later, the first American symphony, Howard Hanson's Third, was heard by concertgoers in Wiesbaden; and shortly thereafter the first ballet danced to an American score was staged before a local audience in Karlsruhe. Chamber works were also easier to get performed and the first U.S. work presented to Germans during the occupation was Quincy Porter's *Music for Strings*. By June 1946 there had been 47 performances of 25 American works in the occupation zone and nine months later the total had reached 173 performances of 57 pieces. Many of these works had, however, been played by orchestras under direct ICD control, such as Radio Frankfurt's.[37]

Although some of the music ICD promoted might rest comfortably among the finest of the century — Thompson's Second and Schuman's Third symphonies, for example, or Copland's *Quiet City* — and some stood, like Barber's *School for Scandal Overture* or Gershwin's *Rhapsody in Blue*, among the most fun, much of what they had to offer was not very memorable. When Otto Matzerath presented Robert McBride's *Strawberry Jam Overture*, the greater part of the audience was "completely horrified by what some Germans referred to as '*Eine amerikanische Schweinerei.*'" This hostile reaction should not be entirely taken as a sign of anti-Americanism, for when Hindemith, four years before, had been asked to review the work, he described it as a "sloppy, tossed-off piece of crap." Piston's *Incredible Flutist* was also received with "puzzlement" by a Mannheim audience, while his *Concertino for Piano and*

Orchestra was greeted in Heidelberg with "energetic whistling" (a sign of disapproval). Some of this negativity was due to the problems German orchestras had with the American musical idiom and with poor preparation and a lack of enthusiasm among artists who only mounted the work in order "to keep in good graces with the Americans." But the results could be horrific. A performance of Gershwin's *Rhapsody* in Karlsruhe was mangled so badly that intelligence officers took it as criticism of the occupation and suggested the military police close down the theater. A few months earlier, "confused" choreography meant to seem broadly American, together with dancers dressed up like cowboys and scenery that looked as though the whole thing were "laid out in New Mexico," badly distorted a production of Copland's ballet *Appalachian Spring*.[38]

ICD did score some real hits in Germany. Barber's *Adagio* was everywhere well received, as was Menotti's *The Old Maid and the Thief*. But the problem of overcoming German apathy toward American classical music remained. As Newell Jenkins conceded, "the trouble involved in placing an American work is tremendous." In an attempt to overcome some of that resistance, in March 1947 Jenkins established a series of chamber concerts of American works preceded by lectures and followed by group discussions. He borrowed the idea from the American composer Virgil Thomson and called the gatherings The Friends and Enemies of Modern Music Society Concerts. The concerts "worked amazingly well," attendance was good, and "precious few enemies" showed up. This inspired John Evarts, who founded similar societies in Karlsruhe in April and in Munich in May. By the end of 1947, Friends and Enemies were meeting in all the major cities where American cultural officials were stationed. Attendance at these concerts remained strong and positive because ICD passed out free tickets to music students and local artists, and it managed to press such pro-American notables as Rosbaud, Hartmann, and the music critic H. H. Stuckenschmidt into service as lecturers. The concerts did much to familiarize the next generation of German musicians with American classical music and helped remove some of the prejudices with which they had been raised.[39]

When it came to indigenous, as opposed to American or other European music, politics strongly influenced official tastes. The Americans in Bavaria regarded Orff with considerable disdain because they saw him as overly *bayerisch*; he was much more popular among the authorities in Stuttgart, where his regionalism carried fewer political implications. In Munich the control officers favored Karl Amadeus Hartmann, a composer of solid political credentials who seemed delighted by the American presence in his city. Hartmann's Musica Viva series got OMGUS support, through block ticket purchase, a subsidy for concerts featuring U.S. works, and free performance space in the Amerika Haus. In Berlin the Americans' darling was Boris Blacher, for whom Bitter managed to secure extra food rations and who became acquainted with a number of wealthy American patrons and influential musicians. In Heidelberg, Pastene befriended and pushed a young Fortner student, Hans Werner Henze. No one gave Egk or Pepping much thought; Strauss and Pfitzner, rightly or wrongly, were regarded as tainted relics from the past. By and large, local governments echoed American preferences so long as the occupiers were watching. Orff was offered a job in Stuttgart, but Munich officials only talked to him in secret; Hartmann's Musica Viva organization received strong backing from the Bavarian and Munich governments, but Strauss and Pfitzner were snubbed. Blacher was the best connected and one of the most performed composers living in the American sector of Berlin. But the man everyone talked about, the dominant composer in both American and German eyes, Paul Hindemith, remained the absent hero in these years. Although politicians and artists begged for his return and his operas and works were performed in his absence as *events* — as a kind of ritual act of invocation and contrition — Hindemith did not visit until 1947 and then quietly and on private business.

For two years, Hindemith maintained that he would only return if Military Government sent him on tour as a visiting expert, something the War Department refused to allow as it considered his "connections with the Nazi Party . . . closer than had been supposed in the early days." Unaware of the blemishes on his record, the field officers continued to promote Hindemith as a symbol of resistance. The Americans urged local musicians to perform his works, especially those composed in America, but the position the composer adopted was that if musicians wanted them, they knew where they could get them: from Schott, his publisher (something they had been able to do throughout the Nazi period).[40] At one and the same time a symbol of Weimar and of America, of resistance to Nazism and of the émigrés' abandonment of their homeland, of new music and old, Hindemith was, in his public image and private dealings, the most complex of composers. And yet, like the others, only more so, he was celebrated by the occupation and the state as a contemporary composer conservative music-lovers might appreciate.

Interestingly, although a great many of the American and modern European composers ICD promoted were Jewish, the division never specifically advertised the fact. Nor did it ever insist that musicians perform works by Mendelssohn or Mahler simply because they had previously been banned on "racial" grounds. No one in ICD ever explained why this was, but one can easily imagine. How would the division have singled out the works of Jewish composers without reinforcing Nazi assertions that "race" mattered? A German population that thought of Jews as different and foreign, and which was now being made to feel guilty for those feelings, would only find reassurance in an Allied program that racially identified its subjects. Moreover, since many of the American and contemporary European works performed were received unfavorably, one risked reinforcing stereotypes by drawing attention to the fact that their composers were Jews. And so, even though a number of the regional branch officers and both deputy chiefs Benno Frank and Walter Hinrischen were Jews, ICD policy pointedly overlooked the issue. Apparently, the music officers believed the case for tolerance was more powerfully made by presenting Toch and Blacher as equally German and Copland, Ives, Stravinsky, and Menotti as equally American. As John Evarts maintained in one of his lectures to German audiences: "America has opened its doors to every type of music from all over the world, and many powerful works have emerged." Pointedly, he added, U.S. music was charting "a new direction, one absolutely American, one that draws as much from African rhythms as from the dissonant chords of Debussy, as much from Negro Spirituals as from Jewish liturgical chants."[41]

What did tend to unite the composers whom the Music Branch advanced was that they were among the more accessible modernists. Although dissonance was part of their twentieth-century musical language, these composers tended to express it without casting away from the traditional tonal moorings; Milhaud and Hindemith and Harris all shared an interest in polytonal, polymodal, and polyrhythmic effects together with an adherence to the tonic. It is notable that the Americans did little until 1949 to promote the more avant-garde music of their time, whether Cowell's or Schoenberg's or Messiaen's. Consequently, the avenues of the avant-garde remained unexplored in the concert halls in 1945–46, and it was not only German conservatism that was to blame. American officials were no more fond of twelve-tone or politically engaged music than were most Germans. Furthermore, neither Americans nor Germans believed popular music belonged in the concert hall, and the only Broadway work ICD reproduced for German use was Kurt Weill's hit *Knickerbocker Holiday*. Some groups, like Hartmann's Musica Viva or Steinecke's Darmstadt Ferienkurse, did present some of the more adventurous contemporary works, and they did received ICD's financial patronage, but the Americans also bemoaned their repertoire. The fact is that the field officers were interested in pushing the boundaries of public taste, not alienating musical conservatives. Although they advanced music they believed would be challenging for audiences, they remained reformers in the concert hall and not revolutionaries.

Without question, however, the Americans seriously misunderstood the recent history of modern music in Germany. Although it is never a bad thing to attack cultural prejudices, and many people must have profited from their exposure to the new music being composed in the United States and other European countries, the principles on which the field officers based their initiatives were flawed. The Americans were convinced that Nazi Germany had been a cultural desert and that the public needed and appreciated them for supplying the refreshing waters of hitherto unavailable music. What they failed to realize was that much good contemporary music was performed in Hitler's Germany and that until the war the country was not closed to the works of British or French or other European composers. Although modern composers like Honegger and Stravinsky were periodically denounced in the Nazi Party press, their compositions continued to be sporadically performed in the 1930s, and some, like Bartók's, never suffered any type of official proscription. As Jenkins remarked a half-century later, "it was ridiculous thinking that we could teach the Germans anything about contemporary music, because they were very good in that themselves. They were very aware of what goes on. Because I remember, even in the early Nazi days, when I was [a student] in Germany, that the contemporary music festivals . . . used to take place in Baden-Baden and they still had a very powerful bunch of people associated with them and performances from international artists."[42] Unfortunately, not only did the Americans fail to realize that that portion of the concertgoing public that was most likely to react favorably to their efforts—students, musicians, and those already interested in contemporary music—was more knowledgeable than they had imagined, but they also made an error in believing that they could force-feed the rest of the audience a diet of contemporary, albeit tonal, music. Ironically, they were attempting to build in Germany what had not developed anywhere: a mass audience for modern music. The field officers were sensible enough to favor in their work composers like Shostakovich and Britten and Copland who were on the more conservative side of the compositional spectrum, but that decision also carried a cost. What the Americans ultimately did was to alienate both the more conservative music lovers, who avoided concerts featuring American and modern works, and many of the new music cognoscenti, who thought the pieces being offered were too old-fashioned. As a result, although commendable in myriad ways, the branch's efforts on the part of new music were predestined to enjoy only modest popularity.

THE DEPENDENCE OF REEDUCATION ON REVOLUTION

Operating without guides or directives, the music officers attempted to achieve the basic goals of the occupation: to eliminate the possibility of resurgent nationalism, to decentralize power, and to encourage democratic thinking. The solutions they improvised—the licensing and management committees—as well as the new music they promoted and the new people they appointed all aimed to reconfigure the relationship of the state to the arts and to reform public attitudes to music. It is a shame that the music officers were hamstrung, throughout the occupation period, by conflicts over policy within OMGUS itself. In the first eighteen months of the occupation, denazification undercut their efforts, and their success was limited by personnel shortages, poor communication, insufficient cash, and their dependence on the New York field office for supplies. But the fact was that branch officers were at the bottom end of a command hierarchy—no more, as Kilenyi put it, than "anonymous little moles." This is why no one at headquarters bothered giving them much in the way of instruction or coordination, and why they found resources so scarce and others in the Military administration so resistant to their needs. The relative unimportance of the Music Branch makes the achievements of its officers all the more remarkable; but it also helps explain why, over time, so many of their initiatives proved insubstantial.

German cultural officials quickly came to understand the limits of the music officers' authority. In the first year of the occupation they used ICD's personnel where they needed them, defied them where they could, and listened to them where they had to. But they were also ready, when the division began to loosen the reins, to reclaim the authority the Americans had seized and reorganized. Because the music officers tended to speak German, to dress in civilian clothes, and to have experience in the arts, they appear to have been generally liked by local artists and administrators. Moreover, German officials appreciated many of the reforms they pressed, such as the need for greater fiscal control over cultural organizations, the importance of encouraging new music, and the necessity of more-democratic governance in the arts. They also appreciated the need to both ensure the *Intendanten*'s creative freedom and their financial responsibility. But they could not be expected to endorse the Americans' attitude to their cultural life: the presumption that they were chauvinistic and narrowminded and inclined toward herd thinking. *Land* officials therefore prepared to reverse those aspects of the ICD program (and the most hated was denazification) that threatened to weaken or diminish the quality or image of the arts in Germany.

So long as the Americans were watching, the impulse to be new and the desire to ingratiate oneself with the occupation forces made artists reasonably receptive to modern, unknown, and even American works. But it was difficult to undo one aspect of the ICD program without unraveling the rest. Reversing denazification decisions, for example, could only harm those artists who had filled the leadership vacuum created by the mandatory removals. And if the old guard was restored to power in music life, how could the program of encouraging new and American music survive? Might one logically expect people like Knappertsbusch or Jochum, whom ICD blacklisted and chased from the zone, to take up the cause of American music once they were back on the podium? And how would the reforms made to the administration of the arts fare when people trained in a different tradition returned to their old jobs? The music officers did not realize it, but the measures they implemented were riding on the coat tails of the ICD revolution. And so the future of the one hinged on the fate of the other.

4 Learning to Keep Quiet
Wilhelm Furtwängler and
the End of Denazification

Wilhelm Furtwängler hesitated until the German offensive in the Ardennes had been crushed and the Russians had liberated Auschwitz before deciding to escape the Third Reich. He resolved to leave after confirming with his friend, Albert Speer, the minister of war production, that a German victory was impossible and after hearing Speer's warning that the Nazis might kill him in the final *Götterdämmerung*. In February 1945, Furtwängler crossed the former Austrian-Swiss border and entered a Sanatorium in Clarens, where he placed himself in the official care of a surgeon of pronounced Nazi sympathies, Dr. Paul Niehans. The timing of his flight to Switzerland was significant because Furtwängler had declined many previous opportunities to leave, most recently in early December 1944 when he had visited his wife and newborn son in Zürich. Amazingly, at that time, the conductor left his family and returned to his work in Berlin and Vienna. Even more remarkably, although the Western Allies were pressing on Bologna, Furtwängler accepted a Foreign Ministry request that he leave the safety of Switzerland and conduct at La Scala in one of the last Italian cities under fascist control. Furtwängler's urge to make music was extraordinary, but his apparent willingness to conduct the dying Reich's dirge has the unpleasant feel of a final act of homage. Goebbels's observation about the maestro, that "the tougher things become, the closer he moves to our regime," appears to carry truth.[1]

To most people at the time, Furtwängler was Germany's greatest living conductor. He had been named music director of the Berlin Philharmonic Orchestra in 1922, was a regular guest at the premier opera houses of Europe, and had even conducted for three seasons in New York. A monumental egoist, vain and jealous of his position and prestige, Furtwängler had attained, by the late 1920s, a towering position within Central European musical life. But he was never free from challengers and felt keenly threatened by such rivals as Busch, Krauss, Knappertsbusch, and even Strauss. Unwilling to give up what he had achieved, Furtwängler decided to remain in Berlin after the Nazi seizure of power. It was a decision that came at a price, but in the end it was not without profit.

In an initial effort to test the limits of his prestige, Furtwängler had publicly defended Paul Hindemith, whom Nazi ideologues were targeting as a degenerate. The conductor lost his job as a result, resigned as vice-president of the Reichsmusikkammer, and was only allowed to resume his duties, with the title of principal guest conductor of the Berlin Philharmonic, after he publicly acknowledged Hitler's supreme authority over the arts. Possibly in the interests of keeping open a line of retreat, possibly in an attempt to rebuild his damaged international reputation, Furtwängler agreed in 1936 to take over the New York Philharmonic Orchestra for a trial season. Unfortunately, the Philharmonic Board was faced with vocal opposition to hiring a man who had already compromised with Hitler and Furtwängler was unwilling to leave one difficult position for another and withdrew from the job. Surprisingly, the years following Furtwängler's humiliating resumption of his post in Berlin proved good ones. Early in 1934 the Berlin Philharmonic had come under state control, and in 1938 its members were lifted to the highest rank in the ToK pay schedule; Furtwängler enjoyed an exceptionally good salary, was the chief music consultant for the Propaganda Ministry, held the honorary title of *Staatsrat*, and, before the war, appeared frequently in the newly annexed territories. He performed at important party functions, became for a time the leading conductor at Bayreuth, and in 1940 was appointed "permanent conductor" in Vienna and the city's cultural "plenipotentiary" with control over all musical activity.[2] Furtwängler was never a party member and found Nazism distasteful, but he was a prominent fellow traveler and profited from his connection to the regime.

Information Control had few illusions about Furtwängler. Intelligence realized that he was not a Nazi and that he had been "more or less in opposition against [*sic*] the Third Reich." The Americans also knew that, by the standards of his time, he was no anti-Semite and that he had disputed the party's racial policies. In fact, Robert McClure declared that he had "distinguished himself" in 1933–35 by "protesting against Nazi edicts." His assistance to Jewish members of his orchestra and, in particular, to Carl Flesch, the violinist whom he saved from a detention camp, was well known. ICD further recognized that Furtwängler's position as *Staatsrat* was largely ceremonial and that he had played no active role in running the Reichsmusikkammer. But the occupiers also knew that Furtwängler was "a man who learned to keep quiet," that he had been handsomely paid by the Nazis, and that he had been granted special permission by Economic Minister Funk to deposit his earnings from foreign appearances in Swiss and Swedish bank accounts. Moreover, they felt that, no matter what Furtwängler had believed or done or not done, he remained a symbol. In the opinion of Nicolas Nabokov, a composer and one of Berlin's intelligence officers, "the most important fact on the negative side of Furtwangler's political background is his position as the outstanding musician of the Third Reich."[3] If Information Control was going to uproot fascism and make May 1945 into a real turning point in German history, Furtwängler had to be barred from the concert halls.

Naturally, the great conductor did not see it this way. Instead, Furtwängler imagined himself a patriotic anti-Nazi German. He repeatedly asserted that his music had not served the Reich but had instead preserved "the other Germany" within the barbaric state. As Furtwängler wrote in his notebook in 1944: "For myself, I am one of the most convincing proofs that the real Germany is alive and will remain alive. The will to live and work in me is, however critically I view myself, that of a completely unbroken nation." The problem with understanding Furtwängler's position in the Third Reich is that one can — and the conductor probably did — assign various meanings to a statement like this. In asserting that he was simply a symbol "for himself," wasn't he acknowledging that his role as the Reich's "sensation" and "box-office draw" (as he put it) had compromised his ability to appear publicly as a dissenter? And what did he mean by the "real" Germany? Furtwängler wrote admiringly about romanticism, Wagner, Bruckner, Beethoven, and Bismarck; but these were equally revered by the Nazi elite. And in the context of 1944, when Germany was obviously losing the war and central Berlin was a bomb-ravaged wreck, how could one be sure that Furtwängler's assertion that he remained "alive" and "unbroken" was directed at the Nazis and not at the Allies (whom he invariably described as "the enemy" in his notebooks)? Furtwängler's wartime Beethoven broadcasts have often been taken as symbols of his indomitable spirit and his defiance of the Nazis, but in their passion and anguish and energy might they not also be heard as inspirational music for a nation tragically straining in war. How else can one read a 1943 diary entry that seems to connect the Wehrmacht with the musical canon: "One cannot play Mozart and Beethoven and turn away from those who live and die for them?"[4] Although the conductor was disdainful of National Socialism, he had few opportunities to reveal his opposition; even in the privacy of his diaries, his expression was ambivalent. His effectiveness as the symbol he aspired to be was limited by his own insecurity and by his failure to communicate what he was afraid to make known. Ultimately, he proved more effective as an icon for the regime. He was the artist who remained: he was proof that great music still resounded in the Reich and that Nazi Germany was heir to the spirit of Beethoven and Wagner. He lent cultural authority to a state shaken by the defection of many of its greatest artists; he embodied the Nazi claim that its political and racial purges had not destroyed Germany's cultural life and gave comfort and hope to a people at war.

Given Furtwängler's position in the Third Reich, as evidenced by his salary and official titles, it was inevitable that he would be blacklisted. But Furtwängler, who believed himself to have been an opponent of Nazism and a spokesman for the "good" Germany, was outraged by the fact. He had done what he could, he insisted, within the parameters he set for himself, to remain free of Nazi contamination: he had not accompanied his orchestra when it toured countries conquered in war, had refused all honors and titles, and had dealt only when necessary with the Propaganda Ministry. He found the presumption of his guilt and the calls for his deportation to Germany appalling. His crime, he concluded, was simply that he was a patriot. From his Swiss sanctuary, Furtwängler railed against ICD's notion of collective guilt more vehemently than he ever had against Nazi ideas: "What is happening today," he proclaimed, is "something even worse" than what happened under Hitler. True, the Nazis "first declared and practiced mass responsibility for the Jewish question . . . [but] the dishonouring of an entire and great people — a people whose inner nobility can compete with that of any other people, for it produced Goethe and Beethoven and innumerable other great men — is not only dangerous, it is terrible."[5]

Determined to rehabilitate himself as quickly as possible, in early 1946 Furtwängler accepted an improbable offer from Egon Hilbert, the man appointed to resuscitate Austria's musical life. Hilbert had had a varied career as a journalist, socialist bureaucrat, and former press secretary at the Austrian legation in Prague, and he had also been for seven years an inmate of Dachau. Now, as artistic director of all of Vienna's state theaters, his primary purpose was to rebuild the philharmonic and the Staatsoper with all possible haste and he took advantage of the disorganized conditions to snap up the best musicians he could. At the opera Hilbert built a remarkable ensemble, but several of those hired — such as Schwarzkopf, Karajan, and Patzak — carried a brown stain. He claimed not to care; as Hilbert told the *New York Times*, "he did not take very seriously any musician's politics. Except in the cases of musicians who were really active Nazis . . . he felt they should be treated as politically irresponsible." Furtwängler, who had a twenty-year connection to Vienna and was never a party member, was the greatest prize of all, and Hilbert convinced the government's denazification commission to hear the conductor's case. The message from Hilbert was delivered, oddly enough, by ISB's music officer, Otto Pasetti, who was in Switzerland discussing permits for visiting artists. Although the branch officer was careful to point out that the invitation was a purely Austrian affair, what Furtwängler knew of the situation clearly raised his hopes. As he noted slyly to Pasetti, "he was pleased that Karajan was in Vienna, although he could not understand why Karajan was called to Vienna before himself."[6]

From the start everyone was expecting the Austrians to recommended the conductor's denazification. Even before his hearing began, Pasetti had been told in confidence by Cultural Ministry officials that the conductor's reinstatement would be recommended. The Vienna Philharmonic went so far as to announce that Furtwängler would be conducting a mid-March concert. In Paris Roger Desormière and Francis Poulenc were trying to arrange for his appearance at the Opéra, the French military government in Germany invited him to conduct in Baden-Baden, Walter Legge contacted him about going to London to make recordings, and in Vienna the Soviet representative on the Allied Cultural Committee told Pasetti that he would support Furtwängler's denazification — and all this before anyone had officially heard any of the evidence against him![7] No surprise, then, that the Austrian commission should interview no one but Furtwängler and accept uncritically the conductor's explanations for all his actions.[8]

The examination concentrated on the period before 1935 and concluded that Furtwängler's defense of Hindemith and subsequent resignation from the Berlin Philharmonic and the RKK, were themselves "sufficient [grounds] for acquitting him." But the commission went further, acknowledging the conductor's support for Jewish musicians and observing that he "never greeted with the Hitler salute in public concerts, not even in the presence of Hitler." Remarkably, the commission also observed that Furtwängler had "refused on principle to conduct in German-occupied European countries" (which could only mean that they did not consider Bohemia "occupied"), and they explained away his two visits to Copenhagen with the observation that the conductor "did not have the impression that Denmark was an occupied country." Furtwängler's insistence that he only performed at "cultural" and not at "party" events also found its way into the final ruling as did his assertion that he had never tried to use his government connections to "silence" anybody and had only agitated against "the unfairness of the critic[s]." What really concerned the commission, however, was the final result. No matter what "reproaches" may be offered, the tribunal concluded, "from the cultural political point of view the Commission was convinced that[,] in the interest of the cultural reconstruction[,] Dr. Furtwängler ought to be acquired for Austria."[9]

Although they knew what was coming, ISB officers were still annoyed at the Austrian verdict. Hilbert and the others, Pasetti observed, "want to start the reconstruction job at the top. They want to have a big cast of great singers at the State opera. They want to have first class performances of the Philharmonics [*sic*]. They are afraid to start from the bottom. They are afraid to take out from the Philharmonics [*sic*] the big Nazis, because they could not continue the splendid performances of this musical body." The newly elected Austrian government, like the German *Länder*, was burdened with the heavy cost of rebuilding wartime ruin while debilitated by scarcities, rationing, and the shortage of social services. Its population was defeated, branded as monstrous and hungry; it craved entertainments that might reconnect it to a comforting past. The rebuilding of art was a relatively cheap way of doing something tangible in the public interest. It would signify to local people and to the world not only that the former nations of the Reich were returning to civilization but that they stood at its cultural apex. The cost of harboring a few Nazis and fascist collaborators—people who most, in populations filled with the same types, felt did nothing criminal — was deemed minimal. All this may be understandable, but it was an affront to ICD's conviction that one could not divorce art from politics, or the artist from society. Pasetti put his finger on the double standard involved: "[I]n 1938 the Nazis did not ask about the greatness of orchestras when the jews had to go out."[10]

Unfortunately, the Allies were never united on this point and no one was much surprised that the Russian delegate on the quadripartite cultural committee endorsed Furtwängler's denazification. The same could be said of the British representative's affirmative vote: Furtwängler was highly regarded in England before the war and a vigorous lobby on his behalf had been waged in that country by Berta Geissmar, Furtwängler's former administrative assistant and, since the mid-1930s, secretary to the most celebrated English conductor, Thomas Beecham. The French supported the U.S. position, which was that as a German national Furtwängler could not be cleared in Austria prior to his denazification in Germany. And so the issue split the committee.[11]

With the Allied Cultural Committee deadlocked, the Russians, who had by now contacted the maestro about assuming the directorship of the Berlin Staatskapelle Orchestra, decided to move things along and, anticipating the U.S. veto in Vienna, launched an admirable campaign to undermine it. The day after the Austrian tribunal acquitted the conductor, an open letter to Furtwängler appeared in the Soviet-licensed *Berliner Zeitung*, the official paper of the city *Magistrat*'s office. Sponsored by the Kulturbund and signed by the mayor and prominent people in the arts, the letter called on Furtwängler to return to Berlin: "We who, in the spirit of humanity, seek to rebuild a new and democratic Germany need you, the highest symbol of artistic perfection, to arouse German self-consciousness against the relapse into barbarism that was National Socialism." Of the twenty-three signatories to the open letter, eighteen worked in the Soviet sector of Berlin, eleven were on the executive of the Kulturbund, and four were known communists. The rump of the Kammer der Kunstschaffenden — the Schlüterstrasse advisory committee — and Berlin ICD protested this effort to circumvent the process, but the Russians demurred and then quietly packed Furtwängler onto a Soviet cargo plane bound for Germany. The conductor had agreed that, should he be cleared, he would make his return in *Tristan* at the Staatsoper. The Berlin press was alerted to his arrival, and on the tarmac the great conductor, flanked by Sergei Barsky, SMAD's music officer, and the

Kulturbund president, Johannes R. Becher, declared that he had come home to face his accusers.[12]

Furtwängler's return to Berlin in mid-March 1946 was a public-relations catastrophe for Information Control. Because he was in Soviet hands (they returned him to his home in Potsdam), he passed through SMAD's denazification procedure, which in his case involved a quick consideration by the Amt für Volksbildung's Prüfungsausschuss. On 14 June 1946 the *Berliner Zeitung* reported the conductor's clearance by "the Allied denazification committee" and announced his upcoming first performance at the Staatsoper. McClure, who had declared in February that Furtwängler "could not possibly hold a prominent position at a time when we are endeavoring to eliminate all vestiges of Nazism," suddenly looked very foolish. Few outside MG were aware of the Soviet break with the Kammer or of the reason behind the formation of the Kulturbund. No one appeared to understand McClure's insistence that Furtwängler had not passed through accepted channels of denazification and that the Schlüterstrasse committee remained the only German vetting organization in the arts that had ever been recognized by all four-powers. Even more ludicrous seemed the all-but-defunct Kulturkammer's announcement that, because of the backlog of artists awaiting hearings, it would not be able to offer its advice on the Furtwängler case before September 1946. The Soviet protest, that it was ridiculous for Germany's greatest living conductor and a man already cleared by two denazification tribunals, "to queue up like everybody else," duly found its way into the press.[13]

Confident of their victory in the public opinion war, the Soviets, in mid-June 1946, brought the Furtwängler case to the Kommandatura's Cultural Affairs Committee, which in deference to Soviet desires to expedite the hearing, established a subcommittee to recommend a course of action. The subcommittee consulted the Schlüterstrasse committee which recommended that Furtwängler not be allowed to conduct or direct an orchestra. Surprisingly, the Kommandatura's Cultural Affairs Committee rejected that recommendation and advised the conductor's clearance. According to the British representatives, the American committee member reversed McClure's position because he hoped to swing the German public back in the Americans' favor and "harness Furtwängler to their own propaganda machine." There is some evidence to support this claim. A week before the meeting, Berlin's Film, Theater and Music Branch chief telephoned Henry Alter, his old colleague, now in Vienna, to advise him that it was "almost certain Furt-wängler will be cleared" and that the conductor would want to conduct first in Vienna before returning "to take over" his old orchestra in Berlin. The chief of ICD's Berlin office, Frederick Leonard, then pressed Henry Alter "most urgently" to "sponsor" the conductor's visit to Vienna and to "take care of his trip from Vienna to Berlin" so as "to prevent the Russians from being the sponsors of F's return . . . make it generally understood that the *U.S. authorities* are bringing F. back and no one else."[14]

In all probability, ICD's divisional headquarters in Bad Homburg called a stop to this currying after public opinion and two days after the Cultural Affairs Committee meeting the Americans again changed course. When the case was referred to the Kommandatura's Denazification Committee, which had to give final approval to all removals from the blacklist, the American representative denied the conductor's clearance. McClure also clamped down on dissent inside the division, and John Bitter received a reprimand for having told the press in late January that he welcomed Furtwängler's "return to his orchestra . . . as that [outcome] corresponds with his intentions as an organizer as well as with his wishes as a listener." Whether because Furtwängler rejected the obvious alternative—to accept denazification in the Soviet zone alone—or because the Russians were as yet unwilling to make so open a break with their Allies, the blacklist stuck and the conductor returned quietly to Switzerland. Furtwängler was informed that he might still pursue his denazification in the proper fashion and that the Schlüter-strasse committee would be ready to hear his case in six months. For the moment the issue was resolved, but ICD had suffered another body blow in the press war, and McClure's revolutionaries sank even further in German estimation.[15]

Furtwängler's trials revealed both the determination of ICD in early 1946 to revolutionize German cultural life and the unpopularity of its program. As in the Knappertsbusch case, Germans were shocked by the arrogance of the Americans and their inability to recognize anti-Nazis when they saw them. For much of the music-loving public, Furtwängler had done all one could possibly do, within the befouling context of the dictatorship, to keep himself clean. If he was a Nazi collaborator, then so, they felt, were they all. What people did not appreciate was that ICD's revolutionaries considered the conductor one of the preeminent symbols of the old Germany and felt that banishing him from the podium was akin to tearing down the swastikas — it was necessary to show that things had changed. It was a hard line to take, especially when the other occupation powers refused to go along with it, and it cost ICD heavily. In fact, the poor publicity and embarrassing criticism it generated doubtless contributed to the military governor's decision that it was time for a change.

THE DEBATE OVER POLICY

The divisions among the Allies were by now obvious to ordinary Germans, especially in Berlin, where they encouraged doubts about the fairness of the American position. Why, people asked themselves, was a singer who was blacklisted in the city's American sector performing twice a week in the Soviet? Who was the more unreasonable in their approach to German guilt, the understanding Russians or the overbearing Americans? Significantly, of all the Allies, the Americans had moved the most rapidly to create outlets for the expression of opinions such as these. Within ICD, an Opinion Survey Branch was created in 1945 to sample popular views on a wide range of issues and to monitor German feelings. Military Government's interest in sampling local attitudes made sense, as it was the only way the occupiers might determine the effectiveness of reeducation, but it was also a sign of a democratic idealism among the American authorities. Right thinking, it was assumed, would emerge naturally among Germans if the chauvinistic and militaristic aspects of their culture were suppressed and if the public was given impartial and balanced information. The opinion surveys were therefore part of the overall strategy of reshaping German society — a surveillance counterpart to American press policy.

Another outlet for the expression of public opinion, the American-licensed German press, was unquestionably the most important element in Information Control's social revolution. The goal of American newspaper policy was to break the pre-Nazi tradition of a party-linked, fundamentally editorializing German press and to establish papers geared to the provision of "objective" reportage. Papers like the *Stuttgarter Zeitung* were created with licensed editors representing the different political parties in an effort to achieve impartiality through checks and balances. This system worked well enough in the American zone, but it broke down in Berlin where each of the powers had their own papers, which served as critics of each others' actions.

And even outside Berlin, where the emphasis was more strictly placed on direct news coverage, and ICD vigilantly monitored the media for any criticisms of occupation policy, there is no doubt that newspapers served as vehicles for political opinion in their coverage of local issues and people.[16]

But it was the American decision to rush ahead with local elections within a year of the war's ending that made the various elements of public and media opinion really volatile. Elections were first held in villages and rural communities in January 1946, and city elections followed in May. *Land* elections were held in June (to elect constituent assemblies that might formulate *Land* constitutions) and in November–December (to elect *Land* governments). The American military governor argued that if Germany was to become a democracy after twelve years of dictatorship, the people had to be involved in the process, and he tended to view the governments appointed by the occupation forces as "artificial political units." As Clay quipped to one political adviser, rapid democratization was necessary because "to learn to swim you have to get into the water." But by moving rapidly to authorize elections, the Americans were establishing rival political entities highly sensitized to popular and press opinion. Over the course of 1946, these would serve as the basis of opposition to such controversial programs as denazification.

Idealism was not the only rationale for rapidly restoring the vote to disenfranchised Germans; cuts to occupation budgets and the manpower shortage in Military Government were also compelling a devolution of power. Even as elections were being organized, MG personnel was being slashed. In September 1945 Lucius Clay was instructed to reduce American personnel from 10,000 to 7,000 within eight months; in April 1946 he was told to cut that number to 6,500, and in January 1947 the size of the zonal administration was fixed at 5,000. In Clay's opinion, for two years "we have followed a deliberate policy of constantly reducing the personnel in military government" and "there can be no further reduction . . . except at the sacrifice of our major objectives." Two months later, in April 1947, he was ordered to make an additional 20 percent cut. By mid-1949 OMGUS was administering its zone with a work force of just 2,500 Americans. Small wonder that Clay would later justify his policy of restoring local control with the observation that "factual analysis of the administrative problem was sufficient to convince me that there was no other solution."[17]

The truth is that McClure and the other advocates of a long, hard peace were riding against the main current of opinion within the occupation government. Although some Americans did remain hostile to the Germans, OMGUS policy was moving in the opposite direction. By the summer of 1946 senior policy makers were advocating a large-scale American pullout. The once punitive aspects of the occupation were becoming more tolerant, less authoritarian. Speaking in Stuttgart in September 1946, the secretary of state explained to occupation officials that Americans had "no desire to enslave the German[s]" and that they were now ready to "return the government of Germany to the German people . . . [and] help the German people to win their way back to an honorable place among the free and peace-loving nations." This was very much in keeping with Lucius Clay's position. As he observed, "no country can regain its self-respect nor progress to maturity in democratic processes in the presence of large occupation forces. No country will recognize its own guilt over a period of years if it lives in economic squalor under the shadow of mighty occupation armies. Basically, the most important objective to the peace of the world is to create a democratic state in Germany. . . . This objective can be accomplished best with a minimum of outside control and with token forces."[18]

For the first eight months of the occupation there had been consistency to America's denazification policy. A product of wartime animosities and horrors, denazification rested on the principle that most Germans were more or less guilty and that their crimes were the inevitable products of their chauvinistic, militaristic, and undemocratic attitudes. As late as Allied Control Council Directive #24, issued in January 1946, the basic principles of denazification as outlined in JCS 1067, the Potsdam Agreement, and MG Law #8 were maintained. Regulations consistently refined and detailed the demarcations of individual responsibility, but the changes only sharpened the basic principle of guilt by association. It did not matter what one had done in a position; the fact of holding office in Nazi Germany was enough to justify mandatory removal. True, occupation law after Potsdam did acknowledge the existence of nonculpable or "nominal" Nazis; but the law clearly stated that those placed within any of the four categories (major Nazis, officeholders, avowed racists, or militarists) as well as those who had given "substantial moral and material support" to the regime could under no circumstances be considered "nominal." Artists might appeal their cases to the people who ordered their dismissal, but the law held that they were considered guilty until they demonstrated their innocence.[19]

Denazification promised to transform German society; but in no time the scale of the task overwhelmed its enthusiasts. Under military law, all those holding a job or seeking employment in a long list of areas had to complete a series of forms, including a *Fragebogen*, each of which would have to be individually studied by divisional and public safety officers. By December 1945, 1.6 million *Fragebögen* had been received, over a million had been submitted to the Public Safety–Special Branch, and 700,000 had been evaluated. Another 900,000 were processed in the first half of 1946, but millions more remained to be collected and reviewed. By December 1945 Public Safety was accumulating a backlog of 50,000 cases per week and only caught up in June 1946 because it stopped the flow some months before. All told, an estimated 13 million *Fragebögen* would need to be reviewed in the American zone, and less than 15 percent had been considered in the first year of the occupation. Clay recognized the scale of the problem and realized that, even with current manpower, denazification would take some eight years to complete. Clearly, the only way to expedite the process was to involve Germans in it, and in the early winter of 1945 he invited the appointed *Länder* governments to submit proposals on how they might denazify their own populations. At the same time, he established a Denazification Policy Board within MG to "formulate a complete and overall program for denazification in the U.S. zone with as much responsibility as possible placed on German officials for the long range."[20] And so, even as Clay signed ACC #24 into law, his senior administrators were working on the complete overhaul of the system.

Ostensibly, the January 1946 Report of the Denazification Policy Board advised combining the victors' principles with the vanquished's personnel. In keeping with past principles, the policy board maintained that Germany must still be revolutionized: the Allies had to "eliminate the fundamental conditions of German life which have made her a recurring menace to the peace of the world." If this represented a continuation of JCS 1067 and Potsdam, the mechanism for achieving the revolution underwent a subtle but decisive shift. In fact, the board proposed nothing less than an abandonment of the basic grounding of denazification policy. Where all earlier documents had described denazification as an Allied responsibility, the report presented the Americans' inability to continue administering the program as a positive development. Instead of forcing change on a population contaminated and collectively guilty, the policy board maintained that "the occupying powers alone cannot bring about such a drastic alteration in the basic pattern of German society. Acceptance by the Germans of a new kind of society . . . must be voluntary and uncoerced." This view had existed in MG from the beginning, to the extent that Military Government relied on *Land* and municipal governments for local administration, but denazification had hitherto been considered too fundamental for German involvement. Now, however, denazification was presented as a means "for assisting in the shift of power and influence from one group of Germans to another."

While this suggestion—that the new elites participate in the decapitation of the old—moved MG subtly away from collective guilt and punitive justice, the policy board's next proposal represented an utter reversal. Following on the premise that Germans must agree in their own transformation, the board suggested that "if we are eventually to turn Germany back to a group of Germans we can trust, that group must retain popular support." In other words, "to ignore German opinion would be fatal, for if we punish those who are not regarded as guilty by their fellow-countrymen, we will succeed only in creating a new class of martyrs." The locals, then, must play a role in determining the meaning of innocence. The clear implication was a retreat from the policy of guilt by association.

The policy board's recommendations presented, within an overall package that seemed compatible with past practice, a dramatic change in denazification policy. The change, which preceded major friction with the Soviets and the onset of the Cold War, was motivated not by the need to ensure the support of a Germany Americans feared losing, or by the need to ease denazification's impact on the German economy, but by the concurrent construction of an independent political system.[21] The position adopted in December 1945 was that elected municipal and *Land* governments could not carry responsibility for a denazification program that was unpopular with the German public. Introducing democracy into one part of the system meant that all activities transferred to German administrations had to meet the standard of popular support.

The *Länder* themselves were satisfied with these aspects of the report but balked at preserving such facets as the presumption of guilt and the notion that certain activities—such as membership in proscribed organizations—made one automatically a Nazi. Even here, denazification's American reformers gave ground. MG liaison officers informed the *Land* officials that the presumption of guilt, manifested in the fact that one was removed from a job first and had to appeal one's dismissal, could be modified in practice by the German courts. Under pressure from German lawmakers, the Americans then went further and agreed to enshrine the notion that individuals had to be judged by their actions and thoughts and not by their positions. The resulting agreement between the *Länder* and OMGUS manifested itself in the Law for Liberation from National Socialism, which the states passed individually in early 1946 and which, in a special celebration, Clay read to the assembled delegates of the American-zone *Länder* in the Munich Rathaus in March. This, in itself, was a startling new direction in MG's approach and showed the degree to which the military was moving toward a joint administrative policy. For Clay, the Law for Liberation was the centerpiece of a new program of encouraging the Germans to participate in the remaking of their own society.[22]

The Law for Liberation was heavily indebted to the course outlined in the Denazification Policy Board Report of January 1946. But it also represented official accommodation with the long-standing German view that people had to be charged with actual crimes and were not guilty simply because they failed to resist the Third Reich and agreed to work within it. The Law for Liberation continued the process of broad coverage by requiring everyone older than eighteen years to fill out a registration form (*Meldebogen*). Following investigation by officials in the *Länder*'s new Ministries for Political Liberation, those considered suspect would have to appear before a German denazification tribunal (*Spruchkammer*). The tribunal would classify the appellant for denazification into one of five categories of offender and apply a sentence. Although the Public Safety Branch was charged with loose "supervision" of the *Spruchkammer* process, only in Berlin, where the Kommandatura retained authority, were German decisions subject to review by the occupation governments. But even more striking than this procedural change was the way in which the law revised the definition of German guilt. The new law maintained the guilt of only those who "actively supported the National Socialist tyranny, or are guilty of having violated the principles of justice and humanity, or of having selfishly exploited the conditions thus created." Ostensibly the categories of offender in the Law for Liberation were similar to the ones presented in ACC #24—active Nazis, those guilty of racial or other crimes, profiteers—though officeholding itself was dropped as a category. But the tone was completely different. Where earlier documents had employed negative categories, indicting all but "nominal" Nazis, Article 3.2 of the new law asserted that it was only a crime to have been an "active" Nazi. The onus therefore shifted from the appellants having to prove they were "nominal" to the court having to demonstrate they were "active," and the court could not take an individual's Nazi sympathies for granted. In fact, "external criteria, such as membership in the NSDAP, any of its formations or other organizations, shall not be decisive by themselves alone. . . . They may be taken as important evidence of a person's conduct as a whole, but may be overcome, wholly or partly, by evidence to the contrary."[23]

Many in MG were outraged by the new policy. In accepting the idea that denazification involved the "reorientation of Nazis who have demonstrated that they are capable of reformation," the new law flew in the face of ICD's notion that denazification implied a sociocultural purge and not an individual catharsis. McClure did not believe the Germans should be allowed anything beyond a minor role in denazification and ICD determined to bear witness to the rightness of its director's position. An ICD survey carried out in March 1946 maintained that while 39 percent of Germans preferred denazification to be the responsibility of German courts, the military governor was wrong to assume that this represented a majority. Almost as many, 35 percent, said they felt the Americans should do the job alone. For its part, ICD Intelligence was deeply concerned that "it will be extremely difficult for us to see that the German boards keep up . . . our de-Nazification standards." And they were not alone in assuming this position. Thomas Handy, the army's G-3 (Operations) chief also protested that the law ran counter to JCS 1067 and the spirit of the Potsdam Agreement. This gave Washington pause and forced Clay to pin his flag to the new approach: "If policies are going to be changed after the fact or if we are to be given instructions on procedures, I am through. . . . I cannot tell you how strongly I feel in this matter," he wrote his superiors in Washington. Indeed, "to change our plan now would indicate a lack of confidence in our German administrations and also a lack of confidence in military government."[24]

The new law had an immediate impact on Information Control. The committees that the Music Branch had organized to assist artists preparing their cases and hear appeals were ordered out of the denazification business and, in August 1946, the Screening Center in Bad Orb was shut down and its psychiatrists sent home. But McClure was unwilling to give up without a fight. Because ICD was certain that the German courts would "use a standard as low as possible," it was determined to do what it could to keep the channels of cultural life clean. The Law for Liberation was imprecise on the procedures for reviewing mandatory removals already imposed by the Americans, and Al Toombs, the intelligence chief, felt that his section's approval would be required for all reclassifications. McClure therefore ordered ICD to defy the spirit of the new law by accelerating its purge of the arts. In June 1946 he announced that cultural organizations had to be subjected to the closest inspection, before the Germans had a chance to vet their members. It was especially important, he insisted, that ICD "make certain that 'prestige' organizations are one hundred percent clean. . . . Therefore, it is requested that immediate steps be taken to eliminate all former party members from positions where they appear before the public." ICD further asked the Public Safety Branch to forward all cases involving information services to ICD, while Toombs tried to pressure the *Spruchkammern* into contacting ICD prior to hearings in order to determine "whether we have any information favorable or unfavorable to the man concerned."[25]

Unfortunately, the efforts of ICD command to short-circuit the Law for Liberation exposed the moderates' discomfort within the division. Benno Frank and his colleagues in the Music Branch worried that speeding the pace of removals would destroy German theaters and orchestras, and he leaked McClure's June order to the Public Safety Branch. Not surprisingly, Public Safety, which under the Law for Liberation had exclusive responsibility for overseeing the *Spruchkammer* process, bristled at ICD's attempt to preserve its authority. The policy of preemptive denazification therefore had to be abandoned, and Clay bluntly informed McClure that "Information Control is not engaged in denazification." The military governor did, however, compromise on one aspect of the division's objections and allowed that its officers might refuse to implement *Spruchkammer* decisions in order to ensure "that the best available personnel are selected to build new, democratic information services." But the veto, Clay maintained, must be based solely on the individual's "professional qualifications and experience." The opening Clay offered provided at least some maneuvering room to Information Control's more zealous commanders. As McClure informed his officers, "even though Germans may be cleared by the Denazification Boards for political background, Information Control will still examine their technical qualifications to determine their suitability for our work."[26]

Given the dynamics of the situation, it is hardly surprising that ICD divided over how to handle pending cases. Throughout the zone, great confusion now reigned as different offices struggled to make sense of the new rules. In Bavaria the district military governor declared, over the division's protest, that ICD would end its supervision of cultural appointments in early October 1946; two months later, in Württemberg-Baden, ICD conceded that it had no further responsibility for hirings and no veto, even over previous blacklist cases. But headquarters in Bad Homburg still insisted that its officers did hold a veto.

In the music field, the Furtwängler case was recognized by all to be the bellwether of policy, and McClure and the Intelligence Branch seemed intent on wielding the Kommandatura's power. But the music officers had their doubts, and they quietly prepared a line of retreat. With Furtwängler's hearing now rescheduled for winter 1946, the conductor was invited to Wiesbaden, placed under Dubensky's care, and interviewed in early November by Benno Frank and the head of the British Theater and Music Section. Hoping to win the conductor back over to the Western Allies, the officers told Furtwängler that his denazification was "probable" and revealed their major concern to be a face-saving way out of the scandalous reversal. Most important was the need to avoid "gratuitous [press] comment," and this meant keeping Furtwängler quiet about his feelings regarding the process. The Americans were anxious to maintain the image, as they had been in March, that decisions were being reached jointly by all four powers. Frank was also concerned over where Furtwängler would go and wanted to prevent his appearing to reward the Russians for their support. So the Americans offered the philharmonic, while stipulating that some arrangement with Sergiu Celibidache had to be found. Furtwängler, no matter what his view of the Western Allies, agreed to cooperate, and said he was "anxious to avoid unnecessary and undesirable publicity, not so much for his own sake, but to avoid prejudicing his usefulness hereafter or emphasizing any particular allegiance."[27] The Theater and Music Branch had now done what it could to contain the damage of Furtwängler's rehabilitation.

DENAZIFYING FURTWÄNGLER

The transfer of responsibility over denazification from ICD to the Germans meant that the revolutionary moment was passing. Few Germans who had remained in the Third Reich would find another guilty simply because he or she refused to quit a job. Few other than émigrés would blame someone for accepting higher pay or failing to protest Nazi policies. Most Germans did not believe profitable cohabitation with the Nazis a crime, although they were critical of those who failed to shoulder their share of wartime hardship. Nor did the average German see the émigrés as models to be emulated; on the contrary, those who fled were often despised for having avoided the pain of total war and the humiliation of total defeat. What mattered to German *Spruchkammer* interrogators was what one had done with one's position: had the accused harmed others, turned people in, participated in racial or political purges? Less tangibly, the *Spruchkammern* wanted to identify those who were ideological Nazis: the anti-Semites, the warmongers, the acolytes of Hitler. Counterbalancing these negative findings was the desire to highlight the positives: the help Germans provided Jews and other victims of fascism and the hardships they endured at the hands of the Nazis. In short, the tribunals were adopting the standards of guilt and innocence that artists had previously, unsuccessfully, presented to ICD Intelligence: they wanted to be judged for what they had done and believed and not for who they were.

Furtwängler's hearing was delayed as the authorities in Berlin sorted out among themselves the implications of the new policy. Clearly, as the first Furtwängler case revealed, the existing process had broken down: there were mutually unrecognized German denazification committees in both the Soviet and British sectors, the *Magistrat*'s office maintained its own consultative committee (which the Western Allies refused to acknowledge) and the Kommandatura still needed to unanimously approve all decisions. Over the summer of 1946 a compromise was reached. The Soviets accepted a newly constituted denazification committee, the Entnazifizierungskommission für Kunstschaffende, on Schlüterstrasse, chaired by a member of the KPD, which was to serve as the equivalent of a *Spruchkammer* and lay officially under the Berlin

Wilhelm Furtwängler conducting the Berlin Philharmonic Orchestra
(Photo courtesy of Mateo Lettunich)

Magistrat's jurisdiction. However, because of Berlin's peculiar governance, the new Schlüterstrasse group would continue past practice in reporting to the Kommandatura's Cultural Affairs Committee (through its Subcommittee of Experts in Cultural Affairs) and that group would forward cases it approved to the four-power Denazification Committee for final clearance. All cases that had not yet received Kommandatura approval (and that meant all of those hitherto cleared in the Soviet sector) would need to be reconsidered by the new Denazification Commission for Artists. This new group held its first meeting on 4 September 1946, considering the application of the Staatsoper's leading bass, Josef Greindl, who had been performing for a year under Soviet clearance but had never received Kommandatura authorization. The Furtwängler case was scheduled to be heard three months later.[28]

The brief in Furtwängler's case was prepared by British ISB, which assembled the documents that would serve as evidence against the maestro. The commission was charged with investigating the prepared charges (and other issues that might arise) and determining, on the basis of the evidence offered by the appellant and witnesses, whether clearance was warranted. Most everyone now considered Furtwängler's denazification, as one British officer explained it, "a foregone conclusion," though the conductor almost managed to upset expectations.[29] The chair of the commission, Alex Vogel, followed the Communist Party line on the conductor. Although he pressed Furtwängler hard on the first day of the hearing, by the second he recognized the conductor's incompetence at self-defense and helped him through the process. Surprisingly, the commission's prosecutor, Wolfgang Schmidt, a Social Democrat who had, like Vogel, been active in the resistance to Hitler, and who could be implacable in his interrogation of appellants, also treated the conductor relatively gently and encouraged him to make statements that would bolster his case. And yet, even with a predetermined outcome and all this help, the new standards provided something of an obstacle.

The commission was aware that the conductor had helped many Jews, that he took a stand against the Nazis in 1934–35, that he did not perform at most of the party functions expected of him, and that some in Hitler's circle disliked him. But was it so clear that he had never used his position as the leading conductor in the Reich to hurt others? One of the main charges against Furtwängler was that he had used his influence to have a Berlin newspaper critic who exorbitantly praised Herbert von Karajan fired from his job and drafted into the air force. Propaganda Ministry records revealed that Furtwängler had complained about Karajan and the critic to Goebbels, although there was only coincidental evidence to suggest that his protest was the cause of the critic's military induction. Nonetheless, the conductor's difficulty in disconnecting his desire (to hinder Karajan's rise) and his actions (in complaining about Karajan's supporters) from the result (Karajan's marginalization in Berlin and the critic's removal) almost derailed the process during its first session. For the second day, Furtwängler prepared a better case. He hoped to find his way clear of difficulty by suggesting that Karajan and his promoters were the real Nazis and that he had been *their* victim. The central figure in this story was Rudolf Vedder, at one time an important Berlin concert agent, a vice-president of the Reichsmusikkammer, and an ss member, who was unscrupulous enough to have even fallen into disrepute in Nazi eyes. Furtwängler charged that Vedder schemed, for political reasons, to have him removed from his job; that Vedder pushed Karajan as his replacement, and that the agent discouraged his clients from performing with the Berlin Philharmonic. The only problem with the conductor's story, once again, was the outcome: Furtwängler won the fight. In 1942, shortly after he complained to Goebbels about Vedder, the agent was dismissed from the Reichsmusikkammer and lost his concert agency. Even Schmidt could not resist drawing the obvious conclusion: how could Furtwängler be regarded as an anti-Nazi and a victim of fascism when Goebbels consistently supported him against his enemies? The conductor had no real answer and, unbelievably, Schmidt let the issue drop.

Furtwängler also barely skirted the shoals when interrogated about his beliefs. One member of the tribunal chastised the conductor for repeatedly using the Nazi expression *Systemzeit* to refer to the Weimar period. The maestro also found himself entrapped in a charge that he had denounced the Italian conductor, Victor de Sabata, as a Jew, and while he did assert, with the help of Vogel's leading questions, that he had nothing against Jews, he could not really deny that he might have made derogatory remarks. No one enquired much into Furtwängler's musical tastes, and his negative remarks about contemporary composers were allowed to slip by. More trouble arose when he tried to explain how he stood as a symbol of "the other Germany" and avoided appearing as an advertisement for the regime. First, Furtwängler insisted, quite falsely, that the press was as one against him; then he asserted that those who came to his concerts understood his music making as the embodiment of the anti-Nazi tradition. Schmidt asked Furtwängler what influence the press had over the public, and the conductor, fearing where this could go, asserted that the press generally determined popular opinions. As it was hard to maintain that Furtwängler lacked a large and loyal public, Schmidt suggested helpfully that most people understood the press to be controlled and that believers in the "other Germany" saw through it. Furtwängler categorically rejected this view in all but select individual cases. Perhaps the conductor still thought he had to prove that the press was powerful and arrayed against him (so justifying his complaints to Goebbels about the pro-Karajan faction); perhaps he thought Schmidt was trying to trap him into saying that because the public disbelieved the newspapers it would suspect that he was not so negatively regarded by the regime as he said. What he probably hoped to suggest was that most Germans shared his opposition to the regime and they were as much resisters in their attendance as he was in his performance. He did not explain how Goebbels or Speer or the other Nazi leaders who attended his concerts felt about his conducting. In any case, Schmidt did not press the point, and no one bothered to clip the newspaper columns needed to discredit Furtwängler's initial premise.[30]

The hearing was over in two days. According to a British ISB observer, it was the "biggest circus we ever had . . . important issues were at stake . . . but they never got round to them."[31] Doubtless, American and British intelligence officers believed that the case should have charted the limits of collaboration and culpability. Certainly they were contemptuous of the commission's apparent fixation on the Karajan question (a rather sore point with the Allies, which KPD members enjoyed pressing) and its willingness to accept uncritically Furtwängler's contention that he was the victim. But at issue here was still the problem of two definitions of guilt: for the Americans, Furtwängler's crime was that he was a great artist who profited during the Third Reich. If denazification was to retain its meaning under the changed legal circumstances, the definition of collaboration had to be established and a precedent set. To Intelligence, it remained fundamentally a moral issue. But the Germans were looking for specific evidence, particular actions that might reveal guilt or innocence. Collaboration was not in itself a crime to them; they wanted proof of the abuse of influence or power. Neither Americans nor Germans accepted, or even fully understood, each other, though both sensed the other's displeasure. For the Schlüterstrasse commission, this awareness—the realization that they had not done the expected thing—coupled with incomprehension over what they were supposed to do, produced a debilitating immobility. Instead of rendering a verdict, the commission voted to leave the case open pending receipt of more information from Frankfurt. It is not clear what was expected; but the reference to Frankfurt probably means they thought the Americans at ICD headquarters in Bad Homburg held further damning evidence. And there the process stopped, for no word came from Bad Homburg.

In fact, Intelligence was itself deadlocked over procedures and had adopted a hands-off policy that, from the German perspective, manifested itself in a frustrating combination of hostility and silence. For ICD, Furtwängler's hearing coincided with further dizzying shifts in the American approach to denazification that left McClure's revolutionaries even more bitter and disillusioned. Through the summer of 1946, ICD attempted, where it could, to retain control over the denazification process. McClure and Toombs battled the Law for Liberation along its fringes, using the licensing system, its "quality control" prerogative, and a fast-track approach to mandatory removal to slow the flow of the politically cleansed. At the same time, ICD busied itself assembling the evidence needed to discredit the policy of Germanification and in September 1946 launched its counterattack. In a substantial report on the success of the Law for Liberation, ICD Intelligence blasted Clay's program. Reviewing the situation in Bavaria, ICD found that of the 163,242 *Spruchkammer* verdicts rendered, 155,267 declared the appellant politically clean (not affected by the law) and of the remaining 8,000 or so, only 49 were judged "major offenders." Adopting an ostensibly balanced perspective, the ICD investigator averred that, while it was necessary and desirable for the Germans to denazify themselves, the assumption had always been "that individuals found to be definitely nazi [*sic*] (i.e. mandatory removals) under the [old] directives would in most cases fall under the same class of offender under the German law." But such was not the case: only 20 of the almost 2,000 people previously classified by the Americans as "mandatory removals" were retained in that category by the *Spruchkammern*. A particular problem was that the Germans appeared uninterested in using party records in Allied hands; a spot check of 2,800 files found that in 500 cases the appellants had falsified their *Meldebogen*, and the crime had not been caught by German authorities. As one CIC officer lamented: "[O]ur reports show that the majority of *Spruchkammern* work has been a gigantic white-washing. . . . we should have retained control of the boards longer . . . with perhaps a German representative on each tribunal."[32]

The ICD report was a complete indictment of the *Spruchkammer* process, and Clay responded with fury. Having already staked his reputation on the success of the Law for Liberation and fought off challenges from senior officers under his command, the military governor had been caught out. He responded aggressively. On 5 November 1946 he swept down on the first anniversary meeting of the *Länderrat* and blasted the assembled delegates for their failure to live up to the spirit of their agreement. "I do not see," Clay stormed, "how you can demonstrate your ability for self-government nor your will for democracy if you are going to evade or shirk the first unpleasant and difficult task that falls on you." He then listed off the evidence assembled by ICD and declared successful denazification imperative. For the time being, he announced, no one who had been removed by the Americans was to be reinstated by the *Spruchkammern* without MG approval. But Clay did not further override the Law for Liberation; on the contrary, he gave the *Länder* sixty more days to make the tribunals work. Only if the *Länder* failed to correct the faults that had entered into the process would he order his units to reassert control over the program.[33]

Taking heart, ICD officials felt they would soon regain responsibility for denazification. In a show of bravado in December 1946, American ICD officers even went so far as to inform their counterparts from the French, British, and Soviet zones that "decisions of the *Spruchkammern* in the U.S. zone were not binding on Information Control Intelligence." But once again, ICD misjudged the intentions of the military governor. Although Clay was angry over German handling of the trials, he did not for a moment consider a change in policy possible. Convinced that the Germans had to do the job themselves, if only because OMGUS now lacked the manpower to do it better, Clay simply continued to pressure the *Länder* to improve their policies. No follow-up study of the success of denazification at the end of the sixty-day period was authorized, and only inconsequential changes in the *Spruchkammer* process were implemented. Instead, Clay cracked down on the insubordinates in ICD.

Although McClure and Toombs believed Clay's November speech restored their untrammeled veto over *Spruchkammer* decisions involving previous blacklists, they were mistaken. In the first place, they were authorized to review the cases only of people interested in holding important jobs. Initially they considered all musicians fell within their purview until MG ruled, in early 1947, that technical personnel, orchestral musicians, and teachers, even if party members, were to be considered on a level with manual workers and therefore not subject to ICD review. From this point on only potential licensees—dramaturges, directors, *Intendanten*, producers, and conductors—would need to have the results of their denazification hearings approved. As Research Chief Schmid made clear: "On the small fry we feel that with the minimum denazification clearance they should be free to enter information services if the licensees and key position men whom we screened permit them to come in." Furthermore, ICD's practice of overturning *Spruchkammer* decisions on the basis of evidence the Germans had neglected to consider ended when, in February 1947, Clay ordered ICD "to make no additional political requirements in Information Control concerning artists, musicians, etc., who might have been cleared by denazification boards." This all but ended ICD's veto authority over previous blacklists. Although the order did not apply in Berlin, it was a clear indication that the military governor was still intent on leaving the denazification of cultural life entirely to the Germans.[34] Like most military men, Clay considered intellectuals and artists too unimportant to bother with in the cull of the Nazi herd, but his decision was yet another rebuke for Information Control.

By now, the division's radical cadre had begun to dismember itself. Until July 1946, ICD could always support its independence from OMGUS through its dependence on the State Department for broad policy direction. Gradually, however, over the fall and winter of 1946–47, the division was forced to accept Clay's authority.[35] The Intelligence Section, which had been largely stripped of its function by the Law for Liberation, had been scheduled by MG for reorganization in the winter of 1946–47. Although Clay's order of 5 November restored some of the section's responsibility, the personnel cuts and the job redefinitions proceeded as originally planned. Under MG orders, the section's Denazification Branch was to be closed down early in the new year and the main job of the unit was to become the gathering of intelligence on German politics, sampling public opinion, and watching the local press. Managing all this was clearly not a job for Alfred Toombs, and in late November 1946 he left Germany. His replacement, Robert Schmid, was little interested in denazification, and the section assumed a new name, the "Research Branch," in early 1947.

Though ICD would continue to engage sporadically in denazification-related matters, purging German society of Nazism and militarism was no longer its central function.

And so, with ICD Intelligence now disentangling, the Americans refused to intervene one way or another in the Furtwängler's case. The drift therefore continued for months, with the Schlüterstrasse commission awaiting guidance and the Americans stonily silent. And all the while German press criticism mounted, and the commission presented one excuse after another to explain its inaction. As the Soviet-licensed *Tägliche Rundschau* snorted: "[W]hat is going on here? . . . all the pretexts, such as a paper shortage, more than 300 pages of minutes, Christmas holidays, new investigations, are not the true reasons for the months of delay. . . . It is evident that there are forces which in contradiction to the existing rules and regulations seem interested in delaying the Furtwängler case as long as possible." Press mockery was too much for the Music Branch, which on 10 March 1947 finally approached the Schlüterstrasse commission through Michael Josselson, the American representative on the Kommandatura's Denazification Committee, in an effort to remove the logjam. Josselson, a former intelligence officer who now spent his time watching the Soviets, informed the Germans that they were to expect no further information from Bad Homburg and suggested to them that the effort to saddle the Americans with responsibility for the delay in rendering judgment might result in an investigation of their actions by the Public Security Review Board.[36] A few days later the commission voted to close the Furtwängler case and to forward its recommendation for denazification to the Kommandatura. Within a week the case passed both Allied committees, and in early April 1947 the great conductor was informed of his successful clearance.

"Greatness," Otto Pasetti had observed in early 1946, "obliges a man with the intelligence of Furtwängler to be judged differently from the small minded people. . . . In the eyes of Germany and the whole world Furtwängler was the exponent of German . . . music. . . . It would create the worst impression if we would allow that such a man come back without punishment." For almost two years, ICD had obstructed the maestro's return because its commander and its intelligence officers had recognized his symbolic importance. Furtwängler had not been blacklisted because the Americans were blunderers or cultural illiterates, as some commentators have suggested. Rather, Information Control fought hard over the Furtwängler case because it conceived of the conductor as he perceived himself: as the preeminent symbol of German musical culture. But where the conductor cherished that culture as the wellspring of civilization, ICD considered it the birthplace of fascism. Furtwängler, one American officer observed, was "the complete tool of the nazis [sic] . . . [because] to the German people . . . he showed that the nazi regime, after all, continued the much-heralded tradition of the superior German culture. . . . Furtwängler is in the mandatory exclusion category for having been a Prussian state councillor, but also for what he stands for."[37] But despite consistent opposition to Furtwängler's rehabilitation, ICD had been forced to give way—not because it wanted to, but because other elements in Military Government declared its revolution to be over. And with his clearance, the music element in ICD's great experiment in cultural engineering came to an end.

THE FLOODGATES OPEN

During the winter of 1947 dozens of blacklist cases were reversed. Most musicians were cleared through the *Spruchkammer* process, but ICD itself, in select instances, sounded its own retreat. One of the most important of these cases, at least for the Music Branch, was that of Hans Knappertsbusch. The Bavarian conductor's blacklisting in October 1945 had raised the first doubts among music officers about the rightness of McClure's revolution; unfortunately, few of the original group remained in Germany to enjoy their vindication. Knappertsbusch applied for denazification under the Law for Liberation in the summer of 1946, but before his case could be heard, the Americans interrupted the proceedings with a request that all material in the court's hands be sent them for review. Six weeks later, in November 1946, ICD Intelligence reversed its position and announced that Knappertsbusch's name was being removed from the blacklist. It is not clear why they chose this moment to do so, given that it could have vetoed the *Spruchkammer* decision, but it is plausible that Intelligence was hoping to avoid the criticism that would flow from the trial of this hard-to-justify removal. In any event, the Bavarian authorities now opted not to proceed with the case against the conductor and declared that he had no need to seek denazification.[38] In other words, an artist who had been fired from his job and blacklisted for over a year was now being informed, without apology, that no one could find good reason for preventing his conducting. Knappertsbusch himself had always maintained that his career had suffered under the fascists, and though his record was far from clean and his clearance was a consequence of a redefinition of complicity, one can understand his bitterness over events.

In the Knappertsbusch case one cannot resist the conclusion that ICD was reversing itself because it did not believe the mandatory removal would hold under German law and it was anxious to avoid embarrassment. But in other cases, different pressures led ICD to alter its position. British lenience, for example, allowed the Music Branch to get several names removed from the blacklist. In September 1946 the British and American zones were fused economically, and all divisions of OMGUS and the British Military Government were ordered to harmonize their policies. That same month, the Intelligence branches of ISB and ICD initiated regular meetings and theater and music officers began attending these three months later. Taking advantage of the gloom in intelligence circles and of the opportunities provided by closer relations with the British, the Music Branch officers started to press for a more energetic clearance of "dubious cases of prominent artists."[39] Dubensky, the officer in Wiesbaden, for example, used the joint committee to do for the pianist Walter Gieseking what public opinion appears to have achieved for Knappertsbusch.

Gieseking was one of Europe's most eminent pianists. Born to German parents in Lyon in 1895, educated in Hanover, and incandescent in his playing of modern French music, Gieseking was in every sense an international artist. Before the war, he enjoyed a tremendous career in both Europe and North America, and he appeared far more often abroad than in Germany. But there was really no question of his allegiance. When interviewed by an intelligence officer in September 1945, he made no apologies for his decision to remain in the Third Reich and spoke openly of his attitude toward Nazism. He was, he acknowledged, a believer "in Hitler's New Order." The Führer, he explained, "was a very gifted person, a clever politician and [he] achieved many things for his country. He used to say he didn't want any war and we believed him." When asked why the war had been fought, Gieseking asserted it had been a war "against communism." As to who had started it, the pianist replied: "I hoped the war would end after the Polish campaign. Germany wanted to reach an agreement.... It was difficult to tell who started the war." On the matter of the extermination of European Jewry and other barbarities, Gieseking was noncommittal: "It was in Switzerland during the early part of 1945 that I heard for the first time about atrocities. Even then we didn't believe [them]" for "I have been hearing all kinds of rumors, but never pay much attention to them. There are very few reliable people in the world."[40]

Gieseking applied to join the ardently Nazi cultural organization, the Kampfbund für deutsche Kultur, in 1933, but he was never in the party itself. He enjoyed excellent relations with the propaganda and foreign ministries, however, performed as often as he could at party functions, and revised his repertoire (adding Russian music in 1939–41 and dropping French after 1939) as he floated on the currents of war. The pianist's income in the Third Reich was handsome, and during the war years almost half of it came from foreign tours. Gieseking was in Belgium and Holland at least three times a year after 1940 and concertized in France (1943–44) and Norway (1944) and Denmark (1943–45); he performed only before Germans during his annual visits to Bohemia and his two tours of Poland. According to the American intelligence officer who interrogated him, "as an artistic emissary of the Third Reich, [Gieseking] could not be bothered with such nonsense as the Alsatian question or the temper of the Danish or Norwegian peoples. Gieseking was an integral part of Nazi musical life long before the war started, and this only became more pronounced during the crucial years of the conflict."[41]

In August 1945 the pianist was discovered by Special Services, and he resumed his concertizing, this time before occupation troops. According to his agent, he performed nine times for the Americans, three times for the French, and in September–October undertook two tours of the British zone. But Gieseking had already been targeted by the ICD. During the war he had been famously denounced by Erika Mann along with Richard Strauss and Wilhelm Furtwängler in the *New York Times*. In September 1945 Intelligence interrogated him and in October his name appeared on the blacklist. An appeal in January 1946 had no impact on his status; in fact, ICD Intelligence appears not to have bothered responding. Three months later, following the passage of the Law for Liberation, Gieseking filed his *Meldebogen* and requested the scheduling of a *Spruchkammer* hearing. In the meantime, with his name still on the blacklist, Gieseking could not perform in the American zone or the British, though the French continued to employ him up until January 1946. As with the other prominent artists prohibited from playing, Gieseking survived on his savings and friends and by providing private music lessons. In Wiesbaden, for example, even the commander of the occupation forces, Major General Frank Milburn, hired him to give his son piano lessons.[42]

But then peculiar things started to happen. Someone in the Hessian minister-president's office, who was apparently unaware that Gieseking had been blacklisted, wrote him asking whether he would volunteer to play at a charity concert. Gieseking said he would do so gladly, but that he could not because of the Americans; he cannily enquired of the minister whether anything could be done. The president's appeal to the Music Branch in May 1946 received the pat reply that nothing could be done as denazification was now to be a German responsibility. But the minister appeared determined to assist the pianist as far as he could, and in July 1946 Gieseking met with Dubensky and Karl Holl, the Hessian music *Referent*. Dubensky again asserted that the MG blacklist order would persist until Gieseking received clearance from a *Spruchkammer*, but he indicated that the Americans would not reject the tribunal's decision. Probably wanting to be sure of his facts, the branch chief then requested a new intelligence report on Gieseking's activities in the Third Reich. Circumstances suddenly changed for the musician in November 1946 when Clay ordered a revision to the Law for Liberation and consequently made the pianist's *Spruchkammer* decision subject to American approval. Apparently this worried Dubensky, as he had more or less given his word that MG would accept the German tribunal's decision, and he was determined to fulfill his promise. Gieseking may have eased Dubensky's conscience when he expressed his willingness to play any number of free concerts and even to learn the piano part in Walter Piston's *Concertino*. At the Berlin meeting of British and American music and intelligence officers in December 1946, Dubensky raised Gieseking's case and managed to convince the others of the pianist's innocence. As a result, his name was officially removed from the U.S. blacklist on 31 January 1947, which liberated his *Spruchkammer* from the need to seek ICD approval. Dubensky had been instructed not to release this information before the publication of the revised blacklist at the end of January, but someone did anyway. On 18 January 1947 the Hessian Ministry for Political Liberation announced that because Gieseking was not a party member, he did not fall under the provisions of the Law for Liberation from

National Socialism and would therefore not even be required to account for his actions before the *Spruchkammer*.[43] And so, in this sudden and curious way, the blacklisted artist was freed to perform in public again without ever undergoing trial.

Gieseking was, like Furtwängler, a collaborator and opportunist. But unlike Furtwängler, he was also impressed by Hitler and believed in the values of the National Socialist state. His clearance may seem to stretch the meaning of a term like "denazification," but it was nowhere near so scandalous as some. From ICD's perspective, it was the Austrians who again proved themselves the least willing to take Nazism seriously, and cases like Karajan's and Böhm's demonstrated how leniently cultural figures were to be treated. The Intelligence Section considered Karl Böhm one of the most "ardent" Nazi supporters among the leading conductors of the Third Reich. Böhm was not a party member, but he frequently conducted at Nazi ceremonies and joined the Kampfbund für deutsche Kultur in 1933. Böhm received several honors in the Reich, including a professorship (bestowed in 1938) and the Martial Order of Merit (awarded in 1933). He succeeded the conductor Fritz Busch at the Dresden Opera, after political demonstrations forced the latter from his post. One contemporary report of the events described the succession possibly falsely, but in a manner that conveyed the common perception of the choreography behind it: "[T]he orchestra members [incited by those in the *Kampfbund*] . . . staged a demonstration against Busch shortly before a concert. After Busch left, Böhm conveniently stepped from the wings in white tie and full dress to take the podium." Although he maintained high standards in Dresden, he was relatively unhappy there, and in 1943 he was transferred to Vienna where he was awarded the music directorship of the Staatsoper.[44]

But it was Böhm's writings that really convinced the Allies of his Nazi sympathies. He wrote letters to Hans Hinkel, the secretary of the RKK, in which "he professed to be a faithful and good Nazi" and made statements to the press in 1938 approving of the Anschluss and expressing utter confidence in "his" Führer. In one autobiographical sketch, he recalled the "unforgettable experience" of watching the "Brown Columns of Adolf Hitler" marching on the Feldherrnhalle in November 1923 and witnessing "the first blood shed for the idea; an idea which triumphed after all." On another occasion he declared his pleasure that "purely artistic experiments, which are opposed to the community's feelings, have been eliminated in the general foundation of our ideology." And at another time he proclaimed: "I recognize only National Socialist performance principles and according to them I carry out all my relations with [Opera] members and organizers. The new regime, and before that our Führer himself, have so often revealed its cultural will that we no longer have to fear for the future of the theater. More than anyone, I, who saw how our most sacred cultural possessions were previously traded in the political cattle-market, am filled with a special feeling of happiness."[45]

Böhm first applied to resume his duties in Vienna in May 1945, but he was prevented from doing so until cleared by an Austrian tribunal. In December 1945 he applied for denazification in Salzburg and was cleared by the Austrian Commission for the Political Investigation of Artists. Once again, ISB revealed its poor judgment, and the Music Section approved the Austrian decision. Margot Pinter, Vienna's music officer, met with city and ministry officials and all but promised the conductor the leadership of the municipal orchestra, the Vienna Symphony. The Soviets were completely hostile, however, and, as they had done in the Karajan case, "refused to even discuss Böhm's" until both Krauss and Furtwängler had been cleared. The Soviets were clearly driving for a quid pro quo with Böhm, whom they believed the Americans favored, being traded off for either of their favorites. But while ISB's officers may have been supportive of the conductor's rehabilitation, their superiors were not. In January 1946 the Kommandatura's Sub-Committee for Entertainment unanimously turned down his application for clearance. One year later Böhm again applied, and this time received the support of the British delegate on the Control Council, and Baron Puthon, the ever energetic organizer of the Salzburg Festival, took the opportunity to sign Böhm to conduct *Arabella*.[46] The conductor's timing proved fortunate, because within weeks of his reapplication for clearance, changes in Austria's denazification law made his exoneration inevitable.

Under the National Socialist Law, which the Austrian Parliament sent forward in June 1946, cases involving musicians were to be heard by a committee of experts composed of artists and cultural administrators appointed by the Ministry of Education. Where three committees charged with investigating musicians had previously existed in the American zone alone, now there was only one for the whole country. In order to facilitate its work, most artists were simply declared "ordinary laborers" and freed from the need for denazification. Music and theater directors, singers, and instrumental soloists still required clearance as did those who previously had been blacklisted.[47] But the fact that Egon Hilbert was the dominant individual on the denazification committee ensured that artistic rather than political considerations would predominate.

The new committee of experts heard some fairly damning evidence about Böhm. Several Vienna Philharmonic members admitted to having "heard rumors" that he sometimes referred to his "good friend Goebbels" and one secretary remembered him threatening: "I do not like this way of behaving, I shall report it to Goebbels with whom I am very good friends." The committee chose to overlook these statement because some were just rumors, and, as the secretary pointed out, what he heard was not addressed to the Vienna Philharmonic but rather to a group of party members in an orchestra in Munich. When confronted with the story that his wife had donated 1 million reichsmarks (RM) from her dowry to a Nazi charitable organization, the Spende Künstlerdank, which Goebbels had founded in 1936, Böhm responded that his wife had received no dowry but rather had inherited her fortune. The committee accepted this explanation. To the charge that the Reich gave him a villa in Vienna that had been seized from a Jew, Böhm answered that he bought the house for RM 70,000 and that at the time Jews were not allowed to own property. Only Böhm's many published statements, which the conductor had to admit "approximated" things he "might have said," gave the denazifiers any pause. As the committee explained in its final report: "It must be affirmed that Dr. Böhm did not always offer the kind of opposition in the print media . . . that one might expect from an Austrian." But far more important to Hilbert's committee than any of these trifling matters was the fact that there was "a dearth of Strauss conductors" and Puthon had already signed him for *Arabella*: "It will not be possible to call off the opera now since all notices and publicity have gone out and the whole cast is under contract," it was observed. Böhm, the committee ruled, had paid a two-year price for his transgressions and was now ready to contribute to the "democratic rebuilding of Austrian cultural life." In short, "Dr. Böhm's appearance in public would have a positive effect on the reestablishment of the cultural and musical life . . . of Austria." The maestro's final clearance was delayed slightly as administrators awaited the passage of the new National Socialists Law, which stripped the

Allies of supervisory responsibility over denazification; still, he was denazified in time to mount the podium for *Arabella* in the 1947 Salzburg Festival.[48]

As the clearance of blacklisted artists became commonplace, ICD took the final steps to end its experiment with denazifying musical life: it decided to eliminate the blacklist altogether. The list had been a rocky proposition for some time, threatened by the Law for Liberation and briefly annulled, salvaged only from total irrelevance by Clay's order of November 1946 regarding the veto. ICD efforts subsequently to entrench its list, by negotiating a quadripartite zonal deal similar to the one in place for Berlin, failed. The Russians asserted that they were not permitted to blacklist people in advance of a German tribunal decision, meaning that a U.S. blacklist could not apply in the Soviet zone unless the individuals named had already failed to be cleared by one of their own denazification courts. The only list the Soviets agreed to recognize was one naming those whom the German tribunals in the other zones had refused to exonerate. The British also maintained that despite bizonal fusion they could not blacklist an individual who had been cleared by a German court just because ICD refused to accept that decision.[49] Without the kind of agreement that could ensure the survival of the blacklist, even on a bizonal basis, ICD opted to cut bait.

In early 1947, the division's Research Branch revised the blacklist, striking from it the names of all musicians not known to have been party members. On 1 June 1947 licensees assumed full responsibility for ensuring the political clearance of their employees, and no ICD oversight was authorized. Further, the division discontinued all registrations of ordinary artists, including conductors, stripping itself of the "quality control" instrument it had so triumphantly negotiated only six months before. In the future, only agents, *Intendanten*, and private music and theater directors were required to hold an MG license. This action removed the last remnants of American control over the denazification of musicians.[50]

With remarkable speed, those most tainted recovered their old positions. The situation at the Stuttgart Opera is typical, but also notable, because of the initial strides taken to denazify that institution by its otherwise ineffectual *Intendant*, Albert Kehm. Kehm had done signal service for the Americans by energetically initiating the opera's denazification, but after his dismissal in February 1946, the program stalled. Acting upon Toombs's June 1946 directive to accelerate the purging of major cultural institutions, Stuttgart's Newell Jenkins ordered the immediate dismissal of sixteen orchestra members. Although this order threatened to utterly destabilize the opera, no amount of pleading from *Intendant* Bertil Wetzelsberger or any other administrator, could budge the resolute American. Although ICD accepted that orchestra members were theoretically "ordinary labor" and therefore under full German responsibility according to the Law for Liberation, at this point in time Intelligence still insisted that "the public position of such workers, and the fact that the [Staatsoper] has a wide reputation and is looked upon as a favorite child of ICD and the German Government, makes the definition of *ordinary labor* in such cases debatable." But while ICD insisted that all dismissals be final and immediate, the Kultministerium stalled, arguing that because it could not replace a position until a contract expired, the blacklisted members would be suspended but not fired. Realizing that ICD's position was no longer supported by OMGUS statutes, the ministry also challenged the Americans over the legality of their order in view of the *Länder*'s responsibility under the Law for Liberation. Six of the blacklisted employees were let go at the end of their contracts, but the delaying tactic worked. In February 1947, ICD had been ordered to discontinue its veto over *Spruchkammer* decisions, even in blacklist cases, and the division promptly informed the ministry that it no longer needed to vet appointments, even for the most senior positions. Although the ministry was cautioned that under the Law for Liberation it was still bound to employ only those of "positive political and moral character," with oversight removed the ministry discontinued the practice of firing people prior to their *Spruchkammer* hearing. Rather, individuals were now considered innocent until their guilt had been affirmed by a tribunal. By the summer of 1947, the Staatsoper had rehired all the former *Parteigenosse* employees it had previously dismissed or suspended.[51]

Prominent artists who had been blacklisted in the American, though not necessarily in the French or Russian or British zones, also made celebrated returns. It was all somewhat painful for the Americans as it appeared to evidence the foresight of their Allies and highlight their own harshness. The fact that the *Spruchkammer* hearing came increasingly to be treated as a formality only worsened the impression. Berlin Staatsoper greats, such as Josef Greindl and Tiana Lemnitz, who had been retained by the Soviets throughout the occupation, were let go only briefly in order that they might pass through denazification proceedings on Schlüterstrasse. The *Parteigenosse* opera leader, Karl-Maria Zwissler, who had been blacklisted by the Americans and worked in Mainz, was offered in 1948 the position of *Generalmusikdirektor* in Wiesbaden as well, contingent only on his obtaining *Spruchkammer* clearance. Some notable people, such as the conductor Joseph Keilberth, who had headed the RKK's music branch in Bohemia and was known as an enthusiastic Nazi, were able to avoid the *Spruchkammer* process entirely. Keilberth was hired by the Russians to lead the opera in Dresden, despite the American blacklist, but after 1949, with the official termination of denazification, he returned to his former Prague orchestra in its new home in Bamberg. Others came back to old jobs and ousted the musicians and administrators whom the Americans had appointed to replace them. Rudolf Hartmann, who had been *Intendant* of the Bavarian Staatstheater under the Nazis was reappointed following his clearance as Munich's State Operetta *Intendant*. Eugen Jochum, whom the Americans were determined to keep on the blacklist, was cleared by a *Spruchkammer* in early 1947 and resumed his career in Bavaria. In August 1948 Jochum was hired as the principal guest conductor of the Munich Philharmonic and a few months later was also contracted to the Staatsoper; through the maneuvering involved in securing these two positions, he was involved in the ousting of both Georg Solti and Hans Rosbaud.

Very few continued to pay professionally for their allegiance to the Third Reich. One who seems to have kept his profile low was the party member Karl Elmendorff. This conductor's career advanced smoothly under Nazi patronage and culminated in his appointment to succeed Karl Böhm in Dresden. Cleared by a German tribunal in April 1947, he accepted the relatively unimportant position of music director at the devastated Kassel Staatstheater and remained there despite several opportunities to move. Others exercised less choice in the matter. The postwar careers of the pianist Elly Ney and the baritone Gerhard Hüsch were haunted by their Nazi pasts. Ney, who was infamous for the National Socialist speeches she made before performances, was cleared to concertize after her *Spruchkammer* hearing in 1947, but because of her celebrity as "*the* Nazi pianist," the city of Bonn, her birthplace (and Beethoven's) and, after 1949, the capital of the Federal Republic, imposed an official ban on her performing there. This kept the Nazi era alive for Ney and forced her off the main stages and into the provinces. Only in 1952, after she publicly declared that "the Nazis had betrayed the German people" and that she had been "deceived by Hitler," was the ban lifted. Hüsch had been an ardent promoter of National Socialism at the Deutsche Oper in Berlin, and though he had never joined the party, he was closely linked to the regime through his mistress, Rosalind (the sister of Baldur) von Schirach. After his denazification in 1947, he enjoyed a respectable career as a professor at the Conservatory of Music in Munich, but he also resumed his career as a soloist only in 1952 (when he toured Japan), at which point he was well past his prime.[52]

Wilhelm Furtwängler made his own triumphant conducting return to Berlin on 25 May 1947. Although the Russians tried to hold him to his earlier promise and announced that the Staatsoper would host his return performance, they were disappointed. His first appearance was with the Berlin Philharmonic, and he led his old orchestra in the same music he conducted in the dying days of the Reich: Beethoven's Fifth and Sixth symphonies. An amused John Bitter noted sarcastically that, contrary to the expectations of many in ICD, the concert "happened . . . [and] it was an honest musical success, no political demonstration and the Philharmonic played beautifully."[53]

Four months later, Furtwängler conducted the concert the Music Branch was waiting for, a benefit for Jewish refugees with the American violinist Yehudi Menuhin. Dubensky, a friend of the violinist's, had negotiated Menuhin's visit as a way of showing the Germans that a page had been turned and that the occupation was entering a new phase. Clay approved Menuhin's appearance before a German audience, though he ordered the nonfraternization rule to remain in force to the extent that Allied personnel were barred from attending the concert. Nonetheless, for the Music Branch, it was a seminal moment in the history of the occupation: it marked the first time an American civilian performed before a local audience, it was a symbol of Furtwängler's rapprochement with ICD, and it was a public testament to the fact that the control phase of the occupation was well and truly over. Unfortunately, in the United States people were unaware of the changes that had, over the course of the previous year, so dramatically altered the character of the occupation. Many were shocked that an American artist was going to Germany to entertain the very same people they bombed just two years before. Even more disturbing was the participation of Furtwängler, whom many Americans considered the preeminent Nazi musician. As a result, the violinist had to endure the bruising insults of fellow musicians and critics in the United States, who accused him of absolving the Nazis and betraying his Jewish faith. Sadly, his brave decision to perform in Berlin damaged his career in America for years to come.

It was evidence that the bad luck that dogged the music officers in their dealings with Furtwängler would continue. Even though the audiences appreciated Menuhin's performance, they were insulted again and again by American heavy-handedness. Military police, out in force for this first local performance by a leading American musician, blocked entry to the theater and insisted on checking the passes of all those entering; they relented only a half hour after the concert was supposed to have begun and in the face of a huge crowd still waiting to be cleared at the door. Their partial sweep, however, had been sufficient to prevent a considerable number of ticket holders, including two of the city's most prominent music critics, from entering. Fortunately, the MPs had the good sense to realize, after extensive interrogation, that the senior Soviet music officer in Berlin, who was dressed in civilian clothes, should be allowed into the hall, even though he did not have a German *Arbeitsbuch*. To make matters worse, throughout the concert, the police moved up and down the aisles, asking for passes and ejecting those without the necessary papers. "This not only disturbed the audience and Mr. Menuhin but completely nullified the effect the concert was supposed to make," an ICD report complained. That the police then cleared the hall before anyone could applaud seems entirely in keeping with the tenor of the event. It was a rather inauspicious launch for the reorientation phase of ICD's activities.[54]

5 From Major to Minor
The Retreat from Reform, 1947–1950

Although most music officers were happy to see an end to the great purge, contrary to their expectations they did not prosper in the aftermath. For the first eighteen months of the occupation, revolution and reform vied with each other for mastery over ICD's program, but the end of the blacklist and the dismemberment of the Intelligence Section proved cold comfort for the moderates in the cultural branch. Instead of enjoying new authority, the music officers found their numbers reduced, their supervisory functions ended, and their influence eroded. New activities did emerge to occupy their attentions — most important being the creation of a program to bring American artists to Germany — but many of the old guard were uncomfortable with the change from conqueror to impresario. Now they supervised the allocation of licenses, decentralized government branches, imposed artistic personnel, and altered the performance repertoire. By mid-1948 they could do no more than comment on the unraveling of the policies and institutions they had forcefully imposed just two years before. Although they never agreed with the Intelligence Section on the need to overhaul German cultural life, they had exercised their power in the shadow of its revolutionary policies. They had not anticipated that their own influence would disappear alongside the revolutionaries'. They continued to warn, to no effect, that the pullback was coming too soon and that authoritarian and chauvinistic forces would reassert themselves within the German theater. Fortunately, in these dire predictions, they were wrong. Contrary to expectations, the German authorities chose to retain many aspects of their program, even in the face of severe economic difficulties.

The Theater and Music Section had no influence over the decisions determining its size and function, but its officers initially hoped to benefit from the shift from control to supervision. In July 1946, shortly after Clay announced that denazification would become a German responsibility, the section proposed a significant expansion of its field activities, branches, and personnel. Arguing that it was "critically understaffed," the section maintained that if "our mission [is] to guide the reconstitution of German theater and music," then "all cities in Bavaria" as well as such centers as Kassel, Frankfurt, and Darmstadt needed one of its officers. Unfortunately, instead of being reinforced, the Music Branch was instructed to make cuts of its own: three officers in Württemberg-Baden, two in Hesse, and two in Bavaria. By July 1947, the branch had been reduced to include just nine Americans. The reductions were vigorously opposed by ICD's cultural officers, who complained of their inability to monitor local activity and warned that because of the layoffs "this medium would in a very short time fall under Governmental control and the progress of a free cultural development would be slowed down to a standstill." But their protests had no effect; disheartened, many of those who had been with ICD from its earliest days—Clarke, Hinrischen, Bitter, Jenkins—retired from government service. In the summer of 1948, John Evarts was placed in charge of the branch headquarters, which was transferred from Bad Homburg to Bad Nauheim, but he was made responsible for the work hitherto done by three men. By the fall, five music officers were retained in the three *Länder*, and one supervised both theater and music in Berlin. When the State Department finally began to assume control in Germany in July 1949, only four of these administrators were left.[1]

The reality of personnel losses and their unavoidable impact on the morale of those remaining served to impair Music Branch operations severely. As early as December 1946, Jenkins anticipated that the projected cuts would "cripple" operations. Already, he warned, ICD was unable to supervise cultural activity outside the major centers and with a further reduction in personnel the process of "checking and [the] investigation of performances and programs will be rendered impossible." Newell Jenkins was one of the more eager and intrusive of ICD's officers, but most of his colleagues shared his conviction that music life "should be kept under strict control for many years to come if democratic ideals and ideologies are ever to take root." Edward Hogan, who had served as a theater officer in Berlin and Vienna, remarked after one official trip to Germany, that to think the Music Branch could achieve results with the manpower allocated "is madness, and I believe they

*John Evarts lecturing in the Amerika Haus, Augsburg, 1947
(Photo courtesy of Jeremiah Evarts)*

will find it out."[2] Even with the discontinuation of registration and the reduction in the categories of persons needing a license, a music officer's duties continued to include monitoring performances and programs, supervising the remaining licensees, disseminating American music, overseeing city and Land cultural administrations and laws, obtaining travel permits and ration cards for artists, lobbying for Military Government resources for cultural institutions, sponsoring local music activities, lecturing on American culture, and reporting on press and public reaction to ICD-sponsored events. An energetic individual with a reliable secretary, a driver, and a jeep might keep abreast of his work in one city, but it was inconceivable that he could adequately supervise the cultural life of an entire *Land*. The price to be paid for this was that branch officers lost almost all contact with artists in the smaller centers — the very people who in 1946 had proved the most willing to experiment with programming American compositions.

More serious than the loss of personnel was the diminution in branch influence. Though a subtle process and one that is hard to measure, this change was nonetheless increasingly evident to the veterans of ICD service. German cultural ministries and branch officers first sensed the reversal in the power relationship in the fall of 1946 when conflicts arose over licensing and appointments. Three factors precipitated the change: first, the *Spruchkammern* were overturning blacklist decisions and releasing prominent artists for employment; second, with *Land* elections scheduled for the end of November 1946, the various ministers of culture were anxious to show voters that entertainment life was returning to normal; third, Military Government decided that the shift from control to supervision should entail a diminution in ICD's clout.

Since the announcement of the Law for Liberation, MG had been redirecting its divisions toward reorientation and away from control. As James Pollock, Clay's deputy, informed McClure, the new policy would be "to give as much latitude [to the Germans] as possible." The change was implemented falteringly, but the overall shift was unmistakable, particularly following Secretary Byrnes's seminal 6 September 1946 address to American personnel in Stuttgart. In Pollock's view the procedure would be one of "telling the Germans what to do and letting them accomplish the action in their own way." Unfortunately, MG gambled that reorientation by example and advice would require fewer people than reform by control and supervision. Consequently, even those units that were best placed to exercise a supervisory function, such as Theater and Music, were ordered to cut personnel and budgets and to revise their approach.[3]

Clay, however, felt that he knew what he was doing. He was committed to the idea that the Germans had to learn to be democrats by wanting to be democrats and by acting like democrats. MG might install "the democratic processes and the guarantees of personal liberties which make democracy have meaning to the individual," but it was up to the people themselves to learn how to use those freedoms and rights. The best the Americans could be were representatives of Western democracy, models for the Germans to emulate. Clay implemented this policy across a broad front: through the Law for Liberation, through local and state elections, and even through the curtailment of ICD activities. For Clay, removing controls was not just efficient in terms of the manpower it saved; it was also a step in the direction of German self-education. "In the reorientation field," explained Clay's aide, "the Occupation Authorities have no power to legislate or direct and/or control the actions of the German . . . governments." Reorientation, in other words, was something the Germans had to undertake willingly.[4]

Figuring out what this might mean in practice was not easy for military men hitherto empowered to order people about. In fact, the job of specifying what each unit might contribute to reorientation—which meant defining the process itself—fell to each of ICD's sections. Over the summer of 1947, Benno Frank drafted a paper on the role of Theater and Music in reeducation, but because branch officers felt they had been engaged in positive control from the beginning, his report was more a summary and defense of past practice than a pointer in new directions.[5] What Frank did not realize was that the context of policy had completely changed. Where ICD's field officers had hitherto directed reforms confident of the guns that backed them up, they now found themselves in the opposite predicament. They were expected to model democracy for the Germans but, as they soon learned, they did not have the authority to insist on compliance. Moreover, with personnel cuts reducing their ability to even monitor local actions, they were incapable of keeping on top of digressions from MG objectives.

THE GERMANS REGAIN THEIR VOICE

For the Music Branch in Bavaria, the new policy assumed form, distressingly enough, at the moment it was trying to install one of its own in the powerful position of Staatsoper *Intendant*. The Americans had appointed the first *Intendant*, Arthur Bauckner, in the summer of 1945, but they found him unsatisfactory and had long pressed for his removal. In his place, they recommended Ferdinand Leitner, a politically clean musician and a man who struck the Americans as a forceful administrator with a relatively stable temperament. The only obstacle was the Kultusministerium, which was cool on Leitner, not because of his artistic or administrative abilities, but because it hoped that the Law for Liberation would facilitate the release of Knappertsbusch or Jochum for employment or make available some other eminent conductor. Complicating matters was the fact that Bauckner was a prominent member of the dominant political party in Bavaria, the conservative Christian Socialist Party (CSU), on whose cooperation in parliament the *Land*'s American-appointed Socialist president and cabinet depended. Replacing Bauckner was therefore a sensitive issue, and the Minister of Culture advanced the pragmatic line that if it could not secure a prominent Bavarian to replace the current *Intendant*, it would renew the old one's contract for another year.

And so, with the November 1946 *Land* election just two months away and the governing Social Democrats under mounting attack from the right for not defending Bavaria's interests, the *Kultusminister*, Franz Fendt, felt constrained to appoint a native son to the symbolically important post of opera *Intendant*. In answer to his protest, Fendt even told Evarts that "the *Intendant* of the opera should by all means be a Bavarian even if the man is less capable than a candidate from *Gross-Hessen* [meaning Leitner]." Theater and Music was outraged by this assertion of provincialism. It knew that MG had in the past taken a dim view of Bavarian autonomy and that Clay had previously rejected the *Land*'s draft constitution for its particularism. Evarts wanted ICD to foist Leitner on the reluctant Bavarians, much as it had imposed Solti and Rosbaud before him, but his superiors refused. At a crucial meeting with Minister Fendt in late September, the chief of the Information Control Division in Bavaria unfurled the new policy: "[I]n matters of State positions in Theater and Music," he explained, "ICD would simply clear the people politically and the entire choice otherwise would be in the hands of the *Kultusminister* and his *Referenten*." Evarts, who was at the meeting, was understandably furious: the division's "wishy washy behavior," he stormed, had "removed our power of control virtually at the high point of conflict, making us look like ineffective school-boys."[6]

Interestingly, ministry officials were now unsure of whether to exploit the American retreat. They were accustomed to receiving contradictory messages from Military Government and hesitated before trying anything unexpected in the anticipation of the decision being overruled. Unlike their colleagues in Württemberg-Baden, the cultural officers in Munich had never enjoyed peaceful relations with *Land* administrators. The Americans suspected the Bavarians for their conservatism, Catholicism, and presumed monarchism, and they were constantly on the alert for manifestations of separatist sentiment. Eric Clarke, the section chief, therefore advised Evarts to remind the ministry that the Bavarian constitution bound the state to protect freedom of expression and to hope that it would have some effect. It was a fairly mild rebuke, but for a Bavarian administration that was used to unusual scrutiny and strained relations, it was a reminder that a compromise was preferable to a confrontation. Seeking to accommodate the occupiers, even though they had not actually required it, Fendt decided to appoint Leitner as opera director and to leave the position of *Intendant* vacant. Bauckner, whom Evarts denounced as "vacillating . . . [and] unsuited for a post where clear decisions must be made," was named "Ministerial administrator and *Referent* responsible for the State Theater." Sidestepping the problem that he no longer had the authority to press the issue, Evarts objected to this sleight of hand and, just days before the *Land* election, successfully negotiated a compromise: the administration agreed to accept a long-standing ICD demand and create separate *Intendanten* for the three theaters and to separate the post of opera *Referent* from that of opera chief. But Bauckner was reappointed as Staatsoper *Intendant*.[7]

Although only a partial victory, the Americans were lucky to have wrung out a deal over the Staatstheater administration before the election, because the newly elected CSU's *Kultusminister*, Alois Hundhammer, would prove to them no friend. By December 1946 all of ICD was complaining that the "current program of turning over nearly all . . . responsibilities to German government" was in conflict with "Military Government policy . . . to the effect that German information services should be independent of governmental domination." Even more worrying to McClure was the atrophy that set in with the decision to rein in Military Government power. "Prior to the extensive transfer of various responsibilities to German governmental authorities, when problems were largely a matter of inter-divisional coordination, solutions were found with gratifying despatch," he informed Clay's deputy. With the onset of the supervisory phase and the containment of American control, however, officers "within [the] present policy framework" were finding it impossible "to concur in the taking of measures that go beyond those policies and practices." This incapacitating reluctance had already silenced ICD's Intelligence Section, which was at that moment refusing to give clear guidance to the Schlüterstrasse committee in the Furtwängler case. But other elements in MG were equally disoriented by the shift. No one, it seemed, knew how to implement the program or how much power to govern they still possessed. Many learned only in trying, as had Evarts, that they were almost powerless to affect local political developments. Morale suffered as officers realized that their superiors considered their work "a very low priority."[8] As a result of all this, a kind of debilitation crept over many MG units during the winter of 1946–47, a not unsurprising by-product of a poorly thought-through change in policy.

Music branches throughout the zone were especially disturbed by what happened to cultural policy following the *Land* elections. Nowhere did the conflict reach the same pitch as in Bavaria, but smaller crises developed with sufficient regularity to convince ICD officers that a widespread attack on artistic freedoms was under way. In Württemberg-Baden, for example, "a city mayor forbid [*sic*] the production of an American play. A Minister of Culture tried to remove a theater *Intendant* without informing this division. City officials forbid all kinds of performances simply because they did not like them, and other city officials tried to combine their governmental position with that of a licensee."[9] None of these were serious breaches, but the inability of the Music Branch to stop them caused frustration and affected morale.

It was in the hiring of formerly blacklisted musicians that local and *Land* governments first tested their newfound autonomy. Many government officers, for whom the blacklist was a nasty expression of victor's justice, doubted whether it was entirely legal to break a contract through a mandatory removal order. Ultimately, the hostility toward radical denazification was a sign that many Germans would not acknowledge the legitimacy of the occupation or accept that the Third Reich had been a culturally abnormal time. By reemploying formerly blacklisted musicians, governments were declaring symbolically that in cultural life it was the occupation, and not the Hitler period, that was the caesura in Germany's history.

Knappertsbusch's return to the Munich concert hall, for example, was a profoundly symbolic moment, a kind of vindication of German art and a condemnation of American philistinism. Evarts, who attended the maestro's first concert, may have denounced the conductor for the "outrageous liberties" he took with the score, but he still had to concede that "Knappertsbusch admirers were wildly enthusiastic about the eye-and-ear-full which they received. An apparently well-organized clique raised their concerted voices at the end with cries of 'We want Knappertsbusch back at the opera.'" Evarts recognized that the protracted cheering was a frontal attack on occupation policies.

The conductor's blacklisting had changed him from a potential symbol of German-American cooperation into a monument to its injustice and a focus of its opposition. Knappertsbusch's return to Munich, and Eugen Jochum's in the fall of 1947, not only provided occasions for the expression of safe and vocal opposition to the Americans, they also made illegitimate the positions of the incumbents at the philharmonic and the opera. As Newell Jenkins remembered, artists now began to come in for criticism simply because they were "too close to the people in Military Government. . . . They were [seen as] pawns of the Americans."[10]

Ferdinand Leitner was the first to feel the pinch and, having failed to secure the *Intendant*'s position and having no heart for the gathering fight, he left Munich for Stuttgart when his contract expired early in 1948. Solti remained at the opera, but a half century later he still recalled "the hysterical screams of approval that greeted Knappertsbusch whenever he got near the podium. Coexisting with him was terribly difficult for me." At the philharmonic, Rosbaud was also acutely conscious of the weakness of his position as political and press criticism mounted in early 1947. The election victory of the CSU moved cultural politics in decidedly more provincial, more confrontational, and more Catholic directions. Rosbaud began to fight with the city's music adviser, Dr. Königsdorfer, and to come under fire from the music critic at the influential *Süddeutsche Zeitung*. Once again, it was Knappertsbusch's hot breath that he felt on his shoulder, while Jochum remained in the shadows. In February 1948 the city, under whose jurisdiction the philharmonic fell, used the excuse of impending currency reform to cancel Rosbaud's still-active contract, a move many interpreted as an attack on the contemporary-music focus of his programming. Munich's mayor Scharnagl was quite specific about why the conductor was going, charging that he had proved unwilling to submit to the city and seemed to regard his authority as derived from elsewhere. Rosbaud, he declared, had refused to accept the appointment of a second *Kapellmeister* and resisted the idea of inviting prominent guest conductors (such as Jochum and Knappertsbusch) to perform, as people "on all sides" were urging him to do. In sum, Rosbaud seemed to believe that the philharmonic was "his orchestra" and that it should be "under his sole direction and answerable only to him." Cruelly turning American policy back on itself, the city now charged that because of the nature of his initial appointment and the freedom that had been allowed him by his MG license, Rosbaud was a musical dictator. A new conductor, appointed by the city and supported by the philharmonic itself, was necessary to restore "the democratic basis" of music life. Luckily for Rosbaud, he had the luxury of another job offer and, choosing flight over submission, moved off to become the director of the Südwestfunk orchestra in the French zone.[11]

Of all the American appointees in Bavaria, Solti hung on the longest. With the election of the CSU, however, his position was also in continual question. His main rival was not really Knappertsbusch, whom state officials regarded as too wayward for the position of opera director, but Jochum. As a now almost helpless Evarts editorialized in the summer of 1947, "the threat of Jochum is like a sword of Damocles over the head of Solti." But the young conductor was not without assets: relative to other leading conductors, he was exceptionally low paid; was extremely dynamic as a performer; was already highly regarded outside of Munich; had several local supporters, including *Ministerpräsident* Hans Ehard; and, most important, he was a Jew. The CSU's new fine arts adviser, Dieter Sattler, acknowledged the peculiarities of his case and asked John Evarts to attend the contract negotiations he initiated in June 1947. Sattler, who was a close friend of Jochum's, wanted the Hungarian gone but felt he had to make him leave voluntarily. Consequently, he appealed to Solti's humanity and his ego, emphasizing Jochum's "wish for a return to his Bavarian roots," while maintaining that the young conductor was far too good to feel fulfilled in place like Munich. Jochum "as a Bavarian" would, he said, remain in the city through thick and thin, but one could not ask the same of Solti who, as a gifted young foreigner, would doubtless "not want to remain in Munich during the coming hard times." For this reason, Sattler continued coyly, "it would not be right to hold him to a contract if his heart were not in it. . . . The fact that Solti is a Jew," the *Kultusreferent* concluded, and "he feels a special obligation to Jews, only adds to his feelings." Mayor Scharnagl echoed these points, insisting that "since they must reckon on Solti either in the long or short run quitting Munich, it would be better to find someone now who through their personal relations with Munich and Bavaria had a special interest in the Staatsoper." The music officer, by this time, could offer Solti nothing except moral support, but the young conductor had nowhere to go, and, as Carl Orff reminded Sattler, the Kultusministerium could not force him out because the world would denounce them as anti-Semites. As a result, Solti survived, and his contract was renewed in August 1948. Jochum, however, was installed as principal guest conductor at the same salary for his fifteen performances that Solti was earning for sixty-two. The 1949–50 season saw Jochum further maneuvered into the heart of the opera when it was decided that he would be appointed to Leitner's old position of music director, with Solti continuing as opera conductor. Now desperate and unhappy, Solti grabbed at the first passing offer and in the fall of 1951 accepted the "demotion and punishment" of a move to Frankfurt.[12]

Although the threat to Sergiu Celibidache, the American-appointed conductor of the Berlin Philharmonic, was greater than that facing his counterparts in Munich, he also kept his job through to the end of the occupation period. For one of the world's most renowned orchestras, the Berlin Philharmonic had a singularly unstable history. A private orchestra for its first years, the BPO had been forced to sacrifice majority share control to the city only during the inflationary crisis following World War I. For the next ten years it operated as a quasi-independent ensemble — self-governing but with voting control resting in the hands of the municipality — until finally nationalized and placed under Propaganda Ministry direction in 1934.[13] In 1945 its status reversed again when the city, under Russian orders, assumed full legal and financial responsibility. After the war, it was the municipality that fixed rates of pay, supervised the schedule, paid the bills, and hired the musicians. This proved a happy turn of affairs for Sergiu Celibidache, because it was the city that bowed to American pressure and offered him a one-year contract in January 1946. But the young conductor was not so fortunate when the time came to renew his contract, because those negotiations coincided with Wilhelm Furtwängler's passage through denazification.

The orchestra wanted Furtwängler, which may explain why its members proposed a vote at this moment to declare themselves a limited-liability corporation. Ownership of the orchestra by the musicians would subvert any effort to press another conductor upon them and would allow members to bypass the well-known American hostility to their former leader. The city government, however, was divided over recognizing the philharmonic's action. The Finance Department was opposed to outright privatization on the grounds that the orchestra would continue to need a municipal subvention, and someone had to manage the purse strings. As an alternative to privatization, the Finance Department favored restoring the philharmonic to its Weimar period constitution. Several senators, in the meantime, hoped to transform the BPO into a municipally owned orchestra that might serve the whole city, possibly by relocating it to the Soviet sector. The Amt für Volksbildung, however, did not want another expensive municipal organization, believed that the Soviet-sponsored Staatskapelle was now the premier Berlin ensemble, and preferred that the BPO merge with the American-controlled RIAS orchestra. What possibly tipped the balance in favor of the musicians' view was a demand from orchestra members that they receive a 20 percent pay increase in order to bring them into line with performers at the Staatsoper. As the musicians argued, they were losing many of their best players to the Russian-sector orchestra because the city set their salaries so low. Cutting the orchestra adrift may have seemed an ideal way of resolving the various demands: it limited the BPO's influence by satisfying its petitions for corporate freedom. But the city's decision placed ICD in an awkward position. Ideologically inclined to favor privatization, the Americans were nonetheless worried that a philharmonic owned by the musicians themselves would dump Celibidache in favor of Furtwängler. Unfortunately, John Bitter's desperate efforts to pressure the municipality into unilaterally renewing Celibidache's contract before a decision was reached on incorporation came to nothing. What was agreed was that Celibidache's contract would be extended on a month-by-month basis until such time as the orchestra decided its future.[14]

After prolonged discussions, the BPO became a limited-liability corporation governed by its musicians in mid-1947 and promptly elected two of its own as its business manager and chief executive. The city, however, continued to exercise considerable behind-the-scenes influence, despite its acceptance of the orchestra's official autonomy. In the first place, Berlin "guaranteed" the orchestra's operating revenue, which meant that it would cover any deficit the BPO might incur. Second, it reserved the right to oversee contracts and season's programs in order to ensure "coordination" with the other municipal ensembles. Finally, it also insisted that it had to approve the programs and conductors for the seven free concerts the orchestra offered as repayment for its subsidy. In the end, the continued involvement of the Amt für Volksbildung in the orchestra may have cost the musicians Furtwängler.

Still hoping for a cost-saving merger between the radio orchestra and the BPO, city officials were cool to the idea of Furtwängler remaking the philharmonic into the city's preeminent band. Moreover, Furtwängler was expensive, and the *Magistrat* could not afford to reimburse him for regularly conducting the philharmonic at the same rate of pay that he was promised for conducting individual productions at the Staatsoper. Ultimately, the great maestro decided to return to the BPO as principal guest conductor, the same position he held under the Nazis, with about a dozen concerts a year, though his contract stipulated that he would lead the orchestra whenever it undertook foreign tours. This arrangement allowed him the freedom to rebuild his reputation internationally while ensuring him a stable German income; it also liberated him from the need to work closely with the Americans, whom he still mistrusted.[15]

Several other factors now played into Celibidache's hand. Luckily, Furtwängler warmed to him and the young conductor was sensible enough to treat his senior with the deference he expected. In addition, the BPO was still performing in the Titania Palast, an art deco movie theater that was fully under MG control. The philharmonic rented this facility from the occupation government for much less than it would have any other hall, an indirect subsidy that the orchestra could ill afford to surrender. The Americans even undertook, at their own expense, a major renovation of the Palast, which greatly improved its comfort and appearance, if not its cramped stage or inadequate staff rooms. On top of all this, Celibidache's annual salary was the equivalent of what Furtwängler got for two concerts, an advantage that was hard to ignore. And so, the young Romanian was reelected chief conductor by the BPO, though in Furtwängler's opinion he hardly deserved the title since so many of the orchestra's concerts were conducted by other people.[16] In artistic terms, the orchestra had made a sound choice, even if Celibidache's survival was linked to the Americans just as surely as was Furtwängler's reluctance to reestablish himself in Berlin.

Of course, because of their ownership of the Titania Palast, the Americans were uniquely important to the BPO and could influence Celibidache's reappointment. In other parts of the American zone, conductors and artists were not so lucky. Everywhere *Parteigenosse* musicians were slipping from the blacklist and supplanting those installed or promoted by Information Control. In Stuttgart, the American-appointed conductor of the philharmonic, Hermann Hildebrand, was ousted in favor of the recently denazified Willem van Hoogstraten, the husband of Elly Ney, and the conductor from 1938 to 1945 of the Mozarteum Orchestra in Salzburg. In Kassel, Richard Kotz, whom ICD had installed as *Generalmusikdirektor* at the opera, lost his job to the former party member Karl Elmendorff.[17] Music Branch officers condemned these machinations, but local politicians and many concertgoers saw the removal of the occupation's appointees as a sign of life returning to normal. In fact, for some postwar politicians music was the "crystallization point" of the entire recovery process, an encapsulation of both reconstruction and restoration. What bothered ICD's officers was that so many Germans seemed to conceive of reconstruction in physical terms and of restoration as the real spiritual challenge.[18]

The disintegration of ICD's revolution was especially galling for Robert McClure. After he left Germany in May 1947 to assume the leadership of the New York field office of the army's Civil Affairs Division, his new post kept him in charge of coordinating the programs of his former division, but he was no longer responsible for implementing policy or directing units. The heart of ICD's challenge to Clay's program of reorientation was thereby stilled. Although he had been defeated in Germany, McClure remained unreconciled to the new course and continued to maintain that Clay had made a mistake in restoring German self-government so quickly. As he told the army newspaper, *Stars and Stripes*, in the summer of 1947, because the Germans "have no confidence in their own government officers," it was preposterous to hand authority over to them. The former commander was especially disturbed by the newly elected governments' assault on the programs his division had implemented. It was proof to him that democracy had failed to take root in Germany and that the country was being allowed to revert to authoritarianism. Sensitive to the fact that people, in difficult times, become nostalgic and that regimes were prone to use culture as an instrument of legitimation, he complained that from his perspective it was impossible to "teach the Germans democracy or any other ideology as long as they were starving under that ideology." At the very least, Military Government "should be running things until they get on their feet."[19]

There was, however, little either McClure or the officers remaining in Germany could do as the forces of resistance to ICD's program gathered strength. And when the Western Allies pressed forward with currency reform in June 1948, the reactionary current appeared unstoppable. Now *Land* and municipal governments were pressured into becoming even more intrusive in arts management in order to control costs and boost sagging ticket sales. In so doing, they threatened to undermine the entire edifice of entrenched cultural freedoms. In the meantime, audiences grew more inclined to shy away from unfamiliar or less popular works and to use their entertainment budget to hear pieces and performers they knew they liked. If unchecked, the consequent narrowing range of musical tastes promised to destroy the American program of repertoire diversification. There was no point, after all, in convincing musicians to perform American or previously banned works if no one went out to hear them. But no matter how loudly ICD's music officers complained, they seemed powerless to prevent it.

THE IMPACT OF CURRENCY REFORM

Since the end of the war, the occupation governments had maintained artificial caps on living costs through comprehensive wage and price controls. In theory, carefully rationed goods were kept cheap and wages low in the hopes of managing the allocation of resources in a mangled country shorn of a third of its industrial capacity and saddled with debilitating reparation payments. But the success of wage and price controls depended on the ability of the Allies to harmonize the supply of goods and money, something they were unable to do. During the war, the Nazis printed vast quantities of reichsmarks (RM), most of which remained in circulation. It was a problem the Allies only compounded by oversupplying their territories with military marks. With four administrations each pursuing individual economic goals, there was no way of controlling the money supply or even finding out how much cash was in circulation. The natural consequence of this surplus was inflation, but rising prices could not find their outlet in the regulated marketplace. And so the black market flourished; goods at official prices disappeared from stores only to reappear at several times their official cost in the back streets and market stalls; industrial productivity collapsed because it was senseless working hard for worthless money at low rates of pay; and absenteeism became rampant. With alarming rapidity, the black market supplanted the official economy as the real arena of commercial activity. For many, bartered goods came to replace cash as the instrument of exchange, and the "cigarette economy" emerged. Millions of Germans found that the only way they could obtain food was to travel out into the country and trade what they owned with farmers for potatoes and meat. Tragically, while black-market traders and many farmers were "rolling in ease," much of the population was forced to divest itself of any remaining possessions.[20]

As early as the summer of 1946 the Americans were grappling with the problem of controlling the runaway black-market economy. What they resolved was to remove Germany's devalued currency from circulation and to replace it with an instrument that better reflected the country's productive capability. As this solution would require the removal of most wage and price controls, the phasing out of rationing, and the coordination of the finance sector by all four military administrations, it was opposed by the Russians. By the time the Soviets modified their position and accepted key features of the OMGUS proposal, the Western Allies had grown tired of their obstructionism. The United States and Great Britain decided to go it alone.

Early in 1948 Control Council discussions became acrimonious with the Soviets charging, correctly as it turns out, that currency reform was a contrivance for dividing Germany. Ultimately, the French reluctantly accepted their Allies' plan for currency reform, but the Russians did not. In June 1948 the old reichsmark was withdrawn in the three western zones and exchanged for the new deutsche mark (DM) at a ratio of 10:1. The immediate shock was terrible: those with cash savings were wiped out and prices soared. Almost overnight, goods disappeared from shops and started to reappear only a few weeks later, but at prices much higher than previous official ones and even than those that had prevailed on the black market. "The old money was worthless," noted one American officer, "but so is this! . . . Real misery is cropping up on a large scale. . . . No one has anything to buy or pay with. A streetcar ride costs ¼ of your whole fortune. God knows how anyone can buy a meal." It took many months for prices and wages to stabilize and during that time the people suffered grievously. As had been expected, the impact of monetary conversion was no less severe politically than economically: the introduction of the deutsche mark induced the Soviets to walk out of the Quadripartite Control Council, blockade Berlin, and accept the country's division into two separate economic entities.[21]

It all made for hard times in the arts. Under the cigarette economy, when money was cheap, people had the resources to attend the theater. Concert tickets were price-controlled and, unlike commodities, were not subject to black-market inflation. As a result, ticket prices were laughably low, and theaters were permanently sold out; goods, not culture, were in short supply. What currency reform did immediately was to make a night out an expensive luxury. People whose savings had been eliminated and who were facing rapid inflation were naturally disinclined to spend money on entertainment. In June 1948 ticket sales collapsed — only four tickets, for example, to the Bavarian Staatsoper's *Die Zauberflöte* on 22 June were sold between the introduction of currency reform and the night of the performance. Then, as wages rose and goods reappeared in shops, consumers began "buying shoes, kitchen utensils, furniture rather than theater and concert tickets." The loss in revenue was felt immediately, because theaters were required to pay bills in deutsche marks with money earnings and subsidies paid in reichsmarks. "The costs of performances are the same," the music officer in Munich reported, "but no one has money to buy a ticket & even if every seat at the opera were sold they wouldn't have enough to pay for a good drum roll from the orchestra." The private theaters were especially hard hit by currency reform, and a "near panic" swept through the sector as dozens closed down and many more survived only by pooling resources. According to one report, 350 private theaters closed in western Germany in the year following currency conversion. The American policy of "over-stocking the country on licensed entertainment, provoking strong competition," had apparently backfired.[22]

For private organizations that were receiving state subsidies, survival depended on increased funding. By December 1948 Karl Münchinger, the director of the celebrated Stuttgarter Kammerorchester, wrote that his ensemble would disband if its government subsidy was not raised from DM 1,800 a month to DM 5,000. By 1953, the orchestra was completely reliant on the monthly subvention of DM 8,000 it received from the two levels of government. Dependency came at a cost, however, as the members of the Berlin Philharmonic learned. The BPO's municipal grant in 1947–48 was RM 350,000; by 1950 it needed DM 1.1 million to cover expenses and was under intense pressure from the city to reduce costs and boost attendance. The management of the philharmonic insisted that it needed a new and bigger concert hall if it were to pull in the crowds necessary to reduce its dependency on the state, but with an overall expenditure of several million deutsche marks a year on musical organizations, the city was hard-pressed to make ends meet and was unable to pay for the new facility. Furtwängler, concluding that another moment of crisis for the philharmonic had arrived, lobbied the newly created Bonn government to support the ensemble on the basis of its "important role in the rebuilding of all of Germany." It was, he insisted, the country's "best known and best loved" orchestra.[23]

Furtwängler, never a strong believer in private orchestras, favored the security of a closer tie to the state. As early as 1949 he was urging the appointment of a municipal *Intendant*, but the west Berlin's *Magistrat* was wary. Furtwängler was expensive, did little to administer the orchestra, and was seldom in Berlin; to have him testily pressing the city on its responsibilities seemed presumptuous. West Berlin's *Senator für Volksbildung* therefore urged him to take a year away in 1951–52 and further insulted him by proposing that his nemesis, the tremendously popular conductor Herbert von Karajan, fill in for some of the orchestra's major concerts. Furtwängler snarled that if Karajan was going to come, it was better to have him do so while he was around, and Celibidache invited his young rival to conduct a series of concerts. Karajan, however, was shrewd enough not to beard the lion in his den and declined to lead more than three concerts in the 1952–53 season. Instead, he took over a refugee orchestra made up of musicians who had quit east Berlin and led them on a Scandinavian tour. His commitment to preserving a noncommunist west Berlin was warmly appreciated in the *Magistrat*, and the chamber orchestra promptly secured a major performance contract with Radio Free Berlin, which broadcast propaganda into the Soviet sector.[24]

Furtwängler was in a tight position. The city wanted the philharmonic to lower salaries, but he feared this would drain off its premier musicians. There was no obvious progress on a new concert hall despite a campaign to finance one through donations, and it was clear that the municipality felt the orchestra needed to update its image. As a condition for continuing its support, the city appointed a director for the orchestra — something less than an *Intendant* but still a sign of increasing control — to oversee accounts and, more important, to handle bookings when financial issues were at stake or when "damage might be done to [the BPO's] reputation" through its choice of guest conductors. This was a slap at Furtwängler, who was notorious for never wanting to see anyone of stature (other than himself) on the podium of his orchestra. The conductor's old trick of offering to resign failed when the *Senator für Volksbildung* indicated that he would regret having to witness his departure. It took a memo from Bonn, in the summer of 1951, indicating that the federal government would be willing to subsidize foreign tours by the philharmonic, so long as Furtwängler continued his association with it, to help lift the darkening cloud. The orchestra, with city backing, now offered Furtwängler a lifetime contract as principal conductor; an *Intendant* was appointed (Furtwängler secured his old friend, Gerhart von Westerman, for the job), and Celibidache was let go. Although the BPO continued to be self-governing, the deal forced it into an even closer relationship with the city and made a municipal appointee (the *Intendant*) its corporate representative. These were hard conditions for Furtwängler because he liked Celibidache and enjoyed his own freedom, and it was only with great reluctance that he again nailed his flag to the BPO's mast. Sadly, he was to die just two years later and, as he had feared, Herbert von Karajan succeeded him as conductor for life.[25]

Not only the private theaters and state-supported ensembles suffered in the months following currency reform, as revenues plunged at *Land* and municipal houses as well. In Frankfurt, attendance at the playhouse and opera averaged 420 people per night in the fall and winter of 1948, while in Wiesbaden, in the deutsche mark's first month, the opera sold 4,500 tickets—for a theater with a monthly seating capacity of 35,000. In Stuttgart, in 1946–47 the Staatstheater had sold almost RM 3 million worth of tickets; in 1948–49 this same theater earned DM 1.6 million. In Munich, theater revenues plummeted a full 60 percent in the six months following currency conversion. Even though the cultural ministers pledged themselves in October 1948 not to raise ticket prices, by December they felt they really had no choice. In Wiesbaden, the ministry ordered an increase in Staatstheater tickets on a sliding scale, with the cheapest rising 5 percent and the most expensive by 10 percent. In Stuttgart, the opposite was tried and the lowest-priced tickets were raised most dramatically in the hopes of driving theatergoers into even more expensive seats. But no matter what was attempted, all theaters continued to suffer from poor attendance and complaints that prices had gone too high. As one angry theatergoer complained, he had come into Stuttgart for a symphony concert with his fourteen-year-old daughter only to find that she was charged full price (which he considered an outrage) and that even the cheap seats cost DM 3 each. Furthermore, he had to pay 25 pfennigs for a program. For his money all he got was a seat so high in the theater that the orchestra, pianist, and conductor looked "minute." The seats, he said, "were not worth it," and he was clearly not alone in thinking so: the house was half empty. It would be another year or two, he snapped, before he would again have enough spare cash to invest in a concert ticket.[26]

The great difficulty for the theater was that, unlike sales, costs did not fall with the conversion from reichsmarks to deutsche marks. Inflation affected most of the things theaters needed to stock, and wages could or would not be forced downward. Although Military Government had demanded that the *Länder* and municipalities not lower wages, they ignored the order. Salaries of orchestra players fell an average of 12 percent in 1948–49, and opera singers saw a pay cut of 17 percent, but even these savings were insufficient. Moreover, the reductions tended to be imposed on those at the bottom of the organizational hierarchy rather than at the top. The concert master of the Stuttgarter Kammerorchester, for example, who earned RM 700 in 1947, was paid DM 800 two years later, while the young *Heldentenor* Wolfgang Windgassen saw his salary at the Württemberg Staatsoper rise over the same period from RM 10,000 to DM 15,000. Some senior officials, like the opera *Intendant* in Stuttgart, took a 15 percent pay cut, but his *Generalmusikdirektor* did not. In other words, market forces determined rates of pay and the salary reductions were not born equally or by all. Consequently, theaters that were now desperate to bring in big names in order to attract audiences tended to see their payroll rise or remain constant rather than decline.[27]

For the state theaters, the sudden collapse in box office revenues was primarily a political problem. Since the majority of the larger classical musical ensembles were either public-sector institutions or had their operating costs guaranteed, a decline in sales revenue meant an increase in the burden on taxpayers. According to Württemberg-Baden's minister of culture, currency reform had eliminated the *Land*'s cash reserves and was forcing extreme economy throughout the public sector. In July 1948 he was already forecasting a "serious cut" in the subsidy granted the state theater.[28] But how could the government reduce its subsidy unless the theaters, which had up to now operated on a guaranteed-cost basis, agreed to work within a fixed budget? A *Land* or city might allocate whatever amounts it chose to the arts, but it was still going to be responsible for any cost overruns. And so it boiled down to a question of how effectively the government could pressure *Intendanten* and their directors into controlling expenditures. Information Control's system of structurally entrenched artistic freedoms and decentralized theater administrations was being massively challenged sooner than any could have anticipated.

Many Americans predicted that currency reform would result in a reassertion of the authoritarian state. The private theaters came under direct attack as municipalities, anxious over the competition they provided to public institutions, did what they could to suppress them. Some productions at state theaters were closed down by cultural ministers on moral grounds, and *Intendanten* found their freedoms suddenly restricted. New and modern works disappeared from the repertoire. In 1952 Fritz Rieger, a former party member who now filled the position at the Munich Philharmonic once occupied by Rosbaud, announced that he was all but eliminating modern music from the subscription concerts. The conservative public, observed the *Neue Zeitung*, had overpowered a half century of art. Rieger was extreme in trying to cater to Munich's conservative tastes, but only in degree. According to one *Kultusreferent*, it was important that opera houses continue to mount one modern work a year, in order to expand and educate public tastes, but to consider doing more would be financial suicide.[29]

Remarkably, although the independence of music organizations was limited by money-pinching officials, the structure of postwar theater management remained in place. *Intendanten* were compelled to tighten their belts, and state and municipal authorities did instruct business managers to slash expenditures and, by implication, reduce repertoire choices, but the all-important arm's-length principle survived. When *Länder* did try to assert direct controls over the theater, they found themselves checked by powerful and entrenched interests: theater committees, the press, strong-willed *Intendanten*, and their own constitutions. American principles also survived because many government officials were themselves committed to finding a democratic way of balancing fiscal responsibility and artistic freedom. Once again state power ended up finding expression largely in the hiring process, and the close management of musical organizations remained rare. The results were admittedly messy, as different solutions were tried in different places, but the overall pattern suggests a search for compromise and balance.

It might not have been this way. In the panic immediately following currency reform, Württemberg-Baden tried a dramatic invasion of arts administration when the cultural and finance ministers obtained cabinet approval for Ordinance 1031. The order granted government the power to do everything necessary to control public expenditures including micromanaging the theaters. In the case of Stuttgart's Staatstheater, the right to impose salary reductions, cancel contracts, and effect other cuts was vested in the hands of the ministers of finance and culture, while in Karlsruhe the ministers could act with the support of the *Landesbezirk* president. When the *Intendant* in Karlsruhe refused to implement a 15 percent pay cut and offered to resign, he was fired instead. Several members of the theater's committee, including the city representatives, immediately protested this action, claiming that they had not been consulted and that contracts could only be changed with the agreement of the local *Betriebsrat*, but the *Kultminister* ignored their protests and appointed a new *Intendant*, who just happened to be the son of his colleague, the finance minister. Although the administration clearly hoped the new *Intendant*, Heinrich Köhler-Helffrich, would be responsive to demands that he lower costs, he defied expectations by agreeing not to impose the salary reductions that had prompted his predecessor's removal. His justification for doing so was that the Americans had pointed out a loophole in the *Land*'s Ordinance 1031 that appeared to exclude the theaters from its provisions. Theater management quickly reverted to its previous character.[30]

The actions of the Württemberg-Baden government, while generating enormous controversy and publicity, did little to reduce costs. In 1948–49 the state theaters' expenditures remained the same as they had been the year before, just over DM 4 million, and the state had to double its initial DM 1 million appropriation. The next fiscal year, expenditures were even higher, and the municipality and state were each contributing DM 1.5 million to the company's support. Clearly, the *Land* had failed to contain theater costs, but it also, in the aftermath of the failure of Ordinance 1031, decided to steer clear of direct interference in theater management.[31] Like governments in Hesse and Bavaria, it would attempt to manage the performing arts through the appointment process and budget controls rather than through direct administration.

Of all the *Länder* in the American zone, Hesse was the least inclined to spend money on the arts. Where Württemberg-Baden officially subsidized its theater to the tune of DM 2 million in 1948–49 and Bavaria provided DM 2.5 million, Hesse budgeted a mere 400,000 for its state theater (although ultimately it, like the other *Länder*, had to spend more than twice that amount to cover losses).[32] Unfortunately, it inherited, through the 1945 reorganization of *Land* borders, three public theaters together with a municipal theater in Giessen anxious to be annexed by the state. By transferring administrative power over the theaters to the municipalities, the *Land* was able to shift primary responsibility for the funding of the houses in Kassel and Darmstadt to the cities and to limit its contribution to a fixed half-million deutsche marks each. This agreement left the municipalities guaranteeing all cost overruns, but it also limited the ministry's influence over the theaters to appointing *Intendanten* on the recommendation of the *Verwaltungsausschussen* of each theater. *Land* meddling in affairs in Kassel and Darmstadt was therefore largely restricted to trying to mediate between their *Intendanten* and the cities and unions as well as ensuring cost-efficient administration. This was not always easy, because the strain of financial hardship produced conflicts of unusual intensity. But the fact remains that in Hesse the competing interests of the various levels of government ensured the chaotic autonomy of the *Intendanten*, at least in Kassel and Darmstadt.

In Kassel, for example, the theater's committees, which were dominated by the municipality, successfully ousted the *Intendant* in December 1949 on the grounds that the productions were "tired" and the public was staying away. Instrumental in forcing him out was the business manager, who, the *Intendant* charged, had undercut his authority with the company. The *Verwaltungsausschuss* then nominated his successor, but the new man ran into difficulty even before the ministry approved his contract. In his first press conference, the new *Intendant*, Paul Rose, a former private theater owner from Berlin, predicted a half-million-mark increase in the deficit unless major changes were instituted. He then announced that there would be a shake-up of the theater personnel and a rejuvenation of the company. The business manager bridled at the implied charge of bad management and decided that the new man must go; so too did the theater's *Betriebsrat*, which was determined to protect the employees. In February 1950, with personnel relations in free fall, the *Land's Kultusreferent*, Karl Holl, was called in to sort out the mess. Since the mayor still supported the *Intendant*, Holl sided with Rose, calmed emotions, and urged that changes be instituted slowly and consultatively. He also convinced the *Intendant* and business manager to sign a protocol of understanding fixing their respective areas of responsibility. Eight months later, however, Holl was back again. Now, on top of all the earlier charges against Rose, he learned that the *Intendant* had hired his mistress to work in his office and that the business manager had been eavesdropping on telephone conversations. As even the mayor was fed up with Rose's difficult personality, the *Kultusreferent* decided that he could not and should not be saved.[33]

The Kassel case shows a ministry determined on mediating battles among the various groups involved in theater administration. Although the ministry could remove an *Intendant*, at least if it had the support of the municipality, it still had to respond to a number of other interests. Theater personnel, the business manager, the public, and the press all had to be accounted for in the process. One result of this is that even unpopular *Intendanten* like Rose could hold onto their jobs for years. This was even true in Wiesbaden, where the Hessian government exercised preponderant influence, paid the bulk of the bills, and was solely responsible for cost overruns.

As in Munich, the *Intendant*'s position in the Hessian capital was a highly political one and governments tended to fill the post with party supporters. Government power was not, however, unlimited. The theater committees, in particular, had been pushing for expanded powers for some time, and the *Betriebsrat*, which was dominated by the theater's unionized workers, had also become militant in the weeks surrounding currency reform. Fearing that the administrative committee would recommend wage cuts, in July 1948 the *Betriebsrat* demanded that all financial meetings involve both committees. This was rejected by the *Verwaltungsausschuss*, although Holl did warn his superiors that the *Betriebsrat*'s opinions were being too often ignored. In recognition of the need to involve different parties in the hiring process, Erwin Stein, the minister of culture in the Christian Democratic Union (CDU) government, agreed that the two committees would be allowed to interview those applying in 1949 for the post of *Intendant*.

What Stein did not say was that he and Wiesbaden's mayor had already decided on whom they wanted to hire: the son of their colleague in Württemberg-Baden's CDU cabinet, Heinrich Köhler-Helffrich. The young *Intendant* had already run into difficulty with the press and public in Karlsruhe, where he was pushing an unpopular merger scheme with Mannheim and Heidelberg. To Stein, however, who favored the idea of saving money in Wiesbaden by amalgamating its theater company with nearby Mainz's, Köhler-Helffrich's troubles were sweet music, and he was apparently willing to overlook the DM 1.2 million deficit the well-connected *Intendant* had run up for Karlsruhe's 120,000 inhabitants. Unfortunately, the Staatstheater's administrative committees were not so forgiving and, despite city and ministry support for Köhler-Helffrich, he failed to secure majority support. Stein appointed him anyway, to the outrage of the theater administration and the opposition Socialists, who denounced his actions as an assault on the democratic process.[34]

Stein weathered a storm of protest in appointing Köhler-Helffrich, and it continued to cost him. Although he had been named *Intendant* in the hopes that he might control expenditures, lift attendance, and keep the repertoire moving down a conservative path, with respect to all of these things Köhler-Helffrich again proved himself a man full of surprises. Unfortunately, for Stein, having braved the rapids in appointing the *Intendant*, he could do little now to control him without attracting public ridicule. It was another sign that, in circuitous ways, the democratic process was working.

Köhler-Helffrich's first surprise came when, after probing the theater and municipal government in Mainz about the prospects for merger, he made the spectacular announcement that he no longer supported the idea. "Do you really think," he told the press, that "putting two sick people in bed together will make them both better?" The new *Intendant* also attacked the *Land* government for insufficiently funding the theater, so much so that Stein came to deeply resent his press criticism. His worries over the new *Intendant* were stoked by Holl, who distrusted Köhler-Helffrich from the beginning and seldom missed a chance to criticize his administration. Köhler-Helffrich also turned out to be more adventuresome in his programming than anticipated and, among other modern works, mounted Britten's *Rape of Lucretia*, *Beggar's Opera*, and *Billy Budd*, Menotti's *The Consul*, and Blacher's *Grossinquisitor*. He also hired the young composer Heinz Werner Henze as

Kapellmeister and staged one of his operas. Anxious to make Wiesbaden into a *Kulturstadt* instead of merely a *Kurstadt*, he staged a major international music festival in the city in 1951 and took the opera company on its first international tour. An expensive and flamboyant *Intendant*, Köhler-Helffrich ended up alienating most of those who had initially supported him, but they could not afford to let it be known. His behavior did not, in consequence, endear him to the Social Democrats (SPD), who won the January 1951 *Land* election and considered him a CDU appointee. But even the Socialists could do nothing to oust him until his contract expired in 1953.[35]

In Hesse the ministry did use its power to hire and fire as a way of shaping the artistic and financial direction of the state theater. But the evidence also suggests that the government had limited power to control artistic directions once it had chosen to employ someone. Unless an *Intendant* was foolish enough to do something that allowed his premature removal (as had Kassel's Paul Rose), he was safe until the expiration of his contract. This was also true in Bavaria, but the ministry there still tried to involve itself in operational decisions, such as those relating to the hiring of conductors.

Although undoubtedly a legacy of American control and the installation of musicians the Bavarians considered foreign or secondrate, ministry scheming over the hiring of Jochum and Knappertsbusch and later Clemens Krauss resulted in its exercising undue influence over management affairs. Furthermore, the Kultusministerium in Bavaria chose to monitor developments in the theater closely through its business manager, Wilhelm Diess, who reported directly to the minister and not, as in other cities, to a *Verwaltungsausschuss*. Fortunately, Diess was a sensible and conscientious administrator and, although he was on occasion asked by the ministry to report on the moral propriety of productions, he was invariably balanced in his views. He took seriously his job of controlling costs, however, and this led him into a running fight with the theater *Intendant*.

In 1949–50 the opera *Intendant*, Georg Hartmann, proposed a *Spielplan* involving fifteen new productions. Diess rated this an impossible number in light of depressed revenues and the one-third reduction in the state subsidy since 1947, and he told Hartmann so. For the moment, the *Intendant* endured cuts, but the next year he was determined to test the manager's authority; instead of presenting his annual budget to the ministry, he announced his unapproved *Spiel-*

plan to the press. His program included two Catholic Bavarian works (Haas's *Tobias Wunderlich* and Orff's *Bernauerin*), one anticlerical piece (Hindemith's *Mathis*), and four modern pieces: a composite of shorter Stravinsky pieces organized into a *Ballettabend*, *Simon Bolivar* by Milhaud, Honegger's *St. Jeanne au bûcher*, and Orff's percussive opera *Antigone*. In order to block Hartmann, Diess now sought political backing for his position; in addition to consulting the ministry, he lobbied the city for support. The politicians, in turn, applied pressure on the *Intendant*. Ultimately, the *Spielplan* was truncated; only *Mathis*, *Bernauerin*, and *Tobias Wunderlich* survived the cost cutting. Hartmann's cut also came when his contract expired in 1951.[36]

Although the involvement of the ministry and the city in obstructing Hartmann's plans reveal that the politicians were not so far removed from the theater as they should have been, Diess was simply doing his job. In fact, the system worked as it was designed to do, with checks and balances ensuring the *Intendant* had artistic freedom *and* was fiscally responsible. The shame is that Hartmann was trying to expand the theater repertoire and public tastes and, in so doing, was continuing the policy promoted by the Americans. But hard times are bad times for experimentation and not just in Bavaria. Across Germany, modern and underplayed music was falling victim to austerity. With high costs limiting the number of new productions, companies felt compelled to revert to "shop-warm [*sic*] and cheap pieces." Furthermore, the public was now unwilling to pay to hear unfamiliar works and wanted pieces that they knew they loved. "Opera houses have played the standard repertoire until it is threadbare, preferring to repeat *Aida* or *Wildschutz* to mounting a new untried work," the American music officer in Wiesbaden observed; while in the concert hall, "the key to a full house is Beethoven . . . [though] Tchaikovsky is also sure-fire as is Strauss." Music theatergoers filled a house only when a big-name star was in town (which tended to push up costs) or when a production was particularly well reviewed in the press. Concertgoers, in turn, became highly selective regarding programming: "[T]he announcement of a work by Hindemith keeps them away in droves, even when padded with Brahms and Wagner."[37]

But the conservative trend in music making was not universal. Radio orchestras, such as RIAS's, tended to remain committed to the modern repertoire, in part because they did not depend on ticket revenues but also because people actually enjoyed hearing unfamiliar

*Audience at a Munich Philharmonic Youth Concert, 1948;
note the winter coats. (Photo courtesy of Carlos Moseley)*

works when they did not have to pay for them. Another exception was
the opera house in Stuttgart, which continued to produce unusual
pieces: Stravinsky's *Rake*, Honegger's *St. Jeanne*, Orff's operas, Hindemith's *Mathis*. The Staatstheater's defense of twentieth-century art
in the late 1940s was notable and exceptional, but it had limits. Despite
the interests of Ferdinand Leitner, the theater committees refused to
experiment with Henze's *Boulevard Solitude*.[38]

Although ministries and municipalities did try to influence the repertoire through appointments and budgets, it did not tell music directors or *Intendanten* what they could or should perform. Rather, a
subtle interaction of forces — the preferences of the artists, the spending habits of the public, and the governments' need to reduce costs —
combined to influence repertoire choices. The contraction of the repertoire was not, therefore, a sign of the failure of democratization,
but it was a tragedy for lovers and advocates of modern music. These
were unhappy times for the theater and concert hall, and the contraction in programming was as understandable as it was regrettable. But
the fact remains that only on a very few occasions can it be said that the
disappearance of a piece of classical music from a program was actually
attributable to direct censorship by the state, rather than to the informal operations of public tastes. Nonetheless, the censorship that did

occur, whether through market or political causes, was deeply worrying to the Music Branch, and its officers repeatedly, though unsuccessfully, urged a Military Government response. In retrospect, however, there was little the occupation government could do, short of paying people to perform modern music, and even in the most explicit cases of political censorship, there were forces at play that both mitigated their impact and ensured they would not be precedent-setting.

CENSORSHIP AND THE MARGINALIZATION OF CONTEMPORARY MUSIC

By the time currency reform was imposed, the Music Branch had lost almost all its administrative influence. No longer empowered to veto hiring decisions, the field officers had also lost control over licensing, registration, and postproduction censorship. The handful of officers who remained in Germany continued to report on local affairs and they bemoaned the constriction of the repertoire after 1948, but they could do little about it apart from urging or paying their German contacts to experiment with unfamiliar works. They often protested that the *Länder* were using their straitened financial situations as a justification for increased interference in the arts, but their warnings were ignored. Even when the states and cities attacked cultural freedom through censorship, the branch officers were unable to do anything more than complain. By 1948 the supervisory phase of the occupation's reform period in the arts had come to an end.

The most notorious censorship case of the postwar period in the art-music field was the cancellation of Werner Egk's ballet *Abraxas* by direct order of the Bavarian cultural minister in the summer of 1948. Egk's work, based on Heinrich Heine's *Faust* fragments, had been commissioned by *Intendant* Hartmann for a Munich premier and its dress rehearsals had been warmly greeted in the press. Munich's bishop, Johann Neuhäusler, however, acting on a complaint from members of the ballet troupe, asked the minister to look into the propriety of the third act, which featured an orgiastic "Black Mass." The minister appointed a commission, made up of Diess and the dramatic theater's *Intendant*, Alois Lippl, which previewed the offensive scene a few days before opening night. The commission suggested that minor changes could be made to render the dance more tasteful. Unfortunately, the changes failed to satisfy the minister who, after just five shows, banned the ballet from performance in all state theaters. Minister Hundhammer justified his action on the basis of Article 110 of the Bavarian constitution which empowered the State to combat "smut and indecency." As the *Land*'s cultural adviser explained, this was not real censorship as the work had not been banned in Bavaria, "only prohibited from being performed in state theaters."[39]

Military Government investigated the case and concluded that it could do nothing to overturn the prohibition and advised Egk to seek restitution in court on the grounds of a breach of contract. Interestingly enough, neither Georg Hartmann, the *Intendant*, nor Dieter Sattler, the *Land*'s *Kultusreferent*, were in Germany at the time of Hundhammer's action and both disapproved of the ban. The *Referent*, when he returned, proposed a new staging of the offensive scene and then tried to buy Egk off with promises to mount *Peer Gynt* the next season. But the minister was adamant and inadvertently undercut compromise efforts by circulating information regarding Egk's successes in the Third Reich. Still, while *Abraxas* was a victim of heavy-handed censorship, its banning came at considerable cost. The press was highly critical of the government, relations with the *Intendant* were strained, and Egk did take the Staatstheater to court and won sizable damages. Moreover, *Abraxas* became a runaway sensation after its Munich cancellation, enjoying 116 performances in Berlin alone. *Abraxas* may have been the clearest case of political interference in the theater, but it was also a warning to politicians not to press too hard.[40]

Another potential censorship case occurred one year after *Abraxas*'s banning, when the *Intendant* in Wiesbaden canceled a scheduled production of Paul Hindemith's *Cardillac*. Realizing that he was powerless to alter this decision, Everett Helm, the music officer in Hesse, gave an interview with the Deutsche Allgemeine Nachrichten-Agentur (DENA) in which he voiced his disappointment in the government, administration, and personnel of the state theater. The theater, he explained, was not like a private enterprise, whose repertoire was determined at the box office. Instead, subsidized theaters had the privilege and mission of programming works on the basis of their artistic quality. This, he announced, the state theater had failed to do. Far from trying to broaden cultural horizons by mounting "modern works of an advanced nature," the theater had catered to the narrow-minded. Helm then went on to blast the Hessian government for improperly involving itself in hiring decisions and for rating candidates' political credentials over their artistic qualifications. And he attacked the *Inten-*

dant, who also happened to be a former Nazi, for allowing himself to be swayed by the opinions of a few "cranks" into banning an important modern work; these same conservatives, the American hinted darkly, had silenced Hindemith once before in Germany.[41]

Helm's comments hardly rippled the political waters. The *Intendant* in Wiesbaden insisted that he had heard a significant number of operagoers would be canceling their subscriptions if *Cardillac* was on the program, but he admitted he had received nothing in writing. The opera had been launched in a school hall the previous year, and the reviews had been cool: there was a perception that interest in the opera was exhausted. The Cultural Ministry, in its own press releases, responded with indignation, observing that the only time it interfered in artistic decisions was when the Military Government asked it to find work for some touring American.[42]

Although it was Helm's job to worry about the role of the government in the arts, in this case the American's fears were not justified. In all likelihood Helm realized that *Cardillac* was not really a censorship case as his comments to the press offered a more broad-based critique of recent developments in music life. What really concerned the branch officer was his realization that *Cardillac* had been struck from the program because of the debt-induced dependence of the Staatstheater on its subscribers rather than on the state. This was why he raised the whole issue of the educational role of the public theater. *Bildung*, or cultural edification, had been an accepted part of the arts tradition in Germany and it was in its interests that the Americans had defended the subsidized theater's continued existence in their zone. For ICD, however, modern and international works had to be the prime constituents in music's *Bildungs* function. By creating an environment congenial to the production of modern works, ICD was trying to turn music institutions into instruments of reorientation. The state theater had a "mission," they argued, that was fundamentally "educational," and the definition of that mission they arrived at—that they had to promote modern and international music because they were "good" for people—was grounded in a conception of German theatergoers as arrogant and chauvinistic and starved of exposure to the cultures of other lands. This was why Everett Helm interpreted the cancellation of *Cardillac* as a reassertion of Nazi tendencies: it was an attack on the theaters' reeducational role as MG had conceived it. After four years of music control, the branch officer in Hesse still felt that the fascistically narrow-minded German public survived unbowed. Indeed, it was again claiming the same victim — and an American citizen no less!

Yet Helm might have admitted that the occupation's music program had never been so unidimensional. In addition to prescribing a course of modern music as therapy for chauvinistic Germans, the Americans always wanted to encourage the arts' greater sensitivity to public tastes. Music, they insisted, should be for the people and not tailored to the needs or tastes of the politicians and community elites. What currency reform did was to reveal the difficulty of reconciling the two objectives of democratization and reorientation; a public empowered by its poverty quite simply did not want to be reeducated. The trouble was that while ICD's officers knew what they wanted to get away from, they did not really know any better than the Germans how to change public attitudes without embracing the dictatorial methods of the past. If they had been honest about it, they would have acknowledged that currency reform in Germany had imposed constraints on the repertoire not dissimilar to those prevailing in the United States. The Americans had been lucky because they had exercised their greatest authority in Germany at a time when the people were still going out to all the concerts and operas that could be mounted. Consequently, the problem of compelling people to accept the unknown had not really troubled them. The German authorities, in contrast, had to assume full control when currency reform was keeping people away. How were states to continue to educate a public that chose not to be educated when governments were trying to control costs and theaters were increasingly dependent on ticket sales?

The solution governments reached was a segregation of the modern and the popular. Although all subsidized music organizations continued to perform some unfamiliar works, they became more incidental in the programming of larger ensembles. The modern and more arcane repertoire reverted to specialist societies that survived entirely on the basis of state support. The Internationale Ferienkurse für neue Musik, for example, which from the summer of 1946 met annually in Darmstadt, would champion first the music of Schoenberg and his circle and later that of Boulez and Stockhausen. The Military Government initially assisted the summer seminar with start-up money, even though the Music Branch was not pleased with the atonalists' prominence. Still, thanks to the energetic support of Everett Helm, a small

MG subsidy was maintained. After OMGUS dissolved itself into the High Commission, U.S. support was kept up, so long as the seminar continued to feature lectures about and performances of American music. Although the amounts contributed were small, American support was critical to the seminar's survival because it placed pressure on local governments to fund the organization. As a result, Hesse and the city of Darmstadt maintained the Ferienkurse with vital subsidies. *Land* contributions of DM 4,500 in the late 1940s were raised to DM 10,000 in 1951, but this amount pales before the municipal subsidy of between DM 50,000 and 85,000 per annum. Because the institute earned only DM 10,000 to 15,000 a year, it was clearly an entirely public organization. Government patronage of the Ferienkurse, as an "international institution . . . with support in American circles," continued in spite of recognition that its market was "relatively small and would remain so."[43]

The Bavarian government was even more generous in its support for such groups and programs as the Musica Viva concert series and the Studio für neue Musik. Like the Darmstadt Ferienkurse, Musica Viva was an early recipient of ICD patronage. In fact, its organizer, the composer Karl Amadeus Hartmann, had long been the Music Branch's favorite. He was an enthusiastic promoter of new and international music, and genuinely open to American suggestions regarding repertoire. Hartmann was also the leading local example of the "inner migrant": his works were not performed in the Third Reich, and he had survived through the kindness of his wife's family, circumstances that stood him in good stead among the occupation forces. After the war Hartmann became ICD's primary consultant on local musical matters in Bavaria and headed a number of MG-sponsored committees, events, and agencies. "Of all the musical people in Munich who deserve support from his fellow citizens," wrote John Evarts gratefully, "Hartmann deserves it as much as any." And in many ways, he got much more. Military Government rented Hartmann a hall in the Amerika Haus at a cut rate; Radio Munich, which the Americans controlled, provided Musica Viva with DM 8,000 a year for broadcast rights; and in 1948 MG started buying DM 400 worth of tickets per concert and distributed them free to students. Although the election of the CSU ended Hartmann's local political influence and bolstered that of his fellow composer, Carl Orff, he continued to be the beneficiary of public largesse. He had become, during the first two years of the occupation, simply too important to ignore or cut loose. The ministry granted the Musica Viva series an annual subsidy of around RM 10,000 before currency reform and DM 6,000 in the later 1940s. In addition, after 1950 the *Land* assumed responsibility for buying block tickets for students and continued the American practice of paying radio performance rights. According to Dieter Sattler, the Bavarian government did all it could for Hartmann because it recognized that "the continued development of international musical relations is very important from a political-cultural perspective and must be supported wherever possible."[44]

Even after currency reform, then, *Land* and local governments maintained their support for new and modern music despite minimal public interest. Occasional efforts were even made to test the extent of popular support, as when Hartmann was engaged to mount a big summer festival of new music at public expense, but the results were generally disastrous in terms of attendance. German administrators seemed content to continue backing small specialist organizations, however, even though they were not themselves interested in hearing the music performed. As Munich's Mayor Scharnagl sniffed, he and "the overwhelming majority of concert-goers reject modernity in music, and its polyphonal twelve-tonisms, will stay away from such so called 'works of art,' and will return to the concert hall only for the real classic music."[45] Given the public's indifference to the products of most twentieth-century classical composers, the validation the Americans provided to new-music organizations was probably crucial to their continuing existence under state sponsorship. But the overall American goal of using modern and international music as a way of creating understanding and harmony among peoples and of encouraging democratic thinking among the music-loving masses was nonetheless a failure.

In 1948, thanks to currency reform, mainstream concert and opera life moved in decidedly conservative directions. The big losers in the reactionary surge were not the avant-garde, which was already entrenching itself in the specialist organizations in Bayreuth and Munich and Darmstadt and Donaueschingen, but the "popular" modernists of 1945–48: Hindemith, Hartmann, Stravinsky, and Milhaud. These were the composers who fell on hard times after currency reform for the simple reason that they had not developed a mass audience. On the edge of public tastes, they were at once rejected by most theater-goers, who had limited money to spend, and by the real avant-garde, which regarded them as too mainstream. Administrators like Karl Holl in Wiesbaden understood what was happening, and he even warned the organizers of the Darmstadt Ferienkurse that if they did not avoid what had become a "notorious shrinking in their musical sources and consequent decline in their public," they could not expect to receive continued funding.[46] Sadly, efforts such as this to maintain ICD's dream of a popular and internationalist music modernism failed. Darmstadt and groups like it continued to explore sound worlds that offered little delight to most music lovers and ticket buyers. And most of the more-tonal modernists, who had never developed a circle of acolytes who would fight on their behalf for state funding, tended to drop out of view.

One of the central pillars of reorientation — the mass reeducation of the German public through modern and international music — therefore crumbled under the weight of the new currency. But other elements in ICD's program of reform proved more durable. Although tested and abused in the catastrophic years following the deutsche mark's introduction, the new structures that had been grafted onto theater administrations continued to function. As we have seen, theater committees did wield significant influence in many places and these helped to hold the *Intendanten* accountable to groups other than the state or municipality. In addition, business managers did accomplish their work as designed, and they served as agents for the public and guarantors of fiscal responsibility, even though many music directors found it impossible to work with them. Finally, politicians and bureaucrats generally accepted that the theater must be free from political influence. Public authority tended to be exercised through the hiring of senior administrators, but most governments refrained from micromanaging the music business. Freedom of expression was enshrined in all state constitutions in the American zone, and while the tyranny of the market did constrain it, politicians, by and large, did not.[47]

Artistic freedom was taken very seriously by most arts advisers, and there were some exceptionally good and influential ones in the late 1940s: Karl Holl, Dieter Sattler, and their Berlin colleague, Franz Wallner-Basté. These men agreed with the American music officers on the need to keep music and vote production separate, and they tried to walk the line between artistic freedom and political responsibility. As Holl explained, artists "are responsible for artistic decisions and are alone answerable for them." An *Intendant* did have to present his annual playbill to the ministry for approval and to keep his theater's committees "advised" on all administrative matters, "but for all that the *Intendant*'s authority cannot be limited." Under the Hessian constitution, Holl declared, "no one might hinder someone in the pursuit or free expression of their art unless that person breaks a law or does harm to children." Still, the Hessian arts *Referent* was the first to attack an *Intendant* who refused to follow established practice. When Köhler-Helffrich, as a budgetary measure, announced to the press that cuts had forced him to cancel a number of orchestra contracts without consulting either the ministry or his theater *Betriebsrat*, Holl was livid. Although it was true that costs had to be brought down, he stormed, the Staatstheater was "not only an economic problem child," it was also "a cultural and political instrument of the state" and "theater leaders should not be allowed to appropriate leadership in the public arena." In short, while an *Intendant* could run a theater as his fiefdom, his authority had to remain sensitive to political considerations. Köhler-Helffrich had provoked the ire of the unions and placed the government on the defensive with its employees, and in Holl's eyes this was overstepping the bounds of his artistic freedom.[48]

One finds similar contradictions in Dieter Sattler's justification for the actions of his minister in the *Abraxas* case. Although Sattler conceded that Hundhammer had been motivated by his Christian beliefs in prohibiting the ballet, to Catholics "there could be no culture without freedom and no freedom without roots." With this in mind, one could not really compare the actions of the *Kultusminister* with those of a dictator, he said, because they were grounded in widely cherished values. To Sattler's mind one only had to ask, "[D]o Bavarians want their cultural-politics based on Christianity?" to recognize that they do, "so long as the majority of the Bavarian people think as Christians and vote as Christians." And so, he concluded, "have we after only five years already forgotten what a real 'commado-culture' is and is it really possible to conceive of a dictatorship of the majority?" To Sattler, Hundhammer was justified in his actions because he represented the cultural will of the people.[49]

It was therefore true that even democratically minded politicians and administrators sometimes justified their decisions to restrict repertoire or dismiss people on spurious grounds. In its most common formulation, the argument boiled down to a belief that because the

voters had freely elected their representatives, the actions of the politicians manifested their will. Arguments like this are not uncommon in
democracies, but they are nonetheless disturbing, and they are especially so in a country recovering from dictatorship and without a real
democratic culture. But it would be wrong to imagine that it was an
easy thing to balance competing loyalties to art and politics. The new
German *Länder* were now in the position of having to pay the piper
and contain the performance without calling the tune. That a balance
had to be struck was something even Bavaria's minister of culture,
Alois Hundhammer, acknowledged. The state, he said, "should not
regiment, but should establish a set of *preventive conditions* regarding
personal and administrative matters in the theater. Only in the case of
nonfulfillment of these conditions should the state be granted the possibility of intervention."[50] Although arts administrators recognized
freedom of expression as an essential of democracy, they also felt perceived limits such as these to be necessary. At a time of profound
economic insecurity, German administrators had to justify their expenditures on classical music without exercising the public's right to
control the way its money was spent. The compromises they reached
did sometimes constrain artistic freedoms, but for music-making institutions, that was a modest price to pay for security. And to be fair,
the Americans, for all their democratic experience and attention to
infractions, were really no better in specifying how the balance was to
be managed.

What the sponsors of the reorientation program did do was to
identify the hypocrisies in the local politicians' excuses. They understood that censorship was being justified as the free expression of the
religious beliefs of a democratic polity, that market forces were serving
to undermine reeducational priorities, and that democratic principles
were justifying the dismissal of OMGUS appointees and the rehiring of
ex-Nazis. What they did not see was that the *Länder* were also committed to maintaining the priorities of their former military governors
and were trying to find responsible solutions to issues of great complexity. The Music Branch officers, who were not sure that the Germans had grown much beyond fascism, tended to interpret government actions they did not like as totalitarian attacks on the free theater.
They were powerless, however, to do anything about them. The very
fact that Everett Helm had to complain to the press about the cancellation of *Cardillac* was a sign of how impotent the Americans had be-

come by 1948. Short-staffed and shorn of the power to push the Germans about, the Music Branch was a shadow of its once potent self. Unwilling to deal with the undoing of their work, most of the branch officers had gone. Theater and Music's transfer, in late July 1948, out of the Information Control Division and into a new Cultural and Educational Relations Division was simply another sign of its diminishing relevance. From here on, the job of the music officer was to approximate that of a cultural affairs officer in the Department of State: to promote American culture rather than to govern German. For the music world, the victory of supervision over control therefore developed into a license for self-government. For the music officers who had been there from the beginning, the only hope was that the safeguards they had imposed and the people they had installed in 1945–46 would be strong enough to uphold democratic cultural principles. To everyone's credit, by and large, they proved to be.

6 Paying Guests
American Artists in Cold War
Germany, 1948–1953

Carlos Moseley greeted the twenty-nine-year-old conductor with bad news. An oboist in the orchestra he was to lead in two days had collapsed from hunger and the musicians had gone on strike, demanding higher food rations. Moreover, the streetcar workers were about to walk out, which would probably stop everyone—musicians and audience alike—from attending his performances. And there was more. The American music officer had to inform Leonard Bernstein that he also had no hotel to stay in and that OMGB was refusing to provide him with assistance. The official line was that Bernstein had come to Munich on the private invitation of Georg Solti, the chief conductor of the Staatsoper, and the Military Government therefore had no obligation to support him. Moseley, however, believed that the young American musician had been snubbed because he was rumored to be a communist.[1]

It took desperate scrambling, pleading, and improvisation on Moseley's part to get Bernstein onto the podium. With his own money, he paid an actor he knew with a house in Geiselgasteig to turn his place over to the visitor for a week. He then made "frantic" phone calls to the ministry, "pleading high and low to make more food available" to the striking orchestra. Finally, two days before the concert, the *Referent*, Dieter Sattler, called Moseley to tell him that the musicians had agreed to perform one night (not the scheduled two), so long as the Americans paid them 115 packs of cigarettes. Moseley considered this "a foul threat but reasonable [as] cigarettes can be exchanged for food." With a dozen packs of his own to start the fund-raising, he called everyone he knew to collect the rest. By the end of the day he had secured the bribe; but even as he overcame this hurdle, he faced another, when the streetcar strike was called. Miraculously, Bernstein, who had recently accepted the post of chief conductor of the Palestine Symphony, was in communication with the Jewish Refugee Committee in Bavaria. When the committee learned of his troubles, it convinced truck drivers from the two refugee camps outside Munich to spend the next days ferrying musicians to and from the theater. It was, Moseley reported, "absolutely unheard of, for the feeling between these two groups [Jews and Germans] is terrifying." But Bernstein was a symbol of the new Jewish homeland for the refugees, and they were inspirited by his appearance. He repaid their generosity warmly, visiting both camps the day after his Munich concert and conducting their small chamber orchestras to "howling, cheering mass[es]." Moseley rated it "one of the most extraordinary experiences of all my life . . . so moving and terrible in its tragedy that I had to hang on for dear life to keep from making an ass of myself."[2]

Moseley's efforts on behalf of the conductor yielded results with the Germans as well. It was, he wrote "a miracle . . . Bernstein, a young Jew and an American, stepped up to rehearse a grumbling, hungry German orchestra for its first rehearsal — in German at that. I was as tense as an E string with Menuhin doing a double stop on it. Within ten minutes his energy and personality and magnificent musical genius (a great and true genius) began to overwhelm the orchestra. By the end of the rehearsal the orchestra was cheering for him, by the time of the concert, they would have died for him." Bernstein felt it too, and after the rehearsal he wrote his secretary that "I have already had my triumph in conquering that orchestra." But he was wrong: the actual performance was received with even greater enthusiasm. So sustained was the cheering that the third movement of the Ravel piano concerto, which he conducted from the keyboard, had to be repeated twice, the closing applause lasted twenty minutes, and the conductor delighted the audience by blowing them kisses. The crowd lingered around the theater after the concert and, as Bernstein departed, applauded him further and "cars escorted him along Prinzregentenstrasse [while people] cheered." Bernstein himself was elated: "[T]he Munich concert was . . . a riotous success," he wrote home; "there is nothing more exciting than an opera house full of Germans screaming with excitement. . . . It means so much for the American Military Government, since music is the Germans' last stand in their 'Master Race' claim and for the first time its been exploded in Munich."[3]

Carlos Moseley had been in Germany for three months when Bernstein arrived, in May 1948. But the concert was his first real local success, and he hoped that "it has turned the tide for me." Unfortunately, it also embittered him against Military Government and convinced him that cultural reorientation was not being taken very seriously. Although Leonard Bernstein was already a star performer in the United States, and although he was the first American-born conductor to perform in Munich before a local audience, MG ignored him. In the hopes of arousing some interest, Moseley distributed 200 free tickets to his colleagues and superiors, but only a dozen Americans accepted the offer. Even Bernstein's rousing success failed to awaken the interest of the administration. A few days after the concert, the music officer hosted a reception for the conductor, and although all the important Bavarian artists and officials came — including the *Kultusminister*, Alois Hundhammer — no senior Military Government representative showed up. It left Moseley "cringing" with embarrassment and "fuming" with anger.[4]

Barred from military service by poor eyesight, the thirty-year-old Moseley had put his own career as a concert pianist on hold during the war and joined the OSS. He underwent training to operate behind German lines but never saw action; after Paris was liberated, he left his secret service job and joined OWI's Music Division. Along with so many other OWI officers, he transferred to the State Department when the information agency was terminated and from 1946 to 1948 headed up the Music Section of the International Lending Libraries' (ILL) branch of IIA. Even before going to Germany, then, Moseley knew a great deal about both American music and ICD's reorientation program. At OWI, he had been in charge of purchasing much of the sheet music that stocked Radio Luxembourg, and at ILL he secured American works for shipment to the Interallied Lending Library in Berlin. He recalled his years in Washington fondly and was especially impressed by the "colleagues of real calibre at all levels of authority" he found there: "dedicated, knowledgeable, eager to do superior work for the general *cause*." He found conditions in Germany very different.[5]

Within three weeks of his arrival in Munich, Moseley was incensed at MG, which he discovered "through its bumbling & through its conflicting policies & because of the jackasses who are able to play Big-Shot-Gods in the occupation, is the greatest stumbling block in the way of 'information control.'" Although he bore none of the scars of the struggle in 1946–47 to preserve ICD's independence and authority, he immediately felt frustrated in his efforts to create a meaningful reorientation program. As someone educated in the OWI–State Department philosophy of cultural relations, Moseley had a firm belief in the value of international understanding. American cultural achievements, and not just its military might and industrial superiority, had to be advertised all around the world in order to show peoples the worth and character of American democracy. Moreover, because international cultural propaganda engendered empathy and goodwill, Moseley believed it helped other countries understand and not fear American objectives and actions. "I so much love America," he wrote his mother, "and I can hardly bear to see it so misunderstood when it is trying to do so much more than any other nation on earth." German reorientation, in his view, was another name for bringing others to an appreciation of America's basic goodness. It was no different in principle from what he had been doing in Washington, although in Germany's case, it had the added benefit of countering the population's aggressive instincts. "The Germans & Austrians think they own music, lock, stock & barrel, think no one else even knows anything about it — aggravated race superiority," he wrote home. This was why revealing to the Germans the importance of American musicality was such a potent weapon in the struggle to destroy the remnants of their militarism, because "music is the ONLY field wherein they think they have not lost face. It is at this time THE ONLY THING left that they can glory in."[6]

Most of those who came to Germany in 1947–48 as replacements for the first generation of ICD Music officers — the Jenkinses, Clarkes, Hinrischens, and Bitters — shared Moseley's attitudes. Only one of them had served in the forces (as a statistician in a bomber group), only one of them spoke fluent German when he arrived, and all who had previous connections to information services had it through OWI or State. As a result, none of them experienced the division's original drive or its difficult second year, and all of them saw ICD's mission in Germany as simply one of promoting America's achievements in the arts. As they did not appreciate the extent of the power their predecessors had exercised, they found the treatment they received from the Germans confusing and funny. When Moseley arrived in Munich, for example, he thought the "reception in my honor was a scream! . . . I was just like Wally & the Duke making the rounds in Nassau. They were bearded & goateed, long & short & FORMAL to a degree you couldn't believe. If I laughed everyone laughed. If I was quiet, they were quiet." It was, he remarked, "ABSURD the way I am treated. The opera house practically disembowels itself whenever I come near the place. Rosbaud stopped the rehearsal of the splendid Munich Philharmonic yesterday when I entered the rehearsal room, called an intermission, talked with me (on business) for 15 minutes, & insisted on walking all the way to the street with me. . . . I sometimes feel like a walking shrine." The new generation of officers saw themselves as cultural attachés, representatives of their country's arts and letters, and not conquerors. Reorientation, to their minds, was to be the consequence rather than the method of their endeavors. Sadly, while they had the drive and imagination to be effective, they did not, in the end receive the tools.[7]

All the new music officers learned quickly that the occupation government had by now become a major obstacle to their work. Moseley was so put off by his experiences with Military Government that he returned stateside in just one year. Mateo Lettunich, who took over John Bitter's job in Berlin, found his superior, Section Chief John C. Thompson, an uninformed and impulsive manipulator. Lettunich was dismayed over the damage Thompson did to the branch's local relations when he tried to block the soprano Erna Berger from traveling to New York. Berger had been contracted to sing Gilda at the Metropolitan and would be the first Berlin artist to perform in an American opera house since the war. According to Berger, Thompson turned against her because she refused his sexual advances. The chief's eventual mistress was the lyric soprano, Irma Beilke, and he reportedly did what he could to advance her career while obstructing her rivals. As the relationship was a poorly kept secret, it did nothing to boost the Americans' questionable reputation when it came to fraternization. Lettunich and Thompson were soon at loggerheads, and the music officer later felt that it was his branch chief who requested a CIC investigation into his moral integrity. No evidence against Lettunich was found, but CIC tactlessly interviewed some of Berlin's leading artists and newspapermen concerning his sexual orientation, much to their amusement.[8]

But it was not just personality conflicts, parochialism, homophobia, and poor leadership that caused problems. Although the Music Branch's transfer out of Information Control and into the newly organized Education and Cultural Relations Division in July 1948 was a promising development, it remained a neglected stepchild. To work, cultural reorientation depended on money. Artists like Bernstein could not be brought to Germany, billeted, toured, and paid without significant resources. Most of the good musicians were booked a year or more in advance and so to tour them required advanced planning and a long-term commitment of funds. Concerts had to be organized, halls reserved, accompanists hired, and advertising managed. The same was true, to a lesser degree, of American compositions. Someone had to buy the scores, ship them, and then market them locally to ensure their performance. All of this took time and money, and without those essentials even the best-intentioned official could achieve little. Military Government, however, refused to commit serious resources to the business of cultural reorientation and left the program, like Germany's musicians, in a malnourished state.

MUDDLING INTO A PROGRAM

Resistance to using music as an instrument of reorientation originated with Clay. The military governor was a strong advocate of German reeducation in action and since 1946 had been pressing ICD and other reluctant divisions to accept it as their primary goal. He had directed the creation of the Education and Cultural Relations Division, armed it with a big budget, and later expressed his "deep conviction" that Germany would only be transformed by "the dissemination . . . of examples of our own cultural life." But to Clay, reorientation was something the Germans had to achieve for themselves, and while the Americans could assist and guide them, the locals had to be responsible for initiating and implementing the programs. The model here was the Law for Liberation from National Socialism under whose terms the Germans undertook their own denazification. Clay applied this approach most forcefully in the cultural sector and insisted that while OMGUS might model democratic arts organizations for the Germans, it could not impose them. This was why he refused to allow Music to overrule decisions of the *Länder's Kultusministers* and also why he prevented the branch from drawing on the regular reorientation funds budgeted to the division. The reorientation deutsche mark funds had been accumulated by ICD from newspaper and magazine publications and from the films it distributed. The moneys were then used to fund reorientation projects: in a sense the Germans were indirectly paying for their own reeducation. But while willing to authorize the expenditure of these funds for projects with clear political, educational, or economic ramifications, Clay refused to allow them to be used to promote American culture or to entertain the population. And he would also not permit reeducation projects designed to "explain America" to be charged to the *Länder* as an "occupation cost" (to do so, he felt, "is not only contrary in all probability to international law but would defeat our purpose"). In consequence, although Washington authorized visits by American artists in May 1946, Clay allocated no money to pay for their travel or expenses and asserted that if the Germans wanted to hear American musicians they would have to either pay for them or find some private organization in the United States that would help. Menuhin, whom the Germans paid (on the understanding that the violinist would then donate his honorarium back to the BPO), was therefore the only visiting U.S. musician to enjoy MG support for performances before locals prior to the spring of 1948. Even when, in the months before the introduction of the new currency, MG found itself with half a million reichsmarks it had to spend or write off, Clay reportedly declared: "[N]o musician would come on any of that money." Not surprisingly, those working in cultural affairs found MG's position confusing, and even the division's chief in Württemberg-Baden took the "lack of funds for reorientation . . . [as] indicat[ive of] passive interest."[9]

What pressure there was to use musicians as instruments of reeducation came, not surprisingly, from the Department of State. For over a decade, Latin America had been listening to U.S. "good will ambassadors," and the department saw no reason why Germany, whose need was so much greater, should be spared similar exposure. Sponsoring tours of U.S. musicians, the department argued, was a valuable element in "the long-range plan for German re-education . . . [as it would] contribute to dispelling Nazi sponsored views of American cultural inferiority." The idea had first been broached by OWI's planners during the war and became part of the State Department's inheritance in the fall of 1945. But at the time McClure was unconcerned about reorientation, and there were just too many obstacles — nonfraternization rules, prohibitions on travel, billeting problems — to allow for foreign visits. Nor was it possible for individual music officers simply to invite someone to Germany. In fact, through 1946 it remained unlawful for U.S. citizens to perform before local audiences without governmental authorization (as there had not yet been a peace treaty, it remained "trading with the enemy"). When the conductor, Otto Klemperer, who had become an American citizen during the war, crossed the border in June 1946 and tried to conduct in Baden-Baden, American military police entered the French zone and escorted him back to the border.[10]

But McClure was being pressed by both his field units in Germany and by some well-connected lobbyists in the United States to implement a program of cultural penetration. One of the *New York Times'* editors, Shepard Stone, for example, who had served in ICD in 1945, denounced McClure and his associates soon after his return to the United States as "misfits in their jobs." As he warned the War Department in early 1946, "unless measures are taken to remedy the situation, there is a danger that the program to reorient the German mind . . . will disintegrate." Already, at a quadripartite meeting in December 1945, McClure had learned that the other three occupying powers were going to lift their prohibitions on local performances by their nationals, and he agreed that, when they did so, OMGUS would have to follow. And so, in March 1946, ICD's commander reluctantly moved to mollify his critics and requested State Department authorization for the employment of American artists in German reeducation. As McClure conceded, the "appearance of a careful selection of artists in the US Zone would disprove the belief, consistently supported by Nazi propaganda, that Americans have no understanding for the arts and would combat the myth that German music is superior to the music of other countries. Because of the heavy emphasis placed on musical and artistic matters by German press and radio, the influence of artists would be expressed in all media of public information." The Department of State sanctioned McClure's proposal at the beginning of May, but Clay remained unconvinced and refused to authorize the project.[11]

With Theater and Music's proposal buried on Clay's desk, Newell Jenkins decided to take matters into his own hands. In May 1946 the section chief learned from one of the French zone's music officers that a wonderful young pianist, Monique de la Brouchollerie, would be performing before a local audience in Baden-Baden. Jenkins drove down, liked what he heard, and promptly invited the French pianist to perform in Stuttgart. With the help of Erwin Russ, the philharmonic, a conductor, and a hall were secured, and the first performance in the American zone by an Allied national before a German audience was heard on 10 May 1946. But MG was furious and reprimanded Jenkins. Never one to give way gracefully, Jenkins immediately invited the pianist back for two concerts in January 1947. But efforts to get an American artists program moving remained stalled. The branch wanted to launch it in September 1946 with Menuhin, who was performing with the BPO before allied troops in Berlin, but Clay refused permission. Menuhin agreed to return as part of his next continental tour in the spring of 1947, but this too fell through when, in February, the Military Government rescinded its three-month-old order allowing U.S. and Allied artists to travel in the zone. It was not until September 1947, a full year after the Soviets first sent musicians to Berlin and eighteen months after the first French tour, that Menuhin was able to launch the U.S. artists program in the company of Furtwängler and the philharmonic. And Clay accepted Menuhin's visit only because Washington ordered the policy change.[12]

The OMGUS roadblock to employing American artists in reorientation had therefore still not cleared when the matter came before the State-War-Navy Coordinating Committee, which replaced the Joint Chiefs as the senior policy making body for the occupied territories in March 1947. The directive the committee issued, SWNCC 269/8, was a revision to a year-old policy statement on German reeducation calling for a freer flow of people in order to end "the Nazi heritage of Germany's spiritual isolation" and to "foster the assimilation of the German people into the society of peaceful nations." The policy statement called for German leaders and youth to be sent to the United States where they would acquire a political and cultural education through exposure to life in a free society. U.S. experts and artists would in turn visit Germany in order to encourage local appreciation of America's cultural achievements.[13] Washington policy makers had been traveling this way for some time, and visiting experts programs were already operating in the educational, financial, and technical fields. But music, which was seen by most military men as entertainment, not uplift, was different. It took a clear statement from above for MG to accept using artists to educate and, even so, serious obstacles remained.

The foremost difficulty was financial. The military governor continued to object to visiting artists on the grounds that he did not want the program financed by either a mandatory MG charge to the Germans or by the American taxpayers. He had reason to feel this way. OMGUS had already run up against public and congressional opposition for softening its policies, and Clay's denazification program had come in for particular criticism. Furtwängler's clearance, which several prominent commentators in the United States considered unconscionable, also attracted an inordinate amount of negative publicity. Even Davidson Taylor, Theater and Music's first chief and a CBS executive, complained, "[W]hen I see the possibility of Gieseking returning . . . and hear about Furtwängler having great triumphs in Berlin, I wonder what role music can fulfill in the political re-education of the German people." So deep was the sentiment against rehabilitating German musicians that when Gieseking attempted a thirty-seven-concert U.S. tour in 1949, there were protests from veterans and Jewish groups, and the Immigration Service detained him pending a hearing into his activities in the Third Reich. Rather than face a reopening of the barely sealed wound, the pianist chose to leave the country, canceling his tour. The Chicago Symphony faced similar opposition when it proposed hiring Furtwängler as its conductor in 1949: not only did vocal Jewish groups protest, but prominent artists such as Anton Rubinstein, Vladimir Horowitz, Nathan Milstein, and Isaac Stern all declared they would not perform with the symphony so long as Furtwängler was associated with it. Unprepared for scandal, the organization's management canceled the conductor's contract. Even as late as 1955, Karajan was greeted by protesters when he took the BPO on its first American tour.[14] Since MG understood the public temper in the United States, it was unwilling to risk paying Americans to concertize before Germans.

This forced the Music Branch to devise a complicated and unwieldy plan to pay for its program. As Jenkins had shown in Stuttgart and Menuhin would show in Berlin, German concert agencies could manage visits, handle the advertising and secure halls, with their expenses being covered by the sale of tickets. The artists themselves, the branch suggested, could be paid in dollars if they also performed at concerts for American GIs under Special Services auspices (their pay would come out of dollar ticket sales). Under these circumstances, Special Services might also cover the costs of travel to and from Germany, as it normally did for the performers it hired. In the end, OMGUS would be liable only for billeting, messing, and transporting the musicians when in Germany.[15]

Unfortunately, although the Music Branch hoped to piggy-back its program on Special Services, the unit proved reluctant to share its entertainers or invite the kind of people ICD wanted. Consequently, when McClure returned to the United States in May 1947 to run the army's New York field office, he took over a visiting artists' program that still had no budget. In order to get things going, McClure ordered Harrison Kerr, the field unit music chief, to secure artists willing to visit Germany and the money needed to pay them. But Kerr, who shared many of McClure's worst attitudes, was a poor choice: short-fused, opinionated, and committed to the idea that American artists should go to Germany to teach the locals a lesson.[16] For Kerr, as for McClure, reorientation did not involve gentle persuasion but was a form of indoctrination: Americans would humiliate the Germans musically and knock them, once and for all, off their cultural pedestal.

Kerr may have had opinions, but he had no cash, and his one effort to get things going by having visiting musicians classified as "technical experts" and so charged to Marshall Plan funds was shot down by the War Department. And so it fell to a charming if somewhat mysterious woman living in the Berlin suburb of Dahlem, Beryl Rogers McClaskey, to find a solution. Officially, McClaskey was employed in the records section of the Military Government, writing a history of religious policy under U.S. administration. But everyone thought she was a spy. One visiting American pianist noted that she was popularly regarded by German artists as Berlin's real military governor and that she was "very close to Clay" (the implication was that she was his mistress, though this was merely a joke of the time). In Berlin, she played the role of the "doyenne of hostesses," and her weekend parties were meeting places for the city's leading artists. With access to a lot of money, she also organized a series of local societies, including the important Dahlem Music Society, which sponsored artistic events, often in her villa. Among her many "discoveries" was the young and brilliantly talented baritone, Dietrich Fischer-Dieskau. McClaskey was immensely influential, but as the visiting American sneered, she displayed the "steam roller like tendency of the whole opulent American middle class, to expand and flatten whatever it comes in contact with." He found it pathetic the way "that artists and musicians lick these bland official asses with every semblance of gratitude and affection."[17]

In November 1947 McClaskey took Benno Frank back to the United States to convince private foundations to fund a visiting-artists program. They returned with a start-up grant of $10,000 from the Oberlander Trust, which had been established in 1930 to underwrite visits by Americans engaged in cultural or civic enterprises to German-speaking countries, and $7,500 from the Rockefeller Foundation. This latter donation was kept secret, however, because at the time the foundation had no official program for sponsoring foreign tours by artists. It was therefore a quiet gift. But despite these promising developments, trouble continued to plague the program. Although the Music Branch hoped that the foundation's dollar account would be refilled with revenues from money earned through ticket sales to GIs, it never happened. Jealous of its turf, the army's entertainment branch refused to use some of the visiting artists ICD secured and the rest simply failed to attract substantial audiences. In Wiesbaden, for example, only $50 worth of tickets were sold to GIs for an American pianist's concert, while a harpsichordist visiting Munich attracted only $15 worth of business.[18] And so the foundations' account was quickly run down while the New York field office squandered away its slim resources, bringing in artists of such limited repute that few Germans, and even fewer Americans, wanted to hear them.

Of course, Harrison Kerr had troubles of his own. The money to pay for artists materialized only in January 1948, too late to secure really important people for the 1948–49 season. Moreover, some of those the branch did approach, such as the conductor Leopold Stokowski, canceled when he learned that Military Government did not really favor musicians' visits and would do nothing to cushion their ride. Others, such as the country's most exciting young violinist, Isaac Stern, was sidelined on Kerr's order because he was not American-born. Some tours, such as one by the Martha Graham Dance Company, simply could not be arranged on short notice. And Kerr refused to spend money on the group most likely to accept an invitation — German-born musicians — on the grounds that they would be seen by audiences as locals, not Americans, and would therefore do little to advance reorientation. This was a disappointment for field officers such as Moseley and Evarts who unsuccessfully pressed Kerr to invite Hindemith and Křenek and Schoenberg.[19]

Moreover, with limited funds at his disposal, Kerr was constrained to divert to Germany performers who were already in Europe and willing to work for next to nothing. In the end he contented himself with a series of unknown musicians: a twenty-year-old violinist, Patricia Travers; a young pianist, Webster Aitken; a university-based string quartet; and the Yale Glee Club. Because Special Services was also bringing over a folksinger, Tom Scott, who Kerr felt was close enough to the American classical music tradition, he hired him as well.

Only a couple of senior musicians were contracted: one of the Metro-politan's baritones, Mack Harrell, and the renowned harpsichordist Ralph Kirkpatrick. Both left good impressions; however, because of his instrument and the timing of his tour, Kirkpatrick's audience was minuscule (in Karlsruhe, for example, only eighty people bought tickets to his 7 July 1948 concert).[20]

It proved enormously frustrating to the music officers: after all their effort and all the delays, the fruits were generally small and underripe. Each visit took a great deal of work to coordinate and the music officers still had to combat intransigence on the part of the military administration (MG, for example, refused to provide mess facilities or a billet for Patricia Travers's German accompanist). Moreover, the program set sail in the summer of the currency reform, at a point when theater attendance was collapsing anyway. For some tours, the results were disastrous. Although Travers had a likable stage presence, she aroused little interest even among the branch officers when she toured the American zone in May–June 1948. In Bremen, although the acting officer had asked Special Services to arrange her concert, when the violinist arrived, she found she had nowhere to play. In Bavaria, Mose-ley got no support from MG and could not convince a local agent to sponsor her; as a result he had to do everything, including sticking up the advertising posters, himself. In Stuttgart, when the orchestra sud-denly refused to accompany the American, Bill Castello had to bribe them to go on.[21] But bad as this was, it was nothing compared with the misfortune that accompanied the pianist Webster Aitken.

Aitken had made a fine impression in his debut Town Hall recital in New York in 1948 and would go on to a solid career as a music peda-gogue, but he was in poor form in Germany in early 1949. Rather boldly, the pianist programmed Beethoven concertos, and this only made his weaknesses the more glaring. Even John Evarts, who was seldom other than cheerfully positive, rated Aitken's playing "insecure, nervous and unexpressive" and the visit "painful and embarrassing." Berlin's Mateo Lettunich was scathing: "[P]laying of the type exhib-ited by Aitken tends to confirm the current impression here that Amer-icans' principal claim to musical distinction is in their technical gym-nastics, and that great interpretation of great music lies outside their grasp." Sadly, because few people paid to hear his concerts — in Wies-baden, only DM 38 worth of tickets were sold, in Darmstadt, DM 68 — the music officers were forced to paper the halls. They were angry to have to engage in this humiliating activity for an unknown artist, and, as an officer in Stuttgart complained, it was "virtually impossible to place the man during the time allotted to Stuttgart and absolutely impossible to get any people to listen to him. The business of sending over second-string people whom nobody over here has ever heard of is just no good and the position of the Military Government desperately peddling its visiting artists is a curious one. I believe it is safe to say the whole program will not achieve its intended purpose if the people sent over will not be better and more prominent than anything Germany has to offer in the respective categories, that means HOROWITS [*sic*], SCHNABEL, TRAUBEL, etc." The added cost of filling the hall through complimentary tickets was that it lent the performer an official cachet, which, in Aitken's case, left some Germans confused and others de-lighted at the poverty of American musicianship. The criticism stung Moseley: "[T]he fact that so few American artists have been sent . . . tends to over-emphasize the importance of those who do appear. If only one or two such artists are to be sent in the course of the year, it becomes even more essential that they be of the first calibre."[22]

The official response to the complaints from the front line was typically unhelpful. In Bavaria, MG was disturbed over the prospect of low ticket sales and asked the Kultusministerium to suggest which U.S. performers German audiences would most likely want to hear. Moseley was outraged: "[T]he Kultmin. is *roaring* up its sleeve!!! WE ask THEM to submit the names of people THEY want to come to reorient them!!!!!" Carping from the field about the quality of the vis-iting performers also antagonized Harrison Kerr, who deemed it an attack on his own musical judgment. Turning the tables, he declared that the music officers' criticism was "so manifestly meaningless as well as unfair . . . that it could hardly have stemmed from any musical inadequacies." In Aitken's case in particular, Kerr continued, the pi-anist "had no suspicion that his work was considered inadequate," and the American reviews of his playing had been universally posi-tive. "I can understand the unfriendly attitude of the German critics, but I cannot so well account for the reaction of Mr. Moseley and Mr. Lettunich. Is it possible that Americans working in Germany ac-quire the German attitudes toward American artists?" Kerr then an-swered his rhetorical question in a memorandum to McClure: "[I]t seems," he wrote, "as though they have been won over to the German viewpoint that there was no outstanding talent outside of Germany."[23]

The Music Branch did score hits with some American artists, but none of them came under the official program as a visiting artist. Leonard Bernstein, who wowed the crowd in Munich, was a private invitation of Moseley's (he knew the conductor from having played with him at Tanglewood) made under Solti's signature. Bernstein was on his way to perform in Vienna and at the Prague Spring Festival, and so the side-trip to Munich was easily arranged. Similarly, the most spectacular of all the tours, that by Paul Hindemith in February 1949, was executed under a program to invite education consultants, the conductor being a professor at Yale. What made these two visits distinct was that they came as close as musicians might to advancing the goals of reorientation. In America, Bernstein was redefining the very image of the conductor: he was improvisational, sensual, and full of snap. Bernstein's very difference from his closest European parallel, the equally young, gifted, and charismatic, but infinitely more calculating and rehearsed, Herbert von Karajan, was itself an education in what American culture was about. Similarly Hindemith, who by his very presence inspired questions about the connection between music and politics, continuity and change, made those topics the focus of his message in Germany.

Hindemith made a particular splash in Munich, where a special gala performance of *Mathis der Maler* was mounted in his honor. By sheer coincidence, Furtwängler was also in the city, and with two such eminent guests to entertain, Hundhammer offered to share his box with them. The *Kultusminister* had banned Egk's *Abraxas* just weeks before to much public criticism, and, as Moseley reported, "when the audience gradually learned the situation," that here was the minister "at a performance of *Mathis*, which has as its subject the freedom of the artist . . . with those other two leaders of the drama from the Hitler days [Furtwängler's defense of Hindemith led to his resignation from the leadership of the BPO in 1934] . . . [t]hey went through the floor. They all rose to their feet and faced us and went wild." There was more scandal to follow. Speaking the next day in the Aula of the University of Munich, the composer "let them have it right between the eyes," attacking the "shallow depth" of what he presented as German music thinking. Hindemith explained to his audience of 1,500 students and intellectuals that European music had traditionally been the servant of political and religious forces. He then called for a new thinking about art and its detachment from those same moorings. This, he felt, could

Sergiu Celibidache, Paul Hindemith, and Carlos Moseley, Berlin, 1949
(Photo courtesy of Carlos Moseley)

only be achieved through nurturing genius and inspiration and not through mere technical training. In fact, he declared, the prevailing preoccupation in schools with teaching form and method was ensuring music's continued subservience to forces alien to itself.[24]

Hindemith clearly wanted to be provocative, and he got what he was after: "[T]here were not too well muffled cries of 'Nicht so! Nicht so!' . . . and there were mutterings during the intermission and after the meeting, and they grew in violence the longer he stayed and the more he talked." Matters became particularly heated when he launched into a critique of other composers and approaches, culminating in his vehement derision of what he saw as the most "shallow" of all the "purely technical" approaches: the twelve-tone method. At his next lecture, given in the form of a dialogue between technique and inspiration, Hindemith continued his assault, arguing that "method" was a completely subordinate concern and that, while genius could shine through poor technique, uninspired music was seldom even worth hearing.[25]

Hindemith offended many people, but from the Americans' perspective, his trip was a stunning success. He pulled big crowds, attracted a lot of publicity, and stirred up controversy within the arts community. But although the branch officers pressed for more of the same, and especially for a tour by Hindemith's opposite number, Arnold Schoenberg, it did not happen. Instead, by the time the army finally passed responsibility for Germany over to the Department of State during the summer of 1949, the visiting artists program had ground to a stop. All of the money McClaskey and Frank had raised was spent, and dollar earnings were too small to replenish the account. The Yale Glee Club had alone drained $2,200 from the kitty and there was nothing left to fund even groups that volunteered to travel, such as New York's Ballet Theater. For the last six months, there had not even been enough cash to buy and ship recordings.[26] Hindemith may have shown what could be done to provoke debate over the connection between music and politics, but there was neither the money nor the imagination to follow through with the project he'd launched.

THE HIGH COMMISSION'S APPROACH TO AMERICAN ARTISTS

Over the summer of 1949, OMGUS was dissolved, the New York field office closed down, and the visiting artists program came to an end. By this time, not much remained of the Music Branch in either the United States or Germany. In July 1949 Moseley resigned from his position, declaring that he had had enough. That same month, Jerome Pastene and twenty-two other cultural officers were declared "surplus" and dismissed from government service. None of these people was replaced. According to the Department of State, it intended to continue Theater and Music operations with just one officer for the zone (John Evarts) and one for Berlin (Mateo Lettunich). In the summer of 1949 the Cultural Branch chief admitted, "utter confusion" now existed in Germany, and "music and theater activities have been discontinued on [the] *Land* level." The department insisted that it wanted to keep the visiting artists program going but recommended that it remain a War Department responsibility (so it could continue its supposed free ride on Special Services). This offer the army declined. A few weeks later, the chief of the Education and Cultural Relations Division in Germany also resigned, claiming that he saw no reason to expect a change in reorientation's neglect. "I have recommended time and again," he wrote, "that we have to send one of our great symphony orchestras, that we control the kinds of motion pictures that are sent over here, that we make available our best authors, and in fact, attempt to work out a cultural cooperation program."

Reorientation, he asserted, had failed because "we are still accused of being materialistic — a nation without culture."[27]

The situation deteriorated further when, in 1951, John Evarts was riffed from the service on the grounds of homosexuality. Unfortunately for Evarts, he was indiscrete when drunk and drank in the wrong company. And so the Branch commander left Germany after more than five years in service with no pension and a record that made it unpleasant for him to return home. He moved to Paris where he survived for four years studying French with money obtained under the Servicemen's Readjustment Act, composing and playing piano in a nightclub. Although some family members begged him to abandon "Gore Vidal's world" and return to the United States, he remained in Europe the rest of his life. In 1954 an old ICD colleague, Nicolas Nabokov, hired him as his secretary, and he then began a long association with UNESCO. But his departure from Germany was a tragedy, because Evarts, whom McClure had earlier rated "trustworthy and a hard worker," was "a good guy, a really good guy" and well liked in Germany. Further, because he was not replaced, his dismissal meant that the Theater and Music Branch actually ceased to exist as a centralized unit.[28]

Despite the crippling losses, things changed fairly dramatically with the State Department now in charge. Although planners realized that "the informational and educational program will be substantially affected by the planned curtailment of activities," they nonetheless cherished big dreams. Unlike the army, the foreign service had some experience with exporting the arts and was not unwilling to use them to promote America's international objectives. Moreover, the new Office of the High Commissioner for Germany (HICOG) proclaimed reorientation one of its primary political objectives and it was prepared to pay for it. As American High Commissioner John McCloy announced, the opportunity was not to be missed for "at this stage in history there is a better chance to influence the German mind than there has been for a century." State Department officials believed that Military Government had made few advances in the field of reorientation and wanted a big program consisting of more exchanges, more visiting artists and experts, more publications and films, and more support for local democratic initiatives. Not surprisingly, it also rejected Clay's notion that the Germans should undertake self-reeducation as naive.[29]

For Department of State planners, it was the "the right of the occupation powers to exercise such powers of persuasion as may be needed to assist German officials and functionaries with the democratization of the German educational system and the system and machinery of public information." They justified their desire to tighten controls over Germany with reference to the Occupation Statute, which the three Western occupying powers had negotiated in early 1949 and which laid out the terms for the end of Military Government and the creation of a west German state. The Occupation Statute officially terminated the occupiers' powers of oversight and control in a series of specified areas, returning them to full German authority. But on the insistence of the French, it was agreed that the high commissioners would retain absolute power over all nonspecified or residual areas. Because the statute contained no reference to reorientation, the State Department's Bureau of German Affairs discovered that it was a residual and that the occupiers had unlimited control over all aspects of education, information, and cultural affairs. Ironically then, although the Occupation Statute shepherded the creation of a new Federal Republic in west Germany in 1949, it also, in what it left unsaid, allowed the allies to exercise more control than at any time since 1946.[30]

On the basis of the Occupation Statute, officials in the Public Affairs Division of the State Department, which assumed control over the cultural program, proposed returning to the notion of directed reorientation as first proposed by OWI and the army's Psychological Warfare Division. MG's rather confusing notion that the Germans had to choose to reorient their own cultural life as modeled by the Americans was to be replaced with the older idea that HICOG had the right to "establish, operate and maintain" information and cultural media. Department officials also advocated replacing what they saw as MG's "indiscriminate approach" to public reeducation with a more carefully targeted program aimed at "special groups and audiences which are the source of political power"—in effect, at members of the social, economic, and cultural elite. If all this made HICOG's approach to reorientation sound very much like PWD's, so too did its objective. The department initially conceived the aim of reorientation in completely traditional ways, as the elimination of the German people's military and antidemocratic impulses and the construction of "a democratic, self-reliant and peaceful Germany" through the encouragement of "all genuinely democratic elements." To Clay's closest advisers, this seemed a return to the "hard-peace" ideas they associated with people like Robert McClure and Henry Morgenthau, the former secretary of the treasury. As one of Clay's aide's despaired, the hard-liners in the State Department had everyone "over a barrel"; and he feared the Germans were going to have to get used again "to being whip-sawed by the Morgenthau crackpots."[31]

It didn't turn out that way. Although officers in the German Affairs Bureau supported the idea of reorientation by American dictate, the High Commission never had the personnel to make it happen. Reorientation by control depends on a lot of workers doing the job, but HICOG was far too lean-limbed and uncoordinated to take on existing policies. As a result, instead of reversing OMGUS's programs, HICOG ended up making them work better. Shepard Stone, who eventually headed HICOG's Public Affairs Division, which directed reorientation activities, sounded very much like one of Clay's officials when in August 1950 he declared his goal was not to "establish, operate and maintain" but to "assist, advise and persuade." Under HICOG, the student and expert exchange programs were dramatically expanded, direction was retained over operations like RIAS and the *Neue Zeitung*, and the film distribution network and the information centers were enriched. And, just as Clay had emphasized that Americans must be guides and not marshals, HICOG officials presented themselves as mentors to the Germans. By December 1949 HICOG's Public Affairs Division had accepted the fact that it was really in the business of teaching the Germans to help themselves: "Our self-help projects are designed to advise, counsel and assist German leaders in encouragement, establishment and administration of democratic organizations and institutions built on the concept of self-help. This concept accepts the premise that little will be accomplished in Germany unless the Germans do it themselves. Self-help leads to self-responsibility. . . . There is a depreciation of character that accompanies any prolonged 'hand-out.' "[32]

As for music, it had already been allowed to slip from American control and the Public Affairs Division made no effort to repossess it. To do so would have required some personnel, and HICOG had no music officers in the *Länder* and, after John Evarts's dismissal, only one official — Mateo Lettunich — left in Berlin. The Public Affairs Division did have cultural advisers in each *Land* — William Dubensky became one of them, and Eric Clarke briefly returned to Germany in late 1949 to set up the unit — and these officials continued to have responsibility for dispensing reorientation funds to artists willing to perform works by American composers and reporting on local concert activity. But the cultural advisers covered a vast territory — film, theater, exchanges, museums, fine arts, music — and had little time to devote to any one area. In the music field, they reported on local activities (by tabulating performances of American works), secured local artists willing to perform U.S. compositions for a fee, made arrangements for visiting Americans and German artists traveling to the United States, and attempted to make their presence felt by hosting and attending musical events. Their primary job was therefore to represent America positively and not to direct operations.

The active promotion of American music culture became the responsibility of the directors of the zone's twelve Amerika Häuser. These information centers, organized by ICD in 1947 on the State Department's Latin American model, were places where Germans could hear recordings, read books, magazines, and newspapers, and attend lectures on American culture and society. The information centers ran English education classes, hosted concerts, and had youth outreach programs. Most of them sponsored chamber concerts on a weekly basis, hiring local artists and inviting Americans, in the interest of providing "what cannot be seen or heard elsewhere." They aimed their music program at university and conservatory students and distributed hundreds of tickets to the schools. Taken over by Public Affairs in 1949, the Häuser continued to devote their time to presenting "a full and fair picture of the United States" to interested Germans. But as with other Public Affairs units, the Häuser repudiated the notion that they were trying to mold German thinking. As their director observed in 1950, "we are making contact with the German communities of a sort that would guide them in creating such work themselves. In other words, all our work is of a self-help nature. We do not do youth work. We guide and assist the Germans in doing it themselves."[33]

The Amerika Häuser did bring a few musicians of distinction to Germany, such as Julius Katchen and William Kapell, and they employed some fine German ensembles, like the Schmid Quartet, which was contracted to tour a series of American works. Thanks to their efforts, a great deal more American music was heard in Germany than ever before. In May 1949, for example, Munich heard Griffes's *Piano Sonata*, Barber's *First Quartet*, MacDowell's *Concerto for Chamber Orchestra*, Piston's *Flute and Piano Sonata*, Bergsma's *First String Quartet*, and Creston's *Suite for Piano and Viola*. Frankfurt's Amerika Haus, in the meantime, presented Griffes's *Two Sketches for Quartet*, Carpenter's *String Quartet*, Piston's *Sonata for Flute and Piano*, and Gershwin's *Three Preludes*. From the end of the war to December 1949, there were 1,400 performances of U.S. works given in fifty-eight cities, but a full quarter of all those performances occurred in the last half of 1949.[34] The increased attention to American works, although occurring within the modest confines of the Amerika Häuser, did represent an improvement over OMGUS policy, even if most members of the audience only came because the concerts cost nothing.

HICOG's reorientation program did therefore succeed in presenting more American music than ICD ever managed, although there was even less coordination and fewer personnel to give it coherence. It remained a haphazard program that extended only as far as local administrators wanted to take it, and little control was exercised with regards to quality. In consequence, while the Amerika Häuser expanded ICD's program of promoting American and contemporary works, they did so in a less noticeable way. A visiting artist performing in an Amerika Haus was obviously not going to attract as much attention as one playing in a municipal concert hall or state theater. Nor did the Public Affairs Division allocate the kind of money needed to do other than continue bringing in young and relatively unknown musicians. Although the $56,000 PAD set aside in 1949–50 to fund guest performers was far more than Harrison Kerr commanded, it was still not a great deal of money, especially when it is considered that the Americans hoped to feature new performers each week. The Amerika Häuser therefore ended up touring groups like a quartet of singers from Bowdoin College; Roy Eaton, a young American piano student; singers studying in Europe, such as Charlotte Milgram and Mildred Mueller; and local GIs, like the jazz band from the Kitzingen base. The results were inevitably discouraging and complaints from the Amerika Häuser's coordinating directors that "we are sponsoring too many second and third rate artists" and that "the US Information Centers cannot be used as sounding boards for aspiring young artists" have a distressingly familiar ring.[35]

With its institutionally linked administrative staff, vague objectives, low profile in the overall program, unknown performers, and weak audience interest, it was unreasonable to expect Public Affairs to entrench American music in the regular repertoire. Consequently, despite the money the High Commission made available, it lacked the people and resources to give meaning to the points it was able to make. Simply paying musicians to give isolated concerts was not really an adequate substitute for sustained working relations, because if a performance was not placed in the context of an ongoing effort to familiarize artists and their audiences with American works, it would be difficult to make them appreciate the works as symbols of an entire culture. Moreover, because German musicians were unfamiliar with some American idioms, Public Affairs continued to complain that much of the music they sponsored came out sounding wrong. Simply increasing the number of performances of works by different composers also did nothing to confront these problems as it simply buried the real gold in the mountain of dross. For local artists and audiences then, the result of the Amerika Häuser's efforts was that American music performances remained a series of forgettable one-night flings.

HICOG also intensified the music program without confronting the questions that ICD's more modest approach had never itself answered: Would simple exposure to the diversity of America's cultural products really promote democratic thinking? Was force-feeding contemporary music, which most audience members did not warm to anyway, the best method of convincing Germans that America was a cultured nation? Even if the target audience was, as Department of State planners now maintained, Germany's intellectuals and opinion makers, did it necessarily follow that a familiarity with American music made elite groups support U.S. ideals and its foreign policy goals? Moreover, as we have seen, the bifurcation that followed currency reform meant that the works of the generation of more accessible American composers — Copland, Harris, Gershwin, Schuman, and Barber — disappeared from the mainstream repertoire anyway. In consequence, outside of the Amerika Häuser and the subsidized specialist-oriented venues, in the early 1950s American music was not performed in west Germany.

Paradoxically then, under HICOG, the dream of using American music to reorient Germany actually came to an end. Although State Department planners initially proposed revitalizing programs first advanced during the war and set money aside for them, they never seriously undertook the task. The belief underpinning the policy of reorientation through music was that Americans had to "uproot the erroneous German idea that German performers were the only ones worthy of upholding the musical traditions of the world and that

[the] contemporary output of other countries was of inferior calibre." The Germans' sense of their cultural superiority, the Americans argued, was a symptom of the "cultural and spiritual isolation imposed by national socialism" and to fight it was therefore to attack the cultural roots of Nazism and militarism.[36] Clearly, the tools needed to wage this kind of war on German attitudes were top-notch performers, compositions that could be broadly accepted as impressive, and a large and enthusiastic audience. The Music Branch tried in 1946–47 to create these winning conditions, but because of the staff and cash shortage, it never broke through on a broad-enough front. The visiting artists program of 1948 might have carried the occupiers some way toward victory, but it failed to recruit artists of the prominence required. Public Affairs then gave up completely, accepting a lower profile for the program and targeting a much smaller audience. In this way, it abandoned the idea of culturally reorienting a people in favor of influencing a small group of artists and students.

Although Public Affairs officers continued into the 1950s to talk about the need to shape German thinking, it moved away from reorientation when it narrowed the market for its product. What the Americans offered in its place was on the surface quite similar but in reality completely different. On the one hand, HICOG's cultural advisers hoped to awaken German elites to America's place on the cutting edge of contemporary music performance and composition; on the other, they wanted to convince ordinary German music lovers that America was a cultured nation. Both of these approaches had been part of earlier reorientation efforts, but they had been elements in a campaign to break down the Germans' belief in their country's musical greatness. The new function of these directives was different: they were to create among Germans, and specifically among members of the elite, a sense of kinship with and admiration for America. Avant-garde circles, it was hoped, would learn to see the United States as a forward-moving musical nation that shared many of their ambitions, while ordinary people would come to regard Americans as just like them. This was why HICOG continued to support such new-music groups as Steinecke's in Darmstadt. Although the effort was in large measure successful, to the extent that Europe's avant-garde composers were kept aware of the activities of like-minded American composers, it remained a far cry from *mass reeducation*. The idea of reorientation — of transforming German culture — through music therefore disappeared quietly by feeding into a new program that shared many of its surface features but which flowed in a different direction. The new cultural affairs program, a senior officer in the State Department's German Affairs Bureau explained, was not about transforming Germany; it was "insurance against defection."[37]

MUSIC AND THE COLD WAR

Encouraging the Germans' identification with the West had been on the minds of occupation authorities for some time. The goal, however, became much more central to American thinking in 1948, when the Cold War began to insinuate itself into ICD directives, and it came to dominate cultural relations in 1949, with the creation of the west German state. Because it feared Soviet aggression—a concern apparently justified after 1950 by the war in Korea—the Americans put a priority on unifying Western Europe democratically and militarily and combating the communist "fifth column." "We face a serious assault," observed Henry Kellerman, the chief of the State Department's Division of German and Austrian Reorientation Affairs, and "a tremendous team effort is overwhelmingly important and crucial to our success." Ensuring that the new German state remained committed to the struggle against communism was now far more important than any psychological warfare against Nazism. "Can we," mused Kellerman, "with the urgent priorities for building integrated strength, afford any large resources for what must, on the scale of relative importance, be of marginal concern?" The answer was clearly negative: "[W]e ought to consider how the German information program is affected by the priorities which now surround our objectives in Europe [i.e., containing communism], and we should, ultimately, fit our activities, including 'psychological' activities, to this perspective."[38]

Although the Americans decided only over the course of 1947 that Germany would have to be divided, they had long been perturbed by Soviet actions. The turning point came early in 1946 when SMAD decided to build public support for the Communist Party in its zone by dissolving the Social Democrats into a new communist-led "united working-class party," the Sozialistische Einheitspartei Deutschlands (SED). Imposed at a time when the SPD was the party most favored by both the British and the Americans, the Soviet decision had the effect of weakening the Socialists (by eliminating them in eastern Germany, where they were traditionally strongest) and ensuring that no one party could dominate German political life. The creation of the SED also alerted the Western Allies to the fact that the Soviets intended to democratize their zone according to a Stalinist model. Subsequent SMAD actions only aggravated these concerns. The Americans were worried by moves to collectivize property and to expropriate the farms of the larger landowners in the eastern zone on the grounds that they were Nazi collaborators. They were antagonized by communist efforts to gain control over trade unions and cultural organizations and to construct a popular front among German intellectuals. They were exasperated by Soviet demands for reparation payments from the other zones and were angered by the openly anticapitalist, anti-American tone of communist propaganda. The tensions were especially concentrated in Berlin, where the powers squeezed together like four colossi in a confined space: any move by one was bound to discomfort the others. In Berlin, SMAD's denazification program had been a major irritant to the Americans from the beginning, its patronage of the arts had long been an embarrassment, and the overt favoritism it showed communists was intensely destabilizing. The Social Democratic victory in the municipal elections in October 1946, for example, was such a blow to the SED that the Soviets simply refused to allow the new administration to exercise full power, thereby gridlocking city governance.[39]

Berlin ICD had been suspiciously gauging SMAD's intentions all this time. The Intelligence Section had several officers—including Nicolas Nabokov, who dealt with theater and music—who were there to determine Soviet intentions. These officers, many of whom were Russian or East European émigrés, were warning in the fall of 1945 that communists were infiltrating or in control of all the major cultural institutions in the city. Using higher pay, exoneration from Nazi associations, and larger food rations, the Soviets drew many of the best artists to their zone. They also spent lavishly on the theater, contributing an estimated DM 24 million to building restoration in their sector by early 1947 (in contrast, U.S. expenditures had been barely half a million). "It is well known," an ICD officer noted in 1946, "that the Russian authorities in Berlin, as well as in the Russian zone, realize the paramount propagandistic importance of the stage for the re-educational tasks of the occupying forces and act accordingly with a vigour that disgraces the hesitancy on the part of the rest of the Allies." As great-power relations deteriorated, the Western Allies were propelled to counter some of the Soviets' advantages. In early 1946 ICD and British sector Information Services Division reactivated the defunct Kammer der Kunstschaffenden, In September, Clay temporarily blocked the circulation of Soviet-licensed print literature in the American zone in retaliation for a similar move on SMAD's part. ICD also declared that artists denazified by the Soviets were not considered cleared by the Americans—a direct attack on their occupation partner's lenience. And, as the Kommandatura deadlocked over currency reform, the Western Allies banned the Kulturbund from operating in their zones.[40]

The Allies might have worked through most of these conflicts had they been limited to Germany, but events elsewhere rendered them insurmountable. In Austria the Soviets were continuing to run their own occupation zone irrespective of the demands of the national government they had themselves pressed into existence. In Poland the communists, backed up by the Red Army, were waging war on the political opposition, despite promises that elections would be free and open. In the summer of 1947 the Communist Party in Bulgaria declared its main rivals illegal and began executing opposition leaders. In December, King Michael of Romania was forced to abdicate and the communists seized power. Two months later, the most devastating takeover of all occurred when a coup in Czechoslovakia turned that country into a one-party state.

The Stalinization of Eastern Europe, preparations for the transfer to State Department administration, and the widening rift in the Control Council made communism into a major theme of reorientation policies in the American zone. Late in October 1947 Clay introduced "Operation Talk Back," which was designed to counter anti-American propaganda emanating from the Soviet zone, to "emphasize divergences in policies and to make explicit the position of the US and western allies, as opposed to that of the Soviet Union." In April 1948 the operation reached a sufficient level of intensity that the Soviets again blocked the distribution of American-licensed newspapers, and one month later OMGUS issued a permanent ban on the circulation and sale of all Soviet-licensed print literature. Over the course of 1948, a heavy-handed information program was revealed "to reaffirm and support United States objectives and actions in Germany" and to combat totalitarianism "whether from former Nazi and fascist or from communistic doctrines." It was, the Americans insisted, a purely defensive campaign to win back the Germans who "are being deliberately utilized in a planned attempt to turn European people against the United States and to bring about the failure of American efforts at European reconstruction." The goal of the new political propaganda campaign was to "impress people with the reliability, consistency and seriousness of United States foreign policy" and to convince them that it was not "selfishly conceived but [is] in the best interests of other peoples." The operation was centrally coordinated and involved radio, film, newspapers, the Amerika Häuser, and traveling lecturers, and a special fund was created to aid in the publication of anticommunist books and pamphlets. "We Are At War," declared one MG directive in February 1948, "Yes we are engaged in an ideological war. The battleground is right here in Germany. On the one side is the American way of life fighting for democracy, freedom, and the brotherhood of man. On the other side is communism fighting desperately for the right of aggression and oppression."[41]

In fact, in light of all this, it is remarkable that the allies in Germany continued to work together, albeit tensely, until early 1948. Even if relations were hardly smooth, it was not until the introduction of the deutsche mark and the consequent Berlin blockade in the summer of 1948 that quadripartite control became utterly impossible. In early October 1948 the Berlin Philharmonic, which was scheduled to tour the eastern zone and was contracted to resume its regular performance broadcasts over the Soviet-licensed Berliner Rundfunk, came under strong pressure from the Americans to shun the East. Although ICD insisted that it was up to the orchestra to decide where it performed, they were gratified when its members voted 73 to 1 not to play again in the Soviet zone, thereby severing a vital musical link. It set the pattern for what was to come. In December 1948 the Music Branch withdrew all American scores from the Interallied Music Lending Library, which had been located for the previous three years in the Soviet sector, and moved them to a new library in Bad Nauheim. Berlin Library administrators promptly announced they would be replacing the lost music with scores by composers from the people's democracies. Although American cultural officers continued to enter the Soviet sector throughout the blockade, their visits were now carefully monitored. Where Berlin's music officers had hitherto simply driven to shows they wanted to see in the East, Lettunich was told he could only go in his own car to the Brandenburg Gate, where a Soviet escort would meet him and take him the rest of the way. Audiences and artists also remained officially free to pass back and forth between the sectors, but stark limitations on the number of ostmarks one could convert to deutsche marks each month soon forced musicians to decide which city they chose to work in and concertgoers to determine which organizations they wanted to patronize. The result was a mass exodus from the East in 1949–51 and a vitalization of musical organizations in the West.[42]

HICOG inherited OMGUS's anti-Soviet propaganda campaign and extended it. In fact, by 1950 the struggle to contain communist influence in Europe had completely supplanted the program to stamp out the traces of Nazism. Within three years, even German observers were acknowledging that "the reeducation episode belongs to the past." Convincing the Germans to resist communism, which included persuading them to rearm, involved fertilizing their fears concerning the Soviet Union and assuaging their doubts about America. The positive theme of American propaganda became the unity of the West — politically, spiritually, militarily, and culturally. By emphasizing the democracies' cultural similarities and the common source of their creativity, public affairs officials hoped to bind Europe and America more closely together. A new mission therefore emerged for American artists: to show Europeans that they were committed, cultured, and congenial. By encouraging "attitudes of mutual respect and an appreciation of the beneficial relationship possible between the United States and Germany" American artists would help foster the Germans' identification "of their cultural and political aspirations with institutions and values of the West rather than with those of the Soviet Union."[43]

From the late 1940s, American officials had been growing increasingly concerned over Moscow's success at building support among Western intellectuals through both the various national communist parties and the international peace movement. A number of prominent European intellectuals, including Jean-Paul Sartre and Maurice Merleau-Ponty, were vaguely or overtly pro-Soviet, often because they feared American cultural imperialism more than they worried about communist dictatorship. In order to counter, through emulation, the Soviets' successes, Washington began to foster, by way of generous (if often covert) financial assistance, prodemocratic feelings among Europe's more transatlantically oriented elite. The most celebrated result of this effort was the Congress for Cultural Freedom, founded in

Berlin in 1950, together with its various print-media spinoffs, which included *Preuves*, *Der Monat*, and *Encounter*. HICOG's support for the Darmstadt Ferienkurse fitted in with this general program as it was seen as a way of reaching intellectual circles within the classical music field. Although never overtly anticommunist, by encouraging identification with the United States through exposure to its music and composers, HICOG's Darmstadt subvention served to advance the broader program of bridging the Atlantic and fostering pro-American sentiments.[44]

In this effort to win over the Germans, however, Berlin was the nodal point. Not only was the city a site for "round the clock propaganda and psychological warfare," it was also here, more than anywhere else, that the continuation of the American presence rested "squarely on the support of the . . . population. If ever we should lose its confidence our position would become untenable." At their London meeting in April 1950, the foreign ministers of the Western occupying powers reaffirmed their commitment to the city's defense and called for new measures that might augment west Berlin's status. In November the Allied Kommandatura (which since the Soviet walkout included only the three Western commands) announced that they would meet this challenge through a Berlin cultural festival to be held in September 1951. The festival would showcase all the performing arts — music, dance, film, and theater — and would display the creativity that west Berlin and its defenders had to offer. But unlike other arts festivals, which were primarily designed to attract foreign tourist income, Berlin's was to be a celebration of Western art for the benefit of the locals from both East and West. At its most basic level, this Cold War festival was aimed at the Soviets, as it "would have a stabilizing and cheering effect on Berlin morale, and West European morale generally" and evidence "Western international solidarity and the confidence of the Western World in Berlin."[45]

The Allies proposed exorbitant contributions to the festival: the Sadler's Wells Ballet, Thomas Beecham and the Royal Philharmonic, a Benjamin Britten opera conducted by the composer; the Comédie Française, the Ballet of the Paris Opéra, the orchestra of the Garde Republicaine; a production of Gershwin's *Porgy and Bess*, Stokowski and the Philadelphia Orchestra, and Toscanini and the NBC Symphony Orchestra. To purchase this wish list, the Kommandatura offered a half million marks and the High Commission threw in a further

DM 400,000 plus an additional DM 400,000 guarantee against losses; Berlin was to provide a further half million from its own budget. On the insistence of the Allies, the *Intendant* of the Städtische Oper, the recently denazified Heinz Tietjen, was placed in charge of organizing the month-long event. Tietjen immediately began spending lavishly on new productions at his own house and promised funds to all of the theaters able to mount new works during the festival weeks. He also lived high, and the Allies were later appalled to discover that Tietjen spent a tenth of his total budget on office expenses.[46]

Real trouble, however, began to arise for the festival in the new year: the cash-strapped Berlin Senat delayed its vote on the appropriation until March 1951, by which time Allied enthusiasm had begun to cool. The High Commission, facing a budget crunch of its own, suddenly cut its subsidy to DM 300,000, and the Kommandatura refused to grant any money, although it still promised to cover the deficit. In addition, the Allies demanded that to help finance the project, they receive 60 percent of earnings on shows by their own nationals. As the French sector's deputy commander observed, "I think we should not forget that if for certain political reasons the Allies are urging to have this Festival arranged, Berlin is still going to derive out of it very big financial and economical advantages, and it would at least seem extraordinary to see the Allies supporting all the expenses of the affair and the Germans drawing all the revenue and benefits from it."[47] Unfortunately, the long delays and squabbling over money meant that many of the performers the festival committee hoped to import could no longer be secured. In place of *Porgy and Bess*, the Americans were forced to offer the New York Theater Guild's production of *Oklahoma!*, and instead of two symphony orchestras, Berlin got the Juilliard String Quartet.

In the end, the American contribution to the 1951 Berlin Festival was respectable rather than inspiring. Shepard Stone considered *Oklahoma!* a "fifth rate" production, a harsh assessment that doubtless partly originated in the failure of Berlin audiences to comprehend this most American of musicals. The play brought over — a melodramatic retelling of *Medea*, which served as a prop for the indigestible acting of Judith Anderson — was even more poorly received by critics: one of them commented that Berlin had not seen anything like it in a hundred years. And everyone realized that they should not have sent the droll pantomimist and comedian Agnes Enters; her material was too particularly American, the audience failed to see the humor, and her performance run had to be cut short. On the other hand, the Juilliard Quartet was an unqualified success in its rather daring all-Bartók program and the brilliant American soprano, Astrid Varnay, was a triumph as Isolde and Brunhilde at the Städtische Oper. Even more impressive was the great African American ensemble, the Hall Johnson Choir, though planners erred in scheduling it for only one recital.[48]

Clearly, HICOG's cultural officials continued to have trouble finding well-known performers in the United States who might appeal to German audiences. It was not that the choices made were poor ones; they were, after all, made on the basis of the artists' critical reputation in the United States, and the Department of State was sufficiently anxious to ensure quality that it contracted the selection process out to an independent theatrical organization, the American National Theater and Academy (ANTA). But success on the New York stage did not necessarily mean a hit in Germany; theater and music idioms and performance styles were as yet too deeply embedded in local custom to be easily transported. Young people might soon be rocking to Elvis Presley and Bill Haley, but the *Bildungs* culture of the Berlin Festival audience remained uncomprehending and vaguely hostile to American products.[49] It is therefore by no means clear from the reception accorded the artists chosen to represent the United States that HICOG achieved its aim of convincing Germans of their kinship to Americans.

Although Berlin's Mayor Reuter was delighted with the political returns on his city's investment, declaring his appreciation of "those who we like to refer to as *our* allies," the financial rewards were also considerably less sizable. The festival cost more than DM 1 million to mount but box office receipts were a depressing DM 100,000. About one-quarter of all ticket sales were in ostmarks, but the number was unfairly inflated by sales to a handful of all-German events (such as a Johann Strauss evening at the *Waldbühne*). Ostmark receipts at shows given by U.S. artists were closer to 10 percent. The failure to attract East German audiences to Allied artists was, however, not nearly so discouraging as the more general need to fill the halls with free seats. As many tickets to *Oklahoma!* and *Medea* were given out free as were sold, while 450 tickets to the Juilliard Quartet were purchased and 330 given away. Yet even with this level of support, when *Oklahoma!* played in the Titania Palast, one-quarter of the hall was empty. According to public affairs analysts, not enough time was provided for securing artists, the festival administration spent too much on itself, and too many events were crammed into too short a period, subdividing and exhausting the audience.[50]

It was with an eye to resolving these problems and getting it right that the High Commission bowed to a request from Berlin's government and agreed to subsidize a second festival in September 1952. The Allies, however, decided to withdraw their guarantee against losses, to offer a lump-sum contribution that could only be used to import their own artists, and to insist that the festival management live within its budget. Yet even with these understandings in place, HICOG was unsure it could convince Washington of the value of the expenditure, and McCloy refused to give it final authorization until Congress voted his budget in June 1952. It was not until early July that Public Affairs was cleared to proceed, by which time the festival program was set, the advertising ready, and the theaters booked. The State Department and ANTA now had to scramble to find artists able to travel to Germany on two months' notice and could place them in only the least appealing houses. In the end, it was a miracle they secured the New York City Ballet (which was luckily ending a European tour), *Porgy and Bess*, Astrid Varnay, and the conductor Eugene Ormandy at all. The playbill offered in 1952 was, by necessity, much more modest than that supplied the previous year and paled in comparison to the ones mounted by the French and the British. But HICOG was lucky this time, because of all the Allied contributions, *Porgy* proved the sensation of the festival, and it played for three weeks to sold-out houses and cheering, foot-stamping audiences. It was undoubtedly Public Affairs' single great success in the somewhat desultory official effort to present American artists to Germans.[51]

Sadly, neither the State Department nor OMGUS can be commended on the way it managed its cultural programs. Although some exceptional talent was introduced to European audiences, the administrators remained completely at sea. For years, MG was a hindrance to the Music Branch's control, refusing to fund visits or allow food rations or billets or ease fraternization regulations. Short of cash and staff, MG rated the reorientation of German music culture not simply as a low priority but as something it really did not want to engage in at all. HICOG was more positive but no more sensible. It too allocated money in a hand-to-mouth fashion and seemed incapable of long-term planning. Once it abandoned reorientation, the whole purpose of its

Everyman Opera Company production of Gershwin's Porgy and Bess, *Final Scene. The picture, taken in London in 1952, shows the same set and cast that visited Berlin. (Photo courtesy of Ella Gerber Kasakoff; source: The Jerome Lawrence and Robert E. Lee Theatre Research Institute)*

program fell out of focus and Public Affairs pursued goodwill almost for its own sake. Anticommunism may have reinvigorated the program on paper, but it did little to enliven it in practice. The chaotic way in which the High Commission managed its subsidy for the two Berlin Festivals was symptomatic of its inability to make things happen in the arts without inviting ridicule.

MUSIC AS AN INSTRUMENT OF REORIENTATION

The question is, even without the policy mismanagement, could it really have worked? America's cultural officers were generally convinced that music had a role to play in changing German attitudes: it might break down prejudices, encourage peaceful and democratic sentiments, and build fraternity among peoples. What led them to these beliefs was music's peculiar mythology—notions that it was an "international language," universally accessible; that it was "above politics"; that it was fundamentally "humanistic"; and that it rocked the cradle of harmony for all peoples. These images remain tremendously powerful even today and they transcend national boundaries — in fact, they are part and parcel of the Western tradition — but the very idea that musicians in 1945 relied on them in order to absolve themselves of Nazi guilt should make us pause over them. Germany's musicians did many things about which they should have been ashamed, but few of them were. Music culture served for them as an excuse, as a therapeutic ideal, which allowed them to preserve their pride in themselves and their connection with their audience. By the same token, the notion that music could cross borders and speak directly to foreign peoples was a widely cherished belief, but one that in postwar Germany's case obscured more than it revealed. To what extent, one must ask, was the visiting artists' program and even the whole concept of using sound as an instrument of reform a product of wishful thinking? To answer this question we might look more closely at the two most overtly successful efforts to promote American classical music: the 1952 *Porgy and Bess* production in Berlin and Leonard Bernstein's 1948 visit to Munich.

Porgy and Bess was in many ways a daring choice for Berlin. George Gershwin was known as a writer of popular songs, and even American critics had generally proved unwilling to take his opera seriously. Gershwin hoped he had composed what would be seen as an authentic opera, a work, he said, that lay somewhere between *Carmen* and *Meistersinger*, but even American audiences were uncomfortable with the notion that this "halfway opera" by a composer of "Broadway entertainments" should be considered the equal of the European masterworks. The critics therefore cheapened their praise of the score, acknowledging the loveliness of the "tunes" even as they disputed its status as an opera. The problem for many American commentators with Gershwin's great work was that it drew on the musical style of a people outside the classical tradition. In assimilating an African American sound and translating it for urban white audiences, Gershwin weakened his claim on the operagoing public and alienated many blacks. In fact, African American critics condemned *Porgy* on both artistic grounds (as an untrue reproduction of their music forms) and for its portrayal of blacks as "a primitive human community." As a writer for the Baltimore *Afro American* stormed, *Porgy* is "delighting the bigots on Broadway and putting the colored race to shame."[52] None of this helped win the opera acceptance, and it remained largely unperformed, awkwardly straddling midtown and uptown.

Unfortunately, from a propagandistic perspective, the story was as challenging as the music. As one public affairs officer discovered to his horror, the show "deals with the seamy side of American life — a tatter-demalion community of Negro paupers and outcasts, often held in the grip of crime, vice and mob hysteria."[53] In fact, *Porgy* tells a story of love and hardship among poor Gullah fishermen and dock workers in South Carolina. Crown, a crude though superhuman force, murders a man during a crap game and is forced to go into hiding. His girlfriend, the beautiful but cocaine-addicted Bess, is left behind and finds shelter with a crippled beggar named Porgy. Under the influence of Porgy's love, Bess becomes a "good" woman, and the community accepts her. But Crown returns, and Porgy is arrested after he kills Bess's former lover by knifing him in the back. Bess, abandoned once again, is se-duced by her cocaine dealer, and, when Porgy gets out of prison, he finds she has gone to New York. Ever faithful in his love, Porgy follows after her in his goat cart.

The unexpected harshness of the story posed a real challenge to PAD's cultural officers. For years, the Soviets had been slamming the United States for the suffering it inflicted on its black population, and *Porgy* seemed to confirm all of the negative images. This had a direct bearing on reeducation because as one widely read proponent ob-served, the German people will be "quick to detect the weaknesses of democracy . . . [and] it is idle to suppose they [will] not know about lynchings and the plight of the Negro in America." Throughout the occupation period, effort had been made to restrict the fraterniza-tion of black troops and to downplay "the problem in the South" in hopes of defusing German criticism of American race relations. But the American efforts to cover up of the country's racial shame proved fertilizer for German prejudice. As one May to November 1952 study of west German newspapers concluded, of 284 articles in which blacks were mentioned, 79 percent reported at least some unfavorable infor-mation.[54] In the hopes of dodging controversy, Berlin's cultural of-ficers therefore decided not to "oversell" *Porgy* and remained tight-lipped about the opera's visit. Press information began to appear only in late August, barely three weeks before opening night, amid panic over the "dearth of material" and "serious fears . . . of lean houses." What information was ultimately released to the press urged Berliners not to see the opera as an "authentic" depiction of American society: "People can no more judge true life in America by the opera *Porgy* than they can judge true life in Italy by some of the more lurid Italian operas," announced one official; "it is a piece of folklore out of our past."[55]

Far from demonstrating the African Americans' continuing repression, Public Affairs argued, the opera was proof of their individual achievements. As the official propaganda made clear, *Porgy* showed "that the negro artist in America has reached a high degree of skill, acceptance and fame and the personnel of this company will demonstrate their achievement as American citizens not only on stage but off." In raising the issue in this way, the Americans at once drew attention to racism and segregation and offered *Porgy* as an answer to it. The very *brutality* of *Porgy* would further allow officials to "demonstrate that the United States is assessing realistically the true importance of Soviet propaganda as far as our ethnical [*sic*] problems are concerned . . . and claims an appreciation of art above politics."[56]

The Americans' preperformance damage control proved, in retrospect, unnecessary. Audiences were enthusiastic, and *Porgy* became the hottest ticket at the 1952 festival. The west Berlin press was overwhelmingly positive and the eastern remained thankfully silent. State Department officials were relieved and gratified; *Porgy*, they concluded, "was the greatest possible propaganda tool that could be sent abroad." Berlin theatergoers were smitten by *Porgy*, more so than they had ever been with any previous American import, which led many observers to conclude that U.S. artists had finally started to win over German audiences. As one of them maintained, although frequently referred to as "boon doggling," the program of touring Americans was proving its importance: "[I]t is difficult to appreciate the value that Europe places on cultures. In the United States, as a young nation, we have a magnificent musical contribution to share with the world. . . . Europe, in general, and Germany in particular, conceive of the United States as being the land of unlimited dollars, unselected commercialized motion pictures and irresponsible tourists. Only recently, in the German press . . . have the critics begun to report that it was an amazing revelation to know that the US had a culture and not simply efficiency and materialism." Moreover, the opera was helping America win the struggle for the German mind by offering "a direct answer to the communists and destroy[ing] their charge that the Negroes [are] enslaved." As a *New York Times* correspondent in Berlin chortled, as an instrument of psychological warfare, *Porgy* "was worth several divisions of troops in the Cold War."[57]

Porgy's reception bears scrutiny because its success was presented as a landmark in American-German cultural relations. But State Department officials clearly exaggerated the opera's success and simplified the critical reaction. The truth was that had they reacted as favorably to *Porgy* as the State Department believed, Berlin audiences would have been off-loading an enormous amount of baggage. First, they would have had to come to terms with the musical idiom. Jazz was a familiar sound in Germany and the country had already produced some considerable artists of its own, but recognizing this as the music of the dance hall and welcoming it into the opera house were two very different matters.[58] Moreover, Berlin critics and audiences would have had to balance their evaluation of the opera, their suppressed resentment of America's supremacy, and, since the blockade, their appreciation of the Western Allies' military presence. Third, they would have had somehow to deal with the talent of the performers, their exoticism, their own prejudices about blacks, and their knowledge of racial inequalities in the United States. The existence of all these preconceptions and predispositions ultimately forced audience members into a delicate negotiation of competing urges. On the one hand, they praised the music and the show as revelatory of great talent. On the other, they dismissed it as artistically unsophisticated and primitive. In fact, it was the primitive nature of the production that critics actually argued made it great. America, in this light, may not have had real *Kultur*, but it was erupting with energy and a kind of unrefined talent. The racial issue stood at the center of this interpretation, because it was the African American presence in the work that facilitated this packaging of excitement and contempt, voyeuristic pleasure and disdain.

For German critics, *Porgy* was an African American work. "Dominating the score," wrote the reviewer for the *Berliner Anzeiger*, "are the Negroid melodies typical in America; it seems that Gershwin took over actual Negro songs or composed in their style." Gershwin, wrote another, "submerged himself in the atmosphere, in the soul of this unrestrained world"; the music is not so much a composition as a "reproduction . . . even down to the bustle of the streets in drumming and percussion solos and the rattling of window shutters." The conviction that Gershwin did not so much write *Porgy* as translate it for the stage underpinned the view that what audiences were watching was authentic. Despite official efforts to contextualize the work and present it as something "out of America's past," critics believed that they were being exposed to the real thing. Even the writer for *Die Neue Zeitung*, HICOG's German-language paper, contradicted his sponsor in proclaiming *Porgy* an authentic work drawn from a "pure" source. Similarly, Friedrich Luft, an artist and critic who also enjoyed official American favor, declared *Porgy* "complete nature . . . full life," an encapsulation of "the whole wild, insoluble longing of the Negro people." To the critic for *Der Kurier*, it was "a piece of life," while another said it was a series of scenes "taken from everyday life," and the correspondent for *Der Abend* became so enthused as to declare that it was not theater at all since "the many colorful inhabitants of Catfish Row are playing themselves."[59]

Acceptance of *Porgy* as real had a major impact on how the show was seen and interpreted by critics and, one can assume, by other audience members as well. The sexuality of the production—which went well beyond tight dresses and bare male chests to include depictions of foreplay and even intercourse—was taken by critics both as titillating and as a sign of African American savagery. That *Porgy* could successfully challenge concert hall proprieties in its depiction of sex was entirely due to the fact that it featured black people. Just as anthropological depictions of black nudity were acceptable in an age when similar images of whites were proscribed, representations of black sexual freedom could be vicariously enjoyed because the people depicted were seen to be fundamentally savage. Even Leontyne Price, who was playing Bess at the start of her magnificent career, was admired not so much for her singing as for her "attractive, hip swinging elemental character." Critical reviews were alive with adjectives like "hot," "ecstatic," "trembling," "lustful," "passionate," and "steaming"; the *Nacht Depesche* critic seemed particularly aroused by the moment when "dark Bess, who goes for all men, tears the shirt off the murderer Crown and he stands half-naked before her, a mighty King Kong, a creature of the primeval forest." Voyeurism was central to the opera's appeal to German critics, but they never considered the racial undertow to their preoccupation with looking. On the contrary, Berlin commentators presented their fascination and pleasure at watching black bodies as evidence of their openness. As *Der Tagesspiegel* explained it, they were willing to accept blacks "just as they are: narrow, hot from miasma and passion from frivolity and gambling, envy and gossip, hatred and murder."[60]

If this was America—oversexed and over here—it was a dark continent, wild and torrid and raw. Here were people, who "dance and enjoy themselves, mend their nets and go fishing, make love and very quickly seize their knives." This world, declared the writer for the Socialist daily, the *Telegraf*, was a real America "different from that which Hollywood sends out into the world. It is vibrating with the pulse of the people. . . . Here lives are thrown together, uncivilized and disordered, placed by fate on the edge of existence . . . a ballad against a real steaming background." It is, announced Florian Krenzl in *Der Tag*, "fantastic. . . . None of us has ever seen anything like it. . . . The vibrating, disturbing passion swarms, it crawls all over the stage, from all windows and doors, in every corner." After years of American troops and radio and films, another critic observed, he thought that he "knew America," but now he had confronted something "never seen before or heard . . . a great unknown . . . [that], my God, we have never known, [that] we've never been able to picture."[61]

The critical reviews of *Porgy* reveal the resilience of racist, anti-American, and xenophobic images. True, Berlin newspapermen were enthusiastic for what they saw, but what they now praised were the very things Nazism had reviled. The approach was more positive, but the images remained the same. Not surprisingly, then, critical enthusiasm for *Porgy* did not translate into a new vision of the United States. Once again, the old stereotypes about America's lack of culture surfaced, although they bubbled up in the most positive of ways. America's greatness, observed the critics, lay in its lack of sophistication, in its abundant primitiveness, in its raw energy. Friedrich Luft, who marveled at the "anthill of life arranged on the overcrowded stage," saw in its "unsifted feeling . . . complete nature, beautiful, disordered, undevastated, life." The choice of words here is intriguing, given that *Porgy*'s set featured a dilapidated alley in a port city, but Luft was reflecting on both Berlin's destruction and America's richness. Once again, postwar Germans were anxious to point out, even when confronted by American racism and poverty, that they had suffered more. The United States remained, as Luft explained it, an "artistic Garden of Eden"; an unsophisticated yet intact world. For all that the opera depicted poverty and hardship, Catfish Row was a "more innocent" place than the *Alleen* of Luft's Berlin. Other critics echoed these views. The *Berliner Anzeiger* thought that the opera revealed "the whole tangled abundance and sultry atmosphere of the Southern States," while Werner Öhlmann in the *Tagesspiegel* saw "the good and strong abundance of life" shining through the poverty.[62] Remarkably then, for Berlin critics, *Porgy* evoked an America unfettered by European cares, unscarred by European hardships, and underdeveloped in the European arts.

Sadly, American officials did not notice the tension in these critical evaluations in part because they shared many of the same racial prejudices. They had always been too ready to believe the worst of black soldiers and were too much the products of a segregated culture to even perceive their own blinkers. The ambiguities of the critical reaction were ignored because State Department officials, while perhaps no longer convinced of black savagery, saw them as different and inferior. Indeed, if the critical reaction to *Porgy* reveals the survival of racist and anti-American attitudes in Berlin, and the strategies used in their disguise, it also highlights the narrow band of assumptions German critics shared with their white American counterparts. As with white critics in America, those in Berlin questioned Gershwin's talents, objectified *Porgy*'s performers, and read the opera's depiction of African Americans as true.[63] Small wonder that State Department officials were pleased with *Porgy*'s propaganda impact. They read only the positive in the reviews and ignored the racist stereotypes that underlay them because they accepted those images as largely accurate. But at this time, years before the *Brown* decision, to expect otherwise would be optimistic. The end result, however, was that American officials were as one in presenting *Porgy* as an untarnished success: they failed to see that for German critics the discourse of primitiveness was not confined to blacks but was being used as a springboard to characterize all of America. But with vision narrowed by their own racial blinker, HICOG officials hailed the opera for having done more to "elevate American cultural prestige in one month than anything we have attempted here in the past seven years."[64]

The cultural officers' inability to understand what the locals were saying speaks to the gulf that remained between America and Germany. Despite years of close contact, a slew of preconceptions influenced the way each nationality saw the other. America's cultural officers continued to feel intimidated by Germany and its cultural heritage; they were nervous about presenting *Porgy* in part because they worried that the locals would not find it up to snuff. Moreover, they still had doubts about the value of popular music and their contributions to both Berlin festivals pointedly excluded anything that might be considered "low culture." In a sense, the Americans continued to box themselves in, insecurely proffering works that fit the central European definition of *Kultur* and expressing deep gratitude when their gifts appeared to be accepted. They still could not bring themselves to see the powerhouse of musical creativity and imagination they represented.

But German critics—and, after all, they were members of the very elite HICOG hoped to influence—tended to see little that was truly praiseworthy in American culture. While race influenced their reading of *Porgy*, their condescending approach was not unique to this production. All visiting Americans were quietly stereotyped, and most were belittled even as they were praised. Although ICD and Public Affairs had been waging war on prejudice in the music field for almost a decade, the critical evidence suggests that the Germans' confidence in their own superiority in music remained unshaken. Anti-Americanism served a vital function in music culture because it justified the defeated's rights and power, even in a divided and occupied land.

Regrettably, *Porgy* was particularly easy to disparage because it was a mongrel work: a white-on-black pastiche of spirituals, Tin Pan Alley tunes, and late romantic arias But even performers and groups of a more purely classical lineage were stereotyped in the German press. American soloists and ensembles were often warmly greeted by German critics, but with uncanny regularity words like "mechanical" or "cold" marred even the most positive reviews. The Boston Symphony, for example, which performed in Berlin in 1952 under the leadership of its French conductor, Charles Munch, was greatly admired but also subtly demeaned. The *Berliner Anzeiger* critic wrote of a "coldness we Germans are not quite used to; we seek to interpret music a little more from the inside. We are not quite accustomed to such extreme perfectionism." *Die Neue Zeitung* similarly found the orchestra's performances "completely different [from what audiences are used to] . . . namely, unsentimental, classically poised, dynamic and with marble cool phrasing," while the *Berliner Zeitung* commented on its "almost mechanical, highly technical, perfection." Comments like these, while not overtly negative, manifested the conviction that where U.S. artists might be fine technicians, they lacked "soul." Music production, for Americans, was thought to be about getting it right, whereas the Germans prided themselves on knowing that a little sloppiness was necessary for the spirit to soar. When an American criticized Furtwängler for overlarding a piece, a German fan shot back: "[Y]ou in your new nationality are perhaps not able to feel the sublimity of such a performance for a down-trodden people."[65]

Not surprisingly, newspaper critics were especially likely to focus on technical elements when reviewing performances by the young musicians touring under the visiting artists and Amerika Haus programs. The Walden Quartet, for example, was praised for its "highly integrated and disciplined playing, homogeneous sound, temperament and the organizational ability to untie even the most problematical knots in the program." Patricia Travers's technique was dissected by the critic for the *Stuttgarter Zeitung* as though she were a student undergoing her conservatory exam: "[S]he gives life to dry passages, shows feeling without becoming sentimental, and reveals a controlled strength; her bowing is very beautiful, her attitude remarkably calm, her tone is not exceptional, but suitable, and her technical ability is admirably developed."[66] Nowhere in these reviews were the quartet's or Travers's interpretations of the music discussed. American artists were generally treated like good copyists: they could reproduce classical music, but they were representatives of too new a culture to feel it.

The contrast between German soul and American technique was made even by Paul Hindemith. Carlos Moseley recalled, with great relish, the composer offering such provocative comments as "[Y]ou think your orchestras are that good? We [in the United States] have high-school orchestras that can play better." In short, "he let them have it. . . . He [laid] it on and let them know that they had missed the *big* boat *musically* and that they were pretty stupid to be down-grading America." But given Hindemith's public assertion that technique was no substitute for spirituality and his repeated attacks on German educators for deadening music by overemphasizing method and neglecting soul, were his comments as positively intended as Moseley believed? In fact, for a paid publicist, the insights Hindemith offered into America were distinctly below proof. In his lecture on American music culture, he told audiences that serious music in the United States was still in its fetal stages and that just twenty years before the only good musicians and conductors in the country were Europeans. "Since then," he continued, "there has developed a new generation of musicians, outstanding especially because of their technique." The composer went on to confirm what many in his audience would have already believed regarding American excess, pointing out that while

Paul Hindemith, Mateo Lettunich, and John Evarts, Berlin, 1949
(Photo courtesy of Mateo Lettunich)

chamber music was not enjoyed in the United States as it was in Europe, the country did boast concert halls that could hold 10,000 and stadiums that could seat 60,000. As for America's composers, Hindemith noted, they "are well trained but they had little time to develop themselves so there does not exist an American style yet." Many of them, he continued, were trying to write music based on folk idioms, but this he felt would not lead them to a new style as the country's folk music was itself derivative, being largely "British in origin [or] . . . Negro spirituals."[67] While Hindemith almost certainly did not mean to run down the United States, his comments and the topics he chose to talk about demonstrate his inability, even after ten years in the United States, to shake off his own Central European predilections. Once again, American officials could not appreciate that what they took to be positive commentary might actually serve to reinforce, rather than challenge, anti-American sentiments.

Only a very few American classical artists put real pressure on German preconceptions. Foremost among them was the young, mop-haired maestro, Leonard Bernstein. The conductor's behavior fascinated, bemused, and appalled critics in Munich and also in Vienna. Conducting without a baton, Bernstein waved his arms, leapt in the air, and, most impressively, punched with his fists. "Hard in his blows, he gives the strongest accents with his fists, which look like boxing punches with which he might K.O. [the] symphony." One Viennese critic found the "messaging and attacking of the orchestra, the getting loose with fists, with poundings, and mewings, and the exaggerated showmanship" utterly distracting, even if he did have to admit that with "fists, feet, [and] shoulders, with turns and twists, and with scrapes and shoves" he really "heats up an orchestra." Dr. Hajas, of the Soviet zone *Oesterreichische Zeitung*, was deeply disturbed by it all, finding in the conductor's Schumann "a rendition, partly wildly move-mented, partly convulsive, which coincided little with one's ideal con-cept of the original, and presented an example, in spite of a few beauti-ful passages, of music being carried on like a boxing bout."[68]

Like *Porgy*, Bernstein manifested the American challenge to Ger-man music culture. And like Gershwin's opera, Bernstein was an un-tidy mass of competing textures: the classical and the popular, the artistic and the commercial, the gay and the straight, the impulse to conduct and the desire to compose. Moreover, just as the *Porgy* pro-duction that visited Berlin tempted critics to confuse the real and the fictional, the actor and the character portrayed, so too did Bernstein erase boundaries. The boxer on the podium drew so much attention to himself that he threatened to eradicate the distinction between the work and its interpreter. But this was his point. Though ostensibly submerging himself in the music — feeling its pulse and revealing it physically — Bernstein in no way wanted to drop out of view. Virgil Thomson observed of him: "Leonard Bernstein knows what American music is all about, but in the western European repertory he is obliged to improvise. . . . That is why, I think, he goes into chorybantic ec-stacies in front of it. He needs to mime, for himself and for others, a conviction that he does not have." Thomson was a prescient critic, but he could not believe that what Bernstein did was done intentionally. Spontaneity, he felt, had to be read as a sign of insecurity. But Bern-stein, with his good looks, long hair, T-shirts, and "bobby-sox fan clubs" was a self-conscious exponent of Cool. Everything he did was designed to keep the audience's gaze fixed on the podium and, in so doing, to reinforce the performance instant itself. In this he was carry-ing forward into classical music what was arguably the most important feature of twentieth-century American culture: the ideal of improvisa-tion. Just as Jackson Pollock's splash and drip paintings or William Carlos Williams's experimental, improvisational poetry was designed to draw attention to the artist's act of creating, Bernstein was trying to convey the impression that he was spontaneously reanimating music even though it had already long before been composed and rehearsed.[69]

As with *Porgy*, Bernstein's challenge to conventional music culture was trivialized by critics through a handful of key images. First they presented him as an innocent youth: in Ravel's concerto, a "whizzing, sparkling, pearl-like" piece, everything was "joy." "Joy shone in the eyes of the pianist-conductor, joy sparkled in the eyes of the musicians, joy on the micro-phone of the radio, joy on the ornaments of the hall. . . . It was all a carefree, happy game." Schumann's Second Symphony was similarly described as having "cried and laughed and sung like probably never before"; Bernstein was the "happy youth," "he does not feel the responsibility of a genius, he plays with the unbent freedom of a 'homo ludens.'" Second, the conductor was presented as the embodiment of American energy. The pugilistic imagery has already been noted, but visions of the atomic age can also be detected. In Munich, one critic noted, Bernstein was an "Electron . . . who put the public in oscillations of enthusiasm." The young American, noted another, "radiates freshness, vitality and unused musical power"; he was "spontaneous, unstaged, elementary, like a bolt of lightning." The Schumann was played with "vitality and drive," the orchestra "let itself be led by the energy-loaded wizard." Finally, there was the sexually potent American, chock-a-block with connotations of blackness and jazz. In Vienna, Hajas wrote of his "rhythmic exoticism" and of an "orchestra released Dionystically [*sic*] by the conductor." Another critic observed that he phrases "by means of pulls and pushes" and so transforms "lyric melodic" music into "dramatic outcries." Yet another thought he played the scherzo in the Schumann as a jazz-inflected (hence blackened) fox-trot. "One almost misses the saxophone." One more saw Bernstein as "an ecstatic and [*sic*] orgiast of the musical form."[70]

In relying on these images, European critics recoded Bernstein according to an accepted Old World–New World dichotomy. He represented the popular not the cultured, the young not the mature, the impulsive not the deeply considered, the black not the white. And yet, while this view simplified and distorted, it nonetheless failed to eliminate. Unlike those artists who could be dismissed as mere technicians, or even *Porgy*'s cast, which could be written off as primitive blacks playing themselves, Bernstein's disruptive message was more challenging. European music critics may have been able to explain him, but containment is never a strategy of obliteration. The guardians of high art could insulate themselves against spontaneity by regarding it as youthful, but in retreating to defend the high ground of art music, they were abandoning the rest of the field. And it went deeper. In failing to deny Bernstein's legitimacy as a classical artist, the critics were also failing to build truly impermeable defenses. Over the long haul, Bernstein's style would become more fashionable, and in time even German high culture would begin to more visibly get hip.

Leonard Bernstein and *Porgy and Bess* carried to Germany some of the energy and brilliance of American music as well as its freshness and maturity. The artistry they revealed was different and disruptive and evocative: as the critics recognized, albeit disdainfully, these artists were really and truly "alive." As one reviewer observed of Bernstein, he "communicates his will to the orchestra by means of a quick-silver like and exaggerated sign-language which is the expression of a fanatically overheated sensibility," and in so doing the music making took on "something of the atmosphere of a big sports event."[71] If groups like the Juilliards and singers like Varnay were taken by Germans critics as illustrations of how skillfully foreigners might imitate them, the *Porgy* cast and Bernstein challenged Europeans to acknowledge American otherness. Realizing that they were dealing with singularly talented artists, the critics reaffirmed the superiority of the German performance tradition by embedding their subjects in a series of demeaning images. In this way, the threat was held at bay, but its potency survived. The cultural officers did well in bringing in these artists to Germany, as they did when they toured quality performers like Varnay and the Boston Symphony and Yehudi Menuhin and Ralph Kirkpatrick and the Juilliards. Art music may not have lived up to its reputation as a carrier of fraternal and humane messages, or as a builder of German-American empathy, but it did allow the Germans a glimpse of an America that was a more interesting place culturally than they had probably imagined.

If the goal of reorientation in the music field had been to teach the Germans that their own culture was flawed and America's superior; it clearly failed. If the purpose of using music in the campaign to solidify Western European defenses was to show Germans their kinship to Americans, it also failed. Anti-Americanism was alive and well among the patrons of art music in the mid-1950s and it would remain so for decades to come. A few American artists in the occupation period had dented German cultural preconceptions and even provided a warning of what was to come, but they had not won elite converts. In time, of course, Europe would become so well supplied with American musicians that they would cease to seem exotic, but even in the concert world, a certain disdain survived, most easily discernible in frequent expressions of longing for a golden age of Austro-German music production (among whose exemplars are an uncomfortably large number of musicians prominent in the Third Reich), when artists embodied "national traditions" and not some faceless "internationalism" (read: America).

Classical music's failure to overcome local resistance was probably untypical. After all, Germany did become the most overtly "American" of European countries. It remained loyal to the West in the Cold War and developed a real and enduring democratic nature. Americanization also succeeded, if judged by dress and style and even popular music, although the latter is more a testament to the power of radio, the recording industry, and advertising. Which underlines the problem: it is extremely difficult to connect directly the development of Germany's postwar culture to specific policies undertaken by OMGUS or HICOG. In terms of the music program, it is even difficult to credit the occupation authorities with "setting the ball in motion," because they created as much resentment and opposition as goodwill. Only in the structural reforms initiated by the Music Branch in 1945–47 can one easily see a lasting contribution. Of course, reorientation must have worked, as did the struggle against communism, but the individual programs seem to have only indirectly influenced the country's evolution. Unfortunately, in the realm of classical music, the successes were never enough to topple the cultural elite's resilient anti-Americanism.

Conclusion
A New Day in Beulah

Van Wagoner was quite insistent. He had just been on the phone to Clay, and MG wanted the music festival in Beulah reopened that very summer. Jim Clark, ICD's director in Bavaria, appeared confused: where exactly was the festival to be held? The *Land*'s military governor repeated his instructions: "in Beulah — the music town up the road." Clay, he explained, had agreed, under repeated pressure from some British muckety-muck, Lady Mabel Dunn, to authorize a reopening of the Wagner Festival in Beulah. Dunn claimed to have already lined up support and money for the festival in the United Kingdom, and she had corresponded with Wolfgang Wagner, the composer's grandson, about his assuming control. Van Wagoner, however, was a canny Wisconsin politician and there was something about the matter that made him uneasy. "What about this fellow, Wagner?" he asked Clark, adding hopefully, "Was his music banned by the Nazis?"[1]

A few days later, on 7 March 1948, Carlos Moseley was on his way up the road to Bayreuth. He had grave misgivings about reopening the festival, because he knew, as Van Wagoner did not, that Hitler had considered it the centerpiece of the arts in National Socialist Germany and had enjoyed a close personal relationship with the Wagner family. He also knew that uncertainty surrounded the whole issue of the Festspielhaus's ownership. Special Services had taken over the opera house in 1945 and used it for GI entertainments, and it had also served to accommodate displaced persons (DPs). In July 1947, when the prewar owner of the house, Winifred Wagner, passed through her *Spruchkammer* hearing, the army transferred the building in trust to a property custodian named by the city. Wagner, who had been blacklisted as a party member, was found guilty by the court and sentenced to 450 days manual labor as well as a fine that eliminated a large proportion of her personal wealth.[2] Consequently, although she wanted to reclaim ownership of the theater, the court not only prevented her from doing so until September 1948 but also made a reopening of the festival by the family financially impossible.

According to the property custodian, Edgar Richter (the son of the *Ring*'s first conductor, Hans Richter, and a close friend of the Wagners) the Festspielhaus had to be repaired immediately and at great cost. Although Moseley doubted that the structural problems were as significant as Richter said and suspected him of trying to make the building seem as unattractive as possible in order to ward off potential buyers, he realized that even without the deterrent of repairs, the theater was a big venture for anyone to contemplate running. The city of Bayreuth did not want it, as its 85,000 residents were already adequately served by their own opera house and concert hall and it could not afford to maintain a building that was only in use for one month a year. The mayor proposed raising money by establishing a "Tanhäuser Charitable Fund" in the United States, but John Evarts nixed that plan. The city then supported turning the house over to one of Winifred Wagner's sons, but the Americans also rejected this. The only politically clean member of the immediate family, Friedelind Wagner, who was living in New York, had been offered control, but she indicated that she was not yet ready.[3] And so, in this indeterminate state, the Festspielhaus festered on its green hill.

Moseley never took seriously the idea of staging a festival in Bayreuth in 1948, let alone a Wagner festival. Before the war, the old management had booked 1,600 rooms for the musicians and their families and the city had available a further 4,000 for the visitors who came during the festival's four-week run. These Bayreuth, which had been badly damaged by bombing and the fanatical resistance of ss troops in the closing days of the war and which was home to thousands of DPs, could simply no longer provide. When discussing the matter with city, state, and OMGB officials, Moseley therefore "stressed the fact that the undertaking should be kept within practical bounds" and promoted the idea that "a total of six simple orchestral concerts with 'selected' soloists spread over not too great a period of time should amply suffice." Eschewing the name "Festival," he recommended the holding of a series to be called "Bayreuth Summer Concerts," largely for the benefit of the locals.[4]

Moseley's report ended plans to revive the Wagner Festival under

American patronage, but Clay's willingness to consider its reopening was not lost on *Land* Bavaria. The *Land* understood the potential long-term benefit of the festival, both in terms of tourist income and prestige, but felt it would only succeed if the tainted Wagner family's connections were severed. Although the CSU government was not adverse to restoring former Nazis to their jobs if it meant ousting American appointees, reinstating the Wagner family was a different matter. Tourists, the Kultusministerium believed, would never come to a festival with such transparent links to the Nazi period.

In April 1948 the *Land's Kultusreferent*, Dieter Sattler, met with Winifred Wagner and indicated Bavaria's willingness to assume financial responsibility for the festival, but only on the condition that ownership be ceded to a committee of state, municipal, and "international friends." This Wagner refused. She did, however, indicate that she would be willing to surrender ownership to her two sons and she agreed with Sattler that under no circumstances should any artistic leaders of the Nazi period, such as Heinz Tietjen, the festival's former director, be involved in the new undertaking. The state rejected these conditions, however, and one month later Hundhammer spoke in Bayreuth on the anniversary of Richard Wagner's birth. The *Kultusminister* pointedly declared that the composer would never have achieved his dream of building a festival house in the first place had it not been for the Bavarians. He then affirmed his own interest in "dispelling the shadow of Nazism that still lay over Wagner's work." Sattler went again to Bayreuth in July 1948, this time with Moseley, and the two met once more with Winifred Wagner. Although Moseley confirmed that MG would prefer to see the festival removed from the control of current family members, he also said — probably in the hope that Friedelind might still prove acceptable — that his superiors were eager for an amicable settlement of the matter. But Winifred refused to consider *Land* control and held fast to her position that the only thing she would exchange for state funding was a transfer of Festspielhaus ownership to her sons. She also warned the two officials about her strength of will and rather tastelessly compared it with the relentlessness of a *Wehrmacht Blitzkrieg*.[5]

Negotiations had reached an impasse: the Wagners could not afford to reopen the festival without external money, and the Bavarian government would not provide the cash so long as the family remained in charge. As Winifred completed her sentence, the Wagners therefore began actively looking for private financing, and, worried that they might succeed, Sattler responded with another proposal: the *Land* would accept Wieland, the oldest son, as license holder as well as the family's ownership of the Festspielhaus, but in exchange for public money, the Wagners would hand over artistic direction to an *Intendant* elected by a committee representing the state, municipality, Bavarian radio, and private donors. This too the family rejected, and it publicly charged the state with trying to seize control of the *Festspiel* and disinherit its rightful owners. Wolfgang, the younger (and more politically clean) son, then launched a major fundraising drive to save his inheritance, and in the end some DM 400,000 from private sources were secured against the projected start-up costs of DM 670,000. Convinced now that the Wagners would not surrender control, the *Land* gave way a little. Instead of assuming the bulk of the costs, Bavaria contributed DM 200,000 to the 1951 festival but refused to guarantee the Wagners against losses (a wise move in retrospect as the festival went considerably over budget and cost DM 1.7 million).[6] Quite probably, the *Land* was keeping its interests in Bayreuth alive so that it could step in if and when the private venture failed. But for the moment at least, Wolfgang Wagner and his brother Wieland, who assumed the *Festspiel*'s artistic direction, had secured a tremendous victory.

The Wagners' single-minded commitment to the Bayreuth Festival was remarkable, and their ability to attract donors attests to the continued popularity of the master's music in postwar Germany. But the new owners had also learned from the fight to retain control that if their inheritance was to survive financially they would have to erase their family's past. As a first and most important step, Winifred quietly removed herself from any connection to the organization. At the same time, Wieland presented himself as the chief spokesperson for the theater, which he christened the "New Bayreuth" and which he asserted had been reborn artistically following the "creative black years" of the occupation. The Bayreuth Festival he created was designed to embody a transformed Germany, and he was anxious to contrast his own vision of the theater with that of his Nazi-period predecessors: Heinz Tietjen and his set designer, Emil Preetorius. These two, Wieland suggested, and not his own family, were the locus of the taint on the hill. "How do you expect me to design my productions," he asked a newspaper correspondent, "as they were done in the Third Reich? Decidedly not. . . . We live in the year 1951 and not in 1876 and must adjust ourselves to our times." Even though Preetorius had famously trimmed down Bayreuth's sets and made the costumes more abstract, Tietjen's productions, Wagner insisted, were artifacts of the past. Unfairly connecting Tietjen's stagings with those of the late nineteenth century, he told a reporter from *Le Figaro* that productions in the 1930s "were antiquated; young people today would laugh at them: too much fabric, too much pasteboard, and excessively absurd costumes."[7]

In a subtle and disturbing way, Wieland Wagner had reconceived the Nazi period as an aesthetic rather than familial or societal deformity. Nazism had been an abomination because it trivialized his grandfather's work. Naturalism in stage production, of the kind popular in the Reich, Wieland wrote, was an "utterly inadequate" way of realizing the composer's "inner vision." Could anyone really believe, he asserted, that Richard Wagner would be happy to see "the airy rainbows of his imagination reduced to a fusty, rickety bridge" or "the demon Klingsor turned into a bourgeois magician?" Bayreuth had to change, he asserted, "if it were not to become anachronistic, in effect, appealing only to a backward-looking public." In these years, Wieland never spoke about his family's relationship with the Führer, his own membership in the party, his work in the Flossenbürg concentration camp, or the special patronage the festival had enjoyed in the Nazi Reich. He never talked about his long conversations with Hitler in Berlin over design matters or his family's creation of a research and publications department in Bayreuth among whose purposes was advertising the composer's Aryan identity. Nor did Wagner own up to the fact that his ideas about how the composer's works should be presented had really begun to take shape during the Third Reich and not thereafter.[8]

The past, like the theater itself, should not, as Wieland explained it, relive reality; it should be magic. In the modern theater one had to escape from the "real, the banal, the everyday," and that meant attempting to represent on stage the "mystical, the legendary, the eternal." Wagner therefore abstracted his confrontation with the past through his art, illuminating with only the thinnest beams of light the darkness that had enveloped him. The results were not altogether comforting. As the writer Geoffrey Skelton observed, the centerpiece of the 1951 festival, Wieland's *Ring* cycle, was presented as a story of ruin: Wotan's dream of perfection — revealed by Wieland as a shimmering, dreamlike projection of Walhalla — was doomed to fail because the god had lied and cheated and countenanced murder to see it constructed. If this was a parable of the Reich, it revealed an artist content to question the methods, but not the values, of his past. And yet, Wieland Wagner did—in this *Ring*, above all—decouple Bayreuth from Nazism by exploiting the fiction that if the thing appeared radically new, then so it was. This was a common enough enterprise among artists in postwar Germany, but Wagner's efforts remain singular because they were so successful. Very few of those who had so greatly enjoyed Hitler's patronage were able to discard their background so completely. Certainly, Heinz Tietjen failed: critics rated his postwar staging of Wagner's operas pretty, but old-fashioned, and he had to console himself with the thought that Berlin audiences just didn't appreciate great art any more.[9]

Strongly influenced by Kurt Overhoff's notion that Wagner's operas had to be stripped of all unnecessary props in order to bring out their "inner meaning," Wieland Wagner, in the "new Bayreuth," denuded the stage of scenery and relied on light instead of pasteboard. Costumes became uncluttered, simple, "architectural" features—there to emphasize, through overall color or shape, a particular dramatic mood. Reality was eschewed and buildings, rocks, and trees reduced to abstract shapes and shadows. The artistic director also made a virtue of casting against type, hiring Clemens Krauss, who prized orchestral lightness and transparency, to conduct the *Ring* in 1952 and Karajan, whom Hitler particularly disliked as a Wagner conductor, to share the podium in the first year with the more conventional Knappertsbusch. Wieland also employed a number of high-profile foreign singers; a Canadian, George London, was the first Amfortas, an American (Swedish-born), Astrid Varnay, the first Brünnhilde, and a Chilean, Ramon Vinay, the first Tristan. As the historian Sabine Henze-Döhring has pointed out, the new Bayreuth seemed to manifest the very internationalism that the Americans had worked so hard to promote.[10]

It is difficult, however, to ignore the irony in this theatrical phoenix. Wieland Wagner, who joined the Nazi Party at the age of twenty-one, was presenting former Nazis like Herbert von Karajan and Josef Greindl and strong Hitler supporters such as Klemens Krauss and Karl Böhm and Erich Witte as annunciators of a new look and sound. The truth is that, while Bayreuth employed some foreigners, it also made use of many old Nazis. Even when they were packaged in startling ways, Günther Treptow and Hans Knappertsbusch and Ludwig

Weber could hardly be regarded as altogether new. Revolutionary though Wagner's art appeared, more of the past lingered about Bayreuth than anyone cared to recognize.

But in the postwar classical music field the fact is that new had become shorthand for exoneration. This is why so many Germans seemed willing to participate in the magic that was the "new Bayreuth." But new had not become the Federal Republic's cultural code word unassisted. It was during the process of their denazification in 1945–47 that artists first discovered the importance of aligning themselves with the new, and there is no reason to expect that, without the pressure applied by the Allies, they would have seen the need to reconfigure themselves at all. Most musicians did not believe they had done anything wrong by performing or composing in the Third Reich and so saw no reason to change. In fact, people like Orff and Furtwängler and Egk and Karajan and Krauss and a host of others believed they and their art were victims of Nazi oppression: they congratulated themselves for carrying on through the dark years and, like Böhm and Zwissler, were proud of having—through their repertoire choices—preserved their integrity. Although most musicians were doubtless happy to see the end of war and dictatorship, none of them seemed to feel that they had compromised with the Reich and, as a result, none of them felt they should be punished for what Hitler had done. It was the Allies who insisted that a new Germany must be constructed on the rubble of the old, and it was the Allies who demanded that artists make a fresh start.

Although the reformers and revolutionaries in ICD were at loggerheads when it came to judging the guilt of musicians, they all agreed on the need to create a new and democratic Germany. Most senior ICD officers in 1945 considered the Germans an arrogant, warmongering people, machinelike in their willingness to follow orders and predisposed to inhumanity by their contempt for others. These character traits, they felt, were present even before the Nazis, but twelve years of indoctrination had made them worse. If the world was ever going to be free of the German menace, it would have to change the Germans' culture. This is what led MG to encourage the new. As far as Germany was concerned, change could only be for the better.

Music made its way onto the list of areas for ICD to re-create relatively late, but its presence there made eminent sense. For many people at the time, and for most Germans, their country was the fountainhead of classical music: German composers dominated the repertoire, German artists were widely regarded as the best, and German values (primarily the notion that music was a force of uplift and education) permeated the culture. The Nazis amplified these ideas and used them to justify both a narrowing of the performance repertoire and the elimination of Jews and other "degenerates" from the stage. And classical music came to serve the regime in other important ways: justifying its claim to greatness, corroborating its racism, and countering its opponents. By 1945 Nazism had tangled itself through the industry: performers had been compromised by their activities on behalf of, or membership in, fascist organizations and causes; the repertoire had suffered; the meaning and image of music's icons had been distorted; and the structures of administration had been corrupted. If German culture was to be set on a completely new course, the occupiers believed, classical music needed to be transformed.

Although the military governor's decision to end radical denazification one year after its implementation put a sorry end to this unfulfilled experiment, the revolutionaries may well have achieved at least part of their goal. The simple threat of the blacklist had been enough to convince many musical artists that they needed to make themselves over, and the telling of lies was their way of making a fresh start. Thanks to ICD's policies, musicians embraced the idea that a cultural page had been turned in 1945. That in itself was something. American policy induced artists to make believe Germany's surrender marked a *Stunde Null* for the arts, and the idea of newness coursed through music culture in the occupation years. This was why artists found it reassuring to conflate different impressions of time passage: the usual one, which held that anything written relatively recently was more or less contemporary, with the specifically German one, which hinged on the idea that 1945 was the point where things began. Werner Egk's 1948 declaration that his *Circe* was "contemporary and modishly modern" implied that it was a postwar work, even though it had been written during the last years of the Reich; similarly, Hindemith's *Mathis der Maler* was proclaimed in 1946 as "banishing to lonely theorizing all those who doubt the value of the utterly new," even though it was a product of the early 1930s. Wieland Wagner had first staged a stripped-down *Ring* in Altenburg during the war.[11]

The image of novelty was also all important to *Land* governments, which pumped money into contemporary music organizations and cultivated new arm's-length relationships with those they appointed to administer public institutions. This too was a legacy of ICD's aborted effort to transform German culture. In fact, like the denazifiers, the music officers' long-term contribution to democratization was partly structural and largely attitudinal. In the interests of artistic freedom, they appointed people they considered democratically minded to head major orchestras and opera houses, they pressed structural reforms designed to distance the state from the concert hall, and they encouraged competition in the shape of private theaters. Much of what they attempted came apart under the blows of currency reform—their appointees were dismissed, the state tightened its financial grip on the arts, and the private organizations folded—but, as with denazification, core values survived. The fact that state control came to be seen as a bad thing was a legacy of ICD's conviction that the Germans were predisposed to kowtow to authority. So too was state support for contemporary music, and it survived currency reform because public officials were convinced that Germany had to look like it was a changed place. The Americans' definition of the Nazi music world—that it was the ultimate expression of the German proclivity for bureaucratization and conservatism—therefore survived in the *Länder*'s anxiety to avoid the appearance of centralization and governmental restriction and cultural chauvinism. As with new music and made-over musicians, ICD's impact on artistic freedom was indirect, transformative, and enduring.

While the inability of the occupation authorities to realize specific goals requires emphasis—and the visiting artists program stands out in this regard—it is also important to acknowledge the scale of the task the Americans had undertaken. Running another country's affairs and governing its people is far from easy and becomes even more daunting when one tries to do it according to democratic principles. A major reason why McClure's hardheaded approach to Germany failed was because it seemed arbitrary to his own music officers, and it struck his superior, Lucius Clay, as undemocratic. Both were uncomfortable with the idea of reforming Germany by force rather than persuasion, prohibition rather than example. At the root of the controversy was not only a different concept of the depth and breadth of the Germans' inhumanity, but also a different image of the attractiveness of American democracy. Although ostensibly more "realistic," Clay's approach—which was also ultimately adopted by the High Commission—was in reality the more "idealistic" because it rested on the belief that the Germans would choose democracy by doing it because it was so much better than dictatorship. In Clay's view, democracy would grow through its own merit, and all the Americans had to do was prevent the bad men from perverting it, as they had done once before. The music officers shared much of this idealism. Although they did not accept the military governor's conviction in 1946 that the Germans were ready to run their own cultural affairs, they did think the defeated could be taught to be free and that even the corrupted could learn to prize liberal values. Needless to say, like Clay and McCloy, their definition of freedom and democracy remained an American one.

In many ways, it is remarkable the Americans succeeded so well, given the size and marginal status of the cultural officers within the occupation hierarchy. But the Music Branch was fortunate in its personnel: mostly hardworking, well-meaning, and knowledgeable people. In fact, the cultural officers' own success, in personal terms, is something of surpassing importance. No matter what else they might have achieved or failed to do, these Americans deserve credit for having generally behaved in trying times and tempting circumstances with uncommon decency. Few of them cheated others or abused their positions or jumped to simple conclusions, even when the opportunities offered themselves. To one contemporary observer, this was ultimately their most important legacy: "[T]hese people—Johnny Bitter, John Evarts, Ginny Pleasants, Carlos Moseley, Newell Jenkins—they themselves and their personalities and the effect that they had on the people with whom they dealt, that was the positive aspect of the program. The program itself, I think, was useless."[12]

Though perhaps not quite useless. Postwar Germany did develop into a stable and peaceful democracy, and freedom of expression was enshrined in the constitutions of its *Länder*. Artists did now struggle to find new sounds and new ways of presenting themselves, and this contributed to the impression that a new day in Germany had dawned. Something had clearly worked. Of curse, the cultural life of the new republic had not really been refreshed in the process of its democratic regeneration. Nazis and fellow travelers still dominated the classical music landscape: Wieland Wagner and Herbert von Karajan, Elizabeth Schwarzkopf and Wilhelm Kempff, Carl Orff and Werner Egk. These artists presented themselves as though newly formed in 1945 because they buried the record of their Nazi-era selves. As Webster

Aitken slyly noted of the artists he met in 1949, their "basic orientation . . . is about the same as it always has been. It only awaits a suitable opportunity to fish out all the trunkfuls [*sic*] of Nazi flags, swastikas, SS uniforms, etc. — patriotic rubbish temporarily relegated to basements and attics of whatever houses still stand, kept alive with significance, by an overwhelming sense of defeat, in the crevices and chasms of an unfathomable national consciousness."[13] This was not a psychologically healthy development, even if Nazism never revived and even if Germany's quick return to international musical celebrity did have a stabilizing effect on the state and society. ICD's contribution to this reality has to be recognized (for good and ill) just as does its role in promoting artistic freedoms and international connections.

Military Government must therefore share responsibility for creating classical music's chiaroscuro in the postwar period. It should be credited with advancing the idea that music's Nazi links had to be severed and a new culture created, and it must also shoulder blame for not taking sufficiently seriously the fascists' contamination of the arts and for allowing musicians with shameful pasts to quietly and collectively rehabilitate themselves. Other options were available, ranging from McClure's purge to the music officers' selective punishment, but MG chose the cheapest, easiest, and most inglorious course: it let the locals decide. If the American occupiers contributed to the development of postwar Germany's rich classical music scene, they failed to prevent the reassertion of German confidence in their own cultural superiority or the cover-up of classical music's collaboration in the crimes of National Socialism. Many of us who love music remain troubled by this legacy.

NOTES

ABBREVIATIONS

In addition to the abbreviations used in the text, the following source abbreviations are used in the notes.

ACA   Allied Control Authority
AdK   Akademie der Künste, Berlin
APA   Author's Private Archive
BDC   Berlin Document Center
BH   Bayerisches Hauptstaatsarchiv, Munich
CAD   Civil Affairs Division
CRB   Cultural Relations Branch
DDEL   Dwight David Eisenhower Library, Abilene
DHQ   Divisional Headquarters
DISCC   District Information Services Control Command
DO   Director's Office
E&CR   Education and Cultural Relations
EO   Executive Office
FT&M   Film, Theatre and Music
HH   Hessisches Hauptstaatsarchiv, Wiesbaden
HI   Hoover Institution on War, Revolution and Peace Archive,
           Palo Alto
HO   Historical Office
HRC   Harry Ransom Center, Austin
HS   Hauptstaatsarchiv Stuttgart
HSTL   Harry S. Truman Library, Independence
IECA   Information, Education and Cultural Affairs
IfZ   Institut für Zeitgeschichte, Munich
ISD   Information Services Division
JEPA   Jeremiah Evarts Private Archive, Cornish, New Hampshire
LB   Landesarchiv Berlin
LC   Library of Congress, Washington, D.C.
NA   National Archives, Washington, D.C.
nd   No Date
OCB   Operations Control Board
ODL   Oskar Diethelm Library, Cornell University, New York, New York
OMGBS   Office of the Military Government Berlin Sector
OMGH   Office of the Military Government Hesse
OMGWB   Office of the Military Government Württemberg-Baden

OSU	Ohio State University Archive, Columbus
PAJB	Private Archive John Bitter, Miami
PAMK	Private Archive Michael Kater, Toronto
PR/ISC	Public Relations/Information Services Control
PRO	Public Records Office, London
Rg	Record Group
RMK	Reichsmusikkammer (Chamber of Music in the Third Reich)
SB	Stadtarchiv Berlin
SL	Staatsarchiv Ludwigsburg
SM	Stadtarchiv München
SS	Stadtarchiv Stuttgart
T&M	Theater and Music
USACA	U.S. Allied Command Austria
WB	Württemberg-Baden
WSU	Washington State University Archive, Pullman
YUA	Yale University Archive, New Haven

INTRODUCTION

1. Deems Taylor, Transcript of Radio Broadcast, 22 February 1942, uncataloged boxes of radio broadcasts, Deems Taylor Papers, YUA.

2. See, for example, Kater, *The Twisted Muse* and *Composers of the Nazi Era*; Wulf, *Musik im Dritten Reich*; Prieberg, *Musik im NS-Staat*; Rathkolb, *Führertreu und gottbegnadet*; and Potter, *Most German of the Arts*.

3. On the central role of music in the nineteenth-century German national identity, Applegate, "What Is German Music?"; on its postwar importance, see Kater, *Composers of the Nazi Era*, 267–70 and 276–79.

4. A number of MG's cultural divisions have now been studied. For film, see Fehrenbach, *Cinema in Democratizing Germany*, ch. 2, and Culbert, "American Film Policy"; the press is covered in Frei, *Amerikanische Lizenzpolitik*, Gienow-Hecht, *Transmission Impossible*, Hurwitz, *Die Stunde Null der deutschen Presse*, and Mosberg, *Reeducation*; on writers, Gehring, *Amerikanische Literaturpolitik*; radio is discussed in Mettler, *Demokratisierung und Kalter Krieg*; for the Amerika Häuser (predominantly the lending libraries), see Hein-Kremer, *Die amerikanische Kulturoffensive*; on education, Bungenstab, *Umerziehung zur Demokratie?*, Müller, *Schulpolitik in Bayern*, Tent, *Mission on the Rhine*, and Remy, *The Heidelberg Myth*, chs. 5–6; for galleries, see Deshmukh, "Recovering Culture"; the only study of the cultural divisions as a whole is an excellent, though *Land*-based, one: Bausch, *Die Kulturpolitik der US-amerikanischen Information Control Division*.

5. On the failure of denazification and its link to economic recovery: Niethammer, *Entnazifizierung in Bayern*; Boehling, *A Question of Priorities*; Eisenberg, *Drawing the Line*, 372–74. Eisenberg dates the major change in de-

nazification policy to 1947 rather than early 1946; Balabkins, *Germany under Direct Controls*, sees the Allies obstructing recovery, and Milward, *The Reconstruction of Western Europe*, doubts the positive contribution of the Americans; on the penetration of American business values, see Berghahn, *The Americanization of West German Industry*, and on consumerism, see Carter, *How German Is She?*

6. The classic critique of OMGUS is Peterson's *The American Occupation of Germany*. Bance, Introduction, 23–24, and Makovits, "Anti-Americanism," show nation building through resistance. Monod, "Internationalism," traces this aspect in the music area.

7. Goedde, *GIs and Germans*; Berghahn, "Recasting Bourgeois Germany"; Rupieper, "Bringing Democracy to the Fräuleins."

8. Maase, *Bravo Amerika*; Fehrenbach, *Cinema in Democratizing Germany*; Poiger, *Jazz, Rock and Rebels*; Höhn, *GIs and Fräuleins*. Peter Breit briefly summarizes the failure of official efforts at "Americanization" in comparison with the success of U.S. popular culture in the 1950s in "Culture as Authority."

9. On politics see Boehling, "US Military Occupation"; the princess analogy can be found in Schivelbusch, *In a Cold Crater*, 183; the quotation is from Glaser, *The Rubble Years*, 334.

CHAPTER I

1. Interview with John Bitter, 9 June 1996. (Interviews by author unless otherwise indicated by archival reference.)

2. Interview with John Bitter, 9 June 1996; interview with John Bitter, 6 November 1981, C Rep 37/82, LB.

3. SHAEF Joint Intelligence Committee Report, 2 July 1945, 37/4, Daniel Lerner Papers, HI.

4. W. D. Haslett to Reinhold Niebuhr, 25 May 1945, 198 misc 1945, Official File, Harry S. Truman Papers, HSTL.

5. PWD SHAEF, "Account of Operations in the Western European Campaign," 13–14, file: PWD, box 73, HO, DHQ, ICD, OMGUS, Rg 260, NA; interview with Virginia Pleasants, 19 May 1996.

6. Gordon, *Mark the Music*, 249; *New York Herald Tribune*, 17 June 1945, in "OWI and Government Information Policy Daily Report," 18 June 1945, Charles M. Hulten Papers, HSTL.

7. *Wheeling Intelligencer*, 30 May 1945, in "OWI and Government Information Policy Daily Report," 7 June 1945; *San Diego Union*, 2 June 1945, in ibid., 12 June 1945; *Rochester Democrat and Chronicle*, 17 June 1945, in ibid., 25 June 1945, Hulten Papers, HSTL. Thacker, "Liberating German Musical Life," 82–85, sees similar conflicts in BBC broadcasts.

8. Marek, *The Good Housekeeping Guide*, 48, cited in Horowitz, *Understanding*

Toscanini, 261; Gelatt, *The Fabulous Phonograph*, 273–77. On classical music's elite associations, see Levine, *Highbrow/Lowbrow*; Ota, *Making Music Modern*, ch. 12; Lynes, *The Lively Audience*, ch. 1. On the meaning of classical music to turn-of-the-century Americans, see Horowitz, *Wagner Nights*.

9. PWD SHAEF, "Account of Operations in the Western European Campaign," 15, file: PWD, box 73, HO, DHQ, ICD, OMGUS, and R. K. Craft, "Psychological Warfare Staff Coordination at all Echelons," November 1945, in file: PWD, box 49, Central Files, HO, DHQ, ICD, OMGUS.

10. PWD SHAEF, "Account of Operations in the Western European Campaign," 18, file: PWD, box 73, HO, DHQ, ICD, OMGUS; *Washington News*, 31 March 1945, in "OWI and Government Information Policy Daily Report," 2 April 1945, Hulten Papers, HSTL. Hein-Kremer's detailed discussion of the lending libraries provides an excellent introduction to the coordination of OWI/PWD activities; see *Die amerikanische Kulturoffensive*, esp. ch. 2. For more on the origins of PWD, see Balfour, "In Retrospect," 142–45.

11. Eisenhower, *Crusade in Europe*, 434–35; Murphy, *Diplomat among Warriors*, 281–82; "Directive for Psychological Warfare and Control of German Information Services," 18 April 1945, entry 87, box 19, PWD, Special Staff, SHAEF, GG331, NA.

12. On the Guild Theater, see Lynes, *The Lively Audience*, 189–91; "Draft Notes on Music in Germany," FO 898/415, PRO (I am grateful to Toby Thacker for the quotation and reference); the PWE report that Munsell forwarded to PWD ultimately appeared as appendix A of the *Manual for the Control of German Information Services*, 34/1, David M. Levy Papers, ODL; interview with Carlos Moseley, 18 March 1996.

13. "Report of the Science, Education and Art Division, Department of State," May–June 1944, box 1, Bryn J. Hovde Papers, HSTL; *Washington Times-Herald*, 8 April 1945, in "OWI and Government Information Policy Daily Report," 9 April 1945, Hulten Papers, HSTL.

14. Davidson Taylor memo, 12 January 1945, entry 87, box 24, PWD, Special Staff, SHAEF; Robert McClure to F. E. Morgan, 25 April 1945, W. S. Paley to Samuel Rosenbaum, 20 January 1945, and Semi-Monthly Report of PWD Sections, 4 April 1945, entry 87, box 17, PWD, Special Staff, SHAEF; "Program Guide for Germany," 1 June 1945, OWI file, Hulten Papers, HSTL.

15. PWD, "Semi Monthly Progress Reports, Entertainment Control Section," 1 February, 1 March, and 15 March 1945, file: PWD, box 78, HO, DHQ, ICD, OMGUS. I am grateful to Toby Thacker for the reference to McClure's March 1945 request for guidance regarding music control. On PWE's approach: Elkes, "Wartime Images of Germany," 38–54; "Control

of Film, Theater & Music in Germany: Music Control," 2 June 1945, file: Germany, box 64, Staff Advisor, ISD, DHQ, ICD, OMGUS; Davidson Taylor to Film, Theater & Music Control Branches, 26 May 1945, entry 87, box 24, PWD, Special Staff, SHAEF.

16. *Manual for the Control of German Information Services*, 28–29, 34/1, Levy Papers, ODL; interview with Henry Pleasants, 2 November 1996.

17. The best study of wartime destruction is Diefendorf, *In the Wake of War*; interview with Edward Kilenyi, 8 June 1996; interview with Carlos Moseley, 18 March 1996.

18. "Special Report: Music Control in Bavaria, June 1945–July 1946," 27 July 1946, file: Reports, box 241, T&M, E&CR, OMGUS; on the postwar fate of the Festspielhaus, Spotts, *Bayreuth*, 198–201.

19. Clay, *Decision in Germany*, 21; Speier, *From the Ashes of Disgrace*, 26; Webster Aitken's Journal, "Journey into Defeat: Germany, April 7–28 1949," Webster Aitken Papers, HRC; Clare, *Before the Wall*, 16.

20. "PWE Intelligence Report," 10 April 1944, 33/5, Lerner Papers, HI.

21. For more on music in Nazi Germany, see Kater's trilogy, *Different Drummers*, *The Twisted Muse*, and *Composers of the Nazi Era*. Also essential are Wulf, *Musik im Dritten Reich*; Prieberg, *Musik im NS-Staat*; Rathkolb, *Führertreu und gottbegnadet*; Steinweis, *Art, Ideology and Economics*; Levi, *Music in the Third Reich*; Walter, *Hitler in der Oper*; Potter, "The Nazi Seizure of the Berlin Philharmonic"; and Potter, *Most German of the Arts*.

22. Goebbels Diary, entry for 31 July 1924, in Fröhlich, *Die Tagebücher von Joseph Goebbels*, 1:56; cited in Heldt, "Hardly Heroes," 118.

23. Interview with Newell Jenkins, 6 July 1996; interview with Mateo Lettunich, 12 August 1996; Zink, *American Military Government*, 160–61; PWD SHAEF, "Account of Operations in the Western European Campaign," 159–60, file: PWD, box 73, HO, DHQ, ICD, OMGUS; *New York Times*, 1 July 1946. The Department of State appropriated $5 million for information work in Germany in 1945–46; William Benton to President Truman, 7 January 1946, file 1, CF 20E, Truman Papers, HSTL.

24. Robert McClure to C. D. Jackson, cited in Alfred Paddock Jr., "Major General Robert Alexis McClure," <www.psywarrior.com/mcclure.html>, accessed 13 October 2002; Henke, *Die amerikanische Besetzung Deutschlands*, 302, notes the "undisciplined" nature of McClure's command.

25. McClure cited in Schivelbusch, *In a Cold Crater*, 32; McClure cited in Gienow-Hecht, *Transmission Impossible*, 48.

26. Speech by Brig. Gen. Robert A. McClure, 27 August 1945, entry 172, box 330, War Department, Rg 165, NA; "Program Guide for Germany," 1 June 1945, OWI file, Hulten Papers, HSTL; John Scott Cable #79, 21 September 1945, file: OWI (2), box 11, C. D. Jackson Papers, DDEL; R. A. McClure, "Guidance on Propaganda Treatment of Individual German Re-

sponsibilities," 31 May 1945, file: Guidance Notes, box 40, Executive Section, PWD, Special Staff, SHAEF.

27. By 1945 two out of three Americans favored imposing a "hard peace" on Germany; see Casey, *Cautious Crusade*, 221. Mauldin, *Up Front*, 50; Speier, *From the Ashes of Disgrace*, 37–38. For more on Speier, see Barnouw, *Germany 1945*, 139–49.

28. "Control of Film, Theater & Music in Germany," 2 June 1945, file: German Information Control, box 64, ISD Staff Advisor, DHQ, ICD, OMGUS; Music Control Instruction No. 1 and Standing Directive No. 1, 20 July 1945, entry 172, box 330, War Department, Rg 165, NA.

29. "Control of Film, Theater & Music in Germany," 2 June 1945, file: German Information Control, box 64, ISD Staff Advisor, DHQ, ICD, OMGUS; *Newsweek*, 6 August 1945, 90; Davidson Taylor memo, 12 January 1945, entry 87, box 24, PWD, Special Staff, SHAEF. Clemens, *Britische Kulturpolitik in Deutschland*, 142–45, correctly notes the division within PWD over how to control the arts in Germany, but she simplifies the debate by ascribing one position to the Americans and the other to the British; Thacker's "Liberating German Musical Life," 86–88, offers a corrective.

30. *Newsweek*, 6 August 1945, 90; "Program Guide for Germany," 1 June 1945, OWI file, Hulten Papers, HSTL.

31. Evarts, "Vom Musikleben in Amerika," 85; *Nachtexpress*, 4 March 1947, clipping in John Bitter Scrapbook, PAJB; "Draft Guidance on Control of Music," 8 June 1945, Central File 353.8, box 134, DHQ, ICD, OMGUS.

32. *New York Times*, 11 May 1946; Bi-Weekly Report, 24 November 1946, file: T&M, box 21, Executive Office, ISB, USACA, Rg 260, NA.

33. Interview with Edward Kilenyi, 8 June 1996, and for a classic example of the music officers' self-portrait (note the contrast Lothar draws between the rabid denazifier and "Lady Killer," Colonel Ladue, and himself), Lothar, *Das Wunder des Überlebens*, 321–22 and 346.

34. "Program Guide for Germany," 1 June 1945, OWI file, Hulten Papers, HSTL.

35. Interview with Edward Kilenyi, 8 June 1996.

CHAPTER 2

1. Annex to Report No. 121 [*sic*], 11 December 1945, file: T&M, box 21, EO, ISB, USACA, Rg 260, NA.

2. Michael Kater offers a sympathetically critical biography of Strauss in *Composers of the Nazi Era*, ch. 8; for Strauss's work in the RMK, see Splitt, *Richard Strauss*; the composer's defenders include Jefferson, *Richard Strauss*, and Kennedy, *Richard Strauss*; critics include Marek, *Richard Strauss*, and Prieberg, *Musik im NS-Staat*, 200–210.

3. Richard Strauss to Willi Schuh, 10 May 1945, in Schuh, *Richard Strauss*, 78; *Milwaukee Journal*, 10 November 1963 (I am grateful to W. Howard Cotton Jr. for this reference); Annex to Report No. 121 [*sic*], 11 December 1945, file: T&M, box 21, EO, ISB, USACA.

4. Minutes of Information Control Conference, 16 October 1946, file: 52A, box 114, ICD Intelligence Records, Intelligence Division, OMGB, OMGUS, Rg 260, NA; "Information Control Policies in the Light of JCS 1067 and the Potsdam Agreement," 29 September 1945, file: Information Committee of the Political Directorate, box 70, HO, DHQ, ICD, OMGUS.

5. "History of Information Control Division, 8 May–30 June 1945," file: ICD Activities, 1945–49, box 454, ICD, EO, OMGUS.

6. "Information Control Policies in the Light of JCS 1067 and the Potsdam Agreement," 29 September 1945, file: Information Committee of the Political Directorate, box 70, HO, DHQ, ICD, OMGUS. The RKK initially included Jews in its membership, and it was not until the late 1930s that it finally excluded all of them.

7. "History of Information Control Division, 8 May–30 June 1945," 89, file: ICD Activities, 1945–49, box 454, ICD, EO, OMGUS.

8. "History of Information Control Division, 8 May–30 June 1945," 89, file: ICD Activities, 1945–49, box 454, ICD, EO, OMGUS; *Manual for the Control of German Information Services*, 34/1, David M. Levy Papers, ODL; Eric Clarke and Benno Frank, "Theater & Music as Principal Parts of Reorientation in Germany," 16 September 1947, file: Reorientation, box 728, T&M, E&CR, OMGH, OMGUS.

9. "Preliminary Report by the Working Committee to the Denazification Policy Board," 20 December 1945, file: Denazification, box 332, Public Safety Branch, CAD Records, OMGUS. According to Rebecca Boehling, ICD was the most "adamantly anti-Nazi" division in Military Government; *A Question of Priorities*, 87. USFET ICD, "Classification list for screening," 11 October 1945, 34/1, Levy Papers, ODL; "Information Control Policies in Light of JCS 1067/6," 1 October 1945, file: Germany, box 64, ISD Staff Advisor, DHQ, ICD, OMGUS.

10. "History of Information Control Division, 8 May–30 June 1945," 61, file: ICD Activities, 1945–49, box 454, ICD, EO, OMGUS; Report on Mission No. 6, 13 June 1945, "Report on Music and Theater Situation in Nürnberg," 2 July 1945, Daily Report No. 18, Nürnberg Mission, 11 July 1945, and Report: Nürnberg Opera, nd [July 1945], file: DISCC 6870, box 75, HO, DHQ, ICD, OMGUS; Wachter, *Kultur in Nürnberg*, 53–56 and 129.

11. "Present Procedure in Issuance of Licenses" (nd), file: Theater Policies, box 242, T&M, E&CR, OMGUS; Memo: CIC check, 25 November 1947, and "Political Clearance of German Personnel," file: Regulations, box 20,

Director's Records, ICD, OMGUS. MG Law #8 was passed in response to pressure in the United States to tighten up on denazification procedures in the wake of the Patton scandal; Niethammer, *Entnazifizierung*, 95–112.

12. Bi-Weekly Report, 24 November 1946, file: T&M, box 21, EO, ISB, USACA; "Berliner Entnazifizierungs-Kommission für Künstler, Zweite Verhandlung über den Antrag von Dr. Wilhelm Furtwängler," 17 December 1946, file: Wilhelm Furtwängler, box 2, General Records, T&M, ISB, USACA; Subject: Herbert Maisch, 12 June 1946, 35/2, Levy Papers, ODL; Interrogation of Heinz Drewes, 18 September 1945, 72/7, Daniel Lerner Papers, HI; Gertrud Marosky to Konzertdirektion Adler, 11 August 1949, file: T&M, box 97, ISB, OMGBS, OMGUS.

13. Goetz to Carl Orff, 3 December 1945, PAMK; Newell Jenkins to Carl Orff, 7 January 1946, box 928, T&M, E&CR, OMGWB, OMGUS; Jenkins to Orff, 26 March 1946, and Jenkins to Orff, 30 January 1946, PAMK.

14. Heinz Tietjen, testimonial, 8 February 1947, file: Tietjen, box 242, T&M, E&CR, OMGUS; Furtwängler, *Aufzeichnungen*, 236; Prieberg accepts Furtwängler's view that his performances of Beethoven Ninth, in particular, were a "challenge" to Hitler in *Trial of Strength*, 211; Karl Maria Zwissler to Karl Holl, 18 June 1948, and Zwissler, "Kommentar zu meinem Schreiben an Herrn, Dr. Ludwig Strecker vom 7 Januar 1948," 504/33a, HH; Otto de Pasetti to Captain Epstein, nd [January 1946], file: Herbert von Karajan, box 8, ISB, EO, USACA.

15. Winifred Wagner, "Denkshrift," nd [1947], APA; Hamann, *Winifred Wagner*, 292–94, refers to her efforts on her children's behalf and for her denazification, 543–58; on Hüsch, see John Evarts's Diary, December 1945, JEPA; Subject: Max Hahn, nd, 37/17, Levy Papers, ODL; H. C. Alter, "Subject: Elisabeth Schwarzkopf," 2 May 1946, box 8, ISB, EO, USACA.

16. Daniel Lerner, "Notes on a Trip through Occupied Germany," 18 April 1945, 37/7, and "PWD Weekly Intelligence Summary" #5, 28 October 1944, 38/3, Daniel Lerner Papers, HI.

17. "Removal from Black List—Karl Böhm," 16 January 1947, box 8, ISB, EO, USACA; "Report on Clemens Krauss," nd [November 1945?], box 2, T&M, ISB, USACA; Otto de Pasetti, "Clemens Kraus [*sic*]: Investigation Munich," 21 December 1945, box 38, Administrative Section, ISB, USACA; "Maria Cebotari," nd [June 1946?], box 42, EO, ISB, USACA.

18. "Notes on Trip to Western Rhineland Area," 21–28 March 1945, entry 87, box 17, PWD, Special Staff, SHAEF, GG331, NA.

19. Rudolf Goette to No. 8 Information Control Unit, 11 January 1946, and Rudolf Goette, "Überblick über die Tätigkeit Walter Giesekings seit 1933," 11 January 1946, file: Gieseking, RKK 2700, BDC, NA; interview with

Edward Kilenyi, 8 June 1996; Annex to Report 121 [*sic*], 11 December 1945, file: T&M, box 21, EO, ISB, USACA.

20. Weekly Situation Report, 20 June 1945, file: DISCC 6871, box 75, HO, DHQ, ICD, OMGUS.

21. Robert McClure to A. G. Neville, 7 June 1945, entry 87, box 7, PWD, Special Staff; SHAEF; "Recommendations of Film, Theater & Music Sub-Section," 18 July 1945, file: Berlin Reports, box 75, HO, DHQ, ICD, OMGUS; Speech by Alonzo Grace, 8 October 1948, file: Berchtesgaden Conference, box 4, DHQ, E&CR, OMGUS; Weekly Situation Report, 20 June 1945, file: DISCC 6871, box 75, HO, DHQ, ICD, OMGUS.

22. Robert McClure to Lewis Daniel, 20 June 1945, entry 87, box 7, PWD, Special Staff, SHAEF; W. Bogner Jr., "Harry Bogner: Biographical Sketch," nd (I am grateful to W. Howard Cotton Jr. for supplying this document); Holger Hagen, "Personal Observations of Operations in 6870th DISCC," 29 September 1945, file: DISCC 6870, box 241, T&M, E&CR, OMGB, OMGUS; interview with Edward Kilenyi, 28 June 1995; memo: Meinzolt, 3 July 1945, MK 50007, BH; Davidson Taylor to Film-Theater-Music Control Branches, 26 May 1945, entry 87, box 24, PWD, Special Staff, SHAEF.

23. Holger Hagen, "Report on Mission to Munich and Nurnberg," 29 September 1945, file: DISCC 6870, box 241, T&M, E&CR, OMGB, OMGUS; Daily Report, 26 June 1945, file: Reports, box 20, T&M, DO, E&CR, OMGB, OMGUS; the true status of Kabasta's party membership is not certain as he claimed at the time of his 1938 application for membership in Germany to have joined the party in Austria in 1932 (I am indebted to Joan Evans for providing this information); E. Kilenyi to Scharnagl, 10 October 1945, Dr. Stadelmayer to O. Kabasta, 11 October 1945, and O. Kabasta to Dr. Stadelmayer, 3 November 1945, Kulturamt 11016, SM.

24. Memo: Meinzolt, 3 July 1945, MK 50007, BH; G. Van Loon to Captain Ross, 27 June 1945, and G. W. Ross, Memo: Munich Philharmonic, 3 July 1945, file: Munich Philharmonic, box 19, CRB, E&CR, OMGB, OMGUS; Holger Hagen, "Personal Observations of Operations in 6870th DISCC," file: DISCC 6870, box 241, T&M, E&CR, OMGB, OMGUS.

25. T&M Reports, 5 August 1945 and 10 July 1945, file: Reports, box 20, DHQ, E&CR, OMGB, OMGUS; "Report on Munich's Music Personalities," 6 July 1945, file: DISCC 6870, box 75, HO, DHQ, ICD, OMGUS; Kilenyi liked Edenhofer, who was only in his late twenties at the time, and was so upset over his October 1945 blacklisting and dismissal that he wrote a letter of support for him declaring that the young man "has permission of this command to perform in public under sponsorship of license. This decision supersedes previous classification." I have found no evidence that Kilenyi had divisional approval for this last assertion. R. Edenhofer to

Ministerialrat Hassinger, 11 December 1945 and 21 January 1946, file 66, EA 3/201, HS; T&M Daily Report #10, 26 June 1945, file: Reports, box 20, DHQ, E&CR, OMGB, OMGUS.

26. Kater, *Twisted Muse*, 40–46.

27. T&M Daily Report, 15 July 1945, file: Reports, box 20, DHQ, E&CR, OMGB, OMGUS; G. W. Ross, "Interview of Hans Knappertsbusch," 20 June 1945, and G. W. Ross to Mr. Roland, 19 July 1945, 353.8, Central Decimal Files, box 134, DHQ, ICD, OMGUS; Edward Kilenyi, "6870 Report on Potential Conductors," nd [July 1945], file: DISCC 6870, box 75, HO, DHQ, ICD, OMGUS.

28. Kater, *Twisted Muse*, 40–46; G. W. Ross, "Interview of Hans Knappertsbusch," 20 June 1945, 353.8, Central Decimal Files, box 134, DHQ, ICD, OMGUS; Alfred Toombs to Colonel Powell, 17 October 1945, file: T&M, box 43, DO, DHQ, ICD, OMGUS.

29. *Süddeutsche Zeitung*, 26 October 1945; A. Vogel, Daily Report, 9 July 1945, file: Daily Reports, box 20, DO, E&CR, OMGB, OMGUS; "History of Theater & Music Control Branch: Wuerttemberg-Baden," 5, file: History, box 242, T&M, E&CR, OMGWB, OMGUS; interview with Carlos Moseley, 18 March 1996; interview with Newell Jenkins, 6 July 1996.

30. T&M Weekly Report, 24 October 1945, file: DISCC 6870, box 75, HO, DHQ, ICD, OMGUS. Because the philharmonic was now under ICD control, the Music Branch appointed Rosbaud on its own authority.

31. Holger Hagen, "Personal Observations of Operations in 6870th DISCC," 29 September 1945, file: DISCC 6870, box 241, T&M, E&CR, OMGB, OMGUS; Music Section, Daily Reports, 15 July and 5 August 1945, and Music Section, Weekly Report, 3 November 1945, files: Daily and Weekly Reports, box 20, DHQ, E&CR, OMGB, OMGUS. Even in Frankfurt, however, Rosbaud had conformed to party wishes, as when he had conducted an anti-jazz program sponsored by the Nazis; see Kater, *Different Drummers*, 49, and *Twisted Muse*, 66–67.

32. A. Vogel, Daily Report, 9 July 1945, file: Daily Reports, box 20, DHQ, E&CR, OMGB, OMGUS; on Rosbaud's career, see Evans, *Hans Rosbaud*, 13–40, and for an assessment that challenges the Americans' opinion that Rosbaud was "truly white," Kater, *Twisted Muse*, 65–69; see also Hans Rosbaud to John Evarts, 8 June 1946, 3/40, and newspaper reviews and playbills of Rosbaud's performance, 9/153, in Hans Rosbaud Papers, WSU. Included in the playbill series is one for an NSDAP-sponsored concert in honor of those killed in "American terror bombing."

33. "Contribution of Psychiatric & Psychological Screening to the ICD Screening Center," nd [1946], 34/4, and "Screening Centers in Germany," 2 August 1946, 34/2, Levy Papers, ODL. Classic works on the authoritarian

personality include Ranulf, *Moral Indignation*; Lasswell, "The Psychology of Hitlerism"; Fromm, *Escape from Freedom*; Abrahamsen, *Men, Mind and Power*; and Adorno et al., *The Authoritarian Personality*; Ludwig, *The Moral Conquest of Germany*, 127; quotations are from "Analysis of a Potential Nazi," "Analysis of a Fascist," and "Analysis of a Near Bundist," nd [1942], 18/39, Levy Papers, ODL.

34. "Evaluation of ICD Screening Center," nd [March 1946?], 34/4, Levy Papers, ODL.

35. Report to Chief, Intelligence Section, "Subject: Rosbaud, Hans," 15 April 1946, 35/2, Levy Papers, ODL.

36. John Evarts's Diary, 19 August 1946, JEPA.

37. Report on Conference "Germany after the War," hosted by the Joint Committee on Postwar Planning, June 1944, 37/29, Levy Papers, ODL.

38. Interview with Newell Jenkins, 6 July 1996.

39. "Memorandum: Exchange of Information Regarding Artists on the Black List," 25 July 1946, file: Reorientation, box 85, DHQ, ICD, OMGUS; Semi-Weekly Report No. 8B, 4 August 1945, file: Berlin Reports, box 75, HO, DHQ, ICD, OMGUS. On American criticism of French policy, see Grohnert, *Die Entnazifizierung in Baden*, 73–79.

40. Nabokov, *Old Friends and New Music*, 265; Janik, "Music in Cold War Berlin," 147. SMAD's senior cultural officer, Alexander Dymschitz, noted that the Russians felt that the Nazis had "misused not destroyed" German art, and that the Soviets' job was to "free it so that it might breathe again"; Dymschitz, "Rückblick und Ausblick," 77. A contrasting perspective on Soviet cultural policy is offered in Pike, *The Politics of Culture*.

41. European CAD, Special Intelligence Bulletin, 5 July 1945, entry 54, box 300, Historical Records, Information Branch, G-5 Division, General Staff, SHAEF; the Soviets entered Berlin with a long list of prominent artists they planned to patronize and win over: Dymschitz, *Ein unvergesslicher Frühling*, 265–66; "Kommentär zum Schreiben Bohnen von 29 September 1945," 1485, C Rep 120, LB; "Recommendations of Film, Theater & Music Sub-Section," 18 July 1945, file: Berlin Reports, box 75, HO, DHQ, ICD, OMGUS; Robert McClure to A. G. Neville, 7 June 1945, entry 87, box 7, PWD, Special Staff, SHAEF.

42. Draft of Command letter, nd, file: T&M Officers, box 243, T&M, E&CR, OMGUS.

43. Report of Reconnaissance for FT&M Control, 8 July 1945, file: Berlin Reports, box 75, HO, DHQ, ICD, OMGUS.

44. Semi-Weekly Report No. 1, 12 July 1945, file: Berlin Reports, box 75, HO, DHQ, ICD, OMGUS; Schivelbusch, *In a Cold Crater*, ch. 2.

45. "The different spheres of the Union and the Chamber," nd, file: Chamber

of Artists, box 84, ISB, OMGBS, OMGUS; Semi-Weekly Report No. 1, 12 July 1945, file: Berlin Reports, box 75, HO, DHQ, ICD, OMGUS; Schivelbusch, *In a Cold Crater*, 42–43.

46. "The *Kulturbund*," 30 January 1947, file: *Kulturbund*, box 86, ISB, OMGBS, OMGUS; Schivelbusch, *In a Cold Crater*, 75; see also Pike, *The Politics of Culture*, 147–57; Genton, *Les Alliés et la culture Berlin*, 38–50.

47. Semi-Weekly Report No. 5, 25 July 1945, and Semi-Weekly Report No. 1, 12 July 1945, and Henry Alter, "Recommendations of Film, Theater & Music Sub-Section," 18 July 1945, file: Berlin Reports, box 75, HO, DHQ, ICD, OMGUS; William Paley to Robert McClure, 12 July 1945, 70/12, Lerner Papers, HI.

48. Heinz Tietjen to Leo Blech, 20 May 1945, box 1, Heinz Tietjen Papers, AdK; Ruth Friedrich statement, 15 September 1945, and Heinz Tietjen, "*Besprechung mit Leo Borchard*," 29 August 1945, file: Tietjen, reel D100, RKK 2700, BDC, NA; Strässner, *Der Dirigent Leo Borchard*, 221–24; "Kommentär zum Schreiben Bohnen von 29 September 1945," 1485, C Rep 120, LB.

49. Michael Bohnen to Herrn Hülsen, 10 September 1945, 1485, C Rep 120, LB; Heinz Tietjen to Leo Blech, 15 February 1946, box 1, Tietjen Papers, AdK; Semi-Weekly Report No. 1, 12 July 1945, file: Berlin Reports, box 75, HO, DHQ, ICD, OMGUS; *Notiz für Vertrauensrat*, 22 April 1946, Abt. 16, *Deutsche Staatsoper*, C Rep 167, LB; Semi-Weekly Report No. 9, 8 August 1945, and Semi-Weekly Report No. 2, 14 July 1945, file: Berlin Reports, box 75, HO, DHQ, ICD, OMGUS.

50. Semi-Weekly Report No. 9, 8 August 1945, and Semi-Weekly Report No. 2, 14 July 1945, file: Berlin Reports, box 75, HO, DHQ, ICD, OMGUS; Weekly Reports, 20 March 1946 and 4 March 1946, file: Berlin Reports, box 239, T&M, CRB, E&CR, OMGUS.

51. Intelligence Section, "Position of the *Kammer der Kunstschaffenden*," 350.09, Central Decimal File, box 136, DHQ, ICD, OMGUS; "Disposition of *Reichskulturkammer* Organizations," 15 October 1945, file: Chamber of Artists, box 84, ISB, OMGBS, OMGUS; Michael Josselson, Recommendations, 1 October 1945, "Report on the Development of the *Neue Berliner Illustrierte*," 29 October 1945, and Minutes of Kommandatura Deputy Commanders Meeting, 15 October 1945, 4/8-2/2-2, B Rep 36, LB; Meeting of *Kulturkammer* Executive, 19 February 1946, Abt. 16, *Deutsche Staatsoper*, C Rep 167, LB; interview with Mateo Lettunich, 12 August 1996.

52. *Austria Military Government Handbook* (April 1945), box 1, U.S. Element of the Allied Commission for Austria, Foreign Service Posts of the Department of State, Austria, Rg 84, NA; "Rehabilitation of Austria Report (1945–1947)," 10 May 1950, file: Theater, box 3, Operations Section, ISB, USACA.

53. *Austria Military Government Handbook*, box 1, U.S. Element of the Allied Commission for Austria, Foreign Service Posts of the Department of State, Austria, Rg 84, NA; on plunder, see Bischof, *Austria in the First Cold War*, 30–43.

54. Cronin, *Great Power Politics*, 18 and 23–32; Clark, *Calculated Risk*, 410–11; Hiscocks, *The Rebirth of Austria*, 22–24; Bader, *Austria between East and West*, 11–25; *Austria Military Government Handbook*, box 1, U.S. Element of the Allied Commission for Austria, Foreign Service Posts of the Department of State, Austria, Rg 84, NA.

55. Weinberg and Coles, *U.S. Army in World War II: Special Studies. Civil Affairs*, 521; R. Barnes to T. L. Barnard, 1 July 1945; Report, 5 August 1945; and Edward Klauber, Acting Director OWI, to the President, 17 August 1945, OWI Reports: Austria, Charles M. Hulten Papers, HSTL.

56. Interview with Virginia Pleasants, 19 May 1996; Semi-Weekly Report, 8 May 1946, file: Berlin Reports, box 75, HO, DHQ, ICD, OMGUS.

57. Henry Alter, "Operational Notes," 3 December 1945, box 38, Administrative Section, ISB, USACA; Bi-Weekly Report on Theater, 24 November 1945, box 21, EO, ISB, USACA.

58. Bi-Weekly Report, 24 November 1945, box 21, EO, ISB, USACA.

59. OMGUS Intelligence: Toombs/Kaven to ISB Vienna: Pasetti, 15 May 1946; on anti-Semitic feeling: H. Alter, "Operational Notes," 3 December 1945, and for the *Mein Kampf* information: Otto Pasetti, "Subject Clemens Krauss, investigation Munich," 21 December 1945, box 38, Administrative Section, ISB, USACA.

60. Schwarzkopf, *On and Off the Record*, 222; Vaughan, *Herbert von Karajan*, 143; Annex to Report No. 25, 5 February 1946, and Report of Conversation with H. C. Alter, 15 March 1946, box 21, General Records, EO, ISB, USACA; interview with Virginia Pleasants, 19 May 1996.

61. Otto Pasetti, "Memo: Meeting with Capt. Epstein concerning Herbert von Karajan," 13 January 1946, box 8, General Records, EO, ISB, USACA; Declaration of Herbert von Karajan, 9 May 1946, 1/2, Nicolas Nabokov Papers, HRC; "Subject Herbert von Karajan," 16 August 1949, file: Karajan, reel D28, RKK 2700, BDC, NA.

62. Report No. 23, 2 January 1946, and Annex to Report No. 24, 19 January 1946, and "T&M Biography: Clemens Krauss," box 38, Administrative Section, ISB, USACA; Annex to Report No. 25, 5 February 1946, box 21, General Records, EO, ISB, USACA.

63. Report of the Ministry of Education Commission, March 6 1946, 1/2, Nabokov Papers, HRC; Minutes of 13 June 1946 Quadripartite Internal Affairs Division Meeting, 18 June 1946, box 1, General Records, Internal Affairs Division: Quadripartite Branch, USACA.

64. Report No. 32, 15 May 1946, and Report No. 33, 31 May 1946, box 38,

Administrative Section, ISB, USACA; Appendix to Semi-Monthly Report, 17 June 1946, box 21, EO, ISB, USACA; Ernst Lothar to Col. Ladue, 6 August 1946, and interview with Col. Hume, 8 August 1946, box 8, EO, ISB, USACA.

65. Minutes of 13 June 1946 Quadripartite Internal Affairs Division Meeting, 18 June 1946, box 1, General Records, Internal Affairs Division: Quadripartite Branch, USACA.

66. "Subject Herbert von Karajan," 16 August 1949, file: Karajan, reel D28, RKK 2700, BDC, NA; Kater, *Twisted Muse*, 60–61; I am grateful to Michael Kater for the information on Karajan's father and for clarifying the issue of his wife's status under the Race Laws; Appendix to Semi-Monthly Report, 17 June 1946, box 21, EO, ISB, USACA. Karajan would assert that it was "routine" for performers to play the *Horst Wessel Lied* when touring; for a good discussion of his case by the T&M officer of the time: Lothar, *Das Wunder des Überlebens*, 309–14.

67. The expression is Hans Werner Henze's in *Music and Politics*, 123.

68. Bi-Weekly Report, 24 November 1945, box 21, EO, ISB, USACA; Otto Pasetti, "Memo: Meeting with Capt. Epstein concerning Herbert von Karajan," 13 January 1946, box 8, EO, ISB, USACA.

CHAPTER 3

1. *Manual for the Control of German Information Services*, 34/1, David M. Levy Papers, ODL; "History Information Control Division, 8 May 1945–30 June 1946," box 454, file: ICD Activities, EO, ICD, OMGUS, Rg 260, NA; Norman, *Our German Policy*, 69; "Theater and Music Accomplishments" and "Reorientation Activities of ODIC in Germany: Theater and Music," 15 April 1947, box 248, General Records, CRB, E&CR, OMGUS.

2. "Reconstruction of Musical Activities in U.S. Zone of Germany since June 1945—A VERY Rough Draft," box 248, General Records, CRB, E&CR, OMGUS.

3. "Reconstruction of Musical Activities in U.S. Zone of Germany since June 1945—A VERY Rough Draft," box 248, General Records, CRB, E&CR, OMGUS; *New York Times*, 2 June 1946.

4. *Manual for the Control of German Information Services*, 34/1, Levy Papers, ODL; Norman, *Our German Policy*, 10.

5. Hans Rosbaud to John Evarts, 8 June 1946, 3/40, Hans Rosbaud Papers, WSU; Report to Chief, Intelligence Section, "Subject: Rosbaud, Hans," 15 April 1946, 35/2, Levy Papers, ODL; "Testimonial of Franz Ringmeir," 15 October 1946, Eugen Jochum—*Fragebogen* Action Sheet, 11 November 1946, and Testimonial of Romane Guardini, 24 October 1945, file: Eugen Jochum, reel C54, RKK 2700, BDC, NA; Otto Pasetti, "Memo: Meeting with Capt. Epstein concerning Herbert von Karajan," 13 January 1946,

box 8, EO, ISB, USACA, Rg 260, NA; "Subject Herbert von Karajan," 16 August 1949, file: Karajan, reel D28, RKK 2700, BDC, NA.

6. Norman, *Our German Policy*, 69–70.

7. *Manual for the Control of German Information Services*, 34/1, Levy Papers, ODL.

8. E. A. Schinske to Chief ICD, 29 November 1945, box 310, Correspondence, ISD, OMGWB, OMGUS; "Draft Guidance on Control of Music," 8 June 1945, 353.8, Central Decimal File, box 134, DHQ, ICD, OMGUS.

9. "Pre-Performance Scrutiny," 18 July 1946, file: FT&M, box 54, HO, DHQ, ICD, OMGUS; "Information Control Policies in Light of JCS 1067/6 . . . and the Potsdam Agreement," 29 September 1945, file: Info Committee of the Political Directorate, box 70, HO, DHQ, ICD, OMGUS.

10. G. E. Textor to Newell Jenkins, 6 June 1947, file: Theater Policies, box 242, T&M, E&CR, OMGUS; Berlin District Monthly Report, 24 July and 20 November 1946, file: Monthly Summary, box 728, T&M, E&CR, OMGH, OMGUS; Film, Theater & Music Report, 29 January 1947, file: Reports, box 82, ISB, OMGBS; *Mitteilung der Theater und Musikkontrolle München*, 1:2 (June 1946), 10–11, 1/3, Rosbaud Papers, WSU.

11. G. E. Textor to Newell Jenkins, 6 June 1947, file: Theater Policies, box 242, T&M, E&CR, OMGUS.

12. Weekly Situation Reports, 23 June and 1 October 1945, file: DISCC 6871, box 75, HO, DHQ, ICD, OMGUS.

13. William Dubensky, "Detailed Licensing Plan for Theater and Music," file: Theater Policies, box 242, and Benno Frank, "Assumption of Information Control Responsibility by German Agencies," 16 January 1946, file: Theater Licenses, box 243, T&M, E&CR, OMGUS.

14. William Dubensky, "Detailed Licensing Plan for Theater and Music," file: Theater Policies, box 242, and Benno Frank, "Assumption of Information Control Responsibility by German Agencies," 16 January 1946, file: Theater Licenses, box 243, T&M, E&CR, OMGUS; Weekly Situation Report (Württemberg-Baden), 12 February 1946, file: Monthly Summary, box 728, T&M, E&CR, OMGH, OMGUS; Lt. Edelman to Chief, Intelligence, 18 December 1945, file: Unions, box 244, T&M, E&CR, OMGUS; Subject: Association of Musicians of the Province of Kurhessen, 25 February 1946, file: Unions, box 729, T&M, E&CR, OMGH, OMGUS; *Newsweek*, 10 September 1945, 96; E. T. Clarke to General McClure, 23 January 1946, file: Theater Licenses, box 243, T&M, E&CR, OMGUS.

15. ICD Branch Chiefs, "Future Provisions for Licensing and Registration," 22 January 1946, file: Theater Licenses, box 243, and "General Licensing Scheme for Theater and Music," nd, file: Theater Policies, box 242, T&M, E&CR, OMGUS.

16. Carl Hagemann to Ministerpräsident Geiler, 18 September 1945, 504/72, HH; Zulauf, *Verwaltung der Kunst oder Kunst der Verwaltung*, 64.

17. Karl Holl, memo, 12 February 1946; Beineke to *Kultminister*, 15 August 1946; Noak, memo of telephone conversation, 4 March 1946; and Otto Henning to Dr. Geiler, 27 March 1946, 504/72, HH.

18. Bi-Monthly Report, 13 September 1946, file: Historical, box 309, General Records, ISD, OMGWB, OMGUS; Subject: Denazification Committee of the *Kultusministerium*, 5 September 1946, file 3, box 106, Intelligence Records ICD, Intelligence, OMGB, OMGUS.

19. Memorandum of Committee Meeting, 29 January 1946, box 102, Activities of *Laenderrat* Committees and Subcommittees, Regional Government Coordinating Committees, Functional Offices and Divisions, OMGUS.

20. *Verwaltungsrat* to Kauffmann, 31 January 1951, 3415-2, HA.Gr.3, SS; "Combined History of the Theater Control Section and the Music Control Section, OMG Bavaria," 28 April 1947, file: History, boxes 77 and 239, file: Reports, Weekly Report, 26 October 1946, HO, DHQ, ICD, OMGUS.

21. In 1948, for example, after the Hessian Kultusministerium refused to recognize a contract the *Intendant* in Darmstadt had signed with the local theater committees without city or state approval, the courts upheld the contract as valid. Attachment 1 to Karl Holl to *Theaterbeirat*, 12 February 1948, 504/48, HH.

22. HH, 504/3, for the *Intendant*'s case.

23. In Württemberg-Baden, it was called the Kult- rather than Kultusministerium. Heuss once answered Jenkins's question as to why this was with the quip: "In Württemberg-Baden we don't need the us." Interview with Newell Jenkins, 6 July 1996.

24. Franz Sauer to Holl, 6 February 1951, 504/772, HH; Ruppel to Heinz Trefzger, 8 December 1945, EA 3/201/91, HS; Klett to Ministerialrat Kauffmann, 15 March 1946, EA 3/201/74, HS; Steiert, "Zur Musik- und Theaterpolitik in Stuttgart," 59; *Sitzung des Theaterbeirats der Württ. Staatstheater*, 31 December 1945, and Heinz Trefzger, "Bericht über das Staatstheater," December 1945, EA 3/201/91, HS; "History of Theater and Music Control Branch—Wuerttemberg-Baden," 3–6, file: History, box 242, T&M, E&CR, OMGUS.

25. "Draft Guidance on Control of Music," 8 June 1945, 353.8, Central Decimal File, box 134, DHQ, ICD, OMGUS; Semi-Weekly Report #2, 14 July 1945, and Recommendations of FT&M Sub-Section, 18 July 1945, file: Berlin Reports, box 75, HO, DHQ, ICD, OMGUS; interview with John Bitter, 9 June 1996.

26. Interview with John Bitter, 9 June 1996; FT&M Report #12, 19 August 1945, Report #7, 4 August 1945, Report #19, 25 January 1946, file: Berlin Reports, box 75, HO, DHQ, ICD, OMGUS.

27. Interview with Edward Kilenyi, 8 June 1996; in his *Memoirs* (New York, 1997) and in an interview with the author, 16 March 1997, Solti maintained that he was invited to perform in Munich only after he had successfully conducted in Stuttgart on 26 April 1946. Bauckner, however, had already engaged him, "at the request of the Military Government," to perform in Fidelio by late March: A. Bauckner to Staatsministerium, 25 March 1946, MK 50204, BH; interview with Newell Jenkins, 6 July 1996.

28. Weekly Report, 29 June and 24 August 1946, file: Monthly Summary, box 728, T&M, E&CR, OMGUS; K. Scharnagl to *Staatsminister*, 15 February 1947, and Eugen Jochum to Alois Hundhammer, 23 July 1947, MK 50187, BH.

29. Interview with Carlos Moseley, 18 March 1996. The same was true in other places. Boris Blacher and his wife were frequent guests of the Bitters, while in Vienna the opera conductor Josef Krips often came to play piano four hands with Virginia Pleasants. Interviews with John Bitter, 9 June 1996, and with Henry Pleasants, 2 November 1996.

30. "Working Program for Democratization in Bavaria," 6 May 1947, file: Bavaria, box 201, Records of the Cultural Exchange Programme, CAD, OMGUS; HQ US Forces, European Theater, "Priority of Information Control Activities," 28 August 1945, Speech by Brig. Gen. Robert A. McClure, 27 August 1945, and ICD Standing Directive No. 1, 20 July 1945, entry 172, box 330, War Department, Rg 165, NA.

31. "Reorientation Activities of ODIC, Theater and Music," 15 April 1947, and "Reconstruction of Musical Activity in U.S. Zone of Germany since June 1945," box 248, General Records, CRB, E&CR, OMGUS.

32. J. F. Edney to Hans Aldenhoff, 18 February 1947, 4/12-2/23, B Rep 36, LB; G. K. Schueller, "STAGMA," 24 October 1945, 4/8-3/12, B Rep 36, LB; Control Officer, "History: ISD, 8 May 1945–30 June 1946," file: History, box 454, EO, OMGUS; FT&M Report, April 1946, file: FTM, box 77, HO, DHQ, ICD, OMGUS.

33. Thacker, "Playing Beethoven Like an Indian," 370–71; "Minutes of Preliminary Meeting of Theater and Music Officers," 20 October 1946, file: Meetings, box 310, T&M, E&CR, OMGWB, OMGUS; "History: ISD, 8 May 1945–30 June 1946," file: History, box 454, EO, OMGUS; Minutes, ICSG, 7 January 1946, and Minutes of Quadripartite Meeting, 10 May 1946, file: Quadripartite, box 77, HO, DHQ, ICD, OMGUS.

34. "Report to the Department of State of the USIE Survey Mission on the OMGUS Reorientation Program in Germany," 21 July 1949, box 205, LOT 53D311, Department of State, Rg 59, NA.

35. For the assistance the officers provided orchestras, see John Bitter to Virgil Thomson, 2 October 1946, 25/35, Virgil Thomson Papers, YUA; Carlos Moseley to Harrison Kerr, 26 February 1948, and Carlos Moseley to Ar-

thur Vogel, 2 March 1948, file: American Personnel, box 18, CRB, E&CR, OMGB, OMGUS; interview with Carlos Moseley, 18 March 1996.

36. John Bitter Scrapbooks, 1945–48, PAJB; Heidelberg Detachment, Semi-Monthly Report, 10 December 1947, file: Württemberg-Baden, box 240, T&M, E&CR, OMGUS; John Evarts's Diary, 28 November 1945, JEPA; Weekly Report, 15 April 1946, file: T&M, box 20, Administrative Records, Director's Office, E&CR, OMGB, OMGUS; interview with Newell Jenkins, 6 July 1996; Heyworth, *Otto Klemperer*, 2:146–47 and 158; Ernst Legal to Otto Klemperer, 29 June 1946, C Rep 167/16, LB; Frederic Mellinger, Weekly Report, 26 June, 3 July, and 5 February 1946, file: Berlin Reports, box 238, T&M, E&CR, OMGUS; interview with Virginia Pleasants, 19 May 1996; Erich Leinsdorf to Harold Spivacke, 25 February 1944, box 9, Joint Army and Navy Committee on Welfare and Recreation: Sub-Committee on Music, LC; Semi-Monthly Report, 31 December 1947, box 20, General Records, EO, ISB, USACA.

37. Dunbar was born in British Guyana and grew up in London. Trained as a band musician, he played in music hall and jazz orchestras and, in the late 1930s, briefly lived in the United States, in Harlem; see interview with Rudolph Dunbar, 29 November 1938, Federal Writers' Project, LC; Bi-Weekly Report, 5 September 1945, file: Berlin Reports, box 75, HO, DHQ, ICD, OMGUS; Dody Bitter to Virgil Thomson, 12 December 1945, 25/35, Thomson Papers, YUA; for Solti: Evarts's Diary, spring/summer 1947, 6, JEPA; I am grateful to Dr. Joan Evans for providing the date of Rosbaud's first performance of an American work; WB T&M Weekly Situation Report, 9 March 1946, file: Weekly Reports, box 239, T&M, E&CR, OMGUS; Film, Theater & Music Consolidated Report, March 1946, file: Reports HO, DHQ, ICD, OMGUS; Holger Hagen to William Dubensky, 11 November 1946, file: American Plays and Music, box 727, T&M, E&CR, OMGH, OMGUS; "Reorientation Activities of ODIC, Theater and Music," 15 April 1947, file: Reorientation, box 248, General Records, CRB, E&CR, OMGUS.

38. Weekly Report, 23 November 1946, file: WB, box 240, T&M, E&CR, OMGUS; Paul Hindemith to Scheich, 19 July 1942, 16/296, Paul Hindemith Papers, YUA; Weekly Report, 25 January 1947, file: Karlsruhe Outpost, box 599, T&M, Field Relations Division, OMGWB, OMGUS; Weekly Report, 2 April 1946, file: Bavaria: Weekly Reports, box 239, and Weekly Report, 16 November 1946, file: WB, box 240, T&M, E&CR, OMGUS.

39. Interview with Newell Jenkins, 6 July 1996; "History of Information Control Division, Württemberg-Baden, to 1 July 1946," 29, file: Historical, box 309, Correspondence and General Records, ISD, OMGUS; Evarts's Diary, spring/summer 1947, 2, JEPA.

40. I am grateful to Toby Thacker for providing the quote regarding Hindemith's dubious past; on his interest in making sales, see Paul Hindemith to Willy Strecker, 15 July 1946, in Skelton, *Selected Letters*, 196–200; on the availability of his works in the Third Reich, Kowalke, "Music Publishing and the Nazis," 181–82; for a balanced treatment of Hindemith, see Kater, *Composers of the Nazi Era*, ch. 2.

41. Evarts, "Vom Musikleben in Amerika," 84–85.

42. Interview with Newell Jenkins, 6 July 1996; for new music in Nazi Germany, see Evans, "International with National Emphasis" and "Die Rezeption der Musik Igor Stravinskys."

CHAPTER 4

1. Prieberg, *Trial of Strength*, 322, 326; Harrison to Secretary of State, 29 August 1946, 862.20254/8-2946, Central Decimal Files, Germany, 1945–49, Department of State, Rg 59, NA; Furtwängler, *Briefe*, 111; Goebbels quoted in Kater, *The Twisted Muse*, 202. The extent of Furtwängler's collaboration has been hotly debated over the years and still excites enormous interest. Recently, it has been the subject of a hit play (by Ronald Harwood) and a major film — *Taking Sides* — by the esteemed Hungarian director István Szabó. The curious may sample a literature that ranges from the extremely positive — Prieberg's *Trial of Strength*, Schönzler's *Furtwängler*, and Gefen's *Wilhelm Furtwängler* — to more probing works like Kater's *Twisted Muse*, Wessling's *Furtwängler*, and Haffner's *Furtwängler*.

2. Prieberg, *Trial of Strength*; Kater, *Twisted Muse*, 196–203; Potter, "The Nazi Seizure of the Berlin Philharmonic," 57–58; OMGUS Information Control Intelligence Summary #32, file: Wilhelm Furtwängler, reel C52, RKK 2700, BDC, NA.

3. "T&M Biog: Dr. Wilhelm Furtwangler [*sic*]," nd, box 2, General Records, T&M, ISB, USACA, Rg 260, NA; "Press Release," 21 February 1946, box 43, Director's Records, DHQ, ICD, OMGUS, Rg 260, NA; OMGUS Information Control Summary #32, file: Wilhelm Furtwängler, reel C52, RKK 2700, BDC, NA; Telegram, H. H. Fowler to American Legation Stockholm, 14 September 1945, 800.515/9-1445, Department of State, Rg 59, NA. The Americans did, however, variously confuse Flesch, Goldberg, and Huberman.

4. Furtwängler, *Notebooks*, 114; Furtwängler quoted in Shirakawa, *The Devil's Music Master*, 439.

5. Declaration by Wilhelm Furtwängler, nd, 1.2, Nicolas Nabokov Papers, HRC; Furtwängler, *Notebooks*, 157.

6. On Hilbert, see Lothar, *Das Wunder des Überlebens*, 302–3; *New York Times*, 10 February 1946; Annex to Report #25 — Trip to Switzerland, 26 January 1946, T&M, box 38, Administrative Section, ISB, USACA. Pasetti had

already visited Furtwängler, in late November 1945, and helped prevent his returning to Vienna at that time: Annex to Report #21, 11 December 1945, box 21, EO, ISB, USACA.

7. Report #26, 19 February 1946, T&M, box 38, Administrative Section, ISB, USACA. I am grateful to Dr. Toby Thacker for the information regarding his invitation to Baden-Baden.

8. "Report of the Investigating Commission of the Austrian Ministry of Education," 9 March 1946, box 42, General Records, EO, ISB, USACA.

9. "Report of the Investigating Commission of the Austrian Ministry of Education," 9 March 1946, box 42, General Records, EO, ISB, USACA.

10. Norbert Frei has demonstrated that the abandonment of denazification was seen as a crucial step in west Germany's political constitution; see *Vergangenheitspolitik*, 54–69; "Subject: Wilhelm Furtwängler," 21 February 1946, box 38, Administrative Section, ISB, USACA.

11. Stanley Grogan to Deputy Commanding General, USA, 23 May 1946, 180/2, B Rep 37, LB.

12. *Prüfungsausschuss* for Cultural Affairs to Allied Denazification Sub-Committee, 20 February 1946, file: Wilhelm Furtwängler, reel C52, RKK 2700, BDC, NA; USFET Press Release, 21 February 1946, file: FT&M, box 15, Director's Records, DHQ, ICD, OMGUS; Information Control Summary, 15 March 1946, file: Berlin Section Reports, box 239, T&M, E&CR, OMGUS.

13. *Berliner Zeitung*, 14 June 1946; USFET Press Release, 21 February 1946, file: FT&M, box 15, Director's Records, DHQ, ICD, OMGUS; *Prüfungsausschuss* for Cultural Affairs to Allied Denazification Sub Committee, 20 February 1946, file: Wilhelm Furtwängler, reel C52, RKK 2700, BDC, NA; Clare, *Before the Wall*, 132.

14. Information Control Summary, 21 June 1946, file: Berlin Section Reports, box 239, T&M, E&CR, OMGUS; Clare, *Before the Wall*, 132, recalls the event differently; "Minutes of 24th meeting of the Advisory Committee to the Cultural Affairs Committee of the Allied *Kommandatura*," 12 June 1946, and K. W. F. Sely, "The Furtwängler case," 4 August 1946, file: Wilhelm Furtwängler, reel C52, RKK 2700, BDC, NA; Memorandum on Telephone Conversation with Lt. Col. Leonard, 13 June 1946, box 38, Administrative Section, ISB, USACA.

15. Gienow-Hecht's *Transmission Impossible* argues that stark differences in attitude existed between recent émigrés and native-born Americans. OMGUS, ICD, DHQ, Semi-Monthly Progress Report, 29 September 1945, file: PWD, box 78, Director's Records, DHQ, ICD, OMGUS; Memorandum to General McClure, 29 January 1946, file: T&M, box 43, Director's Records, DHQ, ICD, OMGUS; *Kurier*, 23 January 1946; "Minutes of 24th

meeting of the Advisory Committee to the Cultural Affairs Committee of the Allied *Kommandatura*," 12 June 1946, and K. W. F. Sely, "The Furt-wängler case," 4 August 1946, file: Wilhelm Furtwängler, reel C52, RKK 2700, BDC.

16. Hurwitz, *Die Stunde Null der deutschen Presse*; Frei, *Amerikanische Lizenz-politik*; Mosberg, *Reeducation*; Hartenian, "The Role of the Media in De-mocratizing Germany"; interview with John Boxer, 20 October 1996.

17. *The Papers of General Lucius D. Clay*, 1:78, 85, 88, 95–96, 138, and 317; Clay, *Decision in Germany*, 65, 70, and 78.

18. "Restatement of U.S. Policy on Germany: Address by Secretary James F. Byrnes," in Department of State, *Germany, 1947–1949*, 8; *The Papers of General Lucius D. Clay*, 1:243.

19. Department of State, *Occupation of Germany*, 113–17; "Subject: JCS Direc-tive 1067/6," 18 July 1945, file: Intelligence, box 21, Director's Records, DHQ, ICD, OMGUS; "Subject: Information Control Policies in Light of JCS 1067," 1 October 1945, file: Information Control, box 64, ISD Staff Advisor, DHQ, ICD, OMGUS.

20. "Preliminary Report of the Working Committee to the Denazification Pol-icy Board," 20 December 1945, file: Denazification, box 332, Public Safety Branch, CAD Records, OMGUS; Clay, *Decision in Germany*, 70; Boehling, *A Question of Priorities*, 58; Zink, *American Military Government*, 143–44; Gimbel, *The American Occupation of Germany*, 102.

21. "Preliminary Report of the Working Committee to the Denazification Pol-icy Board," 20 December 1945, and "Report of the Denazification Policy Board to the Deputy Military Governor," 15 January 1946, file: Denazifica-tion, box 332, Public Safety Branch, CAD Records, OMGUS.

22. Peterson, *The American Occupation of Germany*, 148–49; Gimbel, *The American Occupation of Germany*, 103–6.

23. Department of State, *Occupation of Germany*, 118–20.

24. John Hildring to the Secretary of War, 13 February 1946, entry 463, box 233, War Department, Rg 165, NA; McClure cited in Norman, *Our Ger-man Policy*, 27; George Schueller to Alfred Toombs, 10 April 1946, file: Regulations, box 20, Director's Records, DHQ, ICD, OMGUS; Smith, *Lucius D. Clay*, 383; *The Papers of General Lucius D. Clay*, 1:251–52.

25. Newell Jenkins, Bi-Monthly Report, 13 September 1946, file: Historical, box 309, General Records, ISD, OMGWB, OMGUS; "Minutes of General Meeting, Information Control Zonal Conference," 16 April 1947, file: 52A, box 114, ICD Intelligence Records, Intelligence Division, OMGB, OMGUS; George Schueller to Alfred Toombs, 10 April 1946, file: Regula-tions, box 20, Director's Records, DHQ, ICD, OMGUS; Robert Mc-Clure, memo, Subject: Denazification, 12 June 1946, file: Theater Policies,

box 242, T&M, E&CR, OMGUS; "Minutes of General Information Control Division Meeting," 30 April 1946, file: 52A, box 114, ICD Intelligence Records, Intelligence Division, OMGB, OMGUS.

26. Benno Frank to Eric Clarke, 20 June 1946, and Memo: "OMGUS signed Clay," 8 June 1946, file: Theater Policies, box 242, T&M, E&CR, OMGUS; Minutes of General ODIC Meeting, 14 August 1946, 132:337, Central Files, Director's Records, DHQ, ICD, OMGUS.

27. "Report on a Visit to the American Zone by Head Theater and Music Section, PR/ISC Group, Berlin," nd, file: British Information Policy, box 53, Policy and Planning, DHQ, ICD, OMGUS.

28. "Proces-verbal de la réunion du comité des affaires culturelles," 28 June 1946, box 2, Cultural Affairs Committee, U.S. Mission to Berlin, Rg 84, NA; OMG Berlin District, ICD Report, 4 September 1946, and ICD Monthly Summary, 6 September 1946, file: Berlin Reports, box 728, T&M, E&CR, OMGH, OMGUS.

29. Clare, *Before the Wall*, 197.

30. "Berliner Entnazifizierungs-Kommission für Kunstler, über den Antrag von Dr. Wilhelm Furtwängler," 11 and 17 December 1946, box 2, General Records, T&M, ISB, USACA.

31. Clare, *Before the Wall*, 197.

32. Subject: *Spruchkammern*, 24 September 1946, file 3, box 106, Intelligence Records of ICD, Intelligence Division, OMGB, OMGUS.

33. Gimbel, *The American Occupation*, 106–10; OMGUS signed Keating to Directors OMG, 15 November 1946, file: Regulations, box 20, Director's Records, DHQ, ICD, OMGUS.

34. "Minutes of the Meeting of the Theater and Music Working Party," 19 December 1946, file: Quadripartite, box 237, T&M, E&CR, OMGUS; the first to drop the names of ordinary musicians was ICD, "White, Grey and Black List for IC Purposes," 1 March 1947, file: White, Grey and Blacklists, box 455, EO, ICD, OMGUS. Newell Jenkins to Licensees, 20 May 1947, EA 3/201/98, HS; "Minutes of General Meeting, Information Control Zonal Conference," 16 April 1947, box 927, E&CR, OMGWB, OMGUS; D. T. Jones, "Discontinuance of ICD Registration," 23 May 1947, file: FTM, box 54, DHQ, ICD, OMGUS; "Minutes of General Meeting—Wiesbaden," 5 February 1947, and "Minutes of General Meeting: ICD Zonal Conference," 5 February 1947, file 52A, box 114, Intelligence Division, OMGB, OMGUS; *New York Times*, 2 February 1947.

35. The War Department assumed budgetary responsibility for German information services in mid-1946 and the transfer was formalized in July. William Benton to Harry S. Truman, 7 January 1946, file 1, CF 20E, Harry S. Truman Papers, HSTL.

36. *Tägliche Rundschau*, 16 March 1947; *New York Times*, 18 December 1946;

Borgelt, *Das war der Frühling von Berlin*, 214–19; Genton, *Les Alliés et la culture Berlin*, 123–25; Michael Josselson, "Subject: Case of Wilhelm Furtwängler," 11 March 1947, file: FTM, box 15, Director's Records, DHQ, ICD, OMGUS.

37. Otto de Pasetti, "Re: Wilhelm Furtwängler," 21 February 1946; RKK 2700, file: Wilhelm Furtwängler, OMGUS Information Control Summary #32, box 38, Administration Section, ISB, USACA.

38. FTM Weekly Report, 7 December 1946, file: Monthly Summaries, box 728, T&M, E&CR, OMGH, OMGUS. I am grateful to the Knappertsbusch expert, Kazuhide Okunami, for the information and copies of the documents pertaining to the conductor's *Spruchkammer* application.

39. "Minutes of First Joint Meeting of the U.S. and British Theater and Music Officers," 18 December 1946, file: British T&M, box 243, T&M, E&CR, OMGUS.

40. Severin Kaven, "Interrogation of Walter Gieseking," 21 September 1945, file: Gieseking, RKK 2700, BDC, NA.

41. Severin Kaven, "Report on Walter Gieseking, Pianist," 25 September 1945, file: Gieseking, RKK 2700, BDC, NA. Gieseking later denied having been in the *Kampfbund*; see *New York Times*, 23 January 1949.

42. *New York Times*, 18 February 1942; Transcript of Radio Broadcast, 22 February 1942, and uncatalogued boxes of radio broadcasts, Deems Taylor Papers, YUA; Rudolf Goette to No. 8 Information Control Unit, 11 January 1946, and Rudolf Goette, "Überblick über die Tätigkeit Walter Giesekings seit 1933," 11 January 1946, file: Gieseking, RKK 2700, BDC, NA; "Meldebogen: Walter Gieseking," 24 April 1946, 501/6.2, Hessisches Ministerium für politische Befreiung, HH; interview with Carlos Moseley, 18 March 1996. Gieseking's correspondence with Hinkel concerning his *Kampfbund* membership was even printed in the *New York Times*, 9 January 1949.

43. Walter Gieseking to *Ministerpräsident* Hesse, 30 May 1946, *Ministerpräsident* to Walter Gieseking, 21 June 1946, and Walter Gieseking to *Ministerpräsident*, 26 June 1946; *Notiz für Herrn Ministerpräsident*, 13 June 1946, Karl Holl, "Bericht über die Besprechung mit William Dubensky und Walter Gieseking," 19 July 1946, 504/72, HH; Walter Hinrischen to Dubensky, 26 February 1947, box 727, T&M, E&CR, OMGH, OMGUS; and "Minutes of First Joint Meeting of the U.S. and British Theater and Music Officers," 18 December 1946, file: British T&M, box 243, T&M, E&CR, OMGUS.

44. Kater, *Twisted Muse*, 64–65. In his misleadingly titled memoirs, *A Life Remembered*, 58, Böhm denies having conducted after Busch's departure, insisting it was someone else who was "waiting in the wings"; OMGUS Intelligence: Toombs/Kaven to ISB Vienna: attn. Pasetti, 15 May 1946,

and Henry Alter, Operational Notes, 3 December 1945, and memo to Egon Hilbert, 21 December 1945, box 38, T&M, Administrative Section; ISB, USACA; "Report of Investigation of Karl Böhm," nd [May 1946?], file: Böhm, RKK 2700, BDC, NA.

45. Extract from "Short Biographies" by G. E. Weinschenk; Karl Böhm, "The Trend of Today's Music," and article from *Dresdner Anzeiger*, 5 January 1934, file: Böhm, RKK 2700, BDC, NA. In *A Life Remembered*, 111, Böhm specifically denies having said these things, though he remembered it differently at the time of his denazification hearing.

46. Music Section Report, 14 January 1946, box 21, EO, ISB, USACA, and T&M Report, 2 January 1946, box 38, T&M, Administrative Section, ISB, USACA; Van Eerden to Colonel Ladue, 17 March 1947, box 8, General Records, EO, USACA.

47. *Report of the U.S. High Commissioner for Austria*, March 1947, August 1947, January 1948, May 1948, and August 1948, boxes 2–3, Reports of the U.S. High Commissioner, U.S. Element of the Allied Commission for Austria, Foreign Service Posts of the Department of State, Austria, Rg 84, NA.

48. Report in Böhm case of the Begutachtungskommission für die politische Einstellung . . . die Künstlern, Sängern, etc., 20 December 1946; Van Eerden to Colonel Ladue, 17 March 1947, and Controller ISB to Colonel Ladue, 16 January 1947, box 8, General Records, EO, USACA.

49. Minutes of Meeting of T&M Working Party, 19 December 1946, file: Quadripartite, box 237, T&M, E&CR, OMGUS.

50. "Review of Activities for the Month of June 1947," file: Monthly Reports, box 77, HO, DHQ, ICD, OMGUS; D. T. Jones, "Discontinuance of ICD Registration," 23 May 1947, file: FTM, box 54, HO, DHQ, ICD, OMGUS.

51. Unsigned letter to Albert Kehm, 10 August 1945, and Kehm to *Kultminister*, 30 July 1946, EA 3/201/98, HS; "Minutes of Meeting," 19 June 1946, file: ICD Meetings, box 728, T&M, E&CR, OMGH, OMGUS; *Ministerialrat* Ströle to *Kultministerium*, 12 December 1946; *Aktennotiz*, 23 July 1947, EA 3/201/98, HS.

52. ISIC Report, July 1951, file: Reports, box 1, PAD, *Land* Commissioner Bavaria, HICOG, Rg 466, NA. The ban on Ney was lifted in time for her to perform at the 1952 Beethoven Festival in Bonn, but, in truth, her career never fully recovered; on her postwar career, see Vogel, *Aus den Tagebüchern von Elly Ney*; for the lifting of the ban and her recantation: *New York Times*, 21 May 1952. On Hüsch, see Hunt, *The Lyric Baritone*; Schlesinger, *Gott Sei mit unserem Führer*, 90–91 and 97; Prieberg, *Musik in NS Staat*, 247 and 249; Rathkolb, *Führertreu und gottbegnadet*, 167; Asche, "Gerhard Hüsch," noted that the singer was "all but forgotten" in his homeland.

53. T&M Report, 28 May 1947, file: Berlin Reports, box 241, T&M, E&CR, OMGUS.

54. Menuhin, *Unfinished Journey*, 221–26; Magidoff, *Yehudi Menuhin*, 252–54; "Subject: Concert by Yehudi Menuhin," 30 September 1947, file: visiting artists, box 15, DHQ, ICD, OMGUS.

CHAPTER 5

1. Benno Frank to Eric Clarke, 17 July 1946, and "Memorandum: T&M Functions Eliminated as a Result of Personnel Cuts," file: T&M, box 310, General Records, ISD, OMGWB, OMGUS, Rg 260, NA; Eric Clarke, "Limited Assignment of Officers," February 1947, file T&M Officers, box 243, T&M, E&CR, OMGUS; Harrison Kerr to Chief, 23 July 1948, file: New York Field Office, box 9, Director's Records, DHQ, ICD, OMGUS.

2. Newell Jenkins to Director ICD OMGWB, 19 December 1946, file: T&M, box 310, Correspondence and General Records, ISD, OMGWB, OMGUS; Edward Hogan to Douglas Fox, 24 October 1949, box 3, Operations Section, ISB, USACA, Rg 260, NA.

3. James Pollock to Robert McClure, 8 April 1946, file: *Laenderrat* Committees, box 102, Regional Offices/Regional Government Co-ordinating Committee, OMGUS.

4. CBS Interview with Lucius Clay, 22 December 1948, in *The Papers of General Lucius D. Clay*, 2:966–67; J. Anthony Panuch to George Hays, 20 May 1949, box 205, LOT 53D311, Department of State, Rg 59, NA.

5. Benno Frank, "Draft Report on Reorientation," nd [August 1947], file: Reorientation, box 728, T&M, E&CR, OMGH, OMGUS.

6. John Evarts, Weekly Report, 12 October 1946, box 239, Weekly Reports, T&M, E&CR, OMGB, OMGUS; John Evarts's Diary, September 1946, 6, JEPA.

7. Eric Clarke to Chief FT&M, 27 March 1947, file: FTM, box 54, DHQ, ICD, OMGUS; John Evarts, "Combined History of the Theater Control Section and Music Control Section," 28 April 1947, Inclosure No. 7, "Influence of the State on the Activities of the State Theaters," file: History, box 20, and "Draft: Decentralization of Theater Administration," file: Theater Meetings, box 244, T&M, E&CR, OMGB, OMGUS; Evarts's Diary, September 1946, 6 and 8, JEPA; Weekly Report, 8 November 1946, file: Monthly summary, box 728, and Weekly Report, 12 October 1946, file: Weekly Reports, box 239, T&M, E&CR, OMGUS.

8. Robert A. McClure to Deputy Military Governor, December 1946, file: Dilemma of Information Control, box 80, DHQ, ICD, OMGUS; "Suggestions for Berchtesgaden Meeting," 20 September 1948, box 879, HQ Chief, E&CR, OMGWB.

9. "History of Information Control Division to 1 July 1946," 28, file: Historical, box 309, ISD, OMGWB.

10. John Evarts, Weekly Report, 10 April 1947, box 239, Weekly Reports, T&M, E&CR, OMGB, OMGUS; interview with Newell Jenkins, 6 July 1996.

11. Solti, *Memoirs*, 88. Munich concertgoers' wild affection for Knappertsbusch extended back to the early 1920s, when he had replaced Bruno Walter as *Generalmusikdirektor* of the Staatsoper; Kater, *Twisted Muse*, 40–41; Hans Rosbaud to K. Scharnagl, 16 February 1947, file 89, box 6, and John Evarts to Rosbaud, 16 February 1947, file 40, box 3, Hans Rosbaud Papers, WSU; *Süddeutsche Zeitung*, 26 and 29 June 1948; Memo regarding contract with Hans Rosbaud, 26 February 1948, cited in Krauss, *Nachkriegskultur in München*, 60; Evans, *Hans Rosbaud*, 44.

12. Dieter Sattler to Alois Hundhammer, 7 May 1947, MK 50136, BH; Dieter Sattler, *Vormerkung*, 16 July 1947, and Sattler, "Aussprache mit Carl Orff," 7 November 1949, box 2, Dieter Sattler Papers, IfZ; John Evarts's Diary, spring and summer 1947, 9, JEPA; H. Müller, *Aktennotiz*, 9 August 1948, MK 50187, and Rudolf Hartmann to Dieter Sattler, 28 November 1949, MK 14395, BH; Solti, *Memoirs*, 91.

13. Richard Wolff and Ernst Fuhr to *Hauptpersonalamt*, 3 May 1948, C Rep 120, LB.

14. Kurt Bork to Sergiu Celibidache, 14 January 1947; Bork to *Finanzabteilung*, 1 August 1947; Berner to *Stadtrat* Dr. Nestriepke, 23 June 1947; Richard Wolff and Ernst Fuhr to *Abteilung für Volksbildung*, 24 November 1947; Bork to John Bitter, 14 January 1947, C Rep 120, LB.

15. Haas (Finance) and Kurt Bork to Berlin Philharmonic Orchestra, 11 December 1947; "Memo on the Contract of the Philharmonic Orchestra," 10 January 1947, C Rep 120, LB.

16. Wilhelm Furtwängler to Helmuth Wolfes, 29 December 1949, in Furtwängler, *Briefe*, 204.

17. Interview with Newell Jenkins, 6 July 1996; "History of Theater and Music Control Branch Wuerttemberg-Baden," 20–25, file: Reports 1948, box 242, T&M, E&CR, OMGUS; Vogel, *Aus den Tagebüchern von Elly Ney*, 14. On Kotz, *Oberregierungsrat* Knöppel to Karl Holl, 10 March 1947, 504/769, HH.

18. Dr. Schwink to H. Meinzolt, 14 July 1945; L. Metzger, *Aktennotiz*, 20 July 1945, and F. Fendt to W. Hoegner, 6 May 1946, MK 50007, BH. Messmer makes this same point in "Münchner Tradition," 174.

19. *Stars and Stripes*, 26 May 1947.

20. The Soviet army of occupation was paid in military marks printed in Leipzig and redeemable only in Germany; see Murphy, *Diplomat among Warriors*, 288; Balabkins, *Germany under Direct Controls*, 142–62; Boelcke, *Der Schwarzmarkt*; Erker, *Ernähungskrise und Nachkriegsgesellschaft*, 67–78 and 168–79; Carlos Moseley to Helen, 20 March 1948, APA.

21. Buchheim, "Die Währungsreform 1948," 189–231; Wallich, *Mainsprings of the German Revival*, 68–79; Helman, "Das Wirtschaftswunder in Westdeutschland," 323–44; Carlos Moseley to Helen, 21 June 1948, APA. On the political consequences of monetary reform, see Backer, *The Decision to Divide Germany*, ch. 9; Eisenberg, *Drawing the Line*, 409–10. Clay's view of events is clearly revealed in *Decision in Germany*, chs. 8 and 18.

22. Everett B. Helm, "Report from Germany," file: Articles by Everett B. Helm, box 727, T&M, E&CR, OMGH, OMGUS; Carlos Moseley to Helen, 21 June 1948, APA; *Staatsintendanten* to Hans Ehard, 16 August 1948, MK 50008, BH.

23. *Stuttgarter Kammerorchester to Kultministerium*, 16 October 1953, HA.Gr.3 3350-9, SS; on the new Philharmonie: *Stadträte* Nicklitz und May und *Kämmerer* Dr. Haas to *Senat*, 23 October 1950, B Rep 14/244–47, SB; *Haushalt 1952: Musikpflege*, B Rep 14/362, SB; Wilhelm Furtwängler to Ernst Reuter, 15 May 1951, B Rep 14/1134, SB; Furtwängler to *Stadtrat* May, 31 October 1950, B Rep 14/1499, SB.

24. Karl Münchinger to Arnulf Klett, 7 December 1948, EA 3/203/628, HS; Consolidated Budget, 1950–52, B Rep 14/342, SB; B Rep 14/247, SB Deals with the Construction of the Philharmonie; Wilhelm Furtwängler to Walter May, 31 October 1950, B Rep 14/1499, Furtwängler to Helmuth Wolfes, 29 December 1949, in Furtwängler, *Briefe*, 204; Furtwängler, *Aktennotiz* to May, 21 December 1950, Furtwängler to Boreslaw Barlog, 20 March 1951, Furtwängler to Tiburtius, 14 May 1952, B Rep 14/1499, SB; Members of the Staatskapelle to *Kultusreferent*, 15 May 1953, Karl Heinz Menzel to Wallner-Basté, 26 June 1952; Members of Staatskapelle to Senat Berlin, 29 February 1952, B Rep 14/1377, SB.

25. Joachim Tiburtius to Wilhelm Furtwängler, 19 April 1952; Furtwängler to Tiburtius, 20 April 1952; Furtwängler to Tiburtius, 14 May 1952, B Rep 14/342, SB; Dr. Türk to Tiburtius, 30 June 1951, B Rep 14/1499, SB; Lang, *Lieber Herr Celibidache*, 150–51. The philharmonic did retain the right to vote for its own *Intendant* from a list submitted by the city.

26. *Entwicklung der Besucherzahlen beim Hessischen Staatstheater Wiesbaden*, August 1948–February 1949, 504/108, HH; Staatstheater Profit and Loss Statement, 21 June 1948 to 20 October 1948, EL 221/3 86, and Budget Projection for 1950–51, EL 221/1 19, SL; Dieter Sattler, *Aktennotiz*, 21 February 1949, box 6, Dieter Sattler Papers, IfZ; "Theater and Music 20 June–31 December 1948," file: Historical Reports, box 728, T&M, E&CR, OMGH, OMGUS; *Sitzung des Verwaltungsausschuss* Meeting, 9 December 1948, 504/44, HH; Wirtschaftsministerium to Kultministerium, 19 June 1952, and Wilhelm Riecker to Kultministerium, 11 November 1949, EA 3/203/341, HS.

27. *Landesgewerkschaft Freie Berufe to Minister für Kultur und Unterricht*,

17 June 1948, 504/331, HH; Theodore Bäuerle to Finance Ministry, 4 October 1949, EL 221/3 267, SL; Karl Münchinger to Kultministerium, 1 April 1946, and Stuttgarter Kammerorchester Profit and Loss, August 1948–February 1949, EA 3/203/303, HS; Revised Staatstheater Budget for 1948–49, EL 221/3 86, HS; Staatsoper Payroll Statements, 4 December 1948, and Georg Hartmann to *Staatsminister*, 27 December 1948, MK 50205, BH.

28. Theodore Bäuerle to John Steiner, 29 July 1948, EA 3/201 78, HS.

29. *Neue Zeitung*, 20 June 1952; Georg Hartmann to Dieter Sattler, 20 June 1949, Wilhelm Diess to Ludwig Held, 7 July 1949, and Diess to Georg Hartmann, 20 June 1950, MK 50098, BH.

30. T&M Report, November 1948, box 880, Correspondence 1946–49, HQ Chief, E&CR, OMGWB, OMGUS.

31. Staatstheater Budget for 1949–50, EL 221/3 86, SL.

32. Appendix to Staatstheater Annual Accounts, 1949, 504/108, HH.

33. *Hessische Nachrichten*, 25 November 1949; Carl Müller to Erwin Stein, 13 January 1950, 504/769; Franz Sauer to Carl Holl, 6 February 1951, Report of R. R. Köhler on visit to Kassel, 29–30 January 1951, *Sitzung des Verwaltungsausschuss*, 18 October 1950, *Betriebsrat* to *Verwaltungsausschuss*, 21 October 1950, Ludwig Metzger, "*Unterhaltung mit* Paul Rose," 29 January 1951, 504/772, HH.

34. *Wiesbaden Kurier*, 22 January 1949, 428/1337; Erwin Stein, *Aktennotiz*, 10 March 1949, 1178/100a; *Versammlung*, 28 January 1949, 1178/100b, HH; Zulauf, *Verwaltung der Kunst oder Kunst der Verwaltung*, 92–93.

35. *Dusseldorf Mittag*, 19 July 1951, 428/1341, HH; Heinrich Köhler-Helffrich to Erwin Stein, 22 January 1953, Köhler-Helffrich to Stein, 2 May 1953, 1178/225a, HH.

36. Wilhelm Diess to Minister, 9 October 1950, MK 50052; Diess to Minister, 28 December 1949, and Georg Hartmann to Minister, 16 December 1949, MK 50206; Hartmann to Sattler, 20 June 1949, Diess to Ludwig Held, 7 July 1949, Diess to Hartmann, 29 June 1950, and Diess to Hartmann, 20 June 1950, MK 50098; *Aktennotiz*, 27 June 1949, MK 14395, BH.

37. Everett B. Helm, "Report from Germany" and "Letter from Germany," file: Articles by Everett B. Helm, box 727, T&M, E&CR, OMGH, OMGUS.

38. Walter Erich Schäfer, "Theater in Land Schillers," nd [1952], EL 221/3 16, Hans-Werner Henze to Ferdinand Leitner, 19 May 1952, and Ferdinand Leitner to Hans-Werner Henze, 14 June 1952, EL 221/3 149, SL.

39. Carlos Moseley, "Subject: *Abraxas*," file: Munich State Opera, box 19, E&CR, OMGB, OMGUS; Werner Egk, "Zum Aufführungsverbot des Bayerischen Kultusministeriums gegen das Ballett Abraxas," and Sattler to Ludwig Hartenfells, 18 February 1949, box 6, Dieter Sattler Papers, IfZ.

40. Carlos Moseley, "Subject: *Abraxas*," file: Munich State Opera, box 19,

E&CR, OMGB, OMGUS; Werner Egk, "Zum Aufführungsverbot des Bayerischen Kultusministeriums gegen das Ballett Abraxas," Georg Hartmann to Dieter Sattler, nd [1948], Sattler's memo of conversation with Werner Egk, 23 August 1949, box 6, and *Werner Egk vs Land Bayern*, box 5, Dieter Sattler Papers, IfZ; Egk, *Die Zeit wartet nicht*, 380–86 and 398–402.

41. *Wiesbaden Kurier*, 23 April 1949; Everett B. Helm, "Press Release," file: Everett B. Helm Articles, box 727, T&M, E&CR, OMGH, OMGUS.

42. Karl Holl, "Uraufführung des Cardillac. 17 March 1947," 428/1301; Otto Henning to Karl Holl, 13 May 1949, 504/36, HH; *Frankfurter Neue Presse*, 24 April 1949; *Wiesbaden Kurier*, 28 April 1949.

43. Kranichsteiner Musikinstitut Budget, 1951, 504/536; Ludwig Metzger to Arno Henning, 5 March 1953 and 3 February 1954, Metzger to Erwin Stein, 5 June 1950, Karl Holl to Erwin Stein, 12 October 1950, 504/799, HH. On American involvement in Darmstadt, see Beal, "Negotiating Cultural Allies," and Thacker, "Playing Beethoven Like an Indian," 380–84.

44. Kater, *Composers of the Nazi Era*, ch. 4; Evarts's Diary, spring–summer 1947, 7–8, JEPA; Diess, *Aktennotiz*, 22 October 1948, MK 50129; Dieter Sattler to Karl Amadeus Hartmann, 25 July 1949, and Sattler to Dr. Keim, 9 September 1947, MK 51259, BH.

45. Evarts's Diary, spring–summer 1947, 23, JEPA; Anton Scharnagl to Dieter Sattler, 16 June 1949, box 2, Dieter Sattler Papers, IfZ.

46. Karl Holl to *Bürgermeister* Schröder, 13 December 1950, 504/799, HH.

47. Historians debate the reasons for the success of German democracy and the occupiers' impact on the country's political culture. One school holds that the Federal Republic succeeded because it rooted itself in indigenous liberal traditions; a second argues, like this study, that the Western Allies helped foster democracy by establishing the structures required to support it. For the former, see Prowe, "Foundations of West German Democracy," and Prowe, "German Democratization as Conservative Restabilization." A variant of this holds that democracy was a product of the economic miracle, not the occupation; see Schildt and Sywottek, "Reconstruction and Modernization." For the structural contribution of the Allies, see Merkl, *The Origins of the Federal Republic of Germany*; Niclauss, *Demokratiegründung in Westdeutschland*; and Benz, *Von der Besatzungsherrschaft zur Bundesrepublik Deutschland*. Rupieper's fine study, *Die Wurzeln der westdeutschen Nachkriegsdemokratie*, bridges the interpretations.

48. Karl Holl, "Aufgaben des Theaterbeirats," 12 February 1948, 504/48, and Holl to Erwin Stein, 9 February 1950, 504/373, HH.

49. Dieter Sattler, "Falsch verstehende Minderheit?" box 5, Dieter Sattler Papers, IfZ.

50. Alois Hundhammer to Ständige Konferenz der Kultusminister der Länder in der Bundesrepublik Deutschland, 15 April 1950, EA 3/203, HS.

CHAPTER 6

1. Interview with Carlos Moseley, 17 March 1996; Leonard Bernstein to Helen Coates, 5 May 1948, file: Helen Coates, box 13, Leonard Bernstein Papers, LC.

2. Carlos Moseley to "Mice and Men," 13 May 1948, APA; Leonard Bernstein to Helen Coates, 11 May 1948, file: Helen Coates, box 13, Bernstein Papers, LC.

3. Carlos Moseley to "Mice and Men," 13 May 1948, APA; Leonard Bernstein to Helen Coates, 8 and 11 May 1948, file: Helen Coates, box 13, Bernstein Papers, LC.

4. Interview with Carlos Moseley, 17 March 1996; Carlos Moseley to "Mice and Men," 13 May 1948, APA.

5. Interview with Carlos Moseley, 17 March 1996; Carlos Moseley to author, 9 February 1998; Carlos Moseley curriculum vitae, nd [1951], APA; Libraries of Contemporary Music in Germany and Austria, 13 February 1946, box 3, American Libraries Music Loan Project, LC.

6. Carlos Moseley to Helen, 5 March, 22 April, and 16 July 1948, APA.

7. Carlos Moseley to Mamie, 25 February 1948, and Moseley to Helen, 6 March 1948, APA.

8. Interview with Mateo Lettunich, 12 August 1996; J. C. Thompson to National Concert and Artists Corporation, 19 July 1949, file: visiting artists, box 124, General Records, E&CR, OMGBS, OMGUS, Rg 260, NA; interview with Newell Jenkins, 6 July 1996.

9. Clay, *Decision in Germany*, 303; Tent, *Mission on the Rhine*, ch. 6; Lucius Clay to William Draper, 9 October 1948, in *The Papers of General Lucius D. Clay*, 2:896; Carlos Moseley to Helen, 22 April 1948, APA; Clay to War Department CAD, 30 May 1946, file: US artists, box 83, Staff Studies, DHQ, ICD, OMGUS; J. P. Steiner, "Suggestions for Berchtesgaden meeting," 20 September 1948, file: Berchtesgaden Meeting, box 879, HQ Chief, E&CR, OMGWB, OMGUS.

10. Robert Murphy, Memorandum, 24 May 1946, file: US Artists, box 83, Staff Studies, DHQ, ICD, OMGUS; clipping: "30 jahre SWF 1976," file: articles in German, box 47, Otto Klemperer Papers, LC. Paradoxically, the Americans justified refusing Klemperer permission to conduct in Germany because of his supposed links to the communists and because his boss, the president of the Los Angeles Philharmonic, had pro-Nazi sympathies. Robert Murphy to Secretary of State, 22 October 1945, file: expatriation, box 49, Klemperer Papers, LC.

11. Shepard Stone to Secretary of War, 15 April 1946, cited in Berghahn, *America and the Intellectual Cold War*, 48; Robert McClure to Chief of Staff, 14 May 1946, file: US Artists, box 83, Staff Studies, DHQ, ICD,

OMGUS; Nicolas Nabokov to Eric Clarke, 17 June 1946, file: Theater Policies, box 242, T&M, E&CR, OMGUS.

12. Interview with Newell Jenkins, 6 July 1996; William Kinard to General McClure, 17 May 1946, file: T&M, box 43, Director's Records, DHQ, ICD, OMGUS. Ironically, the French pianist moved on to Berlin where she performed, with Celibidache and the BPO, in the Russian sector. C. Kincaird to Eric Clarke, 15 June 1946, file: Theater Policies, box 242, T&M, E&CR, OMGUS; E. T. Peeples to Director, ICD Württemberg-Baden, 13 July 1946, file: Policies, box 927, T&M, E&CR, OMGWB, OMGUS; Telecon from Eric Clarke, 6 September 1946, file: Telecon, box 242, T&M, E&CR, OMGUS; Menuhin, *Unfinished Journey*, 224; Walter Hinrischen to All Music Officers, 26 February 1947, file: American Plays and Music, box 727, T&M, E&CR, OMGH, OMGUS; Newell Jenkins, "Test Case of Allied Artists," 1 February 1947, file: US artists, box 245, T&M, E&CR, OMGUS; T&M Report, 3 October 1946, file: Monthly Summary, box 728, T&M, E&CR, OMGH, OMGUS, documents the first Russian performances. Otto Klemperer also conducted first in the Russian zone because he could not get into the American. Klemperer conducted *Carmen* at the Komische Oper in 1949. Otto Klemperer, interview with *Berliner Montag*, 29 November 1948, file: Gespräch bei der Rückkehr nach Berlin, box 46, Klemperer Papers, LC.

13. SWNCC 269/8, reprinted in Department of State, *Germany, 1947–1949*, 610–11, and 269/5, reprinted in Department of State, *Occupation of Germany*, 215–16.

14. Lucius Clay to War Department, 5 April 1947, and Davidson Taylor to Robert McClure, 11 February 1948, file: visiting artists, box 7, Director's Records, DHQ, ICD, OMGUS; on Gieseking, *New York Times*, 26 January 1949; on Furtwängler, *New York Times*, 6 January 1949, and Gillis, *Furtwängler and America*; Vaughan, *Herbert von Karajan*, 12–13.

15. Clay for Daniel Noce, 31 January 1947, in *Papers of General Lucius D. Clay*, 1:309; "Plan for Appearance of American Artists in Germany," nd [March 1946], file: US Artists, box 83, Staff Studies, DHQ, ICD, OMGUS.

16. Kerr, "The American Music Center"; interview with Carlos Moseley, 17 March 1996.

17. Daniel Noce to Gordon Textor, 17 July 1947, file: FT&M, box 15, DHQ, ICD, OMGUS; interview with Mateo Lettunich, 12 August 1996; Webster Aitken Journal, "Journey into Defeat: Germany April 7–28 1949," Webster Aitken Papers, HRC.

18. "Request for Travel to the States for Mr. Benno D. Frank," 15 October 1947, file: FT&M, box 15, DHQ, ICD, OMGUS; Dir CO to Dir IC[D], 15 October 1947, file: visiting artists, box 81, Cultural Exchange Rec-

ords, Education Branch, E&CR, OMGUS; Harrison Kerr to John Evarts, 20 May 1949, file: T&M, box 21, CRB, E&CR, OMGB, OMGUS; Everett Helm to Special Service Karlsruhe, 25 June 1948, and Ralph Kirkpatrick concerts: Box Office Receipts and Expenditures, nd [July 1948], file: exchanges, box 928, T&M, E&CR, OMGWB, OMGUS.

19. Lt. Col. Ladue to Harrison Kerr, 29 April 1948, 372.007, Central Decimal Files, CAD, War Department, Rg 165, NA; Carlos Moseley to Louis Miniclier, 28 October 1948, file: American artists, box 21, Cultural Exchange Records, Education Branch, E&CR, OMGUS; interview with Isaac Stern, 29 December 1995; Eric Clarke to Gordon Textor, 2 April 1948, file: Allied Artists, box 238, T&M, E&CR, OMGUS; Louis Miniclier, "Request for Visiting Experts," 14 March 1949, file: visiting experts, box 175, Central Office, Land Director, OMGB, OMGUS.

20. "Box Office Receipts and Expenses of Kirkpatrick Concerts," July 1948, file: visiting artists, box 310, Correspondence, ISD, OMGWB, OMGUS.

21. Harrison Kerr, "Patricia Travers Tour," 23 July 1948, file: NY Field Office, box 9, Director's Records, DHQ, ICD, OMGUS.

22. In his journal Aitken recognized his poor performance but attributed it to the terrible quality of the pianos he was required to play, to the cold, and to the shock of seeing Germany in ruins; see Webster Aitken Journal, "Journey into Defeat: Germany April 7–28 1949," Aitken Papers, HRC; Harrison Kerr to John Evarts, 20 May 1949, file: T&M, box 21, CRB, E&CR, OMGB, OMGUS; "Cost of Webster Aitken Concerts," 6 May 1949, file: visiting artists, box 729, T&M, E&CR, OMGH, OMGUS; T&M Report, April 1949, file: Special Reports, box 20, E&CR, OMGB, OMGUS; John Evarts to Harrison Kerr, 23 April and 6 May 1949, file: musicians, box 211, Visiting Consultants Program, E&CR, OMGUS; P. Beauvais to J. Evarts, 24 March 1949, file: exchanges, box 928, T&M, E&CR, OMGWB, OMGUS.

23. Carlos Moseley to Helen, 27 April 1948, APA; Harrison Kerr to John Evarts, 20 May 1949, file: T&M, box 21, CRB, E&CR, OMGB, OMGUS; Harrison Kerr, "Patricia Travers Tour," 23 July 1948, file: NY Field Office, box 9, Director's Records, DHQ, ICD, OMGUS.

24. Carlos Moseley to Madame X, 19 February 1949, APA; *Süddeutsche Zeitung*, 1 February 1949; *Münchner Merkur*, 2 February 1949; *Frankfurter Rundschau*, 10 February 1949.

25. Carlos Moseley to Dear and Good Woman of Otis Blvd., 20 February 1949, APA; *Die Neue Zeitung*, 8 February 1949.

26. Charles Winning to John Evarts, 3 March 1949, file: E&CR, box 175, Central Office, Land Director, OMGB, OMGUS.

27. Louis Miniclier to John Bitter, 3 October 1949, file: correspondence, box 18, CRB, E&CR, OMGB, OMGUS.

28. Interview with Mateo Lettunich, 12 August 1996; according to Lettunich and Jenkins it was the homophobic Berlin E&CR chief John Thompson who engineered Evarts dismissal; Newell Jenkins thought that it was because Evarts told the wrong person that he had once been Thornton Wilder's lover; telephone interview with Newell Jenkins, 12 March 1997. File: John Evarts, box 32, Thornton Wilder Papers, YUA, contains the correspondence, but while it is clear from the letters (and Evarts's diaries) that he was impressed by and attracted to Wilder, the evidence does not suggest that they had been lovers. On Paris, Edward Cushing to John Evarts, nd [1951], APA; "Explanation of Proposed Reassignments of T&M Officers," 10 March 1947, file: T&M Officers, box 243, T&M, E&CR, OMGUS.

29. Henry Kellerman to Robert Murphy, 13 April 1949, box 205, LOT 53D311, Department of State, Rg 59, NA; McCloy cited in Schwartz, "Reeducation and Democracy," 38.

30. "The Future Status of the Reorientation Program," nd [summer 1949], box 205, LOT 53D311, Department of State, Rg 59, NA.

31. "The Future Status of the Reorientation Program," and Henry Kellerman to Robert Murphy, 13 April 1949, box 205, LOT 53D311, Department of State, Rg 59, NA; J. Anthony Panuch to Fred Searls, nd [January 1949], file: Berlin Occupation, J. Anthony Panuch Papers, HSTL.

32. Stone cited in Berghahn, *America and the Intellectual Cold Wars*, 62; "Memo on Policy for E&CR Division," December 1949, box 11, DHQ Research and Planning Section, E&CR, OMGUS.

33. "General Policy on US Information Centers," 1951, file: America Houses, box 1, subject files, IIA, European Field Program, Department of State, Rg 59, NA; L. E. Norrie to John Pixley, 30 September 1949, file: Amerika Haus, box 112, Branch Chief, Community Education Division, E&CR, OMGUS.

34. OMGUS, *Monthly Report of the Military Governor*, No. 47, July 1949, 36.

35. "Plan and Policy for the Information Centers, 1951," file: Information Centers, box 14, subject files, IIA, European Field Program, Department of State, Rg 59, NA; Louis Miniclier to W. P. Holderman, 6 October 1950, box 2, Miscellaneous Documents, PAD, *Land* Commissioner Bavaria, HICOG, Rg 466, NA.

36. "Work Sheets: Bavarian Situation in ECR," 21 June 1949, file: reorientation, box 16, CRB, E&CR, OMGB, OMGUS.

37. Henry Kellerman, "Reflections on Program Inspired by Reading the Speier-Carroll Report," 28 December 1950, file: Carroll/Speier, box 5, subject files, IIA, European Field Program, Department of State, Rg 59, NA.

38. Henry Kellerman, "Reflections on Program Inspired by Reading the Speier-Carroll Report," 28 December 1950, file: Carroll/Speier, box 5, subject files, IIA, European Field Program, Department of State, Rg 59, NA.

39. On the impact of the merger creating the SED, Annan, *Changing Enemies*, ch. 10, and on the process, Krisch, *German Politics under Soviet Occupation*; on land reform, Sandford, *From Hitler to Ulbricht*; Frederic Mellinger, T&M Report, 24 July 1946, file: Weekly Reports, box 239, T&M, E&CR, OMGUS; Robert McClure to Sergei Tulpanov, 13 January 1947, file: ACA Directives, box 1, Director's Records, DHQ, ICD, OMGUS.

40. Outgoing Cable, signed Clay, 13 September 1946, file: ACA Directives, box 1, Director's Records, DHQ, ICD, OMGUS.

41. On Operation Talk Back, see Gienow-Hecht, *Transmission Impossible*, 124–39; Office of the Deputy Military Governor, "Directive re: Vigorous Information Program," 10 February 1948, and "Radio Branch Implementation of the Vigorous Information Program," 19 July 1948, box 45, Director's Records, DHQ, ICD, OMGUS; C. S. Wright to Fellow Americans, October 1948, file: Info. Programs, box 308, Activities of Information Centers, Records of Information Centers and Exhibits, ICD, OMGUS.

42. Janik, "Music in Cold War Berlin," 316–18; John Evarts to Chief CAD, 6 May 1949, file: Visiting Consultants Program, box 211, CAD, E&CR, OMGUS; *Tägliche Rundschau*, 28 December 1948; interview with Mateo Lettunich, 12 August 1996.

43. Friedrich Abel, "Kultur oder Kultura," *Fortschritt*, July 1953, and "Public Affairs Plan for Germany," January 1953, file: Cultural Affairs, box 6, subject files, IIA, European Field Program, Department of State, Rg 59, NA.

44. On the effort to develop the transatlantic sentiments of European intellectuals, see Coleman, *The Liberal Conspiracy*; Hochgeschwender, *Freiheit in der Offensive?*; Saunders, *The Cultural Cold War*; Berghahn, *America and the Intellectual Cold Wars*; Scott-Smith, *The Politics of Apolitical Culture*. For an interpretive study of the impact of this struggle on fine art in the United States, see Guilbaut, *How New York Stole the Idea of Modern Art*. On Darmstadt, see Beal, "Negotiating Cultural Allies."

45. Allied Kommandatura, "Cultural Festival 1951," 21 December 1950, file: Berlin Cultural Festival, box 1, PAD, Berlin Element, and "Brief: Berlin Cultural Festival, 1951," 1 February 1951, Office of the Executive Secretary, Berlin Element, HICOG, Rg 466, NA.

46. Financial Estimates for Berlin Festival, 1951, and IECA Committee, Allied Kommandatura, "Report on Extraordinary Session of IECA Committee to Consider the Decisions concerning the Berlin Festival, 1951," 29 January 1951, file: Berlin Cultural Festival, box 1, PAD, Berlin Element, HICOG, Rg 466, NA; *Stadtrat* May, *Vormerkung*, 5 December 1950; Minutes of Meeting of IECA Committee, 9 February 1951, B Rep 14/125, SB.

47. John Thompson to Mateo Lettunich, 28 July 1950; Allied Kommandatura, "Cultural Festival 1951," 21 December 1951; Minutes of the First Meeting of the Joint Advisory Committee for the Berlin Festival 1951, 29 November

1950; Minutes of Meeting of Deputy Commanders, Berlin, 13 December 1950, file: Berlin Cultural Festival, box 1, PAD, Berlin Element, HICOG, Rg 466, NA.

48. Henry Kellerman, "American Participation in the Berlin Arts Festival," 3 October 1951, file: Berlin Festival 1951, box 3, subject files, IIA, European Field Program, Department of State, Rg 59, NA; Robert Schnitzer, "Report on United States Participation in the Berlin Festival, 5–30 September 1951," file: Negotiations/Germany, F106, Robert Breen Collection, OSU; Joachim Tiburtius to President House of Representatives, Berlin, 8 June 1951, B Rep 14/156–57, SB.

49. Two first-rate studies of the reception of American popular culture are Maase, *Bravo Amerika!*, and Poiger, *Jazz, Rock and Rebels*.

50. J. Convery Egan, "Berlin Cultural Festival 1951," 4 October 1951, and Balance Sheet for 1951 *Berliner Festwoche*, file: Berlin Cultural Festival, box 2, PAD, Berlin Element, HICOG, Rg 466, NA.

51. J. Convery Egan, "Cultural Festivals Past and Present," 24 November 1951, file: Berlin Festival 1951, box 3, subject files, IIA, European Field Program, Department of State, Rg 59, NA.

52. Alpert, *The Life and Times of Porgy and Bess*, 89; for critical reactions: Woll, *Black Musical Theater*, ch. 10; Gershwin explained his folk conception of the opera in the *New York Times*, 20 October 1935. *Baltimore Afro American* cited in Taylor, "Ambassadors of the Arts," 94.

53. Dowling, "Report on *Porgy and Bess*," box 2, PAD, Berlin Element, HICOG, NA.

54. Davison, *Death and Life of Germany*, 277.

55. Richter, *Re-educating Germany*, 166; E. Thomas to H. Truman, 17 October 1946, folder 2, Subject File: Germany, President's Secretary File, HSTL; Robert Schnitzer to Stephen Munsing, 15 August 1952; R. Schnitzer to R. Breen, 21 August 1952, box 3, IIA, European Field Program, Department of State, Rg 59, NA.

56. Robert Schnitzer to Stephen Munsing, 15 August 1952, box 3, IIA, European Field Program, Department of State, Rg 59, NA; von Eschen, *Race against Empire*; Robert Schnitzer to W. J. Convery Egan, 8 August 1952, box 3, IIA, European Field Program, Department of State, Rg 59, NA; Staff Study: "Proposed Tour of *Porgy and Bess* in the Soviet Union and the European satellite countries," 20 September 1955, 007.2(6), box 15, OCB, DDEL.

57. Robert Schnitzer to Mary French, 30 June 1952, and F5 Pt1: *Porgy and Bess*, 1952–53, Blevins Davis to Wilva Breen, 6 February 1953, file: Vienna and Berlin, F44A, Breen Collection, OSU; *New York Times*, 2 October 1952.

58. For the attitude of "serious" musicians to jazz, see Kater, *Different Drummers*, 276.

59. *Berliner Anzeiger*, 19 September 1952; *Telegraf*, 19 September 1952; *Die Neue Zeitung*, 19 September 1952; RIAS Radio Commentary by Friedrich Luft, box 3, IIA, European Field Program, Department of State, Rg 59, NA; *Der Kurier*, 18 September 1952; *Der Abend*, 18 September 1952.

60. *Telegraf*, 19 September 1952; *Nacht Depesche*, 20 September 1952; *Der Tagesspiegel*, 19 September 1952.

61. *Der Abend*, 18 September 1952; *Telegraf*, 19 September 1952; *Der Tag*, 19 September 1952; *Wiener Kurier*, 8 September 1952; *Die Welt*, 19 September 1952.

62. RIAS Radio Commentary by Friedrich Luft, box 3, IIA, European Field Program, Department of State, Rg 59, NA; *Berliner Anzeiger*, 19 September 1952; *Der Tagesspiegel*, 19 September 1952.

63. In his memoirs, Lucius Clay echoes German criticism of black troops and defends his own decision to reorganize many of them into segregated units; see *Decision in Germany*, 230–31. American reactions to *Porgy* are discussed in Monod, "Disguise, Containment and the *Porgy and Bess* Revival"; for a broader discussion of racial attitudes, see Baker, *From Savage to Negro*.

64. Foreign Service Despatch: Berlin Cultural Festival, 4 December 1952, box 2, PAD, Berlin Element, HICOG.

65. *Berliner Anzeiger*, 16 May 1952; *Die Neue Zeitung*, 18 May 1952; *Berliner Zeitung*, 16 May 1952; E. Goebel, A. Salomon, E. Mehrer, and G. Dembach, open letter, 6 June 1947, file: Furtwängler, box 237, T&M, E&CR, OMGUS.

66. *Frankfurter Rundschau*, 8 July 1949; *Stuttgarter Zeitung*, 5 June 1948.

67. *Frankfurter Rundschau*, 7 October 1949; *Stuttgarter Zeitung*, 5 June 1948; interview with Carlos Moseley, 16 March 1996; Speech on American Music by Paul Hindemith, 28 August 1947, file: Visiting Artists, box 12, Administrative Records, ISB, USACA, Rg 260, NA.

68. *Münchner Tageblatt*, 15 May 1948; *Weltpresse*, 31 May 1948; *Österreichische Zeitung*, 3 June 1948.

69. *New York Herald Tribune*, 19 October 1947; Daniel Belgrad's impressive study, *The Culture of Spontaneity*, locates spontaneity at the center of America's postwar culture.

70. *Világosság*, 22 May 1948; *Münchner Tageblatt*, 15 May 1948; *Wiener Kurier*, 29 May 1948; *Österreichische Zeitung*, 3 June 1948; *Die Presse*, 5 June 1948.

71. *Welt am Abend*, 3 June 1948; *Arbeiterzeitung*, 30 May 1948.

CONCLUSION

1. Carlos Moseley to Helen, 30 March 1948, APA; Mabel Dunn to Lucius Clay, nd [1948], file: Bayreuth, box 19, CRB, E&CR, OMGB, OMGUS,

Rg 260, NA; Mabel Dunn to *Ministerpräsident*, 16 February 1948, MK 50451, BH.

2. Carlos Moseley, memo to James Clark: "Legal Aspects of Proposed Bayreuth Festival," nd [June 1948], file: Bayreuth, box 19, CRB, E&CR, OMGB, OMGUS; *New York Times*, 3 July 1947. On Wagner's *Spruchkammer* hearing, Hamann, *Winifred Wagner*, 543–55.

3. Carlos Moseley to Director ICD, 18 May 1948, Carlos Moseley to William Rogers, 10 March 1948, and *Stadtrat* Bayreuth to MG Bayreuth, memo on Bayreuth Festival, 18 February 1948, file: Bayreuth, box 19, CRB, E&CR, OMGB, OMGUS; Willi Cronauer to Alois Hundhammer, 3 February 1948, MK 50451, BH, for city support of Wolfgang Wagner's claim. Spotts, *Bayreuth*, 202, on Friedelind's refusal. Friedelind did have a circle of supporters in Munich who were working on her behalf to secure her control, and in 1947 she indicated her willingness to run a festival reconstituted to include non-Wagnerian operatic works: Willi Cronauer to Alois Hundhammer, 11 April 1947, MK 50451, BH; the city of Bayreuth, however, vigorously opposed such a move. On the Tannhäuser Fund: *Oberbürgermeister* Meyer to Staatsministerium für Unterricht und Kultur, 27 December 1945, and Fendt to *Finanzminister*, 12 January 1946, MK 50451, BH.

4. Carlos Moseley to Director ICD, 18 May 1948, and Carlos Moseley to William Rogers, 10 March 1948, file: Bayreuth, box 19, CRB, E&CR, OMGB, OMGUS.

5. Dieter Sattler to Alois Hundhammer, 9 April 1948, and speech by Alois Hundhammer, 22 May 1948, MK 50451, BH; Dieter Sattler, "Zukunft der Bayreuther Festspiele," 24 July 1948, box 8, Dieter Sattler Papers, IfZ; interview with Carlos Moseley, 17 March 1996.

6. Dieter Sattler, "Die Zukunft der Bayreuther Wagner-Festspiele," 10 March 1949, box 8, Sattler Papers, IfZ; Spotts, *Bayreuth*, 205–6; Dieter Sattler to Alois Hundhammer, 24 January 1949, and Sattler to Finanzministerium, 11 March 1950; Consolidated Budget for Wagner *Festspiele*, 1953, MK 50451, BH.

7. Clipping, *Le Figaro*, 18 August 1951, and Wieland Wagner interview, 1951, box 5, Sattler Papers, IfZ.

8. Wieland Wagner interview, 1951, box 5, Sattler Papers, IfZ; Wagner, Foreword, 2; Heinz Tietjen to Emil Preetorius, 15 October, 21 November, and 8 December 1946, 21 November 1947, and 22 January 1948, box 5, Heinz Tietjen Papers, AdK. Also on Wagner's visits to Berlin, see also Hamann, *Winifred Wagner*, 440–41. On the research institute, see McClatchie, "Wagner Research."

9. Clipping, *Le Figaro*, 18 August 1951, and Wieland Wagner interview, 1951,

box 5, Sattler Papers, IfZ; Skelton, *Wagner at Bayreuth*, 161; Heinz Tietjen to Emil Preetorius, 15 December 1949, box 5, Tietjen Papers, AdK.

10. Spotts, *Bayreuth*, 232 and ch. 7; Henze-Döhring, "Kulturelle Zentren."

11. Werner Egk to Heinz Tietjen, 18 August 1948; *Stuttgarter Zeitung*, 18 December 1946, box 2, Tietjen Papers, AdK.

12. Interview with Henry Pleasants, 2 November 1996.

13. Webster Aitken Journal, "Journey into Defeat: Germany April 7–28 1949," Webster Aitken Papers, HRC.

BIBLIOGRAPHY

Archival Sources

GERMANY

Bayerisches Hauptstaatsarchiv, Munich
  Ministerium für Unterricht und Kultus
Hauptstaatsarchiv Stuttgart
  EA 1 Staatsministerium
  EA 3 Ministerium für Wissenschaft und Kunst
  Q1/21 Theodore Bäuerle Papers
Hessisches Hauptstaatsarchiv, Wiesbaden
  Abt. 428 Staatstheater
  Abt. 501 Hessisches Ministerium für politische Befreiung
  Abt. 504 Hessischer Minister für Kultus und Unterricht
  Abt. 1178 Erwin Stein Papers
  Abt. 1219 Hans Piroth Collection
Institut für Zeitgeschichte, Munich
  Dieter Sattler Papers
Landesarchiv Berlin
  B Rep 36 Office of Military Government (Berlin Sector)
  B Rep 37 Office of Military Government (Berlin Sector)
  C Rep 37 OMGUS Interviews
  C Rep 120 Magistrat von Berlin/Volksbildung
  C Rep 167 Staatsoper
Staatsarchiv Ludwigsburg
  El 221 Württ. Staatstheater Stuttgart
Stadtarchiv Berlin (now amalgamated with the Landesarchiv)
  B Rep 14 Senatsverwaltung für Wissenschaft und Forschung
  C Rep 126 Städtische oper
Stadtarchiv München
  Kulturamt
Stadtarchiv Stuttgart
  HA.Gr.3 Kulturamt
Stiftung Archiv der Akademie der Künste, Berlin
  Ferdinand Leitner Papers
  H. H. Stuckenschmidt Papers
  Heinz Tietjen Papers
  Gerhart von Westerman Papers

UNITED STATES

Oskar Diethelm Library of Cornell University, New York, New York
  David M. Levy Collection
Dwight David Eisenhower Library, Abilene, Kansas
  C. D. Jackson Papers
  White House Office, National Security Council Special Assistants' Papers,
    Operations Control Board Series
Hoover Institution on War, Revolution and Peace, Palo Alto, California
  Daniel Lerner Collection
Jerome Lawrence and Robert E. Lee Theatre Research Institute at Ohio State
  University, Columbus
  Robert Breen Collection
Library of Congress, Washington, D.C.
  American Libraries Music Loan Project
  Leonard Bernstein Papers
  Federal Writers' Project
  Joint Army and Navy Committee on Welfare and Recreation
  Otto Klemperer Papers
National Archives, Washington, D.C.
  Berlin Document Center: Nachkriegsunterlagen betreffend RKK (series
    2700)
  GG 331 Supreme Headquarters of the Allied Expeditionary Force
  Rg 59 Department of State
    Central Decimal Files, Germany, 1945–49
    General Records of the Department of State
      LOT 53D101 International Information Activities — Germany and
        Austria
      LOT 53D311 International Information Agency
      LOT 53D339 Records Maintained by Chief Brynjold Hovde,
        1944–46
      LOT 55D370 Records of the Assistant Secretary of State for
        Occupied Areas
    International Information Administration, European Field Program
  Rg 84 U.S. Mission Berlin, Cultural Affairs Committee
    Foreign Service Posts of the Department of State, Austria U.S. Element
      of the Allied Commission for Austria
  Rg 165 War Department
  Rg 260 Office of the Military Government United States
  Rg 260 U.S. Allied Command Austria
  Rg 466 Office of the High Commissioner for Germany
Private Archives
  John Bitter, Miami, Florida

Jeremiah Evarts, Cornish, New Hampshire
Michael Kater, Toronto, Ontario
Harry Ransom Center, Austin, Texas
    Webster Aitken Papers
    Nicolas Nabokov Papers
Harry S. Truman Library, Independence, Missouri
    Bryn J. Hovde Papers
    Charles M. Hulten Papers
    J. Anthony Panuch Papers
    President's Secretary File
    Harry S. Truman Papers
Washington State University Archive, Pullman
    Hans Rosbaud Papers
Yale University Archives, New Haven, Connecticut
    Paul Hindemith Papers
    Deems Taylor Papers
    Virgil Thompson Papers
    Thornton Wilder Papers

Works Cited

Abrahamsen, David. *Men, Mind and Power*. New York: Columbia University Press, 1945.

Adorno, Theodor, et al. *The Authoritarian Personality*. New York: Harper & Row, 1950.

Alpert, Herbert. *The Life and Times of Porgy and Bess*. New York: Alfred A. Knopf, 1990.

Annan, Noel. *Changing Enemies: The Defeat and Regeneration of Germany*. Ithaca: Cornell University Press, 1995.

Applegate, Celia. "What Is German Music? Reflections on the Role of Art in the Creation of the German Nation." *German Studies Review* 15 (Winter 1992): 21–32.

Asche, Gerhart. "Gerhard Hüsch." *Opernwelt*, August–September 1981, 8–11.

Backer, John. *The Decision to Divide Germany: American Foreign Policy in Transition*. Durham: Duke University Press, 1978.

Bader, William R. *Austria between East and West, 1945–1955*. Stanford: Stanford University Press, 1966.

Baker, Lee. *From Savage to Negro: Anthropology and the Construction of Race*. Berkeley: University of California Press, 1998.

Balabkins, Nicholas. *Germany under Direct Controls: Economic Aspects of Industrial Disarmament, 1945–1948*. New Brunswick: Rutgers University Press, 1964.

Balfour, Michael. "In Retrospect: Britain's Policy of Re-education." In *The*

Political Re-education of Germany and Her Allies after WWII, ed. Nicholas
  Pronay and Keith Wilson, 139–50. Beckenham: Croom Helm, 1985.

Bance, Alan. Introduction. In *The Cultural Legacy of the British Occupation in
  Germany*, ed. Alan Bance, 4–28. Stuttgart: Hans-Dieter Heinz Verlag,
  1997.

Barnouw, Dagmar. *Germany 1945: Views of War and Violence*. Bloomington:
  Indiana University Press, 1996.

Bausch, Ulrich. *Die Kulturpolitik der US-amerikanischen Information Control
  Division in Württemberg-Baden von 1945 bis 1949*. Stuttgart: Klett-Cotta,
  1992.

Beal, Amy. "Negotiating Cultural Allies: American Music in Darmstadt,
  1946–1956." *Journal of the American Musicological Society* 53 (spring 2000):
  105–27.

Belgrad, Daniel. *The Culture of Spontaneity: Improvisation and the Arts in
  Postwar America*. Chicago: University of Chicago Press, 1998.

Benz, Wolfgang. *Von der Besatzungsherrschaft zur Bundesrepublik Deutschland*.
  Frankfurt: Deutscher Taschenbuch Verlag, 1984.

Berghahn, Volker. *America and the Intellectual Cold War in Europe*. Princeton:
  Princeton University Press, 2001.

———. *The Americanization of West German Industry*. Cambridge: Cambridge
  University Press, 1986.

———. "Recasting Bourgeois Germany." In *The Miracle Years: A Cultural
  History of West Germany, 1949–1968*, ed. Hanna Schissler, 326–40.
  Princeton: Princeton University Press, 2001.

Bischof, Günter. *Austria in the First Cold War, 1945–1955*. London: St. Martin's
  Press, 1999.

Boehling, Rebecca. *A Question of Priorities: Democratic Reform and Economic
  Recovery in Postwar Germany*. New York: Berghahn, 1998.

———. "US Military Occupation, Grass Roots Democracy, and Local
  Government." In *American Policy and the Reconstruction of Western
  Germany, 1945–1955*, ed. Jeffry Diefendorf, Axel Frohn, and Hermann-Josef
  Rupieper, 281–306. Cambridge: Cambridge University Press, 1993.

Boelcke, Willi. *Der Schwarzmarkt 1945–1948*. Brunswick: Westermann, 1986.

Böhm, Karl. *A Life Remembered*. London: M. Boyars, 1992.

Borgelt, Hans. *Das war der Frühling von Berlin*. Munich: Schneekluth, 1993.

Breit, Peter. "Culture as Authority: American and German Transactions." In
  The American Impact on Postwar Germany, ed. Reiner Pommerin, 125–48.
  Providence: Berghahn, 1997.

Buchheim, C. "Die Währungsreform 1948 in Westdeutschland."
  Vierteljahrshefte für Zeitgeschichte 36 (1988): 189–231.

Bungenstab, Karl-Ernst. *Umerziehung zur Demokratie? Re-edukation Politik im Bildungswesen der US Zone, 1945–49.* Düsseldorf: Bertelsmann universitätsverlag, 1970.

Carter, Erica. *How German Is She? Postwar German Reconstruction and the Consuming Woman.* Ann Arbor: University of Michigan Press, 1997.

Casey, Steven. *Cautious Crusade: Franklin D. Roosevelt, American Public Opinion and the War against Nazi Germany.* New York: Oxford University Press, 2001.

Clare, George. *Before the Wall: Berlin Days, 1946–1948.* New York: Dutton, 1990.

Clark, Mark. *Calculated Risk.* New York: G. G. Harrap, 1956.

Clay, Lucius D. *Decision in Germany.* Garden City: Doubleday, 1950.

———. *The Papers of General Lucius D. Clay: Germany, 1945–1949.* Ed. Jean Edward Smith. Bloomington: Indiana University Press, 1974.

Clemens, Gabriele. *Britische Kulturpolitik in Deutschland, 1945–1949.* Stuttgart: Franz Steiner, 1997.

Coleman, Peter. *The Liberal Conspiracy: The Congress for Cultural Freedom and the Struggle for the Mind of Postwar Europe.* New York: Free Press, 1989.

Cronin, Audrey K. *Great Power Politics and the Struggle over Austria, 1945–1955.* Ithaca: Cornell University Press, 1986.

Culbert, David. "American Film Policy in the Re-education of Germany after 1945." In *The Political Re-education of Germany and Her Allies after WWII,* ed. Nicholas Pronay and Keith Wilson, 173–202. Beckenham: Croom Helm, 1985.

Davison, Eugene. *Death and Life of Germany.* New York: Alfred A. Knopf, 1959.

Department of State. *Germany, 1947–1949: The Story in Documents.* Washington: U.S. Government Printing Office, 1950.

———. *Occupation of Germany: Policy and Progress, 1945–46.* Washington: U.S. Government Printing Office, 1947.

Deshmukh, M. "Recovering Culture: The Berlin National Gallery and the US Occupation, 1945–49." *Central European History* 27 (1994): 411–35.

Diefendorf, Jeffry M. *In the Wake of War: The Reconstruction of German Cities after World War II.* New York: Oxford University Press, 1993.

Dymschitz, Alexander. "Rückblick und Ausblick." In *Alexander Dymschitz: Wissenschaftler, Soldat, Internationalist,* ed. Klaus Ziermann and Helmut Baierl. Berlin: Henschelverlag, 1977.

———. *Ein unvergesslicher Frühling: Literarische Porträts und Erinnerungen.* Berlin: Akademie Verlag, 1970.

Egk, Werner. *Die Zeit wartet nicht.* Percha: R. S. Schulz, 1973.

Eisenberg, Carolyn. *Drawing the Line: The American Decision to Divide Germany, 1944–1949.* Cambridge: Cambridge University Press, 1996.

Eisenhower, Dwight D. *Crusade in Europe*. Garden City: Doubleday, 1952.

Elkes, Pauline. "Wartime Images of Germany and the Germans in British Occupation Policy: The Reports of the Political Warfare Executive." In *The Cultural Legacy of the British Occupation in Germany*, ed. Alan Bance, 38–54. Stuttgart: Hans-Dieter Heinz Verlag, 1997.

Erker, Paul. *Ernähungskrise und Nachkriegsgesellschaft: Bauern und Arbeiterschaft in Bayern, 1945–1953*. Munich: Klett-Cotta, 1998.

Evans, Joan. *Hans Rosbaud: A Bio-Bibliography*. New York: Greenwood, 1992.

———. "International with National Emphasis: The Internationales Zeitgenössisches Musikfest in Baden-Baden, 1936–1939." In *Music and Nazism: Art under Tyranny, 1933–1945*, ed. Michael Kater and Albrecht Riethmüller, 102–13. Laaber: Laaber Verlag, 2003.

———. "Die Rezeption der Musik Igor Stravinskys in Hitlerdeutschland." *Archiv für Musikwissenschaft* 55 (1998): 91–109.

Evarts, John. "Vom Musikleben in Amerika." *Neue Musik* 1 (February 1947): 78–85.

Fehrenbach, Heide. *Cinema in Democratizing Germany: Reconstructing National Identity after Hitler*. Chapel Hill: University of North Carolina Press, 1995.

Frei, Norbert. *Amerikanische Lizenzpolitik und deutsche Pressetradition: Die Geschichte der Nachkriegszeitung Südost-Kurier*. Munich: Oldenbourg, 1986.

———. *Vergangenheitspolitik: Die Anfänge der Bundesrepublik und die NS-Vergangenheit*. Frankfurt: Deutscher Taschenbuch Verlag, 1999.

Fröhlich, Elke, ed. *Die Tagebücher von Joseph Goebbels*. Munich: K. G. Saur, 1998.

Fromm, Erich. *Escape from Freedom*. New York: Rinehart, 1941.

Furtwängler, Wilhelm. *Aufzeichnungen, 1924–1954*. Wiesbaden: F. A. Brockhaus, 1980.

———. *Briefe*. Ed. Frank Thiess. Wiesbaden: F. A. Brockhaus, 1964.

———. *Notebooks*. Ed. Michael Tanner. London: Quartet, 1989.

Gefen, Gérard. *Wilhelm Furtwängler: La puissance et la gloire*. Paris: L'Archipel, 2001.

Gehring, Hansjörg. *Amerikanische Literaturpolitik in Deutschland, 1945–1953: Ein Aspekt des Reedukationsprogramms*. Stuttgart: Deutsche Verlags-Anstalt, 1976.

Gelatt, Roland. *The Fabulous Phonograph, 1877–1977*. New York: Collier, 1977.

Genton, Bernard. *Les Alliés et la culture Berlin, 1945–1949*. Paris: Presses universitaires de France, 1998.

Gienow-Hecht, Jessica. *Transmission Impossible: American Journalism as Cultural Diplomacy in Postwar Germany, 1945–1955*. Baton Rouge: Louisiana State University Press, 1999.

Gillis, Daniel. *Furtwängler and America*. New York: Manyland Books, 1970.

Gimbel, John. *The American Occupation of Germany*. Stanford: Stanford University Press, 1968.

Glaser, Hermann. *The Rubble Years: The Cultural Roots of Postwar Germany*. New York: Paragon House, 1986.

Goedde, Petra. *GIs and Germans: Culture, Gender and Foreign Relations, 1945–1949*. New Haven: Yale University Press, 2002.

Gordon, Eric. *Mark the Music: The Life and Work of Marc Blitzstein*. New York: St. Martin's Press, 1989.

Grohnert, Reinhard. *Die Entnazifizierung in Baden, 1945–1949*. Stuttgart: Kohlhammer, 1991.

Guilbaut, Serge. *How New York Stole the Idea of Modern Art: Abstract Expressionism, Freedom and the Cold War*. Chicago: University of Chicago Press, 1983.

Haffner, Herbert. *Furtwängler*. Berlin: Parthas, 2003.

Hamann, Brigitte. *Winifred Wagner oder Hitlers Bayreuth*. Munich: Piper, 2003.

Hartenian, Larry. "The Role of the Media in Democratizing Germany: United States Occupation Policy." *Central European History* 20 (1987): 145–90.

Hein-Kremer, Maritta. *Die amerikanische Kulturoffensive: Gründung und Entwicklung der amerikanischen Information Center in Westdeutschland und West Berlin*. Cologne: Böhlau, 1996.

Heldt, Guido. "Hardly Heroes: Composers as a Subject in National Socialist Cinema." In *Music and Nazism: Art under Tyranny, 1933–1945*, ed. Michael Kater and Albrecht Riethmüller, 114–35. Laaber: Laaber Verlag, 2003.

Helman, Philipp. "Das Wirtschaftswunder in Westdeutschland." *Archiv für Sozialgeschichte* 36 (1986): 323–44.

Henke, Klaus Dietmar. *Die amerikanische Besetzung Deutschlands*. Munich: Oldenbourg, 1995.

Henze, Hans Werner. *Music and Politics: Collected Writings, 1953–1981*. Ithaca: Cornell University Press, 1982.

Henze-Döhring, Sabine. "Kulturelle Zentren in der amerikanischen Besatzungszone: Der Fall Bayreuth." In *Kulturpolitik im besetzten Deutschland, 1945–1949*, ed. Gabriele Clemens, 42–52. Stuttgart: F. Steiner, 1994.

Heyworth, Peter. *Otto Klemperer*. Cambridge: Cambridge University Press, 1996.

Hiscocks, Richard. *The Rebirth of Austria*. London: Oxford University Press, 1953.

Hochgeschwender, Michael. *Freiheit in der Offensive? Der Kongress für Kulturelle Freiheit und die Deutschen*. Munich: Oldenbourg, 1998.

Höhn, Maria. *GIs and Fräuleins: The German-American Encounter in the 1950s*. Chapel Hill: University of North Carolina Press, 2002.

Horowitz, Joseph. *Understanding Toscanini: A Social History of American Concert Life*. Berkeley: University of California Press, 1987.

————. *Wagner Nights: An American History*. Berkeley: University of California Press, 1994.

Hunt, John. *The Lyric Baritone: Reinmer, Hüsch, Metternich, Uhde, Wächter*. London: John Hunt, 1997.

Hurwitz, Harold. *Die Stunde Null der deutschen Presse: Die amerikanische Pressepolitik in Deutschland, 1945–1949*. Cologne: Verlag Wissenschaft und Politik, 1972.

Janik, Elizabeth Koch. "Music in Cold War Berlin: German Tradition and Allied Occupation, 1945–51." Ph.D. dissertation, Georgetown University, 2001.

Jefferson, Alan. *Richard Strauss*. London: Macmillan, 1975.

Kater, Michael. *Composers of the Nazi Era: Eight Portraits*. New York: Oxford University Press, 2000.

————. *Different Drummers: Jazz in the Culture of Nazi Germany*. New York: Oxford University Press, 1992.

————. *The Twisted Muse: Musicians and Their Music in the Third Reich*. New York: Oxford University Press, 1997.

Kennedy, Michael. *Richard Strauss*. London: Dent, 1976.

Kerr, Harrison. "The American Music Center." *Music Journal*, September–October 1946, 31 and 56–59.

Kowalke, Kim. "Music Publishing and the Nazis: Schott, Universal Edition and Their Composers." In *Music and Nazism: Art under Tyranny, 1933–1945*, ed. Michael Kater and Albrecht Riethmüller, 170–218. Laaber: Laaber Verlag, 2003.

Krauss, Marita. *Nachkriegskultur in München: Münchner städtische Kulturpolitik, 1945–54*. Munich: Oldenbourg, 1985.

Krisch, Henry. *German Politics under Soviet Occupation*. New York: Columbia University Press, 1974.

Lang, Klaus. *Lieber Herr Celibidache*. Zürich: M & T Verlag, 1988.

Lasswell, Harold. "The Psychology of Hitlerism." *Political Quarterly* 4 (1933): 369–76.

Levi, Erik. *Music in the Third Reich*. New York: St. Martin's Press, 1994.

Levine, Lawrence. *Highbrow/Lowbrow: The Emergence of a Cultural Hierarchy in America*. Cambridge: Harvard University Press, 1988.

Lothar, Ernst. *Das Wunder des Überlebens: Erinnerungen und Ergebnisse*. Vienna: P. Zsolnay, 1961.

Ludwig, Emil. *The Moral Conquest of Germany*. Garden City: Doubleday, 1945.

Lynes, Russell. *The Lively Audience: A Social History of the Visual and Performing Arts in America*. New York: Harper & Row, 1985.

Maase, Kaspar. *Bravo Amerika! Erkundigungen zur Jugendkultur der Bundesrepublik in den fünfziger Jahren*. Hamburg: Hamburger Edition, 1992.

Magidoff, Robert. *Yehudi Menuhin*. Garden City: Doubleday, 1955.

Makovits, A. S. "Anti-Americanism and the Struggle for a West German Identity." In *The Federal Republic of Germany at Forty*, ed. Peter Merkl, 35–54. New York: New York University Press, 1989.

Marek, George. *The Good Housekeeping Guide to Musical Enjoyment*. New York: Rinehart, 1949.

———. *Richard Strauss: The Life of a Non-Hero*. New York: Gollancz, 1967.

Mauldin, William. *Up Front*. New York: Henry Holt, 1945.

McClatchie, Stephen. "Wagner Research as 'Service to the People': The Richard-Wagner-Forschungsstätte, 1938–1945." In *Music and Nazism: Art under Tyranny, 1933–1945*, ed. Michael Kater and Albrecht Riethmüller, 150–69. Laaber: Laaber Verlag, 2003.

Menuhin, Yehudi. *Unfinished Journey*. New York: Alfred A. Knopf, 1976.

Merkl, Peter. *The Origins of the Federal Republic of Germany*. New York: Oxford University Press, 1963.

Messmer, Franzpeter. "Münchner Tradition und Klassische Moderne — Der musikalische Neuanfang." In *Trümmerzeit in München*, ed. Friedrich Prinz, 207–23. Munich: Beck, 1984.

Mettler, Barbara. *Demokratisierung und Kalter Krieg: Zur amerikanischen Informations und Rundfunkpolitik in Westdeutschland, 1945–1949*. Berlin: Verlag Volker Spiess, 1975.

Milward, Alan. *The Reconstruction of Western Europe, 1945–1951*. London: Methuen, 1984.

Monod, David. "Disguise, Containment and the *Porgy and Bess* Revival of 1952–1956." *Journal of American Studies* 34 (August 2001): 275–312.

———. "Internationalism, Regionalism and Music Culture: Music Control in Bavaria, 1945–48." *Central European History* 33 (November 2000): 339–68.

Mosberg, Helmuth. *Reeducation: Umerziehung und Lizenspresse im Nachkriegsdeutschland*. Munich: Universitas, 1991.

Müller, Winfried. *Schulpolitik in Bayern im Spannungsfeld von Kulturbürokratie und Besatzungsmacht, 1945–1949*. Munich: Oldenbourg, 1995.

Murphy, Robert. *Diplomat among Warriors*. Garden City: Doubleday, 1964.

Nabokov, Nicolas. *Old Friends and New Music*. Boston: Little, Brown, 1951.

Niclauss, Karlheinz. *Demokratiegründung in Westdeutschland*. Munich: R. Piper, 1974.

Niethammer, Lutz. *Entnazifizierung in Bayern: Säuberung und Rehabilitierung unter amerikanischer Besatzung*. Frankfurt: S. Fischer, 1972.

Norman, Albert. *Our German Policy: Propaganda and Culture*. New York: Vantage, 1951.

Ota, Carol. *Making Music Modern: New York in the 1920s*. New York: Oxford University Press, 2000.

Paddock, Alfred, Jr. "Major General Robert Alexis McClure: Forgotten Father of US Army Special Warfare." <www.psywarrior.com/mcclure.html>.

Peterson, Edward. *The American Occupation of Germany: Retreat to Victory*. Detroit: Wayne State University Press, 1978.

Pike, David. *The Politics of Culture in Soviet-Occupied Germany, 1945–1949*. Stanford: Stanford University Press, 1992.

Poiger, Uta. *Jazz, Rock and Rebels: Cold War Politics and American Culture in a Divided Germany*. Berkeley: University of California Press, 2000.

Potter, Pamela. *Most German of the Arts: Musicology and Society from the Weimar Republic to the End of Hitler's Reich*. New Haven: Yale University Press, 1998.

———. "The Nazi Seizure of the Berlin Philharmonic, or the Decline of a Bourgeois Musical Institution." In *National Socialist Cultural Policy*, ed. Glenn Cuomo, 39–66. New York: St. Martin's Press, 1995.

Prieberg, Fred. *Trial of Strength: Wilhelm Furtwängler and the Third Reich*. London: Quartet, 1991.

———, ed. *Musik im NS-Staat*. Frankfurt: Broschiert, 1982.

Prowe, Diethelm. "Foundations of West German Democracy: Corporatist Patterns in the Post-1945 Democratization Process." In *Coping with the Past: Germany and Austria after 1945*, ed. Kathy Harms, Lutz Reuter, and Volker Dürr, 105–29. Madison: University of Wisconsin Press, 1990.

———. "German Democratization as Conservative Restabilization: The Impact of American Policy." In *American Policy and the Reconstruction of West Germany, 1945–1955*, ed. Jeffry Diefendorf, Axel Frohn, and Hermann-Josef Rupieper, 307–30. Cambridge: Cambridge University Press, 1993.

Ranulf, Svend. *Moral Indignation and Middle Class Psychology*. Copenhagen: Levin and Munksqaard, 1938.

Rathkolb, Oliver. *Führertreu und gottbegnadet: Künstlerleiten im Dritten Reich*. Vienna: Krauchenwies, 1991.

Remy, Steven P. *The Heidelberg Myth: The Nazification and Denazification of a German University*. Cambridge: Harvard University Press, 2003.

Richter, Hans Werner. *Re-educating Germany*. Chicago: University of Chicago Press, 1945.

Rupieper, Hermann-Josef. "Bringing Democracy to the Fräuleins: Frauen als Zielgruppe der amerikanischen Demokratisierungspolitik in Deutschland, 1945–1952." *Geschichte und Gesellschaft* 17 (1991): 61–91.

———. *Die Wurzeln der westdeutschen Nachkriegsdemokratie: Der amerikanische Beitrag, 1945–1952*. Opladen: Westdeutscher Verlag, 1993.

Sandford, Gregory. *From Hitler to Ulbricht: The Communist Reconstruction of East Germany*. Princeton: Princeton University Press, 1983.

Saunders, Frances Stonor. *The Cultural Cold War: The CIA and the World of Arts and Letters*. New York: New Press, 1999.

Schildt, Axel, and Arnold Sywottek. "Reconstruction and Modernization: West German Social History during the 1950s." In *West Germany under Construction*, ed. Robert Moeller, 413–40. Ann Arbor: University of Michigan Press, 1997.

Schivelbusch, Wolfgang. *In a Cold Crater: Cultural and Intellectual Life in Berlin, 1945–1948*. Berkeley: University of California Press, 1998.

Schlesinger, Robert. *Gott Sei mit unserem Führer: Der Opernbetrieb im deutschen Faschismus*. Vienna: Löcker, 1997.

Schönzler, Hans-Hubert. *Furtwängler*. London: Duckworth, 1990.

Schuh, Willi, ed. *Richard Strauss: Briefwechsel mit Willi Schuh*. Zürich: Atlantis Verlag, 1969.

Schwartz, Thomas. "Reeducation and Democracy: The Politics of the United States High Commission in Germany." In *America and the Shaping of German Society, 1945–1955*, ed. Michael Ermath, 35–46. Providence: Berg, 1993.

Schwarzkopf, Elisabeth. *On and Off the Record: A Memoir of Walter Legge*. New York: Scribner's, 1982.

Scott-Smith, Giles. *The Politics of Apolitical Culture: The Congress for Cultural Freedom, the CIA and Post-War American Hegemony*. London: Routledge, 2002.

Shirakawa, Sam H. *The Devil's Music Master: The Controversial Life and Career of Wilhelm Furtwängler*. New York: Oxford University Press, 1992.

Skelton, Geoffrey. *Wagner at Bayreuth: Experiment and Tradition*. New York: Da Capo, 1983.

———, ed. *Selected Letters of Paul Hindemith*. New Haven: Yale University Press, 1995.

Smith, Jean. *Lucius D. Clay: An American Life*. New York: Henry Holt, 1990.

Solti, Georg. *Memoirs*. New York: Alfred A. Knopf, 1997.

Speier, Hans. *From the Ashes of Disgrace: A Journal from Germany, 1945–1955*. Amherst: University of Massachusetts Press, 1981.

Splitt, Gerhard. *Richard Strauss, 1933–1935: Ästhetik und Musikpolitik zu Beginn der nationalsozialistischen Herrschaft*. Pfaffenweiler: Centauras Verlag, 1987.

Spotts, Frederic. *Bayreuth, a History of the Wagner Festival*. New Haven: Yale University Press, 1994.

Steiert, Thomas. "Zur Musik- und Theaterpolitik in Stuttgart während der amerikanischen Besatzungszeit." In *Kulturpolitik im besetzten Deutschland, 1945–1949*, ed. Gabriele Clemens, 55–68. Stuttgart: F. Steiner, 1994.

Steinweis, Alan. *Art, Ideology and Economics in Nazi Germany: The Reich Chambers of Music, Theater and the Visual Arts*. Chapel Hill: University of North Carolina Press, 1993.

Strässner, Matthias. *Der Dirigent Leo Borchard: Eine unvollendete Karriere*. Berlin: Transit Buchverlag, 1999.

Taylor, John H. "Ambassadors of the Arts: An Analysis of the Eisenhower Administration's Incorporation of *Porgy and Bess* into Cold War Foreign Policy." Ph.D. dissertation, Ohio State University, 1994.

Tent, James. *Mission on the Rhine: Reeducation and Denazification in American Occupied Germany*. Chicago: University of Chicago Press, 1982.

Thacker, Toby. "Liberating German Musical Life: The BBC German Service and Planning for Music Control in Occupied Germany, 1944–1949." In *Stimme der Wahrheit: German-Language Broadcasting by the BBC. Yearbook of the Research Centre for German and Austrian Exile Studies*, ed. Charmian Brinson and Richard Dove, 77–92. Amsterdam: Editions Rodopi, 2003.

———. "Playing Beethoven Like an Indian: American Music and Reorientation in Germany, 1945–1955." In *The Postwar Challenge: Cultural, Social and Political Change in Western Europe, 1945–1958*, ed. Dominik Geppert, 365–86. Oxford: Oxford University Press, 2003.

Vaughan, Roger. *Herbert von Karajan*. New York: W. W. Norton, 1986.

Vogel, Heinrich. *Aus den Tagebüchern von Elly Ney*. Tutzing: Hans Schneider Verlag, 1979.

von Eschen, Penny. *Race against Empire: Black Americans and Anticolonialism, 1937–57*. Ithaca: Cornell University Press, 1997.

Wachter, Clement. *Kultur in Nürnberg, 1945–1950*. Nuremburg: Stadtarchiv Nuremburg, 1999.

Wagner, Wieland. Foreword. In *Wagner at Bayreuth: Experiment and Tradition*, by Geoffrey Skelton. New York: Da Capo, 1983.

Wallich, H. C. *Mainsprings of the German Revival*. New Haven: Yale University Press, 1955.

Walter, Michael. *Hitler in der Oper: Deutsches Musikleben, 1919–1945*. Stuttgart: Metzler, 1995.

Weinberg, Albert, and Henry Coles. *U.S. Army in World War II: Special Studies. Civil Affairs: Soldiers Become Governors*. Washington: U.S. Government Printing Office, 1961.

Wessling, Berndt. *Furtwängler: Eine kritische Biographie*. Stuttgart: Deutsche Verlags-Anstalt, 1985.

Woll, Allen. *Black Musical Theater: From Coontown to Dreamgirls*. Baton Rouge: Louisiana State University Press, 1989.

Wulf, Josef, ed. *Musik im Dritten Reich: Eine Dokumentation*. Reinbeck: S. Mohn, 1966.

Zink, Harold. *American Military Government in Germany*. New York: Macmillan, 1947.

Zulauf, Jochen. *Verwaltung der Kunst oder Kunst der Verwaltung: Kulturverwaltung, Kulturförderung und Kulturpolitik des Landes Hessen, 1945–1960*. Wiesbaden: Historische Kommission für Nassau, 1995.

INDEX